FOUNDATIONS OF INDIAN CULTURE

VOLUME I

FOUNDATIONS OF INDIAN CULTURE

VOLUME I

Spiritual Vision and Symbolic Forms in Ancient India

G. C. PANDE

MOTILAL BANARSIDASS PUBLISHERS
PRIVATE LIMITED • DELHI

Reprint : Delhi; 1995, 2005, 2007
Second Edition : Delhi, 1990
First Edition : Delhi, 1984

ISBN: 978-81-208-0710-5 (Vol. I)
ISBN: 978-81-208-0712-9 (Set)

MOTILAL BANARSIDASS
41 U.A. Bungalow Road, Jawahar Nagar, Delhi 110 007
8 Mahalaxmi Chamber, 22 Bhulabhai Desai Road, Mumbai 400 026
203 Royapettah High Road, Mylapore, Chennai 600 004
236, 9th Main III Block, Jayanagar, Bangalore 560 011
Sanas Plaza, 1302 Baji Rao Road, Pune 411 002
8 Camac Street, Kolkata 700 017
Ashok Rajpath, Patna 800 004
Chowk, Varanasi 221 001

Printed in India

BY JAINENDRA PRAKASH JAIN AT SHRI JAINENDRA PRESS,
A-45 NARAINA, PHASE-I, NEW DELHI 110 028
AND PUBLISHED BY NARENDRA PRAKASH JAIN FOR
MOTILAL BANARSIDASS PUBLISHERS PRIVATE LIMITED,
BUNGALOW ROAD, DELHI 110 007

श्रीमातृचरणाम्भोज-सेवातत्परमानसः ।
तस्या एवार्पये ग्रन्थं तल्लीलास्मरणात्मकम् ।।

PREFACE TO THE SECOND EDITION

It is a matter of some gratification that the first edition of the book published in 1984 was exhausted in three years and that the book was generally received with appreciation. I am particularly grateful to my learned friends and students whose kind encouragement has made this second edition possible. The work has been carefully corrected, up-dated and, where necessary, enlarged.

I am thankful to Motilal Banarsidass Publishers Pvt. Ltd. for taking up the publication of this edition. Dr. S.P. Gupta has made me keep a tight time-schedule in finalizing the edition for the press and I am grateful to him. Sri Raghuvansh Tiwari has been of great help in typing and other matters and my sincere thanks are due to him.

"*Ā paritoṣād viduṣāṁ na sādhu manye prayoga-vijñānam.*"

G. C. Pande

29.8.1989
Allahabad

PREFACE

The search for the historical explanation of human life and thought has led historians to the attempt to go beyond the surface happenings of short duration to analyse the deeper structures of longer duration. These have been sought to be identified as economic or social or even geographical. Many of these formulations are vitiated by conscious or unconscious assumptions of a positivistic character. Social formations are not like natural formations given independently of the subject. They are in fact subjective-objective in character. As a consequence social formations and idea formations cannot really be separated. Being and thought are two inevitably co-present dimensions. Despite this undeniable duality of cultural factors it is common nowadays to find many historians emphasizing their social origins exclusively. It may be said that ideas do not simply spring from the head like 'Minerva in panoply' but that they derive from a historically given state of social being. But this social being itself is discernible only through reflection over experience and as such, is related to the self-awareness of the subject. In particular the historian cannot discover social formations except as revealed in a historical record which is directly expressive of some consciousness. Thus, despite the radical significance of social being, it has to be reached and understood in terms of a tradition of social experience and awareness. In a profound sense, thus, while social structures underlie surface events, they are themselves inwardly constituted by a historical world of ideas. *'Manopubbaṅgamā dhammā'*, all phenomena presuppose the mind.

The present work attempts to analyse the social and ideational foundation of Indian culture. The second part of the work concentrates on the analysis of the social world which is presupposed by the intellectual and the symbolic formulations of the Indian tradition. The present volume seeks to reconstruct Indian culture, not as a museum-model from the scrap-heap of time but as a tradition of value-seeking expressing itself in concepts and symbols, as a perpetual theme for hermeneutic commentary. The history as well as the interior dialectic of the tradition is sought to be brought out by noticing the interaction of theory, practice and experience as also the ever-dissatisfied seeking for expressing imponderable feelings symbolically. *Sādhanā, Vidyā* and *Kalā* constitute the three interacting levels of the cultural process, of *saṁskṛti* in the original sense.

Apart from the publishers and the printers I am thankful to Dr. S. P. Gupta, Dr. S. K. Gupta, Sri U. C. Chattopadhyaya, Dr. L. M. Dubey and Sri A. P. Ojha for helping me in various ways to see this volume through the press.

11 Balrampur House,
Allahabad.
July 10, 1983

G. C. Pande

CONTENTS

PART I : SPIRITUAL PRAXIS (SĀDHANĀ) AND VISION (PARĀVIDYĀ)

1

APPROACH : TRANSCENDENTAL ROOTS AND HISTORICITY OF SPIRITUAL PRAXIS AND THE INDIAN CONCEPTION OF CULTURAL TRADITION

Tradition and spiritual praxis (*sādhanā*)

Ultimate spiritual authority in India is in practice held to belong not to ancient books or their learned expositions, but to those who are believed to have personal experience of spiritual truth. Spiritual truth is not held to be something totally beyond the human ken, revealed once for all to some incarnation or prophet of God. Nor is it something to which man can attain only in the life after death. Spiritual truth is capable of being reached while a man yet lives ; this attainment of spiritual truth is profoundly different from its apprehension in merely faith or philosophy. It is a living vision which transforms the inner life, faculties and powers of the person who attains to it. Authority belongs to one 'who has attained' (*apta*). The Vedic seer (*rsi*), the enlightened one (*Buddha*) or the perfected one (*Siddha*) or the worthy one (*Arhant*) among the Buddhists or the Jainas, or the Adept (*Siddha*) among the Tantrikas or the *Sant* in the Bhakti schools, are all variations of the same ideal figure. The process of seeking and obtaining spiritual vision and inner transformation has been variously called, the commonest expressions being *Sadhana*, or *Yoga*.[1]

It may be felt that what has been described as *Sadhana* here is nothing different from religious life or mystical practice. While it is true that all moral or religious or mystical life could be subsumed within *sadhana,* the converse of this would not be true. *Sadhana* is a term of greater generality and its use betokens the perception of a continuity running through all human effort aiming at the realization of higher values alongwith a sense of their gradation. Values are undoubtedly relative to human needs and desires but they are equally the objects of rational discrimination.[2] Behind the diversity of limited needs and desires, running through them there is the sense of a deeper and unending quest of which the object continually transforms itself but continues to beckon like an ever renewing horizon. The true nature of man is covered by a series of *accidents* or assumed personae. To each of these corresponds a way of viewing the world and of seeking and valuing it. The gamut of human experience runs from the inmost and highest level of purely spiritual knowledge to the almost purely physical level of instinctive life. Appropriately lived, life at each level is a preparation for transcending it, as if a valve were to open upwards enabling a movement beyond the vortex below it. This process of appropriate living and ascent to higher levels is *sadhana.* *Yogaḥ karmasu kauśalam*[3]—Yoga is skill in action. *Bhūmā Vai sukhaṁ nālpe sukhamasti*[4]—Infinity alone satisfies. There is no satisfaction in what is limited. *Yatsānoh sānumāruhat bhūri aspaṣṭa kartvam*[5]—as he climbed from peak to peak, he espied evermore what was to be done. The *Bhagavadgita* is the most explicit exposition of this and is the *Yogasastra* par excellence.

Sadhana is thus as extensive as life itself, expressing itself in the upward aspiration and effort organised as a deep and persistent point of view. It is not merely the ascetic and the mystic, the wholetime religieux who is a Sadhaka. A person engaged in his work in any walk of life becomes a *Sadhaka* by adopting an attitude of detatchment and dedication. The *Mahabharata* relates how a pious hunter Dharmvyadha instructs a Brahmin ascetic. Similarly the merchant Tuladhara gives instruction to the ascetic Jajali. The *Devi-Bhagavata* shows us the king Janaka to advantage over the famous mendicant Suka. The tradition is widespread and well accepted that the spiritual goal may be striven after in any kind of social situation in the midst of any kind of life. The *Gita* declares that a man ought to continue attending to the duties of his station without even aspiring to change his station and status. *Svakarmaṇā tamabhyarcya sidhiṁvindatimānavaḥ*—man obtains perfection by worshipping Him with his own work. As ordinarily understood, religion is only a part of life; whereas *Sadhana* embracing the whole of life may be described as a non-dogmatic, universal religion of man coterminus with life in so far as it seeks spiritual elevation. The standpoint of *sadhana* recognizes the pervasive unity of human spiritual efforts in the midst of the most diverse conditions of existence. On the other hand, it recognizes that corresponding to the differences of the individual temparament, social situation and cultural tradition, men may engage in the most diverse practices and ways of living seeking to elevate themselves spiritually.

"*Rucīnām vaicitryādṛjukuṭilanānāpathajuṣāṃ*"—'Just as different rivers flow towards the same ocean, so with their diverse tastes and inclinations do men approach the Lord.' "*Vineya-bhedāt deśanā-bhedaḥ*"—'teaching differs according to the individuality of the recipients.' This catholicity not only tolerates moral and religious differences, it discovers a rationale for such diversity. It rejects the notion that there is one true religion, a single spiritual straight-jacket. Contrary to the religious monolithism and consequent conflict which have prevailed in the western world from ancient times, India has upheld through the ages the free dissemination and commingling of different creeds and sects. Saints of whatever religion receive the same respect from the people irrespective of their creed. It took centuries of blood shed and repeated holocausts to enable the west to effect a distinction between religion and politics, without however wholly eradicating the seeking after ideological uniformity. The western concept of secularism merely refused to support religion by political force. Transported to India even the concept of secularism has come to be interpreted not merely as the religious neutrality of the state, but as the catholicity of a multi-religious culture, not *dharma-nirapeksata* but *sarva-dharma-samabhava.* Efforts are sometimes made to question this broad-minded tolerance and to belittle it as the result of a lack of earnestness or as merely confused syncretism. Doubtless, in the long history of India there have been episodes of intolerance and with the intrusion of the Semitic tradition, occasionally bloody conflicts; nevertheless the difference in this respect between the histories of India and of the West can hardly be missed by any impartial observer. As far as the argument from religious earnestness is concerned, it mistakes the actual situation in India. The different schools and sects neither give quarter, ideologically speaking, nor expect it. The fiercest controversies and debates have raged among the followers of different schools and sects. At the same time, they admit the equal right of others to practise their own beliefs, and it was abhorrent to them to seek to gain converts for themselves by force. There was no lack of earnestness, but there was a counter-balancing recognition of the diversity of men and their ways.

It was fully realised that in some sense *Sadhana* constitutes a universal and a unique path or process. *'Nānyah panthā vidyate ayanāya'*, there is no other path for, treading. *'Ekāyanoyaṁ maggo bhikkave'*—'O monks this is the only way.' The recognition of a single universal spiritual process follows from the basic spirituality of human nature and the unity of its ultimate goal. Nevertheless, it has to be recognised that what divides man from his goal is a differentiating factor and varies from man to man. The human condition is an individualised condition, and consequently there is an individual way for every one to emerge from his shell or historically constructed psychic scenario into the royal highway of spiritual life. From the 'house' to the 'high way' everyone must construct his own path joining other pilgrims at different points and tending to identify the highway with their path. In a way every pilgrim feels himself a lonely wayfarer; in another he feels himself incomplete. Tradition, holy books, teachers, prescriptions and ritual, symbols and maps of the journey, all these give one confidence and assurance that he is not alone, that he has the weight and support of others behind him.

This attitude can easily degenerate into an over-reliance which confuses symbolism with description, spiritual inspiration with magical communion, or into a narrow-minded attitude which confounds a particular tradition with an only permissible spiritual fellowship.

Sadhana and World View

While *Sadhana* like science or art does not presuppose any fixed theoretic or dogmatic system of thought but rather progressively discovers and reinterprets its presuppositions in the light of spiritual and cultural experience, nevertheless *Sadhana* does imply a certain angle of vision (*drsti*) on life. Here, again, the analogy of science or art is helpful. Science presupposes rational objectivity and a spirit of enquiry and experimentation, though its theoretic formulations keep changing. Art similarly does presuppose a felt and imaginative experience of the world which is quite distinct from any rational or practical point of view. Religion presupposes an intense awareness of human mortality and of a super-human reality lying beyond it. Moral life presupposes the sense of individual freedom as well as of universal humanity. As already stated, Sadhana includes all these dimensions and more in a unique integration. It presupposes a general approach to life rather than any definite system of beliefs. It assumes the detached truth seeking (*jijñāsā*) of the scientist, the sensitiveness (*akṣipātrakalpatā*) of the artist to the experiences of life and the earnestness (*saṁvega*) of the moral and religious person. It presupposes a certain maturity and wisdom (*viveka*) towards life, a realization of the inadequacy and unsatisfactoriness of the life of egoism and acquisitiveness (*duhkhabodha, uparati, mumuksa*). It presupposes an unvarnished perception of the inherent limitations of worldly satisfactions, along with a firm faith in the capacity of man to attain to values of a lasting and universal character (*sraddha*). It requires fortitude and determination (*dhrti, virya*).

The cultivation of such moral attitudes is itself the initial phase of the process of *Sadhana.* About the need and direction of such moral life there is little disagreement among the different systems of Sadhana. On the other hand, about the theoretical presuppositions of *Sadhana,* there are naturally many alternative formulations. It is, however, often stated that *Sadhana* takes for granted the doctrine of *samsara* which is accepted by practically all the schools and systems of Indian thought. The doctrine of *samsara* includes the ideas of *Karman* and *Punarjanman, dukkha, ajnana* and *moksa.* In this form the doctrine of *samsara* was a Sramanic contribution and did not belong to the earliest Vedic tradition. Although it was accepted later on by all schools and sects, it is doubtful if explicit belief in it can be described as a necessary presupposition of all types of *Sadhana.* One can only say that as a matter of fact a good deal of *Sadhana* came to recognise the force of existential suffering as also the validity of transmigration.

Sadhana means 'making'. It is the 'making of oneself', a process of self-transformation. The great acarya Sankara has remarked that while making in the natural world depends on the use of means distinct from the end itself, making in the spiritual world requires only the contemplation of the end or ideal for its realization.[6] That human nature can be transformed and raised above the shackles of greed, hatred and fear, is certainly an assumption implicit in the practice of Yoga. But this is not a merely theoretical assumption. It is a well attested fact of Yogic experience and tradition. In this sense it is an assumption built into the texture of spiritual culture. Similarly, that such purification of the mind gives it a qualitatively superior state of enlightenment, happiness and well being, is again a fact of experience in terms of tradition and an initial assumption for the individual.

Another fundamental assumption of Yoga is the existence of an immemorial tradition of *yogic* guidance and teaching. It is not a matter of mere speculation, opinion or social attitude, ritual or symbolism. It is a matter of personal realisation in the course of which a tradition is at once verified and modified. It is in this sense that Vivekanand described *yoga* to be science.

It is this scientific attitude towards spiritual life and truth which was responsible for the fact that while religious faith in Europe chafed against scientific doctrines in the nineteenth century, there was no such opposition to science in India at the same time. The great religious leaders and thinkers of India in the 19th and 20th centuries have accepted the truth of science in the natural sphere without feeling that this jeopardized the tradition of spiritual seeking in any sense. The acceptance of modern social philosophies based on the apotheosis of the natural man and of his individual or collective egoism or of social history seeking the realization of utopias through the aid of technology, creates more problems. These philosophies or "social sciences" express an attitude towards life which is naturalistic, egoistic and historicist. If this attitude were to be absolutized, it would certainly cut across the domination of any spiritual *Weltanschauung*. On the other hand, the practice of spiritual life does not require the social absolutization of any kind of dogmatic philosophy but rather an openness of the mind inconsistent with too much speculation.

* * *

The Indian conception of cultural tradition

The modern conception of culture is descriptive and empirical whereas the ancient awareness of tradition is that of an essentially suprasensuous or rational knowledge which lays down norms to be followed. *Nigama* and *Āgama* thus constitute two branches of *Sampradāya* or *Āmnāya*. *Nigama* is constituted by the *Veda*. *Āgama,* on the other hand, stands not only for the gnostic and the mystical traditions of the Buddhists, the Jainas, the Śaivas, the Śāktas and the Vaiṣṇavas etc., but also includes secular traditions such as of grammar, *daṇḍanīti, śilpaśāstra, āyurveda,* or even *kāmaśāstra*. In fact all the *śāstras* are held to originate from some supra-empirical revelation.[7] They are rationally intelligible and empirically applicable, but their authority does not depend upon the vagaries of human experience and logic.[8] In essence this conception of tradition is comparable with that of science as understood in the west in pre-Modern times, wherein experience, reason and revelation were united in a hierarchy of sciences.[9]

According to traditional awareness, thus, culture subsists as an authentic wisdom of human ends and means and its origin lies in the experience and activity of Prophets and Masters. Culture, thus, is nothing except the perennial tradition of wisdom informing the various aspects of human life and activities. If we do not stick to an intellectualist or literalist conception of tradition, we should find its essence in an insight into imponderable truth and value which subsists basically as personal communication but is expressed and elaborated through symbolic and intellectual activity. For example, Uddalaka's communication *'tattvamasi'* to Śvetaketu gets elaborated in the schools of Advaita philosophy or in the symbology of Śrīvidyā or the poetry of *Yogavāsiṣṭha.*

It is more difficult to appreciate the claim of secular traditions of knowledge to posses a supra-empirical authority. In practice the sciences did in fact advance by empirical observations and kept revising themselves upto a point.[10] Still, they did start from fundamental conceptual frameworks which have to be taken for granted. Such, for example, is the case with the Paninian enumeration of phonemes or the Ayurvedic conception of *tridoṣa.* Although these conceptions underlie the rest of these systems they are hardly open to complete empirical testing. In this sense transcendental ideal concepts form the starting point of even empirical sciences and it is possible to feel that such original ideas of the system were grasped in a primary act of insight analogus to revelation. It is, of course, not to be denied that in lesser minds the appeal to a supra-empirical source was possibly an attempt to win easy approval.

Yet another aspect of this traditional conception is that it does not create any barrier between the secular and the religious. The so called secular sciences and activities are of a piece with religious inspiration and claim to end in it. For example, while it is true that the grammarian studies language as it is given, he seeks to discover in it an implicit ideal model the perfect knowledge of which has a liberating effect on him. "One word properly known produces the fulfilment of all the wishes here and hereafter." "The imperishable word is ultimately the beginningless and endless *brahman*."[11] The student of grammar studies words as a means to knowing their ultimate divine nature. This unity of the secular and the spiritual, the empirical and the ideal extends universally. From the traditional point of view, thus, culture is not the image of the natural man nor the merely historical product of his natural activities. Culture includes but is not the mere refinement of empirical nature.[12] It is rather a divinely given archetype, an ideal model which man needs to follow and in the process fulfil as well as transcend his mere humanity or historic actuality. From a point in time man has to seek the perennial, not merely to contribute to another point of time in the future.[13] Starting from his given empirical identity man has to seek his true transcendental identity. This process of self-realization is called sadhana. While a cultured man was generally called *Arya*, which implied not only the education of manners but also of morals, the Buddhists held that in truth only a spiritually enlightened person can be called *Arya*. Indian culture or *Aryadharma* thus stands not only for a traditional social code[14] but beyond that for its spiritual ground.

REFERENCES

1. Among modern expositions may be seen Vivekanand's *Rajayoga*, Sri Aurobindo's *Synthesis of Yoga*, Sri Krishna Prem's *Initiation into Yoga*, Tagore's *Sadhana*.

2. See the author's *Mūlyamīmāṁsā.*

3. *BG.* II.

4. *Ch. up.* 7.

5. *Ṛ.* I.10.2.

6. Com. on the *Gītā,* II.54.

7. *Vākyapadīya,* 1.30; cf. MM. G. N. Kaviraj, *Bharatiya Samskrti Aur Sadhana,* Vol. I, pp. 214-15.

8. *Vākayapadīya,* 1.34-43.

9. Cf. De Wulf, *Philosophy and Civilization in the Middle Ages,* pp 85ff.

10. Cf. *Mahabhasya,* ad Panini 1.1., *prathamāhnika,* which discusses the relationship between *loka* and *śāstra.*

11. *Vākyapadīya,* 1.1.

12. Cf. The concept of *saṁskāra* in *Mīmāṁsā* and *Dharmaśāstra.*

13. Cf. "In the sacrificial interpretation of life, acts of all kinds are reduced to their paradigms and archetypes... The reference of all activities to their archetypes...is what we ought to mean when we speak of rationalizing our conduct ...", Coomaraswamy quoted by Prof. A. K. Saran, *The Traditional Vision of Man,* prepared for UNESCO, 1978.

14. Cf. *"Rekhāmātramapi Kṣuṇṇād ā manor vartmanaḥ param/*
Na uyatiyuḥ prajās tasya niyantur nemi-vṛttayaḥ//"
(Raghu, 1.17)

2

VEDIC INTERPRETATION

The *Vedas* have been held in the highest veneration by the Hindus for millennia. They have been regarded as a timeless revelation and as the most authentic source of knowledge. It is, therefore, curious that apparently no overt, authentic tradition of understanding the Vedic *Saṁhitās* can be discerned to have been available at least as far back as the *Nirukta* of Yāska. The emphasis laid in *Mīmaṁsā* texts on the unbroken tradition of the Vedic study refers apparently only to the tradition of memorizing and reciting the *Vedas*. The language of the earliest Vedic hymns had become significantly transformed by the time the *Brāhmaṇas* were composed. By the time of Yāska the Vedic hymns had become at least partly unintelligible and a number of views had been formulated in relation to their interpretation.[1] In the 5th century B.C. Pāṇini carefully records the principles of Vedic accent but appears to despair of reducing Vedic grammar to an intelligible regularity.[2] When Sāyaṇa in the 14th century attempted the renaissance of the Vedic tradition, he takes it for granted that Vedic hymns are to be understood strictly in the context of Vedic ritual.[3] Max Müller's publication of Sāyaṇa's commentary on the Ṛgveda Saṁhitā in the 19th century was an early milestone in the modern attempt to understand the *Veda*. The resources of comparative philology, comparative mythology and religion and of comparative history have been employed by a host of scholars all over the world for more than a century now[4] to discover the true meaning of the *Veda* and its religion. It cannot, however, be said that the quest for Vedic truth has reached any final stage.

There is no doubt that our understanding of the Vedic language has made considerable progress. The principal uncertainty of Vedic interpretation is not now linguistic or philological. The uncertainty arises from the fact that there is enough ambiguity in the Vedic hymns to allow a diversity of interpretation as to their exact significance. It is true that the meanings of many words and lines have been disputed and yet there are far more lines and words where the plain meaning or *abhidhā* hardly lends itself to dispute. Nevertheless, unresolved controversies continue to exist not only about the general nature of the Vedic gods but also about the significance of many of the important individual gods.[5]

Vedic language was extremely rich in its variety of particles and forms, especially verbal forms. Many of these like the subjunctive '*leṭ*' became obsolete with time and, as already mentioned, even Pāṇini finds them just a mass of irregularities. Comparative grammar culminating in the monumental works of Brugmann and Wackernagel has, however, been able to reconstruct the phonology and morphology of Vedic language and in this respect the modern investigator is in a happier position than his predecessors over the last two thousand years.[6] Considerably greater difficulties have, however, been engendered by the fact that many Vedic words became obsolete and still others changed their meaning in later times. *Nighaṇṭu* already essayed the task of listing such archaic words. Of modern lexicographic attempts Grassmann's *Wörterbuch* is perhaps the most valuable.[7] Similarly the knowledge of grammatical forms or plain meanings does not suffice to understand idiomatic usage. And the poetic character of the hymns makes matters even more difficult as does our uncertainty about the exact context of the belief and sentiments which the hymns presuppose. This gives to their interpretation a certain conjectural or speculative character. Grassmann's translation is itself a glowing example of the gulf that separates lexicography from contextual interpretation. The sheer task of construing the lines presents detailed problems needing endless revision. A brilliant example of such effort is to be found in Geldner's translation just as Ludwig's comments and Oldenberg's notes[8] represent masterly probings. The general interpretation of Vedic ideas, however, remains as controversial as ever.

The earliest stratum of Vedic literature consists of hymns addressed to the gods invoking them to be present at the sacrifice and seeking their blessings. While some interesting hymns do not show this character and appear to be instead expressive of simply poetic or philosophical experience or, on the other hand, of magical beliefs, most of the hymns clearly relate to some ritual occasion and are prayers of glorification and petition. The ritualistic tradition tended to survive in later times though with increasing attenuation and the use of the hymns continued in this context though they were now used more for their magical and incantatory effect than as prayers fully understood by those who used them. In later times more significant than the use of the hymns in the *śrauta* ritual has been their use in domestic or sacramental ritual. *Upanayana,* marriage and funerary ceremonies continue to use the ancient Vedic rites and hymns even now although the purity of usage and the intelligent use of the hymns has largely disappeared through the ignorance of the priests.

The hymns were always regarded as revealed to the Seers and thus having an inspired character and a power of conveying truths beyond the ken of ordinary mortals, and there is some evidence of ancient efforts at determining the esoteric or mystical significance of the hymns. In the *Brāhmaṇas* and the *Nirukta* we meet with such interpretations occasionally. It has been generally assumed that these texts reflect a later stage of development when the character of the Vedic gods was undergoing reinterpretation. While this is true, there may well have been an ancient tradition of esoteric interpretation which these texts continue though it could have been confined to a smaller circle and generally overlooked in favour of the common ritualistic usage. In fact, the priests gradually tended to understand the Vedic revelation strictly in terms of ritual. What the *Vedas* reveal is what rites one must perform and how so that one attains satisfaction here as well as a supernatural end hereafter. The Mīmāṁsakas went so far as to define the *Vedas* as consisting essentially of practical injunctions, everything else being subordinate to them. While the professional priests sought to preserve the Vedas literally as revelation but confined their understanding within the context of ritual, the search after spiritual meaning culminated in the *Upaniṣads*. In fact, ritual is essentially symbolical and the Vidyās and *Upāsanās* of the *Āraṇyakas* and the *Upaniṣads* only evince the re-emergence of ritual symbolism in a new mode.

The ancient tradition regards the *Upaniṣads* also as revelation or *Śruti*, but there is an obvious difference between the hymns and the *Upaniṣads*. The hymns are distinctly much earlier. The Upaniṣadic sages are not only later, they plainly owe the origin of their ideas at least in part to what may be found in the *Veda*. Nevertheless, a good deal of the ancient *Upaniṣads* is expressive of what was personally realized or intuited by the sages. The fact that the *Upaniṣads* expound spiritual truth directly and clearly had the effect of eclipsing the earlier revelation of which the language was archaic and the mode of expression ambiguous. Thus, it came about that while the earlier hymns were preserved by professional priests in the ritualistic contexts with their spiritual meaning largely forgotten, the seekers after spritual truth turned to the *Upaniṣads* as the more relevant and easily accessible revelation. The *Veda* thus came to be regarded as relevant in a twofold manner with respect to its two parts.

Since the 19th century, however, there have been attempts to interpret the Vedic hymns in a broader or profounder sense than had been traditionally current. Modern scholarship tends to regard the Vedic hymns primarily as historical or anthropological documents which are to be valued for the light they shed on ancient man in general, ancient Indians in particular, and for tracing the origins of later religious and cultural developments in India. While this approach has undoubted value for the historian, its difficulty lies in the fact that it assumes the *Vedas* to belong to a certain level of development which is somewhat arbitrarily assumed. The Vedic hymns show a well developed tradition of versification and mythology. The hymns are by no means primitive or untutored verses. They reflect an age of developed moral consciousness and there is no reason to assume that their religious beliefs ought to be primitive and animistic or analogous to the religious beliefs of ancient Indo-European tribes living far from developed civilisations. In fact, if it were to be accepted that the Vedic hymns were composed by the 'Aryans' in the 2nd millennium B.C. in India, it would have to be accepted that the tradition of Harappan civilization already existed in the background. What the historical position of the Aryans was and what their relationship to the Harappan civilization, remain, however, uncertain.[8]

The most widely current assumption in modern scholarship about Vedic religion is that it represents a primitive and polytheistic nature worship which was followed by a speculative monism on the one hand and a magical or quasi-magical ritualism on the other. Against this several modern Indian savants like Dayanand, Aurobindo, Kapali Shastri, Anirvan, Coomaraswamy, Madhusudan Ojha and Motilal Shastri have attempted to interpret the hymns in quite different ways.[9] They have assumed a background of developed knowledge or mysticism. All these interpretations, however, seek to approach the Vedic hymns without the burden of later tradition. For all of them, the Vedas are the primary source of knowledge about their own meaning. In this respect they all agree with modern critical scholarship. The difference lies in the general assumption with which these several attempts start. Whether the hymns belong to an age of primitive ignorance or pristine innocence, animistic superstition or spiritual illumination, represent sharply divided points of view. What is the true perspective for the *Vedas*, is however, a question that cannot be decided *a priori* but must depend on the unprejudiced collation of all the evidence, a process which is still incomplete, mainly because the different schools of Vedic scholarship are tied to ideological and methodological prejudices of one sort or another. The chief ideological prejudice of westernized modern scholarship is the assumption that the *Vedas* are essentially the expressions of primitive ignorance and superstition. This prejudice stems from that rationalistic-positivistic and evolutionist hypothesis about the origin of religion which Tylor and others made the basis of modern anthropology and which has left its mark on comparative religion and mythology. Max Muller, thus, saw the origin of Vedic mythology in the metaphorical and ambiguous character of poetic language. French Vedicists see in Vedic mythology and ritual the aspect of magical superstition about solar and meteorological phenomena.[10] The vast corpus of modern researches in the *Vedas* is full of such fanciful hypotheses claiming to shed light on that ancient literature. They are all distinguished by being as fantastic as the myths they claim to elucidate but happily for their authors they remain essentially unfalsifiable and hence beyond proof also. They all confound the mythical notions of space, time, causality and identity with those intended in science and hence have no difficulty in 'showing' that the myths are prescientific 'magical' substitutes for science. It is equally plausible, however, to hold that like poetry and drama myth and ritual are not to be understood on the analogy of science and technology but as autonomous realms of symbolic expression.[11]

On the other side, the traditional assumption of the *Vedas* being divine revelations tells us nothing about their meaning though it has led to the neglect of historical records relating to the Vedic age. The ancient 'historians and antiquarians' (*aitihāsikas and paurāṇikas*) did claim to preserve some tradition about Vedic sages and rulers and some *nidānas* have been preserved for the hymns. Nevertheless, such traditions remain uncorroborated and probably suffered from the same 'anthropomorphizing' tendency which assails modern historians who discover in the *Veda* references to the wars between Aryan and non-Aryan races and tribes. The tendency to understand the *Vedas* in terms of imperfectly understood archeological 'cultures' is an instance of a similar kind. Thus Indra, has been pronounced guilty of destroying the Harappan culture, when we do not really know who the authors of the Harappan culture were and how they were related to the authors of the *Vedas*.

In conclusion one is apt to feel that some of the current assuptions in Vedic interpretation seem to proceed more from prejudice than from evidence. Such is the assumption that the *Ṛgveda* is a document of the invading 'aryan' tribes praying for victory against the 'non-aryans'. The fact is that the 'Aryan' race is simply a hypothesis to account for various degrees of similarity between widely distributed ancient languages. If it is assumed that a number of connected 'Indo-European dialects were spoken in contiguous areas at some time, we do not know with any certainty as to the people or group of peoples who spoke them. Nor do we know of their migrations and history. It is difficult to connect preliterate archaeological cultures with 'Indo-European' communities except hypothetically. When in the second millennium B.C. we find definite epigraphic evidence of people speaking or using Indo-European languages or at least words and names belonging to such languages, such peoples are already distributed far and wide from the Aegian to the Indus and have been in close connection with other ethnic and cultural communities. We do not know that a conquering Aryan race migrated into India. The region from the Indus to the Oxus might well have been part of that original habitat in which some of the Indo-European dialects were anciently spoken. Even if there were migrations into India we do not know the character of these migrations. Nor do we know that the *Ṛgveda* was composed by any originally Indo-European speaking people or migrants. The *Ṛgveda* might well belong to a stage when much commingling of races and communities had already taken place. The fact is that the Vedic people, speaking Sanskrit, did not have any distinct racial or ethnic consciousness. Nor is there any reason to suppose that the eastward expansion of the Vedic people was an essentially warlike process, especially of war against peoples speaking a different language.

Similarly the interpretation of Vedic religion as the worship of natural forces suffers from a Christian as well as a naturalist bias. The truth of Vedic religion is grounded in the genuineness of its own experience. It does not have to conform to Christian revelation or to modern rationalism. Nor does it follow that an age of primitive science must also be an age of primitive religion. To assume that Vedic religion must be polytheistic or monotheistic, is to assume that Godhead must be numerable. Yaska and Badarayana see no contradiction in the gods being one and many, personal and impersonal, a point of view which has been traditionally accepted in India. Is it unreasonable to suppose that this tradition existed from more ancient times? Within the *Ṛgveda* itself such a tradition finds expression. Should it be regarded *ipso facto* late? The realization of the unity of the gods does not have to be an achievement of speculative reason undergoing the process of gradual development in the course of a historical tradition. It is more simply and more fundamentally understood as part of the basic religious experience which senses divinity behind the mysterious forms of nature. It is only a sacrilegeous cynicism, positivistic or Christian, which can describe such experience as merely poetical and hence as no more than an imaginative and emotional platform for vague speculative thought. Suppose we deny to the Vedic seers the title to be the recipients of any genuine Revelation such as was vouchsafed to Moses, Jesus or Mohammad, and hold them merely to be moved Caliban-like by occasional impulses of what has been called 'natural religion', even so does it follow that their vague and poetic speculations should be precisely definable as polytheistic or monotheistic? Or are we to say further that monotheism, however vague, cannot possibly be reached without a clear history of anterior speculative development? The fact is that the whole history of Indian religious experience and thought disagrees with the Semitic conception of man's religious history. And both disagree profoundly from the modern naturalistic theories of the origin and growth of religion. It would be a pity if the historiography of religion in India to be 'scientific' has to be tied to naturalistic or Semitic religious ideologies. The only reasonable course for it would be to seek to interpret ancient Indian texts in the light of the tradition of religious experience in India.[12] Vedic gods, thus, ought to be understood as images and constructs seeking to express and interpret the Vedic experience of worship which formed a rich and growing tradition.[13] In particular, we must guard against purely naturalistic theories of the origin of religion[14] since such theories disregard the existential concern of religion and its inwardness.[15]

REFERENCES

1. Cf. *Nirukta,* 1.5 ; Cf. Jaimini, 1.2.31-45 ; *Nirukta,* 2.5 mentions *Nairuktas* and *Aitihāsikas* as two schools of interpretation. Sāyaṇa in his introduction to the commentary of the *Ṛgveda* mentions the Cārvākas as an example of those who disputed the very existence of the *Veda.*

2. Pāṇini's aphorism–*'Vyatyayo bahulam'* (3.1.85) is expressive of such despair.

3. Cf. Sāyaṇa, *"arthajñānasya tu yajñānuṣṭhānārthatvāt."* (Vol. I, p. 2, Poona).

4. A recent summary of this tradition of scholarship may be seen in Gonda, *A History of Indian Literature,* Vol. I : *Vedic Literature.* My review of the work may be seen in *History and Archaeology,* Vol. I, 1-2. Winternitz, *History of Indian Literature,* Vol. I, is earlier but more widely used. Dandekar's three-volumed *Vedic Bibliography* aims at being comprehensive. So Renou's *Bibliographie Védique.*

5. Macdonell's *Vedic Mythology* is a commonly used survey which contains references to diverse views also. Keith's *Religion and Philosophy of the Vedas and the Upaniṣads* is similar in tenor. Prof. K. Chattopadhyaya's *Vedic Religion* may be seen for a quite different approach. His Presidential Address to the Vedic Section of the AIOC, Trivandrum, formulates his approach to Vedic interpretation.

6. Brugmann, *Grundriss der vergleichenden Grammatik der indogermanischen Sprachen ; Wackernagel, Altindische*

Grammatik, Macdonell's *Vedic Grammar* may also be mentioned here.

7. Grassmann, *Wörterbuch des Ṛgveda.*

8. Ludwig, *Der Rigveda,* 6 Vols.
Oldenberg, *Rigveda, Textkritische und exegetischen Noten,* 2 Vols.

8a. Cf. B. B. Lal and S. P. Gupta, *Frontiers of the Indus Civilisation.*

9. Dayananda, *Ṛgvedādibhāṣyabhūmikā,* his commentary on *Ṛgveda ;* Aurobindo, *Hymns to the Mystic Fire ;* Kapali Sastrin, *Siddhāñjanabhāṣyam ;* Anirvāṇa, *Veda mīmāṁsā,* (Calcutta Sanskrit Research Series) ; Coomaraswamy, *A New Approach to the Vedas,* Moti Lal Sastrin, *Śatapatha brāhmaṇa-bhāṣya, Upaniṣad-Vijñāna-bhāṣya.* Recently Karapatriji has produced *Vedārtha saurabham* in 2 Vols. but it is totally conservative and traditional.

10. Bergaigne, *Vedic Religion* (tr. Paranjape).

11. *e. g.,* Cf. Cassirer, *Philosophy of Symbolic Forms,* 3 Volumes.

12. Piggott, *Prehistoric India.*

13. Vide my paper "The Idea of God and the historical Tradition" presented at the International Symposium on 'God the modern discussion' at Maui (Hawaii), December 26-30, 1981.

14. Cf. Keith, RPV, Vol. I, pp. 42ff. Despite his assertion that the origin of religion cannot be empirically decided, Keith's interpretations of Vedic gods are undoubtedly influenced by the kind of thinking which underlies naturalistic theories of the origin of religion. For a new approach, Cf. Prof. K. Chattopadhyaya, *Vedic Religion.* Panikkar's *Vedic Experience* may also be mentioned as an example of a new departure.

15. Vide my paper "Two Aspects of Religion" presented at the Sixth East-West Conference of Philosophers, Honalulu.

3

VEDIC TRADITION AND ITS UNITIVE VISION

The development of the Vedic Unitive Vision

Traditionally the sage Kṛṣṇa Dvaipāyana Vyāsa is supposed to have accomplished the task of collecting the Vedic hymns in the form of *Saṁhitās*. Apparently this compilation took place in the later Vedic age and perhaps was the result of a desire to preserve the hymns to ensure their authenticity in a period of change, especially linguistic change. It must be confessed, however, that if writing was not known, it is not easy to see what 'compilation could have meant.[1] In recent times when Bhatkhande collected songs from different families of musicians his efforts bore success only because he was assisted by a system of notation which enabled him to write down music and compile, however, imperfectly, a public document. It must be remembered that musical notations were unknown to traditional musicians who continued to spurn it. The difficulty and hostility which Bhatkhande faced must surely pale into insignificance compared to what Vyāsa must have faced.

The family *maṇḍalas* of the *Ṛksaṁhitā* are generally regarded as its ancient kernel.[2] These *maṇḍalas,* however, themselves show a stage when the Vedic gods formed a well developed pantheon worshipped within a system of sacrificial ritual. Possibly there was an earlier period when separate cults existed for the various gods among different groups of worshippers, the pantheon developing as the separate clans and tribes gradually fused into a larger society. Within these original cults, too, the real kernel of their tradition must lie in the primaeval myths which would be the expressions of the first revelations of the gods. Out of these myths presumably came some of the basic adjectives, names and descriptions of the gods which together with the ritual context must have provided the staple material for the composers of the hymns in the form in which they are found today.[3] The present form of the hymns, thus, would appear to draw upon a more ancient tradition of myths which is fragmentarily embedded in them. This supposition is doubtless contrary to the tradition of a literal revelation but is perhaps more in consonance with what is likely to have happened in history. Mythically expressed vision of the ancient seers, ritualistic systematization and symbolism of the priests, and the cognitive enquiry of the sages, these appear to be the three broad stages through which the development of Vedic literature and thought has passed.

One became a seer (*ṛsi*), not through heredity or office, but only through actually attaining to the vision of *mantras.*[4] The revelation is at once a form of thought as well as of speech. The *Veda,* constituted by the *mantras,* is thus at once wisdom as well as word. In later terminology it may be described as the 'seeing speech' (*Paśyantī vāk*). Inasmuch as speech arises from the innate, self-expressive aspect of knowledge,[5] Vedic revelation or vision may be described as at once intuitive and expressive. This duality of aspect can be seen in the meaning of the word *dhī* which has been explained as action as well as vision.[6] The radical contrast of knowledge and action which became a characteristic feature of later *Vedānta* is absent here.

A simplistic view of revelation would be that it is a mental quickening inspired by the gods but such a view seems to lose sight of the fact that the Vedic revelation is traditionally held to have a cosmic status or correspondence. The creativity of the gods also involves the operation of the word. In fact, creation *is* a revelation of what is eternally true, a disposition of objects in accordance with the paradigms in heaven.[7] The creativity of the seers in terms of word and vision thus corresponds to the creativity of the gods and the two are linked in a common wavelength. The gods are themselves seers and priests, sacrificers and artificers. It is only through the nearness of the human priest to the divine that the former becomes a seer, privileged for the moment to participate at the human level in the cosmic process of the manifestation of Truth.[8]

Human beings, thus, become seers only through the favour of the Divine Seer and the Vedic revelation is only the expression at the humtn level or articulation of the eternally self-expressive Seeing Speech, the matrix of divine creativity. Tradition specially mentions the Seven Seers and regards them as the founders of the original Brahmanical clans or *gotras*. In the ancient legends they appear as mythical, semi-divine figures. It has been suggested that their names were simply the names of the divine priest, Agni.[9] The figure seven has, again, been referred to the number of priests in the sacrifice but that would itself need a further explanation. The sacrifice on earth imitates the sacrifice in heaven and the Seven Seers should, thus, ultimately refer to their celestial counterparts. They may have had originally some kind of astral significance. Or, the same divine seer reflected in each of the seven worlds would become seven and this would provide the pattern for the human seers.

It would be obvious that in the legendary account of the seers the historical and the mythical are difficult to disentangle and the reason is fundamental. The whole world-view of the ancient Vedic age consistently superimposes the mythical on the historical because it seeks to understand the realities of human life in terms of celestial paradigms. The modern historical view of man which seeks to explain even the gods of the ancients in terms of human realities and ideas is in total contrast to the ancient view. The deficiency of historical material pertaining to the Vedic age makes it difficult to substantiate any significant hypotheses about the social origins or the supposedly underlying historical facts or beliefs of that age.[10] The only thing possible is to seek to reconstruct the complex of ideas held in that period and examine what reality may be glimpsed through its translucence. The glimpses we would attain to would be largely of ideal constructs of religious experience and only incidentally and occasionally of idealized or symbolized socio-historical realities.[11] This should hardly be surprizing because the *Vedas* have been preserved not as historical records but as a revelation claiming perennial validity.

It has been, of course, claimed that side by side with the priestly tradition of the *Vedas* there was a more historical *Kṣattriya* tradition of the same age preserved in the *Itihāsa-Purāṇa*.[12] Even if this were true, the trouble is that the extant corpus of *Itihāsa-Purāṇa* appears to have undergone extensive transformation in the post-Vedic age and hence ceases to be reliable with respect to the Vedic age unless independent corroboration were to be found for it.

The most fundamental Vedic concept is that of *Ṛta*. The concept arises from the basic Vedic *sādhanā* and experience of the holy word or prayer. The *Brahman* or Prayer wells up from the heart and carries with it a revelation of the immutable power and self-governing nature of the gods. The power of *Brahman* and the power of the gods are bound up together as aspects of the same reality. It is *Ṛta* that is reflected in the cosmic order[13] and governs the will of the gods who are thus called *Ṛta-Vrata*. It is *Ṛta* again, that is enacted in ritual.[14] *Ṛta* is thus the ideal principle of ordering, the paradigmatic principle of ultimate reality. It may be imaged as the law of the celestial and primordial ritual which creates and ordains the cosmos.[15] Conceptually it may be assimilated to Natural Law, at once cosmic, moral and ritualistic. It must be remembered that the distinction effected by modern thought between being, and being right and of both from being in accordance with rite or law did not obtain in that earlier period. The modern distinction, in fact, arises from the distinction between knowledge and will, the latter being free to follow any fiat within the bounds of desire and impulse which are regarded as non-rational. On this view the will becomes arbitrary or non-rationally determined and thus the principles which it follows cease to have any reason or connection with reason just as the latter remains concerned only with the nature of things and contains no directive principle for the will. The ancient view had a richer conception of reason which made it reveal facts as well as values, 'natural' as well as moral laws. The notion of reality itself was not held in contrast to that of value or ideality. The reality of any object was held to lie in its participation in an ideal principle.[16] The notion of perfection applied at once to reality and ideality joined together in fullness.[17] The gods are at once wise and good and mighty. That is the celestial perfection, the fullness yonder. All creatures, created along with the principle of *Ṛta* (as ritual), are joined to the gods in a continuous process or cycle of transformation and constitute a natural fullness or completeness. That is the perfection here—*'Pūrṇam adaḥ pūrṇam idam'*.

It would be natural to seek the content of *Ṛta* but the quest would be doomed to failure because *Ṛta* is not accessible to intellectual reason and discursive speech. It is neither a single law or form nor any system of laws or forms. It is rather the ultimate presupposition of all specific types of order or systems of laws belonging to different realms of objects. It is the celestial matrix of terrestrial forms, itself not a limited form but a whole that is self-determined and self-expressive in infinite variety.[18]

Ṛta cannot be conceived apart from the gods. Belonging to the highest heaven, it is inseparable from the highest divinity, our Father in the highest heaven, the source of all the functional gods who underlie the cosmic process. In the nature and functioning of the various gods, in fact, we may see the reflection of *Ṛta* at various levels of reality. This intuitive perception of *Ṛta* in its dynamics or manifestation is expressed in the *Vedas* in the language of myth and ritual. These have an undoubted connection with the phenomena of nature and human life and it is tempting to interpret them as a kind of primitive science or, again, as poetry inspired by the observation of phenomena. This temptation, however must be eschewed. The Vedic religion is not at heart a rain-making or sun-raising magic but rather an insight into the divinity which underlies all phenomena and has been described as a joyous celebration of its epiphany in terms of the cosmos.[19] In contrast to science which tends to objectivize reality and proceeds to analyze and synthesize what it has already delimited and despiritualized, religion cleaves to the living and pulsating reality which holds subject and object together. This divine reality is one and yet capable of manifesting itself as many, it is formless and has infinite forms, it is personal and at the same time impersonal.[20] Its infinite majesty defies the attempt of discursive speech and thought to define it or sum it up in formulae.

The notion of a supreme god, sometimes identified with Heaven, is an ancient one in the hymns.[21] Heaven and Earth as the original divine pair[22] also appear to antedate the later proliferation of the gods, which was easily seen to be the result of treating the different aspects, names and attributes of one or more gods as different gods.[23] If the hymns show a monotheism super-imposed on polytheism, they show equally the multiplication of the gods who are transparently identical. To argue that the notion of multiplicity is earlier than that of unity is unconvincing in the absence of any reliable stratigraphy of the hymns based on criteria which do not presuppose what is sought to be proved. The general idea of conceptual evolution within a tradition may be granted as a safe assumption but the sense of the unity of godhead is not simply an intellectual conception. As an intellectual conception it was doubtless formulated in later Vedic times, but that does not amount to saying that the religious feeling and mythical language of the earlier epoch had not been aware of the truth which was analytically formulated later. As an 'ism' monotheism may be later Vedic, but there is no earlier polytheism either. The early Vedic perception of deity is intuitive and imaginative. It focussed on a specific 'attribute' and name but glimpsed in and through it a transcendent reality. It is from this fact that the fluidity and imperfect anthropomorphization of the Vedic gods result.

If *Ṛta* is the archetypal principle determining the cosmos as an ordered whole, the gods are its superintending powers. The pattern of *Ṛta* and the functioning of the gods have been sought to be presented in terms of myth and ritual. This representation or symbolism presupposes a certain correspondence between human and natural phenomena, a correspondence which was highlighted in ritual. Myth personifies, ritual imitates. Both serve to remind man of spiritual verities so that he may regulate and orient his life and thought as ordained by the gods. The apprehension of *Ṛta* and the gods was part of a religious experience of an intuitive or revelatory kind which is to be distinguished from the sense perception of natural phenomena or fanciful surmises based on it. The mode of expression of this experience was necessarily symbolic but the symbols were not conceptual and abstract. The Vedic seers expressed their vision poetically. For them revelation and poetry, vision and prayer have the same meaning. The reality which they apprehend is superhuman and immortal and yet capable of entering into a personal relationship with man. It is approachable through worship, illumining the heart of the worshipper and showering blessedness on him.

The most important Vedic myth is related to creation. It is the myth of Indra destroying Vṛtra and releasing the cows and the streams of water which had been obstructed by the latter.[24] Vṛtra is the power of chaos and darkness, of sterility as opposed to creativity. The cows are the same as beams of light and, again, the same as the streams of water symbolizing the forces of life and creation. The struggle of Indra and Vṛtra is the struggle of light and darkness, of creativity and chaos. Later on, the more general idea of the struggle of gods and demons, *devāsurasaṅgrāma* came to overshadow this particular myth.[25] The cosmos and its order represent the victory of the gods over the titanic forces of chaos which is symbolized in the later *Nāsadīya* as waters covered by darkness. Still another hymn says that *Ṛta* and *Satya* were succeeded by Night and Night, by the Wavy Ocean. Then arose the Year and then the Sun and the Moon with the procession of days and nights.[26] These hymns, like the Brahmanic and Puranic versions of the *Devāsurasaṅgrāma,* represent a conceptual development over the ancient Indra-Vṛtra myth but they only serve to explicate what was latent in it.

Early Vedic religion was one of active piety, and worship consisted in offering prayers and sacrifices. True prayer was held to arise from the heart with spontaneous feeling. It included petition as well as glorification.[27] It recalled the attributes and deeds of the god and entreated him to favour the worshipper by giving him virtue as well as happiness. It is the strength of prayer that ensured its effectiveness but prayer itself needed an inspiration from the god to attain its proper stature. The sacrifice had a material side but that does not turn it into a soulless, mechanical device. In course of time, undoubtedly, growing ritualism tended to invest the sacrifice with a virtually magical character—but such was hardly the case in the early Vedic age. Nor would it be correct to say that the sacrifices were grossly materialistic in outlook seeking worldly good from the gods on a *quid pro quo basis,* or that they sought to magically counter the primitive fear about the sun failing to rise or the rain failing to fall. Such interpretations arise partly from a prejudice *ab initio* based on modern agnosticism or the Christian reluctance to accept any revelation which would be pre-Christian and non-Hebraic.* Partly it arises from accepting the later ritualistic interpretations of words like *Vāja, iṣ,* and *rai* as booty, food and wealth respectively when it would be equally tenable to interpret them as prize, vigour and things desired to be obtained. It must also be remembered that the blessings sought from the gods are often sought by the priest at the sacrifice for the ruler or the people on whose behalf he is officiating. Material welfare was undoubtedly sought but it was not felt to be in opposition to either virtue or knowledge. Again, the references to struggle and victory do not need to be interpreted literally or historically. The Aryas are only the pious people, the Dāsas are the godless people of darkness i. e., the demoniac powers.[28] The seers pray for strength and victory in the perennial moral and spiritual struggle in which heroes would always need the support of gods against the forces of evil and darkness. Man is a weak mortal, liable to error by his very humanity.[29] It is only through the

*The Christian faith accepts the principle of sacrifice and may be said to be based on the self-sacrifice of Jesus Christ.

divine power by prayer in his heart that he can enlist the support of the gods, rise to a vision of superhuman reality, adjust himself to the inner law and harmony of the universe and fulfil the task ordained for him on earth by the gods.

In fine, the early Vedic religion was centred in prayer, inspiration and vision and envisaged the ideal of a full and happy human life lived virtuously and piously. Virtue and piety were actively conceived. There is a perpetual struggle of right and wrong, light and darkness in which man must fight and serve and pray so that he may attain to the vision of light and participate on earth in the heroic victory of the gods. In this task man needs truth and sincerity, charity and magnanimity, resolution and courage, prayer and piety. The most famous of Vedic prayers and one which has continued to be offered over the millennia, is a prayer for Light.

Tradition represents the Vedic age as a golden age of truth and righteousness when men, led by mighty heroes and seers, enjoyed the companionship of gods. Modern historians represent the Vedic age as one of Aryan expansion into India from Afghanistan to the Gangā, an age of constant tribal warfare, of migrations and settlements. If the traditional view is just mythical, the current historical reconstruction based on comparative philology from the last century remains speculative till some reliable links are forged between the literary and the archaeological sides of the evidence relating to the second millennium B.C. The difficulties in this task arise as much from the deficiency of the archaeological record up to date as from the fact that the *Ṛgvedasaṁhitā* is primarily a collection of prayers and hymns rather than a historical record of tribal affairs. Nevertheless, however patchy and idealized, we do glimpse a certain social scenario in hymns in terms of their symbols and images.

The people were settled in villages "which occupied clearings in the forests spreading all round as a deep green sea. fearful at dark when all tracks got doubly obliterated."[30] Out of the mass of the people called *viśah* two classes were distinguished the priests or *Brāhmaṇas* and the rulers called *Kṣat-*

triyas or *Rājanyas*. These classes were generally, though not invariably, hereditary. Elective Kingship was not unknown nor was republican polity unknown.[31] Apart from kingship and religious ritual, the family was the principal institution. Although the family was patrilineal, women enjoyed a high degree of freedom and social esteem.[32] The cultivation of barley, cattle-rearing, working in leather, cotton, wool, wood, stone and copper constituted the main elements of economic life.[32a] Barter was common though the use of cattle or the precious metals as a measure of value was known. People lived in houses of wood or thatched huts and travelled in ox-drawn carts or horse-driven chariots.

It is from this simple state of society and its natural setting that the hymns draw their symbols and images. Sun beams at dawn are represented as herds of cows rushing out of the stall. Dawn itself is a lovely maiden waking up men and beasts. The sun is the eye of the gods or a glorious chariot racing across the sky. As Pūṣan he is the protector of paths and pastures. As Savitṛ he appears in a golden chariot in the darkling twilight firmament and sends men and beasts home. The victory of Indra over the demons is announced by the crash of thunder which is his mighty weapon. The Maruts are a band of impetuous warriors riding through the billowing clouds and showering rain in their tempestuous wake. They wear glittering ornaments and carry gleaming axes and lances. The clouds are frequently imaged as mountain peaks and the atmosphere as a sea. Rudra is the archer par excellence and his arrows are entreated to avoid the settlements of the people. The settlements are contrasted with the woodland where tracks get lost especially when the spirit of Night is abroad at twilight. Trees are stately. Fire eats them up. The god of fire is the master of hearth and home, a loving father, a wise priest and the poet par excellence. Heaven and Earth are the primaeval couple. The priests weave the sacrifice in patterned ways. They toil and sing. Skilful fingers are like sisters. Barley rejoices in the rain. The streams are like laughing maidens. Happiness is imaged in spaciousness, in the smoothness of the well-fitted cart. Divine help is like a boat enabling one to cross the watery expanse. Indra is a mighty ruler. Mitra and Varuṇa hold an imperial sway and judge men in accordance with their unerring ordinances. The Nāsatyas are twin horsemen heralding the sun. They are also divine physicians and surgeons. Tvaṣṭṛ is the divine artificer. Ṛbhus are marvellously skilled in the mechanical arts. The unbounded expanse of nature is symbolized in Aditi. Sacrifice symbolizes the process of creative transformation in nature where gods are the sacrificers. Fire is the High Priest. Rain from heaven is ritually imaged in the filtering of the *soma* through a woolen filter. Fire is hidden in water and, falling from heaven, nourishes the plants. Wood thus becomes another hiding place for fire whence it is discovered through forceful friction. The succession of night and day, the cycle of seasons and the year manifest the regulative power of *Ṛta*.

Vedic imagination is moved by the sublimity of nature, its might and grandeur, the victory of light over darkness. The particular circumstances which tangentially enter into their inspired songs as images and symbols have crumbled away into the dust of history. The very words which gave them expression are archaic, even to the point where their meanings have to be re-discovered through painstaking and still uncertain research. Nevertheless, the spiritual vision of a sublime cosmic order which requires man to join the perpetual struggle for Light may still be gleaned from the hymns and has a universal appeal. It has continuously inspired the Indian tradition which considers the Vedic hymns as the basic source of *Dharma* or Law, but its meaning is relevant to the human heart as such and in essentials has little reference to the accidents of a lost socio-historical epoch.

The later *Saṁhitās,* the *Brāhmaṇas* and the *Upaniṣads* constitute the principal sources of the later Vedic age. The *Kalpasūtras* too derive their basic material from the later Vedic age though their actual composition should be placed in the next age when a need was felt to systematize the institutions and practices of the Vedic age. We meet now with a wider geographical horizon and a more complex and materially more advanced society. The knowledge of iron has been gained, settlements are bigger and towns are beginning to emerge. Kings are powerful and ambitious and have to contend with their own kinsmen. Kings and their kinsmen constitute a numerous ruling class engaged in hunting, fighting and amorous affairs and at the same time celebrating large-scale sacrifices to win or proclaim their power. They also patronized philosophy and even laid claims to wisdom. The priests were a highly professionalized class, learned and proud, maintaining an ancient tradition and developing it through interpretation, ritual experimentation and speculation.

As mentioned above the heart of the early Vedic religion lay in *Brahman* as prayer, the holy inspired word which was felt to be at once an expression of the human heart and a vision of divine or cosmic law. The ritual accompanying the prayer tended to become more elaborate and regulated in greater detail in the later Vedic age. This was partly the result of a natural growth of priestly tradition and consequent specialization. Partly it was the result of a sense of holy awe at the time of ritual demanding that every detail should be determined and meaningful so that all mistakes and irrelevancies could be avoided. It should also be remembered that the details produce an exaggerated impression when they are simply *read* or read about. In actual enactment the details are mostly routine except that the alternatives have often been firmly determined and sometimes a symbolic significance is indicated for some of the details, or some quaint ones indicated.

Later Vedic ritual has moved away from simple feeling and transparent symbolism. It is now dominated by the sense of ritual obligation and of profound meaning discoverable in terms of special knowledge. Ritual tends to develop as if it were a science with precise practical injunctions oriented to specific ends. Modern scholarship describes such an outlook as magical, or supersitious or, worse, as a cunning device of the priests to strengthen their social hold. Tradition considers the ritual prescriptions to reveal the means for gaining supernatural ends or natural ends supernaturally. The supernatural ends include the winning of heaven after death and accumulating an unseen merit or avoiding sin and demerit.[33] It is assumed that actions not only have a natural but also a supernatural, imperceptible consequence. There is no way of knowing this latter category of things except through the Vedic injunctions. It is assumed that these must be purposive and when no rational purpose can be discovered in them, some supernatural purpose must be assumed. This might sound a bit circular to a sceptical mind, but then faith in the unseen is the essential postulate of all religions. Faith itself survives on the basis of actual or imaginary success gained from ritual action. As far as supernatural gains are concerned, it is obvious that no assurance can be gained about them before death. In practice, then, the assurance has to come from gaining natural ends. Whether such success comes from ritual or from natural causes remains rationally indeterminate. Such, however, is the force of fear and desire in situations of crucial importance but rational uncertainty that men are willing to catch at a straw, whether of ritualistic magic or social science jargon. This psychological explanation of the appeal of ritual does not, of course, constitute a refutation of the reality or effectiveness of ritual. Nor is it intended as such.

Sacrifice consists of three elements-deity, material offering, sacrificing or giving up. The deity is addressed, invoked, praised and entreated in terms of Vedic hymns and formulae. The word or *mantra* and the deity cannot be conceived separately according to the traditional school of Vedic exegesis which tends to identify the two. The principal deities which figure in the more important sacrifices are Agni and Soma, Indra and Varuṇa, Rudra and Maruts, Savitṛ and Prajāpati, Sarasvatī, Vāyu and Dyāvā-pṛthvī. Material offerings are of various kinds—cereals, milk and milk products, *soma* and animal flesh. The sacrificing or giving up of the offering is a mental resolve and announcement to that effect by the sacrificer who gives up his proprietory right over the substance which is permanently taken away from his use.[33a] Sacrificial ritual, thus, consists in invoking the presence of the deity, addressing it and giving up a material offering for its sake. Faith in the sacred word as ensuring contact with the deity, faith in the power and presence of the deity and sincerity in the offering are the obvious psychic components of the ritual. The essential role of the priests is not that of a monopolist, exploiter or professional, but rather of a person at once dedicated and wise whose presence inspires confidence in the correctness and efficacy of the ritual.

Vedic ritual is divisible into three main types[34] domestic (*pāka-yajña*), offerings with or without *soma* (*haviryajña,* and *soma-yāga*). *Pāka-yajñas* were seven—*aupāsana-homa, Vaiśvadeva, pārvaṇa, aṣṭakā, māsika śrāddha, śrāvaṇa,* and *śūlagava.* Although this domestic ritual is not discussed in the *Brāhmaṇas,* its antiquity may be presumed. This ritual was performed in the domestic (*āvasathya* or *gṛhya*) fire as distinguished from both the ordinary secular fire as well as the sacred Vedic (*śrauta*) fire. *Aupāsana homa* was the daily offering of curd and rice, morning and evening, to Agni as the principal deity and Prajāpati as secondary deity. Vaiśvadeva consisted of the five 'great sacrifices' (*mahāyajñas*)—*deva-yajña, bhūta-yajña, pitṛ-yajña, manuṣya-yajña,* and *brahma-yajña.* This codification was possibly of a later date, an attempt to sum up the most important ritual obligations of any ordinary householder. It recognises the claims on him not only of gods, men and ancestors but of all living beings. The next three *pāka-yajñas* are concerned with offerings to the ancestors. *Śrāvaṇaka* was a daily offering during the rainy season to the snakes. It is worth noting that *aṣṭakā-śrāddha* and *śūlagava,* both require the employment of beef and hence went out of use in course of time.

The *pāka-yajñas* are essentially daily acts of reverent remembrance and homage to gods, ancestors, humanity and life as a whole. It is a recognition of man's grateful dependence on others and a celebration of the harmony of nature.

The *Haviryajñas* are—*agnihotra, darśapūrṇamāsa, āgrayaṇa, cāturmāsya, paśu, sautrāmaṇi,* and *piṇḍapitṛyāga. Agnihotra* was homage to Fire and the Sun every evening and morning respectively. Prajāpati was worshipped alongside both in the second place. Milk was the principal offering though other substances like rice could also be used for securing specific gains. One who desired to secure "a village or plenty of food, or strength or brilliance may employ respectively *yavāgū* (gruel), cooked rice, curd or clarified butter". (Kane, II, 2, p. 1001). Being the most obligatory, *Agnihotra* may be said to have been the most important rite. Its similarity to the more popular and handy *aupāsana homa* is obvious. It could be performed without the help of any priest also. In the Vedic age *Agnihotra* seems to have occupied the position which *sandhyāvandana* came to do in later times.

Darśa and *Pūrṇamāsa* were sacrifices on every New Moon day. In the former a cooked cereal offering was made to Agni and milk and curd were offered to Indra. In the latter Agni and Soma were worshipped with cooked cereal cake and clarified butter. *Āgrayaṇa* was a sacrifice of first fruits. The *Cāturmāsyas* performed every fourth month were seasonal sacrifices. *Paśu* was the sacrifice of a goat to Agni, Indra, Sūrya and Prajāpati annually during the rainy season. *Sautrāmaṇi* was also an animal sacrifice where three animals were sacrificed and liquor also was offered although this went out of use in later times. *Piṇḍa-pitṛyajña* was a sacrifice to the ancestors.

The Soma sacrifices were *Agniṣṭoma, Atyagniṣṭoma, Ukthya, Ṣoḍaśī, Vājapeya, Atirātra* and *Aptoryama. Soma* appears to have been a plant with brown juice when crushed and this juice was drunk with water and milk and had an exhilerating effect. Soma was regarded as a deity, especially of the Brāhmaṇas, and also as the dearest nourishment of the gods especially of Indra. The whole of the ninth *maṇḍala* of the *Ṛgvedasaṁhitā* consists of hymns addressed to Soma. Some of these hymns contain unmistakable elements of devotional fervour or of mystical or symbolic intimation. Soma is held to have descended from heaven. Its purification through a woolen strainer is compared to the falling of rain from the clouds. It must be noted, moreover, that Soma is mentioned only in the religious context of offering to the gods. It is not, therefore, to be interpreted as a popular drink, In the sacrifices where Soma was used the hymns of the *Ṛgveda* were sung on sacred melodies called *sāmans*. This must have strengthened the atmosphere of exhileration already present on account of *Soma*.

"The simplest of the *Soma* sacrifices is *Agniṣṭoma* or *Jyotiṣṭoma*. It lasts for several preparatory days called *Upasad* and a final day of *sutyā* when *Soma* was thrice pressed and offered. The householder who wished to perform the sacrifice had to undergo a rigorous period of abstinence, which might be long, and ritual seclusion by way of initiation or *Dīkṣā*. *Soma* was symbolically purchased and ceremoniously received as a guest. The priests pledged mutual loyalty in the *Tānūnaptra* rite and the *Pravargya* rite was performed. The *Pravargya* consisted chiefly of heating an earthen pot called *Mahāvīra* in which butter and milk were later poured and offered to the Aśvins. The preparation for the *Agniṣṭoma* then proceeded by the construction of the Mahāvedi to which *Soma* was brought. Elaborate arrangements were then made for the ceremonious pressing of *Soma*. On the trial day the ceremonies of pressing *Soma,* filtering it to the accompaniment of the *Pavamāna stotras,* filling the various cups or *grahas* with it and offering *Soma* and *puroḍāśa* were repeated thrice—morning, mid-day and evening. The ceremonies involved various priestly processions and chants and animal sacrifice."[35] Some of these ceremonies like *Pravargya* and the filtering of the *Soma* had obvious symbolic meanings. The long preparation through self-discipline of the sacrificer as part of his initiation also deserves to be noted. The famous *Rājasūya, Aśvamedha* and *Vājapeya* sacrifices were special elaborations of the *Soma* sacrifice intended for securing special gains for their patrons.

The early Vedic religion was one of simple piety and prayer from the heart. The *Brāhmaṇa* texts emphasize the performance of ritual obligations which were precisely and elaborately formulated. This made the assistance of priestly specialists necessary and promised absolution from sin, a place in heaven and also worldly success and gains. This certainly looks like a complication and distortion introduced by the growing power of priestcraft, although the Brāhmaṇa-texts are full of symbolism and wisdom. Tradition, of course, clubs together the faith of the hymns and the faith of the *Brāhmaṇas*, regarding them as complementary but presents them as ritualism, a faith oriented to ephemeral gains (*karmakāṇḍa, pravṛttilakṣaṇa dharma*).

While *Ṛta* came to be interpreted as a complex order of ritual prescriptions which one could disregard only at the peril of one's supernatural though imperceptible discomfiture, the gods came to be interpreted as elements in a cosmology symbolized in the principles of sacrifice. The Vedic word or logos was itself interpreted cosmologically. The principle of correspondence between the human, the ritual and the cosmic orders was most clearly emphasized. The *Puruṣa-sūkta* contains a clear indication of these trends. It conceives of a primordial Person (*Puruṣa*) who pervades the whole universe and exceeds it. It attributes creation to an original sacrifice by the gods where the sacrifice was its professed offering as well as its deity. It then identifies human society with the cosmic Person, social differentiation corresponding to the organic structure of Man.

The *Brāhmaṇas* contain much speculation on the sacrifice as the original principle of creation. Without quite annulling the diversity of gods, they tend to supersede it by emphasizing an original creating god called Prajāpati. The famous Ṛgvedic *sūkta* addressed to *Ka* is an early example of the emergence of this deity. There the god is called Hiraṇyagarbha, golden child or child of a golden womb. The *Brāhmaṇas* continue this tendency to identify the creator god with the sun. This is probably the reason why solar gods tend to rise in prominence in the later Vedic age.[36] Viṣṇu was the most important of these and He was often identified with the principle of sacrifice itself.

Prajāpati, however, remained on abstract deity. In fact, the rise in importance of abstract deities is another feature of this age. Viśvakarman, Manyu, Kāma, Śraddhā, Kāla, Skambha and Prāṇa are other similar gods.[37] This, again, ought to be attributed to the speculative tendency so evident in the *Brāhmaṇas.* The form of this speculation is mythical and it is embedded in ritualistic contexts. For example, to explain why an offering to Prajāpati is made silently, it is recalled that Speech was once annoyed with Prajāpati because the latter gave a decision against her when she and the Mind had been disputing who was the greater of the two.[38] The concern with the relation between Mind and Speech is more than mythical but the form of the discussion is mythical. In fact, the *Brāhmaṇas* contain a good deal of reflection over Speech, Thought and Breath, and also on the sun, time and creation. A natural consequence of this concern was an increasing preoccupation with the question of death and immortality. Besides, as this speculative interest increased, there was a tendency to view the sacrificial process in terms of its symbolic meaning. What one does is significant in terms of what one knows about the ritual. This tendency reached its climax in the construction of special fire altars (*agni-cayana*). Here the process of external ritual is virtually superseded by that of symbolical knowledge and meditation (*vidyā, upāsanā*).[39]

The funerary hymns of the *Ṛgvedasaṁhitā* (X.14-16) suggest that the righteous man who has been properly cremated regains the use of his faculties and traversing the path beyond the heights attains to the world of departed ancestors and there dwells in lasting happiness. Thus it is said that it is the unwolfish, the righteous that attain to life after death—*'asuṁ va īyu-ravṛkā ṛtajñāḥ'* (*Ṛg.* X.15.1). The moral law obtains as much in afterlife as here. The *pitṛloka* is won by good deeds here—*vāste śivāstanvo jātavedas tābhirvahainaṁ sukṛtāmu lokam* (*Ib.* X.16.4). The *Pitṛs* themselves are god like in being invoked and in bestowing their grace and good will—"*upahūtāḥ pitaraḥ somyāso barhiṣyeṣu nidhiṣu priyeṣu ta ā gamantu ta iha śruvantvadhi bruvantu tevantvasmān*" (X.15.5). The world of the departed ancestors is ruled by

Yama or by Yama and Varuṇa jointly–*ubhā rājānā svadhayā madantā yamaṁ paśyasi varuṇaṁ ca devam.* (Ṛg. X.14.7). The *Pitṛs* are however, sharply distinguished from the gods–*svāhānye svadhayānye madanti* (Ṛg. X.14.3). At death men follow the same path which the ancestors followed–*pathibhiḥ pūrvyebhiḥ* (Ṛg. X.14.7). This path shown by Yama goes beyond the heights *'Pareyivāṁsam pravato mahīranu bahubhyaḥ panthām anupaspaśānam'* (Ṛg. X.14.1). The world which one reaches through this path is expected to last for ever *'naiṣā gavyūti rapabhartavāu'* (Ṛg. X.14.2). There one meets the departed ancestors all delighting with Yama *saṅgacchasva pitṛbhiḥ saṁ yamena* (Ṛg. X.14.8). The *Pitṛloka* is described to be in the highest heaven or in the middle heaven (*parame vyoman*, Ṛg. X.14.8 or *madhye divaḥ*, Ṛg. X.14.15). In that world one regains the fruits of sacrifices and charities here (*iṣṭāpūrta*, Ṛg. X.14.8). Evil is left behind and one returns home again. There one regains a glorious body, *hitvāyāvadyaṁ punarastamehi saṁgacchasva tanvā suvarcāḥ* (Ṛg. X.14.8).

This hope that they should be able to find another life in another world where they would be god-like and will not again be deprived of felicity, had to contend with the obvious fact that the body, breath and faculties are all destroyed at death *sūryaṁ cakṣurgacchati vātamātmā* (Ṛg. X.16.3). Fire itself burns away with the body. So prayer is made to fire not to really destroy the body but to bake it or mature it so that it will be ripe for the world of ancestors–*mainam agne vi daho mābhi śoco māsya tvacaṁ cikṣipo mā śarīram. yadā śṛtaṁ kṛṇavo jātavedo themenaṁ prahiṇutāt pitṛbhyaḥ* (Ṛg. X.16.1). In the ritual the dead body is even covered by other animal flesh so as to suggest that fire may be satisfied with substitutes. Whether such ritual and prayers are survivals from a remote age or were deemed to have some magical efficacy, is difficult to say. In any case it is obvious that the human body, its faculties and its frailty (*puruṣatā* Ṛg. X.15.6) are seen and felt to be left behind and what the righteous person properly cremated hopes for from the grace of gods, specially Agni, Yama and Varuṇa, is a new life (*asu*), immortal, happy, good and wise like that of the gods. What is the principle linking the dead here and hereafter is not quite clear. The notion of an immortal and individual human soul distinct from the body is not to be found here. *Ātmā* is clearly used for the breath. The word *asu* is significant but its meaning is not precisely definable. It is clear, however, that in some sense man can survive death.

The *Pitṛloka* or the status of the *Pitṛ* was not a necessary fate for everybody. Although the immortality of the human soul is not to be discerned clearly, the inevitability of the moral law is quite clear. Only the righteous have a future in heaven. The evil may merely lose their limbs and have some kind of non-descript existence in the earth or water or vegetation (*Sūryaṁ cakṣur gacchatu vātamātmā dyāṁ ca gaccha pṛthviñ ca dharmaṇā. Apo vā gaccha yadi tatra te hitam oṣadhīṣu prati tiṣṭha śarīraiḥ-Ṛg.* X.16.3). This verse, however, should not be taken as an intimation of the doctrine of rebirth. The idea found here is only this that one may, after death, exist in some form on earth, water or vegetation but that through the favour of the gods one may attain to an exalted condition in heaven.[40] What distinguishes this doctrine from that of rebirth is that it does not recognise the innate immortality of the soul and the inexorability of *Karman* as well as the transience of its results. Nor does it understand the mechanism which joins and separates the soul from the body.

The *Brāhmaṇas* dwell upon the cosmic significance of the sacrifice as a representation of the creative act of Prajāpati who is sometimes identified with the Year, the basic unit of the cycle of time.[41] This movement of time is subject to the Sun and hence it came to be held that the worlds under the Sun are subject to passing away or death. While this was naturally well recognised for the human world, it came to be surmised that the world after death may also be transient if it was this side of the Sun. Thus arose the idea of Punarmṛtyu or Death in Afterlife.[42] At the same time it was clearly recognised that afterlife depends on the gaining of a new life from fire after cremation. Since the Sun is the fire in heaven, it was imagined that some special fire ritual may enable one to pass to real immortality after death.

Thus we are told in the *Śatapatha* that during cremation the fire burns only the body of the dead who is himself reborn from the fire even as he is born from his parents. However, in order that the new life may be permanent one must have performed the *Agnihotra*—"*Sa yatra mriyate yatrainam agnāvabhyādadhati tadeṣogneradhijāyaṭe'athāsya śarīramevāgnir dahati tadyathā piturvā māturvājāyeta evameṣo'gner adhijāyate śaśvaddha vā eṣa na sambhavati yognihotraṁ na juhoti tasmād vāgnihotraṁ hotavyam.*"[43] The immortal principle contrasted with the mortal body is *Prāṇa*, "*Yajamāna ubhayameva bhavati martyañcaivāmṛtañca tasya prāṇā evāmṛtā bhavanti śarīram martyam sa etena karmaṇaitayā vṛtaikadhājaram amṛtam ātmānaṁ kurute.*"[44] To gain this immortality in afterlife one should ritually represent the golden or *hiraṇmaya Prajāpati* (*Ib.*). It may be remembered here that in the *Brāhmaṇas* representation is a means to identification.

The sun being the source of time is identified with death.[45] Similarly whatever is this side of the Sun is all pervaded by deaths'.[46] To the world of time and death belongs the physical body. Life after death arises from ritual performed here or its mysteries meditated over here.[47]

The ideas of the *Brāhmaṇas* about afterlife may thus be seen to have logically evolved from the earlier Vedic ideas. It is ritual that ensures immortality in afterlife, otherwise death may recur even in the other world. The ordinary ritual of cremation gives one life after death but it is only a special ritual which can make that life everlasting. This notion of *Punarmṛtyu* thus is quite different from the later notion of *Punarjanman*.

There are, however, certain passages in the *Brāhmaṇas* which suggest an awareness of the doctrine of Rebirth but then the later portions of the *Brāhmaṇas* overlap with the *Āraṇyakas* and do not need to be too far removed in time from the *Upaniṣads*. Thus the *Śatapatha* in a section towards the end speaks of retaliatory action in another existence.[48] The *Tāṇḍya* speaks of departing for six months and returning in another six months,[49] of descending from heaven,[50] of climbing heaven like a tree and descending to this world.[51] It even speaks of this world being born repeatedly.[52]

There is no doubt, however, that when the Brahmanical thinkers became acquainted with the idea of Rebirth, the old and the new were woven together in the thought of the Upaniṣadic Age. The notion of *asu-prāṇa* became assimilated with the notion of *Jiva,* the notion of ritual action with moral action, and birth and death in the other world with rebirth in this world. The old *Pitṛyāna* was now interpreted as the ordinary path of reincarnation, while *Devayāna* became the path to immortality and corresponds to the conquest of *Punarmṛtyu* through the identity with the Sun. The *Kauṣītakī* says "Then just as one driving a chariot looks down upon the two chariot wheels, thus he looks down upon day and night, thus upon good deeds and evil deeds, and upon all the pairs of opposites. This one, devoid of good deeds, devoid of evil deeds, a Knower of Brahma, unto very Brahma goes on."[53] This image of the chariot wheels and the man on the chariot goes back to the *Śatapatha Brāhmaṇa* where it is used to illustrate the immortality of the Sun and the mortality of the worlds under Him. The old and the new thus smoothly flow together.[54]

This transition in the conception of afterlife was closely interwoven with the transition from external ritual to symbolic meditation and a corresponding change in the conception of the nature of man and his relationship to the cosmos. The later *Brāhmaṇa* texts, the *Āraṇyakas* and the earlier portions of the *Upaniṣads* emphasize symbolic knowledge and meditation. It is, of course, not to be supposed that meditation *replaced* ritual, except for a few who felt themselves qualified to enter an esoteric path. It may be mentioned here that some modern scholars think that this tradition of symbolism and meditation may be very ancient. This suggestion can only be considered unproved, though unrefuted. Some kind of symbolism, of course, was ancient as is proved by the famous *asyavāmīya sūkta* of the *Ṛgvedasaṁhitā*. Similarly, the contemplation of Inspiring Light was an essential part of the ancient revelation and in the form of *Sandhyāvandana* continues down to the present day. Nevertheless, whether a *systemized* symbolic meditation was practised as a *regular* method before the *Āraṇyaka* period remains, to say the least, unproved.

"As examples of these esoteric *Vidyās* may be mentioned *Suparṇaciti* in which the eagle-shaped altar symbolizes a solar cosmogony, the *Nāciketagni-cayana,* the *Sāvitracayana* which symbolizes the mystery of solar time or the Āruṇaketuka where water is the only material used."[55] In this symbolism there is a correspondence between the elements of ritual, cosmic elements and elements of human personality. This correspondence produces a threefold meaning for the actions and constructions viz., *adhiyajña* or ritualistic, *adhidaiva* or cosmical and *adhyātma* or subjective. Thus the various layers of the altar correspond to the various planes—terrestrial, atmospheric, celestial and several intermediate ones—of cosmic being and at the same time to the various elements of personality, physical and vital, and constructing the various layers of the altar is like ascending the various levels of existence and reconstructing for oneself an immortal being beyond death. From *vidyās* in terms of *Agni-cayana* to *vidyā* more generally in the sense of hidden wisdom and *Upāsanā* as meditation upon it was a natural further step. The central idea of these meditations is that while man must give up his mortal body, his *Prāṇa* is capable of gaining immortality by uniting with the solar logos. This is a mystical union arising from symbolic meditation. It cannot be attained by simply external ritual.

Symbolic meditation represents a point of transition between the path of ritual action and that of wisdom, *Karma-yoga* and *Jñāna-yoga* as they are to be found in ancient Vedic literature. The ancient principles of the hierarchy and correspondence of planes of being find their most articulate expression and utilization here. Similarly it was now fully understood that the creative process is one of formation and transformation, multiplication and manifestation and that its source was Light or Logos, or rather, the Luminous Logos beyond which lay the wholly inconceivable Unmanifest. The process of *Upāsanā* also confirmed what was implicit in the ancient hymns viz., that the human mind contained a principle capable of rising to cosmic wisdom and revealing to man his true immortality. The principles of hierarchy and correspondence, unity in difference, centrality of the luminous mind or *nous,* these constituted the basic elements of the impressive structure of wisdom which was clearly articulated in the later *Brāhmaṇas, Āraṇyakas,* and early *Upaniṣads*. These have continued to be permanent elements of the tradition of spiritual wisdom in India and have been repeated and realized in diverse ways in different ages and schools. They are, indeed, elements belonging to *philosophia perennis, sanātana dharma* or *Ārya dharma*.

So far enquiry was the culmination of ritualistic action and discovered its answers in terms of meanings to be discerned in forms and structures, ritualistic, cosmic and human. The wisdom of *Agni-cayana* and *Upāsanā* cannot be separated from action and symbolism. What is more the attitude towards values which lay behind earlier ritualism tends to spill over into *Upāsanā*. Success in this world and immortality in the other are assured in *Upāsanā* as well, although the nature of immortality is better understood and it is emphasized more than temporal gain. As the Upaniṣadic period grows to its maturity, a marked change now takes place. Enquiry now becomes the starting point of spiritual life. Dissatisfaction is expressed with mere ritual and worldly gain. The search for an *archê* without and within leads to the revolutionary perception that it is Knowledge that is the supreme principle of being and with this the search for self-knowledge is completed in the realization of the identity of *Ātman* and *Brahman*. Towards the end of the Upaniṣadic period there are intimations of an ascetic outlook towards life and of the doctrines of *Karman* and Rebirth. At the same time, the older conception of *devatā* culminates in a monotheistic doctrine emphasizing the importance of faith and grace. Then, again, the *Upaniṣads* lay repeated emphasis on moral action and virtues in place of ritual action. In so far as the terms in which the Upaniṣadic enquiry is conducted are conceptual rather than symbolic, its mode of thought may be described as one of intuitive philosophy.

If the spiritual life of the ancient Vedic period was one of simple but active piety centering round the experience of divinity in the phenomena of illumination and prayer, and that of the middle and later Vedic period one of ritualistic action with its experience of solemn holiness and mysterious meaning leading to symbolic meditation, the spiritual quest of the *Upaniṣads* may be described as one of *Jñāna-yoga* and *Adhyātma-yoga* leading to the realization of the unity of spiritual being.

The later *Vedānta-sūtras* which seek to systematize and expound the doctrines of the *Upaniṣads* describe their quest as *Brahma-jijñāsā* or Enquiry into *Brahman*. This is a fitting description of the Upaniṣadic quest also. *Jijñāsā* is desire for knowledge and is comparable to Greek 'philosophia' or 'love of knowledge'. The *Upaniṣads* belong to an age of considerable intellectual development. of growing specialization and debate. "The *Chāndogya* refers to a wide variety of disciplines then pursued by the learned—the four *Vedas*, *Itihāsa* and *Purāṇa*, the lore of departed ancestors, arithmetic, astrology, accountancy, dialectic, theology, metaphysics, physics, politics, astronomy and toxicology."[56] The *Upaniṣads* show how thinkers and sages travelled far and wide in search of knowledge and relate many famous symposia and debates which gathered participants even from distant places. We hear of the kings of Videha and Kāśī, Pāñcāla and Kekaya taking a keen interest in the debate and themselves participating in it. In fact, the view has been advanced that the Kṣattriyas were rivals of the Brāhmaṇas in this age. Actually, "It is only the *Pañcāgnividyā* which is specifically attributed to the Kṣattriyas. On the other hand, the greatest Upaniṣadic teachers are all Brāhmaṇas. It must also be mentioned that the *Upaniṣads* do not attach too great a value to caste. They rather show that the love of truth was placed above the usual pretensions of caste. The story of Satyakāma who was declared a Brāhmaṇa for his love of truth, of *Raikva,* and of Uddālaka Āruṇi who went to Pravāhaṇa Jaivali for learning what he did not know, are instances in point."[57] Nevertheless, it is quite clear that *Brahma-vidyā* is no longer a prerogative of the Brāhmaṇas and that the encouragement which kings gave to its pursuit as patrons and participants must have been a significant factor in attracting the priestly class towards it. In the royal courts debate was clearly moving away from traditional priestly concerns. It has even been argued that the *Upaniṣads* represent an antiritualistic movement. This is true in a sense. "The *Upaniṣads* continue the symbolic interpretation of ritual or discard them as 'frail rafts'. They substitute '*Ātma-yajana*' for '*Deva-yajana*' and the value they seek is not the continuation of worldly happiness here and hereafter but 'eternity' (*amṛtatva*) or 'beatitude' (*ānanda*) or freedom (*mukti*)."[58] Nevertheless, as already argued, these new tendencies were largely interpretative developments within the older tradition. The priests themselves helped these in their search for the spiritual meaning (*adhyātma*) of the ritual (*adhidaiva* and *adhiyajña*). Traditional priestly learning and ritual and the newer and freer, more rational spiritual enquiry developed hand in hand as two learnings, lower and higher, which seems to foreshadow the later theory of two standpoints, pragmatic and absolute. At the same time. the present author has argued elsewhere that the later *Upaniṣads* undoubtedly show the impact of a new circle of ideas and hence presumably of contact with a new circle of thinkers, 'wanderers', 'sages' and mystics who condemned ritual without reservations.[59] The figure of Sayugvā Raikva is much nearer the later *Parivrājakas* of whom Kabandhī Kātyāyana is already mentioned in the *Praśnopaniṣad.*[60]

Although the quest for *Brahman* developed in an age of intellectual enquiry, it was itself not a purely intellectual quest. The truth (*sat*) it sought was not a value-neutral truth. *Brahmavidyā* or metaphysics (in contrast to *bhūta-*

vidyā) was interpreted as *Ātmavidyā* or spiritual science. Although dialectical in the original Socratic sense, its method was at times intuitive rather than purely logical and conceptual. That is partly because of the nature of the truth which is sought. It sought a spiritual truth and it sought to experience it. Naturally the literary means employed for communicating this experience are dialogue, parable and poetry rather than strict ratiocination. The *Upaniṣads* thus contain a mixture of the mystical and the philosophical since they are an heir to an earlier search for cosmological truth as well as for the 'mystery' which would lead to personal immortality. Both these tendencies have been mentioned above.

The Vedic search for *Brahman* was like the Greek search for *phusis* or *archê,* the original substance out of which the universe has emerged. It is tempting indeed to draw a parallel between the views of Thales and the *Nāsadīyasūkta,* Anaximenes and Sayugvā Raikva, Parmenides and Uddālaka Āruṇi. And yet the parallelism is apt to be superficial. Following Aristotle the Greek philosophers have been understood as propounding speculative cosmologies, identifying elements from nature as ultimate causes. Greek "natural philosophies" thus remain only as landmarks in the historical development of philosophical speculation. Vedic thought, on the other hand, is throughout impregnated with religious and mystical significance. For the *Nāsadīya* the original 'waters' pulsated with their innate power, "breathed without breath". For Raikva, air is essentially sentience. The original principle for the Vedic seers is, in fact, never wholly natural. It is always sentient, holy, divine.[61] In this sense it may be said that the Upaniṣadic answers to the cosmological enquiry are, more 'primitive' or more 'mystical' than the Greek, according to one's point of view.

It is also possible to represent the situation in a slightly different manner. In the case of Greece the historical relationship between the thinkers is known much better than in the case of Vedic India. In the case of Greece we can clearly distinguish the 'natural philosophers' from those in whom the similarity to the natural philosophers is really deceptive. For example, Heraclitus is not really a natural philosopher. Nor probably was Parmenides. In the case of India while there is no doubt that the mainstream of Vedic thought held the First Principle to be spiritual, it is just possible that there were thinkers who tended towards some kind of natural First Principles and yet adopted the mode of expression and life characteristic of the sages following a holy life. In the Age of Buddha we find the materialistic philosopher Ajita Kesakambalin living and preaching like the non-materialistic sages. In the present century we have the example of Sadhu Santinatha. In fact, the *Vedāntasūtras* felt the need of distinguishing *Brahman,* the Upaniṣadic first principle from Nature as upheld by *Sāṅkhya* by pointing out that *Brahman* is a sentient creative principle. This need could only arise in the context of at least apparently naturalistic principles being mentioned in the *Upaniṣads*. The possibility cannot be ruled out that some of these are echoes of genuine 'natural philosophies'. There might have been others which have not been preserved in the *Upaniṣads* which were fundamentally religious documents. It should be remembered that the *Upaniṣads* do mention materialism but only to reject it.

Upaniṣadic enquiry follows two directions which ultimately converge. On the one hand, Upaniṣadic sages and thinkers experienced the sense of unity in nature. This experience was at once one of mystical vision as of philosophical conviction. The sense of wonder and the conviction of unity are, in fact, common to both. The notion of Prajāpati or Puruṣa creating the world had already been formulated. The *Upaniṣads* draw the conclusion that there must be a continuity in the whole universe and that existence itself must be spiritual in nature. All diversity must be regarded as only apparent. Just as the same material cause appears differently in different effects, for example, clay in various pots and other articles, similarly the same *Brahman* appears in different forms of existence differently. *Brahman,* thus, is the very being—*sat*—of all things. At the same time, *Brahman* is the creator, the original Person, who wills the world into existence. *Brahman,* thus, is both the efficient as well as the material cause of the world. Just as the spider spins a web out of itself, so does *Brahman* manifest the world out of His own being. *Brahman* is both the being and the sentience of the Universe, the Centre from which it emanates and the radii which spring up in all directions. In the language of Vedāntic philosophy, *Brahman* is the *abhinnanimittopadāna-kāraṇa* of the world. As the seed contains the tree, so does *Brahman* contain the diversity of the world within Himself. As salt dissolved in water pervades every part of it unseen, so does *Brahman* pervade the whole world as an invisible presence.

Brahman meant originally a 'laud' or 'prayer' and hence the word with its holy power, *logos,* the principle of creation. Later it came to mean any principle of creation, *archê.* Hence, came the classical definition of *Brahman* viz., "that from which all beings are born, in which they subsist and into which they return."[62] As already mentioned, *Brahman* is not only the First cause of things but their sole cause, substance, and destiny. It is not only being without difference and limitation but this being is the same as an infinite and homogenous consciousness. Again, *Brahman* as infinite Being—Consciousness is identified with *Bliss* or Beatitude. Bliss is where consciousness gives up its seeking and rests. It is not something different from consciousness but its own self-realization or infinity. "Where there is infinity there is happiness."[63] The Being of *Brahman* is indeterminate and immanent, the source of all the reality that there is in the world. His consciousness is not a psychic function, a relation of subject and object ;[64] it is a timeless, non-relational self-consciousness. His Bliss is not the satisfaction yielded by an object but the autonomy and infinity of consciousness in its self-realization. The Being is consciousness, the consciousness Bliss. Being-consciousness-Bliss, an infinite and universal unity, 'one without a second', the source of all things, their explanation and destiny, the ever-realized end of all seekings, that is *Brahman.* He is the final principle of cosmology and ontology, epistemology and axiology. He is thus the First Cause,

Prime Substance, foundational consciousness and Supreme Value. Different lines of enquiry culminate in Him.

Philosophically, the task of identifying these different categories or first principles presents a difficult task. Cause and substance are logically near and both the categories emerge as part of a cosmological enquiry. The connection with consciousness historically rested on the theistic character of the cosmology. Whether there has to be a First cause, and whether this First cause has to be a person, are questions which were debated endlessly in later times. The connection between consciousness and value in this context also arose originally from the divine character of the creative consciousness. It follows, thus, that although various types of reflection led up to *Brahman* in His various aspects or attributes, the fundamental line of enquiry which led to the concept of *Brahman* was cosmological and theistic. *Brahmavāda* may best be described as a kind of pantheism. *Brahman* is at once the creator and the created things. He is the sole reality. Although there are two aspects of *Brahman,* unmanifest and manifest, transcendent and immanent.[65] He is in essence the supreme divine Person, the object of all worship.[66] Upaniṣadic thought reflects diverse philosophical tendencies but remains close to its original religious direction.

What makes the Upaniṣadic thought unique is the identification of *Brahman* with *Ātman*. Philosophically, the *Upaniṣads* combine the cosmological enquiry for the First cause with the psychological enquiry for the Self. At first the two lines of enquiry proceeded in an independent and parallel manner till an epistemological revolution led to their being joined in what may be described as a spiritual phenomenology. "The problem of identifying the self of man was an ancient one. What is the nature of man or *Puruṣa*—this question was often asked. But the more frequent question was, what is the nature of the self or *Ātman?* This latter formulation has given a distinctive direction to Indian philosophy. It has preserved it from an object-centred behaviourism, from thinking of man simply as one object among others in nature'.[67]

In ancient Vedic thought man was regarded as constituted of body and limbs, breath and mind, feeling and reason or intuition (*dhī*). It was recognized that man survives in some sense and the question, thus, was to distinguish the immortal from the mortal part of man. This quest for the immortal part in man and that for the self as the "self-referring focus of all sentient life and experience,[68] tended naturally to coalesce. The two enquiries were conceptually distinct but both consisted in a process of discrimination, the discrimination of the immortal from the mortal and of the self from the non-self in man. The discrimination of the immortal from the mortal relates to types of being, human and divine. It is ontological and theological, rather than psychological or epistemological, concerned with a distinction between objects, natural or spiritual, rather than with a distinction between the subject and the world of objects.

The older enquiry culminated in the discovery that the immortal constituent of man was *Prāṇa*—'breath' or 'vital force'. At the cosmic level *Prāṇa* is what constitutes the substance of the gods, their unity and essence.[69] The moving wind is as much its symbol as the yonder sun. It is the cosmic regulator and also the principle of life, energy and movement in man. It is a luminous and pervasive principle revealed above all in rhythm.[70] Access to it lies through the luminous mind and the rhythmic word. The various modes of the worship of the gods-prayer, ritual, symbolic meditation are really nothing but approaching *Prāṇa*, the source of life and light.

The *Upaniṣads*, however, distinguish *Ātman* from *Prāṇa* by calling the former the source of the latter. The approach to the *Ātman* usually begins differently, though the search for the source of *Prāṇa* can also lead to it.[71] Naciketas, thus wants to know what survives death, if anything. This is the ancient and perennial query. In answer to this, Death points to the 'ancient god deep in the cave of the heart', who is 'unborn, eternal, perpetual, ancient, never dying with the dying body'. He is 'smaller than the smallest', 'bigger than the biggest', 'incorporeal, all-pervasive'. If the body were to be compared to a chariot, the *Ātman* is like the person driven in it, the senses being like the horses, the mind like the reins and Reason like the charioteer. The objects of experience may be compared to the way on which the chariot runs.[72] The approach to the *Ātman* becomes distinctive here. The experience of mortality is doubtless the starting point but one seeks the immortal self by delving into the heart and withdrawing consciousness from the lower and exterior objects. Corresponding to the hierarchy of being there is the hierarchy of planes of consciousness. The Self is the highest and innermost point whence all consciousness, movement and objectivity start. *Buddhi* and *Manas, Prāṇa,* and *Ākāśa,* all have their ground there. The *Ātman* is like the nave of the wheel of being and consciousness.[73] Thinking of the Self as the innermost, the highest, the subtlest, is a way of abstracting the mind and distinguishing its true goal from outwardly given objects. But it has the defect of turning the Self into some kind of object, however supreme. Hence the *Upaniṣads* turn to a radically negative way of indicating and searching the Self. The Self is neither any object of sensation or thought nor any state of the mind representing or seeking any object. It is the eternal ground or transcendental condition of all experience. Within experience we are limited selves physical, vital, mental, intellectual, 'ecstatic' (*ānanda maya*). The true or noumenal self lies beyond them, though these would not be possible without Him. Just as the Self alone is uncreated and immortal, existing before all things and outlasting them all, the Self alone is unnegatable epistemically. If all objects were to be negated, the Self alone will remain as the ultimate subject, the subject presupposed in every negation as much as in every affirmation. To reach the Self, then, one has simply to 'unreach' all objects. The Self is ever-manifest, self-revealing. One cannot speak of it or point to it without engendering some misconception or the other. *'Upaśānto'yam ātmā'.*

What prevented the *Upaniṣadic Adhyātma-yoga* from leading to nihilism or a denial of the world, was the identification of the *Ātman* with the *Brahman* where *Brahman* was the creative, cosmic principle. The eternal spiritual principle is at once the ground of subjective as well as of objective being. That the two quests, for the ground of one's own empirical and psychic being within and for the ground of the world without, meet at the same point, is the final spiritual experience which the *Upaniṣads* give expression to. Speculative reasoning may have helped in this, but the principle of *Advaita* really rests on spiritual testimony.

As the *Āraṇyakas* had developed the notion of sacrifice into that of symbolic meditation or *Upāsanā,* the *Upaniṣads* went beyond *Upāsanā* to the pure path of enquiry or *Jñāna-mārga.* *Upāsanā* is still a variety of *Karma-yoga.* The search for the Self is essentially an enquiry, a seeking to know. Doubtless, the *Upaniṣads* emphasize the role of right action and the practice of a virtuous life as a necessary preparation for the attainment of spiritual knowledge which is distinguished sharply from the morally indifferent, purely intellectual knowledge. "No one who has not turned away from sin, or disquiet or mental agitation can gain the self through the intellect."[74] Yama tests Naciketas by tempting him with worldly pleasures and success and later pleased with the indifference of Naciketas towards such temptations, declares that the good and the pleasant are quite different kinds of objects and it is only the wise who can choose the good and it is only they who are fit for the spiritual journey. Elsewhere the *Upaniṣads* extend the concept of sacrifice and speak of the whole of life as a sacrifice,[75] an idea which the *Gītā* develops fully. The wise and good man who is indifferent to the world and seeks with inner calm and poise the Self as the immortal principle, as the source of everlasting life and happiness, must approach a proper spiritual teacher, for "knowledge is gained from the teacher."[76] He must hear the revealing word, ponder over it and meditate till the truth heard from the Master becomes a personal realization. It is only when the mind is turned away from objects and is still and one-pointed that it becomes illuminated by the intuitive realization of the Self. The final leap into realization requires the grace of the Self for the identity of the *Ātman* and the *Brahman* implies that the Sel is the divine reality.[77]

Some of the *Upaniṣads* stress the divinity of the Self anc in them monism acquires the aspect of theism. In the *Īśo panișad* and occasionally in *Kaṭha* the Self is a personal goc who pervades the whole universe and is at the same time the spirit in man. To know the Self, then, is to know one's identity with all, something more than mere universal brotherhood. At some other places, most significantly in *Śvetāśvatara* God is distinguished from the individual soul. Human soul and nature are here regarded as two orders controlled by God whose grace given through the Teacher in the process of Yoga liberates and illumines the individual. Here we have a clear adumbration of *Yoga* as well as *Bhakti* which is mentioned by name in this *Upaniṣad* for the first time.

REFERENCES

1. On writing in the Vedic age, cf. K. Chattopadhyaya, *Studies in Vedic and Indo-Iranian Religion and Literature*, Vol. II, pp. 63ff; V. S. Pathak, Presidential Address, Epigrahic Section, Indian History Congress (Aligarh Session).

2. Cf. K. Chattopadhyaya, *op. cit.*, pp. 17-18.

3. Cf. *Bṛhaddevatā*, 1.80. "*na hi nāmānyavijñāya mantrah śakyo hi veditum*".

4. Cf. *Ib*. 5.58ff.

5. Vide my article on 'The Life and Death of Languages' in *Diogenes*, 1965.

6. Cf. Gonda, *The Vision of the Vedic Poets*; Sāyaṇa often equates *dhī* to *Karman*. Also cf. my *Mūlyamīmāmsā*, Chap. I.

7. Cf. *"Kavir manīṣī paribhūḥ svayambhūr yāthātathyatorthān vyadadhāc Chāśvatībhyaḥ samābhyaḥ."*—*Vājasaneyī saṁ*, Chap. 40; Cf. Coomaraswamy, *Selected Papers*, (ed. Lipsey), Vol. II, p. 179.

8. On the nature of revelation see my 'Religion and Historicity', *Manthana*, Sept. 1978. Cf. V. S. Agrawal's *Sparks from the Vedic Fire*, p. 51.

9. Cf. Abel Bergaigne, *Vedic Religion* (tr. V. G. Paranjape), Vol. I, pp. 46-47.

10. *Bṛhaddevatā* records certain traditions about the Vedic seers. The *Purāṇas* claim to record the happenings of Vedic times too. As for modern historical researches, they may be sampled in (1) Dandekar, *Vedic Bibliography*, 4 vols., (2) Gonda, *History of Indian Literature*, Vols. I and II, (3) Keith, *Religion and Philosophy of the Veda and Upaniṣads*, 2 vols., (4) Ludwig, *Der Rigveda*, 6 vols., (5) R. C. Majumdar (ed.), *The Vedic Age*, (6) Macdonell & Keith, *Vedic Index*, 2 vols., (7) Oldenberg, *Textkritische und exegetische Noten*, 2 vols., *Die Religion des Veda*, (8) L. Renou, *Bibliographie Védique*, *Religions of Ancient India*, (9) Winternitz, *History of Indian Literature*, Vol. 1.

11. *e. g.*, we get an image of the poet and priest in Agni, of the warrior in Indra, of the ruler in Mitra and Varuṇa. Nevertheless, these gods stand primarily for spiritual verities accessible to the prayerful and intuitive intelligence.

12. Vide Pargiter, *Ancient Indian Historical Tradition*. P. L. Bhargav has sought to collate Vedic and Puraṇic evidence—*India in the Vedic Age*.

13. *e. g. R.* 4.23.8-10, *Ib.* 4.3.9-12, *Ib.* 10.190.

14. Cf. *R.* 9.73. 6, 9; *Ib.* 10.5.

15. The most celeberated description of this may be seen in the *Puruṣa-sūkta* which speaks of the 'primordial ordinances.

16. *Ṛta* and *Satya* are born together. *R.* 10.5. When heaven and earth are said to be upheld by Truth, it is implied that all things derive their reality from an original principle—*R.* 10.85.1.

17. Cf. *Pūrṇamadaḥ pūrṇam idaṁ pūrṇāt pūrṇam Udacyate.* (*Śāntipāṭha* to *Īśāvāsya*).

18. Cf. *R.* 10.82.6—"*ajasya nābhāvadhyekam arpitam yasmin viśvāni bhuvanāni tasthuh*" and Coomaraswamy's comments, *op. cit.*, Vol. II, p. 179 and fn.

19. See R. Panikkar, *The Vedic Experience,* pp. 26-29. Also my review of the work in *Book Chronicle,* 1978.

20. Cf. *Nirukta,* 7th *adhyāya.*

21. *e. g., R.* 4.1.10: '*dyauṣpitā janitā*'.

22. *e. g., R.* 6.51.5: "*dyauṣpitaḥ pṛthivi mātar*".

23. Ram Swarup's *The word as Revelation, Names of God,* Chaps. X-XI, contain some interesting reflections.

24. The hymns to Indra frequently recount the myth.

25. This may be seen clearly in the *Brāhmaṇas.*

26. *R.* 10.190.

27. Classifications of hymns and types of prayer may be seen in the *Nirukta* and *Bṛhaddevatā.*

28. See Prof. K. Chattopadhyaya, '*Dāsa & Dasyu* in the *Ṛgveda*', *Proceedings of the Nineteenth International Congress of Orientalists,* Rome.

29. Cf. *R.* 7.57.4: '*Yad vā āgaḥ puruṣatā karāma*'.

30. G. C. Pande in *History of the Panjab,* Vol. I.

31. On Vedic republics, see J. P. Sharma, *Ancient Indian Republics.*

32. Cf. Shakuntala Rao Shastri, *Women in the Vedic Age.*

32a. Vedic knowledge of cotton has been forcefully, denied—vide Sethna, *karpāsa.*

33. These ideas have been expounded in *Mīmāṁsā* texts.

33a. Essentially the sacrificer has to sacrifice himself--*havirvai dīkṣitaḥ*—*T. S.,* 6.1.4.5. Spiritually all sacrifice is self-sacrifice—vide my *Bhāratīya Paramparā Ke Mūla Svara,* pp. 42ff, Coomaraswamy, *op. cit.*, II, pp. 107ff.

34. G. C. Pande, *Studies in the Origins of Buddhism*, pp. 274ff ; Keith, *op. cit.*, II, pp. 313ff ; *Kātyāyana Śrautasūtras* (Acyutagrantha mālā), Sanskrit introduction ; Kane, *History of the Dharmaśāstras,* Vol. II, pt. 2.

35. G. C. Pande in *History of the Punjab,* Vol. I, p. 99.

36. Cf. G. C. Pande, *Studies in the Origins of Buddhism,* p. 270.

37. Cf. *R.* 10.83-84 ; 10.151 ; 1.164 ; *Atharva,* 11.4, 2.35 ; 9.2, 19.52.

38. Prajāpati's decision is not surprising since he is often identified with the mind, *e. g., TS.* 6.6.10.3 ; *Ib.* 1.6.10.4.

39. See, *e. g. Śatapatha*—6th *Kāṇḍa* onwards.

40. Cf. Tylor, *Primitive Culture,* II, p. 16 ; Contra Garbe, *ERE* XII, p. 434.

41. *e. g., Ś. B.* II, pp. 1061, 1084.

42. *e. g., Ib.* Vol. II, pp. 1050-53, 1089-91.

43. *Ib.* I, p 175.

44. *Ib.* II, p. 1050.

45. *Ś. B.* I, p. 188 : *"Tadvā eṣa eva mṛtyuḥ ya eṣa tapati tad eṣa eva mṛtyuḥ tasmād yathā etasmād arvācyaḥ prajās tā mriyante atha yāh parācyaste devāstasmādu te'mṛtāh... amuṣmiṁlloke punaḥ punareva pramārayati."*

46. *Ib.* II, p. 1096 : *"Yat kiñca arvācīnam ādityāt sarvaṁ tan mṛtyunāptam."*

47. *Ib.* II, p. 1090 : *"Atha vyāvṛtya śarīreṇāmṛto sadyomṛtosad vidyayā vā Karmaṇā veti. Ye vai tat karma kurvate mṛtvā punaḥ sambhavanti te sambhavanta evamṛtatvam abhisambhavanti."*

48. *Ś. B.* II, p. 1193 : *'Itthaṁ vā ime 'smānamuṣmiṁlloke sacanta tān vayamidamiha pratisacāmahā iti.'*

49. *Tāṇḍya*, I, p. 122, "*Yat tvityāhuḥ ṣaḍbhirito māsair adhvānaṁ yanti ṣaḍbhiḥ punarāyanti.*"

50. *Ib.* I, p. 123, '*Yad ato nyāsu syād ava svargāllokāt padyeran.*'

51. *Ib.* I, p. 126, "*Yathā vā ito vṛkṣaṁ rohantyevamenaṁ pratyavarohanti svargam eva tallokaṁ rudhvāsmiṁlloke pratitiṣṭhanti.*"

52. *Ib.* I, p. 214, "*Tasmād ayaṁ lokaḥ punaḥ punaḥ prajāyate.*"

53. *Kauṣītakī*, 1.4.

54. Cf. G. C. Pande, *Śramaṇa Tradition : its history and contribution to Indian Culture.*

55. G. C. Pande in *The History of the Punjab, l. c.*

56. G. C. Pande in *The History of the Punjab*, Vol. 1, p. 101.

57. *Ib.*, p. 102.

58. *Ib.*, p. 102.

59. G. C. Pande, *Studies in the Origins of Buddhism ; Śramaṇa Tradition : its history and contribution to Indian Culture.*

60. Prof. H. C. Raichaudhury would like to identify him with the famous Parivrājaka Pakkudha Kaccāyana–*PHAI.*

61. Sentience distinguishes *Brahman* or *sat* from *Prakṛti* or *Pradhāna*. So *Brahmasūtras–īkṣaternāśabdam.*

62. *Tai.*, 3.1 ; *Vedāntasūtras*, 1.2.

63. *Chāndogya*, 7.23.

64. *Bṛhadāraṇyaka*, 2.4.14.

65. *Bṛ.*, 2.3.

66. *Kaṭha*, 1.2.11 ; *Śveta.*, 6.20.

67. G. C. Pande in '*History of the Punjab*, Vol. I, p. 103.

68. *Ib.*, *l. c.*

69. *Bṛ.*, 3.9.9 ; *Chā.*, 4.3.

70. Cf. G. C. Pande, *Mūlyamīmāṁsā.*

71. Ramana Maharṣi sometime suggested enquiry into the source of breath as a means for discovering the self.

72. Sri Krishna Prem's *The Yoga of the Kaṭhopaniṣad* is easily the profoundest modern work on the *Upaniṣad.*

73. *Kauṣītakī,* 3.9.

74. *Kaṭha,* 1.2.23.

75. *Chā.*, 3.16-17.

76. *Chā.*, 6.14.2 ; *Śveta.*, 6.23.

77. *Kaṭha,* 1.2.22.

4

ŚRAMAṆIC NEGATION

Śramaṇism : General features

The Vedic search for the spirit did not deny the world. It rather accepted the world as a gift and expression of a divine reality.[1] Even in the *Upaniṣads* while the spiritual is distinguished from the material, the two are still joined together by a series of intermediate and connecting planes and form a whole that is divine.[2] There is thus no fundamental ontic distinction between spirit and matter. Their distinction is only a distinction resting on the direction in which consciousness is turned and the level at which it functions.[3] Turned outwards and downwards consciousness projects the material world or rather different worlds of different degrees of subtlety and luminosity at different points. Turned inwards and upwards it returns into its own eternal and inexpressible nature. As a practical consequence the Upaniṣadic quest seeks to go beyond the life of worldliness and ritualism centred in action but does not usually advocate the radical renunciation of all life of action.[4] Nor does it condemn the world as a vale of tears although it recognizes the unsatisfactory character of worldly goods and gains[5] and stresses the need for spiritual enlightenment for realising that Bliss is the essence of being.

A quite different *Weltanschauung* is expressed in the spiritual quest and thought of the wandering ascetics and mendicants whom we meet in the 6th Cent. B.C. in north eastern

India. The mode of life and thought of these Śramaṇas as they are called, is in sharp contrast to that of the Brāhmaṇas.[6] In fact, the opposition of the Brāhmaṇas and Śramaṇas was well known and held to be as natural as that of 'the snake and the mongoose'. The Brāhmaṇas had been traditionally priests and counsellors, hermits and philosophers but they had not preached renunciation of all family life and property. Ritual, even for the hermit, required a wife and some wealth.[7] Although there was a gradual acceptance of renunciation by the Brāhmaṇas in the form of the fourth *Āśrama,* it was a consequence of Śramaṇic impact achieved in the early post-Vedic or *sūtra* period.[8] The idea that the world is evil and must be given up sooner or later if one is to search for lasting spiritual welfare, institutionalized in *Sannyāsa* or mendicancy, is the lasting contribution of Śramaṇism to Indian Culture.

The Śramaṇas believed that life is basically painful and spiritually evil. The all-pervasiveness of *Duhkha* has since become a by-word in the Indian tradition and makes pessimism its hall-mark. Ancient civilizations in general were not pessimistic, nor was the Vedic outlook so. They all regard natural life, even though destined to end, as a favour of the gods. Its enjoyments were felt to be good and desirable when obtained within the bounds of moral law. The Śramaṇas claimed greater spiritual sensitivity and wisdom. They looked open-eyed at the transitoriness of pleasures and it seemed to them to cancel the very existence of pleasures. When pleasures end they leave behind pain. They appear, thus, to be merely the foretaste of pain. Not merely is the greater part of experience directly painful, the remaining is heavily ringed with pain. This is not all. Even while they last, pleasures are enjoyable only in a state of mental agitation since they represent a constant change and alteration in the psyche. Hence the pleasures may themselves be directly described as painful. Life, then, is not pleasure and pain but pain through and through.[9]

At this point it may occur to a modern reader that this pessimism may be the reflection of dark social conditions, or a sentimental exaggeration, or if true, easily mended by death or suicide. With reference to the first alternative it has been suggested that apart from the general incidence of social misery caused by conditions of poor development, there may have been unusual social distress for some groups caused by processes of social change supposed to be then operating e. g., the break-down of tribal organization, urbanization, rise of monarchic imperialism etc. It is very difficult to take such speculations seriously.[10] Developmental conditions were, if anything, poorer in the Vedic age and yet the Vedic seers did not see nature as hostile nor human life as painful. The history of the movements of social change is too little known for those times in India to speak confidently of the psychological consequences which they might or might not have produced. In any case, the Śramaṇas do not speak of misery in terms of any specific social forms like poverty, unemployment, indebtedness, harsh treatment by slave-owners, harsh condition of life in general etc. The suffering they speak of is not social suffering in the modern sense, which is dependent on some special social situation and is removed by a change of organization or application of technology. They speak of the existential misery of life, its liability to disease and decay, old age and death. They speak, not of any particular and alterable social relationship, but of social relationship in general which causes distress by the clash of interests and egoism, the bondage of obligations and the changeability of situations and relations. They speak not of the limitations of social ability, which can be removed by science and technology, but of the inherent limitation of human ability to satisfy human desires and of the torment which desires and the attempt to satisfy them must inflict on man. The misery of which the Śramaṇas speak is not accidental but essential to life. Its appreciation undoubtedly requires a certain sensitivity just as the appreciation of the tragic vision does.[10a]

Let us now advert to the last suggestion of the modern critic. If life is so full of suffering, why not court death ? For the Śramaṇas, this would be foolish since birth and death are only punctuations in the beginningless process of life called *saṁsāra.* This belief in the doctrine of transmigration constitutes one of the most characteristic tenets of Śramaṇism, which has since become perhaps the most characteristic feature of the tradition of Indian thought. I have argued elsewhere that the doctrine of transmigration appears to have been accepted readymade in some of the *Upaniṣads.*[11] The earlier Vedic notion of Death in Afterlife or *Punarmṛtyu* perhaps prepared the ground for the doctrine of *Punarjanman,* unless it was itself inspired by the latter. The doctrine of Rebirth does not play much part in Vedic thought but assumed a fundamental importance in the post-Vedic age and this apparently ought to be attributed to the impact of the Śramaṇas. The doctrine of *Saṁsāra* is a complex of a number of ideas viz., of soul as distinguished from the body, of *Karman* as binding the soul, and of the repeated incarnations of the soul in accordance with its *Karman.* The distinction of the soul from the body was in some sense an ancient distinction, belonging in various measures to all ancient civilizations and religions. In the ancient doctrine of *saṁsāra* this distinction was made radical. The human soul was considered not to have any essential connection with the body which wholly perished at death and was never to be renewed. The soul could incarnate in any other body, human or non-human. In this sense it would not be correct to speak of the soul as human in any essential sense. Humanity is as much an accident for it as a particular human body. This radical distinction between the soul and the body is thorough enough to include a clear distinction between the soul and the mind also. The soul is not the mind, neither *psyche* nor *nous.* The mind is tied up with the body whatever the kind of body it might be. Mental faculties differ according to the bodies. In a way mental faculties are as extraneous to the soul as physical faculties. In another way, mental and physical faculties are so many veils on the innate powers of the soul. The nature of the soul transcends the body and the mind but it is not a powerless and featureless blank. The soul is neither a breath nor a shadow, nor any other rarified material image. Nor is it a hypostatization of mental and vital faculties. The soul is fundamentally suprasensible and immaterial. Its nature being wholly different from that of the objects of ordinary experience, it cannot be adequately grasped by reason or expounded in human language which has been fashioned by our experience of the material world. The soul is a spiritual being to reach which we must think away from sensuous experience or rational abstractions.[12]

But the soul gets into bondage through being incarnated in a body, which clouds its powers and true nature by giving it a physical, vital and psychic identity and in the case of man, at least an additional social identity. The bondage of the soul consists in its liability to act and suffer in obedience to the laws of the body and its world in which the soul has found its incarnation. The circumstances of birth, the length of life and the experiences of pleasure or pain which accrue in its course are all determined by a force arising out of the actions in which the soul was involved in earlier lives.[13] This force arising out of past actions and determining the birth and experiences of the soul in the future is the force of *Karman.* While the exact nature of *karman* has been as diversely explained as the nature of the soul, there is no doubt that *Karman* arises from action, persists as a force leading to future consequences for the agent, survives death and determines life after death generally. What is more, *karman* follows the principle of moral retribution in working out consequences. It is not a simple causal force, physical or psychic. It is a moral force which operates with reference to the character and past actions of the soul. In what form *karman* survives to produce its effect and whence it derives the power to do so and to follow a moral law in so doing, are controversial questions. Nevertheless, it is accepted that *karman* has its source and effectiveness in the structure of desires and feelings and belief which constitute the conative structure of an individual self-consciousness. One could say that *Karman* arises out of the force of desire and requires that force and a consequent structure as a necessary support to its own functioning.[14]

The modern conception of action emphasizes its natural and

social consequences. The ancient Śramaṇic concept, on the other hand, emphasized its effect on the character and destiny of the agent. The concept of *karman* is thus extremely individualistic within the Śramaṇic context. Individual souls are regarded as essentially separate and unconnected. It is, only during Karmic bondage that they enter into relationship with other souls and the world. Their spiritual destiny is to reach the state of the essential Aloneness (*kaivalya*). It will be obvious that the bondage of the soul is in terms of its involvement in morally significant social behaviour. The bondage is a psycho-spiritual liability produced by socio-ethical activity. According to modern ideas the human individual acquires freedom as he advances from the instinctive to the socio-ethical plane of behaviour. Śramaṇism too considers such freedom as necessary for *karman* which is possible only for man and yet considers the descent of the soul to the plane of moral or instinctive behaviour itself as a bondage in a deeper sense. It recognizes, however, a hierarchy in terms of value between different planes of behaviour. What is nearer the spiritual goal is higher, what is further away lower in value. The various forms of being-insentient and sentient, vegetable, animal and rational—are like rungs in the ladder of spiritual. evolution. At the pre-rational levels the soul merely experiences sensations without being able to act in a morally significant manner. Hence at these levels it does not produce fresh *karman* since it cannot really 'act'. It is only at the rational human level that the soul acts in a morally significant manner and becomes liable to future moral consequences. Thus although human social and moral life is a state of bondage for the soul, it is the only state where it can strive for freedom in the spiritual sense and represents a much higher state than if it were to be born in other species. The principle of spiritual evolution is recognized in the sense of an evolution of the individual soul through the gradation of species rather than as an evolution of the species.[15] But this spiritual evolution is not natural, nor does it represent an unalterable sequence of beginning at the lowest level and ascending up necessarily step by step. The species represent an unalterable hierarchy of being.

The soul has to ascend to be free but the vicissitudes of its destiny are tortuous and unpredictable though in a fundamental sense the soul is the master of its destiny which depends on its behaviour at the plane of moral significance.

It will be obvious that the conception of *karman* implies a conception of morality. If the law of *karman* is the law of retributive morality–good action being rewarded by hapiness and evil action punished by unhappiness–moral distinctions could not be conventional and subjective but must be in some sense natural and objective. Śramaṇism held the distinction between good and evil to rest on spiritual discrimination. Good and evil are characteristics of action ultimately of its psychological roots. Some basic psychological propensities are good, others evil. Thus benevolence, compassion and detachment are good while greed, hatred, deceit and attachment are evil. The distinction between these two classes rests on whether they help or injure life or sentient being. Whatever injures life is evil, whatever helps it is good. *Hiṁsā* is the radical evil and goodness must avoid it.[16] One may go further and state that the distinction between good and evil is ultimately one of the recognition or disregard of spiritual being. Evil arises from disregarding the spiritual nature of being. It is only through overlooking the spiritual sameness of other beings that one can proceed to injure them for the sake of oneself.[17] Such action not only further obscures the spiritual perception of the agent but also tends to drag it in rebound towards a state of suffering which would be the natural expiation of the evil action. That such a retribution inevitably takes place and can take place at remote times and places even after death and that all this happens in accordance with an invisible law without the assistance of any human or social agency, these are dogams of the *Karman* theory which have been widely held on the authority of supernatural wisdom. Popular versions have indeed gone on to give picturesque and even gruesome details of the laws of *karman* and their application with a suggestion of omniscience best calculated to impress the credulous.

Apparently the principle of *Karman* as one of moral retribution is a moral explanation of the vicissitudes of life and its puzzling distribution of pleasures and pains. It appears to be an attempt to rectify in thought the balance of life in favour of the moral order by formulating hypothetical causes and consequences belonging to past and future lives. Such a doctrine was apparently calculated to encourage the common man to act by moral rules and shed his doubts about them. It converts moral laws into natural laws and ascribes to them causal efficacy.[16a] This would make moral behaviour merely intelligent and rational behaviour but for the fact that the knowledge of moral laws can be gained only from faith and is quite distinct in form from any kind of empirical or rational knowledge. Whether the law of *karman* understood in this sense serves to make men moral or merely distorts the moral sense of mankind by perpetrating a category-confusion in thought and an obscuration of moral freedom and responsibility by adding psychological inducements, or whether it has transcendental validity, cannot perhaps be unequivocally decided in the face of an appeal to faith which cannot be rationally evaluated. The charge, however, of the doctrine of *Karman* encouraging passivity, fatalism and pessimism does not really apply because it does not deny the freedom of action or man's capacity to shape his own future. Technically, it is the *Vipāka* that is determined by past *karman* which does not determine future *karman.* Man remains free to act as he pleases, only the results of his action as determining his own future do not depend on his calculations alone. Similarly while the conditions of birth are determined by *Karman,* it has not been maintained that social conditions as such are determined by only past *Karman.* The doctrine of *Karman* has been conceived in the context of the individual; there is no notion of collective *karman* such as would amount to a moral justification of history or social conditions. The *Vipāka* of *karman* is in terms of individual reaction of *sukha* and *duhkha*; it does not entail any specific social situations or forms of experience, much less general conditions of social experience. Properly understood the doctrine of *Karman* does not encourage fatalism or passivity but rather serenity and equanimity in the face of the vicissitudes of life and an active determination to be good.

It cannot, however, be denied that the doctrine of *Karman* could have been popularly misunderstood and become a factor in the growth of social resignation and passivity. The doctrine of *Karman* in its original Śramaṇic form was wholly individualistic and had little direct interest in social welfare. Its encouragement of moral welfare among the laity undoubtedly amounted to an indirect promotion of social well-being, harmony and justice but it stressed the ideal of the individual making himself a more enlightened spiritual being rather than the ideal of the individual creating an ideal society. In fact, the Śramaṇic idea is the polar opposite of the modern idea that the way to improve a man is to improve his society. On the Śramaṇic view man must improve himself individually and prepare for a trans-social destiny. On this view man is not a rational or social animal to be improved by science and legislation in the course of historical ages. He is a pure spiritual being enmeshed temporarily in a rational-irrational, social-asocial nature which belongs to humanity as a rational animal species.

The real and original force of the principle of *Karman*, however, was not to give a moral explanation of the world, to reconcile the vicissitudes of life with the expectations of morality, but to point out the cause of bondage. Good action and evil action may have different consequences in terms of pleasure and pain but are similar as far as causing bondage is concerned. From that profound point of view which regards all experiences as suffering, the difference between apparent pleasures and pains is of small account. 'Pleasure' and 'pain', 'sin' and 'virtue' all serve to bind the soul. The essence of *Karman* lies in its being an expression of desire or appetite, a force of extraversion which takes the soul away from itself towards non-spiritual objects and ends. Desire itself rests on a condition of delusion or ignorance in which the soul identifies itself with the body and mind. These three-ignorance, desire and action—represent three interlocked and mutually supportive bonds that constitute the nexus between the soul and matter.

In this sense Śramaṇism is not only pessimistic and pluralistic but fundamentally ascetical. Since it recognizes a reality opposed to the soul and independent of it, it may also be described as realistic in its metaphysics. The Vedic vision of the unity of man and nature stands broken in favour of a philosophy alienating man from nature spiritually, which makes the spirit transcendent, nature non-spiritual. The spiritual quest of the Śramaṇas was thus purely negative viz., to transcend the realm of suffering and transience.[18] In a sense it could also be called subjective since it required man to withdraw from all contact with society and nature. It conceived spiritual pilgrimage as "the flight of the alone to the alone". Rejecting the world it rejected God as well and tended to be, in contrast to Vedic thought, atheistic. This atheism did not mean the rejection of gods as cosmic functionaries but it did mean the rejection of an ultimate creator. In fact, the Śramaṇas placed the spiritually perfected man above the gods. In this sense Śramaṇism gave a new dignity and status to man and its asceticism instead of rejecting humanity exalts it. The man who is perfected (*Siddha*), enlightened (*Buddha*), victorious over the passions (*Jina*) is greater than the gods because while they are subject to *Karman,* he is not. He is free from all attachments and desires, from all sense of possession. He does not distinguish between himself and others but regards all beings from the standpoint of their essential spiritual sameness. He has compassion and friendliness for all and does not hate or dislike even those who hate and oppose him. He is unaffected by heat and cold, pain and pleasure and utterly beyond physical cravings of any kind. In particular his freedom from lust or sexual attractions is total. He is free from all vanity and egoism and has no family or property. He has superhuman knowledge and wisdom and supernatural powers but he does not use them for any selfish purpose since he has none. He lives in imperturbable peace and radiates it. He is the spiritual teacher and that is the sole mission for which he lives and works.[19]

This ideal of the spiritually enlightened man is remarkable in more ways than one. The purely negative quest of transcendence here emerges into the realization of the sublimest ideal of humanity, the ideal of a divine man, pure and selfless, compassionate and wise. It is proved here that when all the dross of physical attachment and mental bias, desire and egoism is shed, the soul shines forth refulgent in its divine glory and raises man to the level of ideal perfection. The idea of a cosmic god is disregarded but instead the idea of a saintly teacher with superhuman wisdom comes up as a more visible and approachable substitute. Spiritual authority now belongs not to an immemorial revelation but to personal testimony and a tradition going back to the word of a human Master. Spiritual authenticity thus depends on a historical tradition and the possibility of personal verification. The importance of the seer and the sagely human teacher was doubtless held to be inestimable even in the Vedic tradition but the Vedic seer claimed to see only what was freely revealed to him by a god. The Upaniṣadic sage is nearer to the Śramaṇic sage in the sense that he attains wisdom from within by spiritual enquiry as a personal attainment. Nevertheless, he is not generally an ascetic and does not claim superhuman power or perfection, although high moral attainment is implied.

Vedic spiritual seeking makes *Brahmacarya* an essential precondition before the seeker can be admitted to the knowledge of *Brahman*. For the path of ritualistic action the status of a married householder, coming after *Brahmacarya*, is additionally required while some ritual and meditation belonged to the condition of a sylvan hermit. Thus although Vedic ritualism required the full performance of social duties and obligations, even the Upaniṣadic gnosticism generally required that the debt to the sages should be repaid by acquiring Vedic learning in terms of long years spent at a teacher's house under conditions of strict discipline. Spiritual life in the Vedic tradition thus does not negate social life and its obligations. A period of educational discipline—physical, moral and intellectual—was in fact regarded as a common necessity for both a proper secular as well as a spiritual life. This condition of *Brahmacarya* implied the vows of continence and poverty and of humble obedience to the teacher for whom the student had to toil while learning from him. In the *Upaniṣads,* however, *Brahmacarya* seems to occur at places in a more general signification, apparently standing for discipline preparatory to receiving spiritual knowledge. Thus when Indra and Vairocana approached Prajāpati for instruction they were both required to undergo a period of *Brahmacarya* which could hardly have meant a period of Vedic study. Just as *Brahman* came to mean the ultimate principle rather than the *Veda* or a Vedic hymn in the *Upaniṣads,* similarly *Brahmacarya* came to acquire a more general meaning of moral and spiritual discipline. At the same time the *Upaniṣads* stressed the relevance of *tapas* or austerities for *Brahmavidyā.* The *Brāhmaṇas* had regarded *tapas* or energizing as a part of the creative effort of Prajāpati but it seems now to have come to refer to austerities especially practised in the forest hermitages and characterizing a distinct stage of life. Again, while in the *Brāhmaṇas* vows of continence, silence, sleeping on the ground etc., were prescribed during periods of initiation, and the virtues of truth, liberality and piety admired generally, the *Upaniṣads* make the practice of virtues, including in them clearly self-control and compassion, a *sine qua non* for the spiritual seeker. In short, while the notion of discipline, at once educational and moral, was a general Vedic notion and inbuilt into the Vedic scheme of social life itself, the notion of a special preparatory discipline for the spiritual seeker described as *Brahmacarya* or *tapaścaryā* came to be formulated in the *Upaniṣads* which even contain a reference to *bhaikṣacarya* or mendicancy but that is rare.

Mendicancy was, in fact, a Śramaṇic institution. The śramaṇa or toiler was a mendicant, a wanderer (*bhikṣu Parivrājaka*). His spiritual quest was in sharp contrast to the Vedic one in its attitude towards action and social obligations. Mendicancy implied an irreversible and final rejection of all social claims and obligations and of the efficacy of natural or ritual action in the context of spiritual seeking.

Curiously the term *Brahmacarya* is found applied to this condition in Śramaṇic writings, a usage which seems to develop the Upaniṣadic usage even further in a more generalized direction. It seems to mean simply the condition of serving under a master and following his rule of discipline. This confusion between *Brahmacarya* and *Bhaikṣacarya* is, in contrast, carefully avoided in the Brahmanical *sūtras.*

Since the Śramaṇic disciple followed the Master, not only in terms of the rules of conduct but also in dogma, these bands of Masters and disciples called *gaṇas* amounted to so many sects practising diverse rules of mendicancy and asceticism and upholding different metaphysical and spiritual dogmas.[20] Behind the diversities of dogma and practice, however, we can discern the common principles of *Saṁsāra* and liberation from it through the eradication of the force of *Karman.* Bondage and liberation, *bandha* and *mokṣa,* sum up the world view of the Śramaṇas. Unlike the Vedic spiritual ideal of felicity here and hereafter or eternally, the Śramaṇic spiritual ideal was primarily one of freedom from pain and restlessness. There may be a substantive identity between the Upaniṣadic ideal and the Śramaṇic ideal. Both are, indeed, traditionally held to be of 'liberation or *mokṣa*' and modern opinion too is sometimes similar. While a substantive identity between them may well be the case, it is undeniable that they represented originally distinct approaches and conceptions. It is only through the interaction between the two traditions that the *Upaniṣads* came to be understood as *nivṛttilakṣaṇa* and opposed to the earlier Vedic tradition characterised as *pravṛttilakṣaṇa* by the great Vedāntic *ācārya* Śaṅkara.

Śramaṇism represents the original *Nivṛttimārga,* the path of Return. During the course of ordinary worldly life, the spirit remains in bondage to the force of action and moves further and further away from its original nature. This path of worldliness and activity is *Pravṛtti* which may be rendered as natural or instinctive activity and all other activity based upon it. When the experience of suffering begins to appear as an ineradicable contingency of the life of *pravṛtti* and a developed spiritual sensitivity begins to regard it as insufferable and seeks a way out of it with the urgency of a man feeling suffocated under water, the opening has been achieved for treading upon the path of *nivṛtti.* Such was the condition of Buddha or Mahāvīra when they left home and embarked on the loneliest of paths.[21]

The ascetical nature of this path is obvious. Not only did it mean the formal renunciation of family and property, it meant at the very outset the adoption of a rigorous regulation of behaviour and training of the will. The Five Great Vows (*mahāvratas*) were common to all the ascetics, viz., *ahiṁsā* or non-violence, *satya* or truth, *asteya* or non-stealing, *brahmacarya* or chastity, and *aparigraha* or non-possession. This disciplining of the conduct and character, *askēsis,* was a necessary though not a sufficient condition for overcoming the force of past *karman.* Many considered the practice of physical austerities indispensable for the destruction of at least the grosser forms of *karman.* That is the view of *Sāṅkhya-yoga.* The Buddha frowned upon austerities as merely physical torture. It is the Jainas who laid the greatest stress upon austerities or *tapas* and regarded them as the prime means of eradicating past *karman.* Ascetic discipline or *saṁyama* is only a barring of the gates against the influx of further *Karman,* a *saṁvara* against *āsrava.* To shake out the old accumulation, *tapas* is necessary. Of all Indian ascetic sects, the Jainas have developed the practice of austerities with the greatest detail and system and have maintained a long and living tradition of such practices. It should be interesting to note that the Jainas do not stress the infliction of pain on the body but rather the principle of deprivation. Even in the paradigmatic account of Mahāvīra's *tapas,* the Master is seen to bear pain and harassment as they came to him from others or the environment with equanimity and to refuse to seek comfort, pleasure and safety or even the fulfilment of the ordinary needs of life, rather than to set himself about to devise elaborate ways of positively inflicting pain on himself. His *tapas* seems to be above all an exercise in the practice of *titikṣā* or *kṣānti*, forbearance, the cultivation of indifference towards all stimuli, external and internal. Jaina *tapas*, thus, cannot really be described as *Kāya-Kleśalakṣaṇa* i. e., torture of the body.

Withdrawing from worldly activity and inuring the body to hardship serve to check the grosser behaviourally expressed tendencies to indulge the appetites. This does not eradicate the force of desires and passions and latent habits. For eliminating them it is necessary to track them inwardly and abandon them through the practice of meditation.[22] Buddhist texts detail such practices at length[23] and their systematic theory from a Sāṅkhyan stand point may be found in the *Yoga-sūtras* of Patañjali. The essence of any meditational practice consists in the stilling of the mind and such practice not only reduces the power of desires and passions to grip the mind but also enables the soul to realize its own innate desirelessness and the ineffable peace of such a condition. This practice of deep peace is the real and lasting basis of ascetic life.

Even this, however, is not sufficient to bring real liberation to the soul. That can come only from spiritual illumination or self-realization. This illumination—*prajñā* or *jñāna* —as a direct experience or intuition shows the radical difference between the real spiritual nature of the self and the false identity in terms of the body and the mind under which it habitually labours. So long this false identity remains, desire and passions arise from it spontaneously and irrepressibly. It is only when the true identity of the self is revealed as a living experience that the self is enabled to function as a wholly spiritual being or soul. This is the state of enlightenment realized by the ideal spiritual teacher as described before, a state of passionless wisdom and compassion.

In the *Upaniṣads* the state of spiritual realization is described as one of beatitude and fulfilment, of cosmic identification, although the *Brahmasūtras* state quite specifically that the liberated soul does not acquire any hand in the running of the world. In the Śramaṇic conception liberation has two phases. While alive the liberated soul has peace, compassion and wisdom. After death it is totally isolated from the world, returning to itself for all eternity. Such a conception might sound frightful to the modern mind till one were to contrast what Milton called "this intellectual being" with the cold grave of inconscience lying beyond death.[24]

This general sketch of the nature and course of the spiritual quest among the Śramaṇas would have to be considerably diversified to apply exactly to their different sects and schools. The Ājīvakas, for example, were a prominent sect of wandering mendicants led by Makkhali Gosala in the sixth century B.C., and in some form the sect continued till classical times. Gosala believed in total predestination. *Karman* is like a potential force which works itself out in the course of time. Every soul must pass through many births in different species and exhaust the force of *karman* before it can be emancipated. There is no such thing as free will. Realizing his predicament man can only cultivate resignation to the point of letting himself die without seeking to eat or drink. Such extreme fatalism can only be regarded as a curiousity.[25]

Nirgranthas

The Nirgranthas or Jainas were among the most ancient Śramaṇic sects. Already in the 6th century B.C. they claimed a hoary antiquity and of their long line of Tīrthaṅkaras before Mahāvīra, at least *Pārśva* is now generally admitted to have been historical. Mahāvīra himself was a scion of the Jñātṛka clan and was brought up in an ancient noble family. At the age of thirty he left home and practised the severest *tapas* for twelve years and after obtaining Pure Knowledge (*Kevala jñāna*) preached the truth as a naked and wandering ascetic till the age of seventy-two when he did at *Pāvā*. His teachings are supposed to be preserved in the ancient Jaina canon which, however, was very faultily preserved. Parts of it were lost and the remainder was subjected to interpolations and elaborations till it was finally redacted in its present form in the Gupta period. Still in the *Āyāraṅga*, the *Sūyagaḍaṁga*, the *Viyāhapannatti* and the *Uttarajjhayaṇa* we get glimpses of the ancient doctrine and practices of the Nigaṇṭhas in the days of Mahāvīra.[26]

Mahāvīra claimed to be an *āyāvāi, loyāvāi,* and *Kiriyāvāi,* i. e., a believer in the reality of the soul, the world and the freedom of the will. The soul and the world are both real and the mark of reality is to change as well as to endure. The two principal substances, spirit and matter, are at once permanent and impermanent, permanent as substances and impermanent as modes. It will be noticed that Mahāvīra like some of his contemporaries did not shirk paradoxes but rather adjudged knowledge in terms of its capacity to include such paradoxes as aspects of an infinite truth. Knowledge thus has many grades from sense perception to the infinite intuition innate in the spirit in its purity. Only the last kind of knowledge–*Kevala Jñāna*–can really comprehend the truth in its entirety. As a result of this, discursive knowledge is bound to be dialectical if it is not to be one-sided and false.[27]

The doctrine of Mahāvīra may be summarized as a doctrine of the soul's bondage in the world by the force of *Karman* and its emancipation by the exercise of its free will in the form of asceticism. In fact, the Nirgrantha doctrine in its main features may be described as the most ancient form of Śramaṇic ideology. The Nirgrantha conception of *Karman* is quite peculiar in the sense that it regards *Karman* to be a kind of material substance of which different kinds of aggregates enmesh the soul as it were. The formation of these Karmic structures and their infiltration in the soul is produced and sustained by a mental activity prompted by the basic passions or *kaṣāyas.* This mental basis of the material structure of *karman* is described as *Bhāva-karman.*[28]

Liberation requires not merely the cessation of *Bhāvakarman* but also the dismantling of the structures reared by the ignorant soul in the past. The soul is the architect of its own fate. It is in a state of bondage because of its own thoughts, feelings and actions in the past and it can liberate itself in the future only by its own resolve and determined action. In the first place the influx of *karman* must be stopped by adopting ascetic restrictions called *saṁvara*. This must be followed by the shedding of past *karman* through the practice of austerities. It is only through this *Nirjara* that the soul attains to the intuitive knowledge of its own nature, which finally liberates it and restores it to its own eternal condition. This condition of final liberation called *Kaivalya* is, however, not conceived negatively in Jainism. It is a state of perfection, of perfect knowledge, will and beatitude. The perfected souls are the spiritual teachers of mankind and their words are the basis of that faith in spiritual verities which leads to Right Practice leading in turn to liberation.

Among the peculiarities of the Jaina doctrine and practice some have been mentioned above already. The Jaina notion of *karman* as material (*paudgalika*) and their stress on *tapas* were always considered distinctive. Their belief in the almost ubiquitous presence of the soul is another peculiar tenet. The Jainas not only believe in souls for men, animals and plants, gods and demons but also for material elements. These elemental souls make almost everything ensouled for the Jainas. This makes the practice of *Ahiṁsā* a particularly exacting task for them and they drew up elaborate rules, and precautions to avoid injury to life. So great was the importance of *Ahiṁsā* for them that it seems to assume the role of their cardinal principle in ancient texts like *Āyāraṁga*. In modern times, again, many Jaina thinkers have stressed *Ahiṁsā* as constituting the keystone to the arch of their world-view. Here *ahiṁsā* ceases to be a merely negative conception and acquires the sense of universal law and becomes a principle to be applied in all aspects of life, not merely individual but social. Thus it even becomes a principle of political life and action.[20]

Among the external practices of the Jaina mendicants which attracted the curiousity of observers may be mentioned nudity and the plucking out of hair from the roots. Nudity was practised by the great Mahāvīra himself and is the hallmark of the Digambara sect among the Jainas. The other sect of the Śvetāmbaras, however, does not regard nudity as an essential requirement for the monks.

After the death of Mahāvīra the Jainas remained united till the Maurya age when the split between the Digambaras and the Śvetāmbaras occurred after the Council of Pāṭaliputra. During the early centuries of the Christian era the Jainas gradually moved towards the west. Mathura became an important Jaina centre and thence the sect moved towards Gujrat across Rajasthan. It also travelled owards the Deccan and South. At the Council of Valabhi in the Gupta age the canon was redacted and given a final shape. During these centuries the Jaina doctrine was also given a systematic shape. The lists of the *Tattvas* and *Padārthas,* of the types of knowledge and *karman,* and of ascetic practices were standardized and finally determined. From this point onwards, there was an increasing focus on the dialectical defence of the doctrine against rival sects and schools. The original dialectical interest received full development and in the process notable contributions were made to the science of logic. *Syādvāda* became the intellectual hallmark of Jainism.

Buddha and the Buddhists

If the Nirgranthas represent pure Śramaṇism, Buddhism already shows a certain contact with Brahmanical thought, a contact which continued to grow on both sides and gradually transformed both. Like Mahāvīra, again, Buddha left home after some experience of domestic life more or less about the same age. He also was attracted to the homeless life and its wandering teachers, from many of whom he sought to learn their doctrines and practices. He too practised extreme austerities but here the similarity with Mahāvīra's course of spiritual search ceased. Buddha became convinced that extreme asceticism only weakens the body and mind and gave up fasting. He then turned to the practice of *dhyāna* or meditation of which he had some spontaneous experience as a child. Cultivating the stillness of the mind Buddha reached inner illumination called *Sambodhi.*[20] He realized the contingency and relativity of the world of transience and finitude and the ineffable peace which follows such a realization. He realized the nature of truth to be really beyond thought and speech and accessible only to the innate light of the mind, a light which becomes manifest only when the mind is cleansed of its desires and passions, egoism and distractions, images and constructs. Standing on the peak of enlightenment, with the world on one side and *Nirvāṇa* on the other, Buddha was moved by compassion to preach to mankind.[31]

The *dharma* or principle which Buddha preached has been described as the Middle way (*madhyamā pratipad*).[32] In the famous First Sermon the 'middle way' has been described as a path of moderation avoiding the extremes of sensual indulgence and asceticism. Elsewhere, for example, in the famous exhortation to Kātyāyana (*Kātyāyanāvavāda*) in the *Saṁyutta Nikāya*, the 'middle way' has been given a metaphysical meaning. It is described there as the insight which does not cling to the extremes of Eternalism or Annihilationism. This Middle between *Śāśvata* and *Uccheda* is sometimes interpreted in terms of the doctrine of constant change or flux. It is then held to deny a permanent substratum in all processes of change without denying the reality of things altogether. Permanence is an illusion. Everything changes and there is nothing which underlies this change. The human mind thus is a stream of consciousness without any permanent spiritual substance just as the physical substances are not permanent entities, but merely causal processes implied in experience. We live within a stream of experience dependent on causal forces of a psychic and physical nature. Only the process of change and the laws regulating it are real. Permanent identities are a mere construct.

Applied to human life this conception of the metaphysical Middle Way implies the doctrine of *Anātmavāda* or No-soul.[33] The traditional doctrine of the soul posited an identical spiritual substance passing from life to life regulated by the force of *Karman*. On the Buddhist view there is no such stable substance; personal identity rests merely on a process of psychic life which continues from life to life and is regulated by the force which binds actions to their moral consequences. The force and laws of *Karman* are recognised but no permanent or identical agent is accepted. Man is entirely made up of his actions and experiences. His happiness and suffering, his goodness and evil depend merely on the kind of causal factors which are operative. The ascetic emphasis on will here seems to give place to emphasis on knowledge. Buddha appears as the first psychologist who analyzes the mind as an objective, causal process and discards the obstructive and supervenient notion of the soul acting upon natural elements. Buddha was thus called an Analyst, *vibhajyavādin*. Everything was analyzed into natural elements and processes subject to the law of causation. *Dharma* was used for elements and laws and *Pratītyasamutpāda* was the supreme law. Applied to psychic life it implied that the egoistic structure of personality depends on the mutually supportive forces of ignorance and desire. Actions, suffering and rebirth are consequences following the egoistically structured functioning of personality. This causal sequence naturally suggests a scientific way out of the suffering of life. One must objectively watch and discern the procession of psychic life instead of identifying oneself with it and jumping into the fray and becoming merely an element helplessly carried away and lost. One must watch how pleasure and pain cause desire and aversion and how imagination invests experiences with fantastic hues and shapes and constructs delusive objects of seeming permanence like individual selves and their social worlds. Such inner observation and analysis gradually lead to growing discernment, detachment and quiescence.

What is the end in which this process culminates? When all the factors leading to rebirth have become quiet and death supervenes, what happens to the stream of consciousness? A logical and natural interpretation would be that in such a case death would really be the end. Spiritual effort thus would lead to extinction and deny to man the only kind of immortality open to him. Some modern interpretations of Buddhism seem to accept this conclusion. However, the doctrine of the Middle way clearly denies this. Not only does it deny the permanence of the soul, it denies spiritual annihilation (*Uccheda*) equally. The materialists held the doctrine of man's annihilation at death. This was rejected by Buddha as much as the 'eternalism' of the 'Animists'. Did, then, Buddha deny extinction only to accept it for the spiritually liberated? This is really to misconstrue the Buddhist view. For the materialist physical elements alone are real and the 'soul' or psychic functioning simply the result of bodily constitution and functioning. For the Buddhist psychic factors are as real as physical factors. Indeed, they are more real because they determine the conditions of bodily birth and vicissitudes. The basic determinants of psychic life are psychic, not physical and the stream of psychic life does not depend on the body for its survival. The mind can indeed project a body for its external manifestation and incarnation but it may withdraw from all such support and manifestation just as fire may withdraw from its visible manifestation as a flame. When the faggot has burnt down and the flame has ceased to be visible, shall we say that fire itself has ceased, or rather, that it has returned to a state of non-manifestation? Similarly, the sage, when dead, is not annihilated; only there are no 'names and forms' by which he may be specified.

"Accī yathā vātavegena khitto atthaṃ paleti na upeti saṅkhaṁ Evam munī nāma-kāyā vimutto atthaṁ paleti na Upeti saṅkhaṁ."[34]

Nirvāṇa, thus, is not annihilation but the realization of spiritual eternity. This realization occurs as an insight in the psychic stream moving towards enlightenment. *Nirvāṇa* is the object of this insight and its content an ineffable and infinite reality capable of being described only as the ultimate goal of all spiritual effort, where all thought and speech sink in total quiescence. It would be much nearer the mark to think of *Nirvāṇa* as a psychic transfiguration, as a *'metanoia'*, rather than as a psychic state or extinction.

There is another and deeper interpretation of the Middle Way according to which it is the principle of the relativity and dialectical limitation of concepts. *Pratītyasamutpāda,* then, is not a mere causal law but the principle of the utter interdependence of all things and thoughts. Being and non-being are only modes of objectivity or phenomenality which being transcended there cease to apply.[34a] From this point of view, *Nirvāṇa* is truly the Absolute. Its distinction from the Upaniṣadic Absolute lies in the fact that it is neither characterized as cosmic ground like *Brahman,* nor as the ground of subjective life like the *Atman*. Its only characterization is in terms of being the ultimate value, or rather the exclusion of all disvalue.

Vedic *sādhanā* rested on the principle of the spiritual nature and unity of being differentiated into connected planes of experience where seeking from below was responded to by a revelation from above and where the parallelism of the planes of being connected individual with cosmic existence and led to the identification of the search for the Self with the search for God. In Buddhism the principle of the sovereignty of the mind finds its classic expression. All spiritual seeking rests on the direction and regulation of the mind and it is more a matter of knowledge than of will or action. If Vedic *sādhanā* may be described as the understanding of natural and sacred symbolism, Buddhist *sādhanā* must be described as the practice of a psychic science. If the former unites man to his cosmic source, the latter frees him from the delusions which the human ego projects and which sustain it. The two paths are distinct only in terms of approach, accent and expression.

For nearly a century after Buddha's *nirvāṇa* his followers remained more or less united though they spread outwards from Magadha, Kosala and the Vatsa Kingdoms. The Second council at Vaiśalī in the reign of king Kālāśoka saw the first appearance of serious schism and in the following century, the Buddhists were divided into as many as eighteen sects. Aśoka tried to heal the schism and is said to have convened a council for the purpose.[35] In any case, Aśoka's patronage turned Buddhism into a faith which expanded rapidly within and outside India. This expansion of Buddhism and the new contacts which worked upon it as well as the controversies between the different sects which led them to develop their doctrines, produced in course of time a veritable revolution in the aspect of Buddhism.[36] It came to respect the common man's need for a god who can be worshipped by some kind of ritual with its visible symbols and ceremonies. As a result the apatheosis of the Buddha as a more than human and mortal saviour, proceeded apace. This was obviously a powerful factor in the rise of Mahāyāna. Nevertheless it would be wrong to think of Mahāyāna as simply a popular adaptation of the earlier and sterner doctrine of the Buddha. Mahāyāna was also the manifestation and elaboration of an essential aspect of original Buddhism. Buddha's emphasis on the mind and on the relativity of phenomena contained powerful idealistic implications and his own career and personality illustrated the idea of a superhuman saviour. In retrospective reflection and reminiscence both these factors repidly grew in dimension and led to Mahāyāna which, thus, has a historical as well as a metapsychic or spiritual origin.[37]

Sāṅkhya

Sāṅkhya[38] is a theory as well as a method of spiritual life, seeking the liberation of the Spirit from Nature.[39] Belonging to the Śramaṇic *Weltanschauung*[40] it exercised a most powerful influence on the whole course of the development of spiritual seeking in Indian life. The antiquity of Sāṅkhya is undoubted. *The Arthaśāstra* refers to Sāṅkhya as one of the branches of philosophy (*Ānvīkṣikī*) and an earlier reference can be traced in the Jaina *Sūyagaḍaṁga*. Earlier still, the *Śvetāśvataropaniṣad* refers to Sāṅkhya alongwith Yoga. The Buddha appears to have had a Sāṅkhyan teacher and the *Mahābhārata* and the *Gītā* presuppose the existence of the Sāṅkhya tradition. It may thus be reasonably argued that the origin of Sāṅkhya must be prior to the sixth century B.C.

Some modern scholars have expressed the opinion that the Sāṅkhya system gradually developed from the doctrines mentioned especially in the *Kaṭha, Chāndogya* and *Śvetāśvatara Upaniṣads*.[41] This does not appear plausible because the Sāṅkhya principle of *Pradhāna-kāraṇavāda* is totally at variance with the Upaniṣadic or Vedāntic principle of *Puruṣa-kāraṇavāda*. That is why Bādarāyaṇa rejects the identification of the First Cause with *Prakṛti* and describes the latter as a non-Vedic principle (*aśabda*).[42] The Sāṅkhya on its side rejects the

Vedic way equally with the way of the world—'*dṛṣṭavad ānuśravikaḥ*'. The Sāṅkhya is atheistic, pluralistic, pessimistic and ascetic. In all these features it is typically Śramaṇic and different from the ancient Vedic tradition. Hence, rather than seek the origin of Sāṅkhya in the *Upaniṣads,* we ought to see an influence of the former on the latter. The usual attempts to trace the 'development' of Sāṅkhya refuse to see in it either a fundamental philosophical or religious thought. The development they trace is neither logical nor spiritual, it is rather a process of syncretism, emerging from a series of conflations and confusion. Seeking to discover history, this ends up with personal myths about lost forms and stages of Sāṅkhya, which are unfortunately unverifiable.[43] One wonders whether Sāṅkhya is a conglomeration of myths and supersititions or a system of spiritual philosophy growing through the creative and critical work of individual minds.

The classical text of Sāṅkhya is the *Sāṅkhya-Kārikā* of Īśvarakṛṣṇa. Takakusu has unconvincingly argued that this Īśvarakṛṣṇa was the same as Vindhyavāsa who was sought to be refuted by Vasubandhu.[44] There is thus no sure ground for placing the composition of the *Sāṅkhya-kārikā* in the Gupta period. Besides, the *Sāṅkhya-Kārikā* only claims to be the summary of another work called *Ṣaṣṭhitantra* which unfortunately is lost. The classical doctrines of Sāṅkhya as known from the *Kārikās* must in any case be deemed much older than Īśvarakṛṣṇa. In fact, Garbe has rightly suggested that the Sāṅkhya has been a conservative system and its classical doctrines ought to be regarded as its original ones. Against this a number of scholars have sought to reconstruct a 'pre-classical' Sāṅkhya from fragmentary notices in the *Mahābhārata, Caraka-Saṁhitā* and the *Buddhacarita.* Since these notices do not claim to be scientific expositions of the Sāṅkhya system as such but represent the views of sages whose connection with it is not always clear, they can hardly be considered as sufficient evidence for postulating an earlier stage of the classical system. It is, however, not impossible that several thinkers may have interpreted or modified the principles of Sāṅkhya in the light of their individual experience and reason just as in post-classical times such modifications were attempted more than once. An ancient school or sect would undoubtedly ramify in time and place but these ramifications are not the sources out of which the original school may be regarded as having grown.

The sage Kapila is traditionally regarded as the founder of the Sāṅhkya tradition. The great commentator on the *Yogasūtras* quotes an ancient tradition to the effect that the supreme and divine sage (Kapila) who was the first enlightened being, out of compassion, expounded the system to the enquiring Āsuri by taking recourse to a psychically manifested form. On this Kaviraj ji comments "The assumption of *nirmāṇakāya* implies that the Master had not a physical body and his appearance before Āsuri does not therefore represent a historical fact." As the best of the *Siddhas,* Kapila can hardly be placed within empirical history.[45] Myth makes him one of the seven sons of Brahmā while a Purāṇic legend makes him a son of Kardama and Devahūti.[46] Śaṅkara takes pains to point out that the Sāṅkhya Kapila is not the Vedic Kapila.

Kapila is said to have taught Āsuri and Āsuri taught Pañcaśikha who appears to have diversified the original *Tantra* into one with sixty divisions viz., *Ṣaṣṭhitantra.*[47] Some fragments from Pañcaśikha have been quoted by later commentators, though the *Ṣaṣṭhitantra* itself is lost.[48] Pañcaśikha occurs in the *Mbh* as a teacher of one Janaka. If the Pārāśarya Brāhmaṇa mentioned in the Buddhist canon was his disciple Pañcaśikha could be an elder contemporary of Buddha.[49] Vācaspati Miśra gives us a list of the sixty principles where the ten radical categories are: "The existence of Nature; its singleness; objectiveness; distinctiveness (of Nature from Spirit); subordination (of Nature to Spirit); plurality (of Spirits); disjunction (of Spirit from Nature in the end) conjunction (of Spirit and Nature in the beginning); duration; inactivity (of the Spirit)."[50] The other fifty categories are called *Pratyaya-sargas.* Udayavira Shastri has justly remarked that the former ten categories represent the *ādhibhautika,* the latter fifty the *ādhyātmika* aspect of the Sāṅkhya.

Among the later teachers of Sāṅkhya, the names of Vārṣagaṇya and Vindhyavāsa are prominent. The identity of the former and a quotation attributed to him have been disputed. Some other fragments too have been ascribed to him. About Vindhyavāsa we gather that he denied the principle of *antarābhava* or 'intermediate' birth between the incarnations of the soul on earth.[51]

According to the Chinese tradition, between Pañcaśikha and Vārṣagaṇa there were Gārgya and Ulūka,[52] and Vārṣagaṇa transmitted the tradition for Īśvarakṛṣṇa whom as already mentioned Takakusu identifies with Vindhyavāsa, which is refuted by Kaviraj ji. Whether Vārṣagaṇa is the same as Vārṣagaṇya and whether the transmission from him to Īśvarakṛṣṇa was an immediate or personal one, are subjects fit for doubt. In any case, it is Īśvarakṛṣṇa's summary in seventy verses which constitutes the basic and classical account of Sāṅkhya. Īśvarakṛṣṇa claims to have left out "the stories and polemics" of the older *Ṣaṣṭhitantra* which obviously contained them.[53] It seems that the Sāṅkhya originally propounded its wisdom in stories and parables, a method which betokens its great antiquity and also that it arose as the simple and popular exposition of spiritual truth rather than as philosophical reflection and subtlety. This is how Buddha and Christ preached and the saints and sages in India have continued to follow the method through the ages.

The *Sāṅkhya-Kārikās* begin by stating that the universal fact of suffering and the inadequacy of 'positive as well as ritual methods in this context lead to an enquiry into its transcendental cause.' This cause is the ignorance of Man of his true self with his consequent involvement in Nature. Human bondage arises through the non-discrimination of the spiritual and the natural and is a process of passion and action, birth and death. The spirit is pure and unchanging consciousness, Nature unconscious and constantly changing. Nature is constituted by three strands or forces (*guṇas*) viz., *sattva*, *rajas* and *tamas*. The exact interpretation of the *guṇas* in modern terms is not easy. The three are always present together though in varying proportions. They are distinguished by the functions of 'illumination', 'motion' and 'inertia'. Since all the substances of the manifested world are particular products of the *guṇas,* the latter cannot be identified with any one of them. The ultimate nature of the *guṇas* remains unmanifest-"*Guṇānām paramaṁ rūpaṁ na dṛṣṭipatham ṛchhati.*" As a result Nature too is ultimately unmanifest. Its manifestation in the form of the world is a process of evolution (*pariṇāma*) where the effect is really latent in the cause. The reason for this process of manifestation or creation is the destiny of the Spirit for the bondage and release of which Nature functions. The process of evolution is thus described—unmanifest (*Avyakta*), *Mahat* (universal Mind), *Ahaṁkāra* (principle of ego or individuation), eleven tools of cognition (individual mind, five afferent senses, five efferent senses) and the five pure sensibilia (sound, colour etc.), five material elements. These twenty-four elements (*tattvas*) constitute the world of Nature. In particular they constitute the psychophysical apparatus of man. The spiritual element is the transcendental apperception which is implicit in all experience. The mind belongs to Nature. It represents objects on the basis of the stimulation of the senses and its representations are presented to the spirit which in reality only witnesses them but in the state of ignorance fails to discriminate between its own witnessing and the mental representations being witnessed. As a result the function of transcendental apperception becomes a psychological fact of appropriation and sustains the sense of the empirical ego. The Sāṅkhya holds the Spirit to be individual and plural in reality but all its determinations or personal identities to be psychic appearances.

While the *Tattvasamāsa* is of uncertain date,[54] the *Sāṅkhya-sūtras* in their present form may have been compiled in the late 14th or 15th centuries.[55] *Nevertheless* the *Sūtras* undoubtedly contain much ancient material especially in their parables and illustrations. A series of commentators on the *Kārikās* and the *Sūtras* down to modern times attest the significance and vitality of the tradition. Frauwallner argues for the decline of the system between Dignāga and Dharmakīrti

(*Geschichte*, Vol. I, p. 474ff. quoted by Hulin *op. cit.*, p. 142).[55a] Vijñāna-Bhikṣu in the 16th century refers to the languishing state of Sāṅkhya and seeks to revive it (*Pravacanabhāṣya*). From the philosophical point of view Vācaspati Miśra's commentary on the *Kārikās* is the most important though the *Yuktidīpikā* contains much material about the different views current among Sāṅkhya thinkers. However, the spiritual meaning of Sāṅkhya in the context of its practical *sādhanā* has been best brought out by the modern savant and sage Hariharānanda Āraṇya who has not only written copiously on Sāṅkhya-Yoga but also established the Kapilāśrama for practical instructions. The revival attempted by the Svamiji is, however, already flagging since the spiritual *Weltanschauung* of Sāṅkhya hardly agrees with the current Indian craze for imitating the West. In this the fate of Sāṅkhya is no different from that of Buddhism.

Philosophically, the *tattvas* of Sāṅkhya are abstractions into which experience may be analysed but it is the claim of Sāṅkhya that these principles are no mere verbal or speculative constructs. They are real essences revealed in the course of developing spiritual experience. The spiritual seeker must cultivate 'disidentification' from his own psychophysical apparatus and from the world which belongs to it. He must 'disown' the experiences which he habitually regards as his own and adopt towards them an attitude of detached witnessing. As the process of withdrawal proceeds, he will reach increasingly subtler essences or *tattvas*. From the sensuous experience of the material world he will move to the experience of the pure sensuous qualities or *tanmātras* viz., sound, colour, smell, taste and touch. Higher still he will reach the level of the Ego, and beyond that the level of pure or universal Intelligence. It is only at this level that the detachment from the object leads to the realization of the self.

The influence of Sāṅkhya on other systems has been profound. Ārāḍa Kālāma, a teacher of Buddha, is supposed to have held doctrines resembling the Sāṅkhya. Early Buddhism is similar to Sāṅkhya in the sense that both seek to do away with the illusion that the empirical ego is the real self, though Buddha remained silent over the real self. The spiritual effort in the two cases, however, has a great deal of similarity. In both cases the effort is to 'disown' the psycho-physical apparatus and functioning.

The interaction of Sāṅkhya with Vedānta was deep and continued. Vijñāna Bhikṣu tried to reconcile Sāṅkhya with Vedānta by making it theistic. On the other hand, the Purāṇas and the Vaiṣṇava and Śaiva Āgamas generally incorporated the *tattvas* of Sāṅkhya in their cosmogonic schemes. So close came to be the interaction of Sāṅkhya and Vedānta that it has led many to think of them as originally identical! The two, however, remain radically distinct in their outlook.

Sāṅkhya and classical Vedānta

Sāṅkhya and Vedānta are appellations of historically given systems of thought which have evolved through a long process of exposition and criticism. Both of them are philosophical expressions of characteristic spiritual experiences. What gives unity and authenticity to the doctrines and history of each is its underlying spiritual vision. Sāṅkhya and Vedānta are neither dogmatic theologies nor simply exercises in hypothetical reasoning. They are attempts at the coherent expression of profoundly realized facts of spiritual life. To use an older term, they are parts of *Adhyātmavidyā* or spiritual wisdom. They both pronounce on the metaphysical verities underlying human life and experience.

To ascertain the nature of Sāṅkhya and Vedānta and their inter-relationship we have to rely on their own authoritative texts. The classical authority for Sāṅkhya is the *Sāṅkhya-Kārikā* of Īśvarakṛṣṇa. This work defines Sāṅkhya as an enquiry into the origin and final end of suffering and distinguishes it both from the positive knowledge of natural causation as well as from the ritualism of the Vedic Tradition. The summum bonum is here conceived as a total turning away from life which is conceived as full of suffering. The Sāṅkhya doctrine thus appears to be similar to such Śramaṇic doctrines as of Buddhism and Jainism. Like them, again, it does not base itself on the authority of any Vedic text. And, again, like them it denies the existence of God. Independence from Vedic revelation, complete pessimism about natural life, atheism, and rejection of Vedic ritualism, all these features of the Sāṅkhya doctrine attest its origin among the non-Vedic ascetics and mendicants called the Śramaṇas. 'Kapila' may itself be an eponymous name for these ochre-robed mendicants (*Kapilaḥ*). The *Brahmasūtras* on their part equally reject the authenticity of the Sāṅkhya by calling their principle of Pradhāna as 'contradictory to Vedic revelation' (*aśabda*) and including in the Tarkapāda a section on the refutation of Sāṅkhya doctrines. Historically, thus, Sāṅkhya and Vedānta are quite independent and were often hostile. They enshrine quite different types of cultural Weltanschauung. This remains true inspite of the fact that the Vedānta borrowed a lot from Sāṅkhya and attempts were made from time to time to create synthetic systems which would remove the contradiction between Sāṅkhya and Vedānta. As mentioned above many even think that classical Sāṅkhya is simply a development out of the 'Sāṅkhyan' doctrines in the *Upaniṣads*.

The *Upaniṣads* represent the great fountainhead of Vedāntic thought. They trace the origin of the manifold of natural life and existence to the Spirit called *Ātman, Puruṣa* or *Brahman*. All cosmos is the expression of the Spirit, this is the central tenet of Vedānta. Different schools of Vedānta differ in the definition of the exact sense in which the cosmos expresses the Spirit. All of them, however, agree in rejecting the Sāṅkhyan contention that an insentient but autonomous principle ultimately explains the manifold aspects of natural existence. Sāṅkhyan atheism and Vedāntic theism remain basically incompatible. While Sāṅkhya and Vedānta disagree profoundly about the ultimate status of Nature, they agree in holding that it is a basic error to regard the 'self' as just another finite, natural object. For both the real nature of the 'self' is pure consciousness. Both make a fundamental distinction between object-knowledge and pure consciousness or self.

All object-knowledge is relational, determinate, temporal and dependent. All these features are negated in pure consciousness. The former always presupposes the latter and this is the 'transcendental proof' of the self acceptable to both Sāṅkhya and Vedānta. All object-knowledge presupposes consciousness. Since object-knowledge is a fact, it follows that consciousness is real. This remains valid even if all object-knowledge were erroneous. On the other hand, pure consciousness has reality by itself and is intelligible through itself. It does not depend on object-knowledge in any sense. The recognition of the self as pure consciousness, ultimately real and independent and also the presupposition of object-knowledge i.e. the detached witness of phenomena, is common to Sāṅkhya and Vedānta. That the self subsists apart from all knowledge of objects is indeed common to most systems of Indian philosophy though the identification of the self with pure consciousness is distinctive of Sāṅkhya and Vedānta. It is equivalent to the assertion that despite its intermediable status, the 'mind' is nearer insentience than sentience ; it belongs to nature, not to the Spirit. Knowing objects is not the essential mode of being for the Spirit.

For Sāṅkhya pure consciousness is the self but not by itself self-conscious. Even its ultimate self-consciousness is a 'discriminative knowledge' of the non-selfhood of the mind in contrast to the selfhood of consciousness reflected in it. On the other hand, the objects are as independent of the self as the self is of them, though the knowledge of objects depends on the self. When objects and the self cease to be related, the objects lose manifestation or determinate being while the self loses the bondage of empirical knowledge. For Vedānta, on the other hand, the self is innately self-conscious and the objects ultimately depend upon it. It is the transcendent ground of all differences the apparent reality of which presupposes the apparent partial obscuration of the self-consciousness of the self by a positive and beginningless ignorance leading to the Ego which is self and not-self tied together. The partial obscuration of the self, the mutual superimposition of the self and the not-self and the manifestation of the Ego are different expressions of the same situation which does not originate in time nor is eternally real. Ego-consciousness is the seed of 'personality' which develops through a process of secondary identifications of the Ego with the objects.

Like Sāṅkhya, Vedānta stresses the opposition between subject and object so that the hard shell of the Ego may be broken. But unlike Sāṅkhya, Vedānta gives a different description of the ultimate reality and status of things. Consciousness is the sole reality and if anything appears different, the appearance of difference must be a false appearance. In fact, consciousness is being while appearing is for it and can only be described as pseudo-being. In this sense appearance is identical with unreality. When we think of the necessity or ground of appearance we think of its reality which is identical with consciousness. On the other hand, when we think of appearance as a determinate and finite object which has a distinctive nature of its own our thought is merely enmeshed in a self-constructed net of unreality. Unconsciousness, finitude, change and objectivity are for Vedānta marks of unreality. The real must be eternal and infinite, self-conscious and self-grounded. If *Puruṣa* were single and self-conscious and *Prakṛti* unreal, Sāṅkhya and Advaita Vedānta would be hard to distinguish. On the other hand, if a supreme *Puruṣa* were postulated and *Prakṛti* held to be His will and creation, Sāṅkhya would be akin to various dualistic systems of Vedānta. What makes Sāṅkhya distinctive is the limitation with which it invests *Puruṣa* and the ultimacy with which it endows *Prakṛti*. For Vedānta this is true only of a penultimate level of being and knowledge though it is accepted that the isolation of *Puruṣa* from *Prakṛti* is a necessary though not final stage in the realization of the truth. The ultimate Vedāntic realization transfigures *Prakṛti* and *Puruṣa* into a single Spirit or Deity.

To the common man Nature appears as real and desirable. To the spiritual beginner Nature appears an undesirable reality from which to seek riddance. To the most advanced spiritual seeker Nature appears as the manifestation of the self.

Spiritual life is like the 'Dream of Vāsavadattā' which begins with fiery despair and ends with all losses made up.

Patañjali's interpretation of Yoga

Yoga is the universal method of spiritual life and the *Yoga-śāstra* attempts its self-conscious and systematic delineation. Patañjali's *Yoga-Sūtras* contain a classic though particular version of *Yoga-śāstra*.[56] The usage of the word Yoga oscillates between its basic general meaning of spiritual method such as in the expression *Jñāna Yoga, Bhakti Yoga,* etc., and the narrower meaning of Pātañjala Yoga. It will be argued here that while Patañjali must be given the credit for creating the first extant *scientific* system of Yoga or spiritual practice as such, he erred in parts owing to his peculiar philosophical predilections. Taking for granted a rich variety of spiritual practices, Patañjali defines their universal essence and classifies the practices in an ascending order of subtlety and inwardness. He thus succeeds in adumbrating a truly universal science of spiritual culture. At its highest point, however, where the realm of nature is completely transcended, Patañjali's exposition tends to wobble on account of its Sāṅkhyan orientation.

There are some who believe that spiritual life is, in its nature, a negation of science and system. If the spirit is free and transcendent, how can it be made the object of logical thought? Is not the effectiveness of spiritual means purely subjective and individual, a matter of psychic suggestion dependent on personal associations and socio-cultural symbolism? Or, as an alternative, is not spiritual life simply the unpredictable expression of divine grace? One may even think of spiritual life as simply human value-seeking considered as such, or as any kind of idealistic aspiration and effort.[57] Generally speaking, considered in the context of much Western or Semitic moral and mystical speculation, the very possibility of yoga as a unique and universal science appears doubtful since such a science presupposes a certain theory of the relation of Mind to Nature and Spirit.[57a]

The fact is that if we give unpredictable freedom to man as well as to God no science of any kind, and no philosophy either, would be possible. The very concept of method presupposes the determinateness of events. If man or God could act arbitrarily i.e., wholly unpredictably, it would be futile to expect any order in human life and all human endeavour would be in perpetual jeopardy. Without going further into the philosophical paradox of freedom and order, it may be stated here that ultimately the opposition of spontaneity and determinateness must be resolved in terms of self-determination. Man, God and the natural world must ultimately be united as a single self-determining organism which in its temporal aspect appears as a multiplex causal sequence. On any other supposition, insuperable philosophical difficulties are bound to emerge. What appears at first as a purely physical order indifferent to human aspirations and purpose—so much so that man's moral nature is provoked to revolt against it and stake a claim for freedom, apparently spurious since it cannot be validated in the court of natural reason—must appear ultimately as a spiritual order arising out of the very nature of the Spirit. This is implicitly recognized in the *Sāṅkhya-Kārikās* as well as the *Yoga-Sūtras* of Patañjali because both of them concede the inevitability of the spiritual goal and make it the destiny of man. Nature and God work so that the human spirit may be liberated.[58] Spiritual life and natural life are both the functionings of the same psyche though in different directions. We must not think that while natural science explains natural events, spiritual life merely transcends science and intelligibility. Spiritual life uses and develops natural science differently. It needs the science of subtle physical, psychic and parapsychic phenomena. Yoga begins with the control of physical behaviour and culminates in self-knowledge. Throughout it requires the application of the will in the light of a systematic theory. Being genuinely scientific its true theory is open-ended and progressive. At a certain point in his development the Yogī necessarily becomes an experimentalist who cannot be adequately guided by existing theory and has to amend it by fresh discovery. That is why despite the amazing achievement of Patañjali it is now possible to see his limitations in the light of later and continuing developments in Yoga.

Patañjali discovers the essence of Yoga in psychic inhibition[59] which includes concentration. Normally the mind constantly functions in response to external and internal stimuli. A stream of consciousness is thus set in motion where a thousand different thoughts flash past in unending array. Certain empirical as well as transcendental conditions underlie this course of experience. On the empirical level we have the contacts with physical objects mediated through the senses, the cumulative force of past experiences manifesting itself in predispositions and memories, and the reactive force of past actions. These forces are all empirical in the sense that they are all the products of experience, have a definite origin in time and have an objective status. On the other hand, the non-discrimination of the self and the non-self is a transcendental illusion and is neither an object nor an effect. It is, however, the necessary ground of natural experience and can be removed only by self-knowledge. In seeking to attain to true freedom man merely seeks to become aware of his innate and inalienable supernatural status. As a way to freedom, Yoga is thus essentially a way to self-knowledge. This self-knowledge, being innate or eternal is not really produced but merely attained in the temporal order through a manifestation at the psychic level. Since in its purity the psyche or mind is all-reflecting this manifestation is spontaneous as soon as the obscuring factors are removed. The obscuring factors are the distracting empirical forces mentioned above. Normally man's self-consciousness is obscured by his object-consciousness. This produces a restless extrovert stream of awareness. Yoga thus involves a series of inhibitory processes which lead to the abstraction, introversion and concentration of consciousness. From the standpoint of objective forces and its own normal reactions, the mind may thus be said to have been inhibited. It has, however, to be saved from lapsing into inconscience. Only then can supernal wisdom or *Prajñā* dawn. The process of Yoga requires the withdrawal of the senses from the objects and their subordination to the mind, the withdrawal of the mind from the senses and its subordination to the individual self and finally the withdrawal of the individual self from its beginningless companion, the mind, and its merger in the universal self.[60] Throughout this process, consciousness becomes increasingly concentrated and spiritually transfigured.

What is the causal process underlying this spiritual transfiguration of the mind? The mind mediates between Nature and Spirit. It has apparently no nature of its own except limitless plasticity and transparency. Just as light, itself remaining invisible, renders objects visible, so mind, instead of presenting itself, presents the objects by assuming their forms. It is through Mind that Nature evolves out of its utter inchoateness into an ordered world but in the process the mind becomes extrovert and the Spirit finds its very means of self-realization obscured and as a result sinks into natural bondage. The senses are channels through which the mind becomes externalized while the discursive agitation and dull inconscience of the mind keep it in a periodic rhythm which helps to produce the sense of a stable and defined world as the proper content of consciousness. In Yoga, the mind must become withdrawn, stilled, pointed and luminous. The senses must become quiescent, the discursive activities of the mind stopped, its sleepy dullness prevented from supervening, and its natural agitative distraction substituted by a one-pointed flow of awareness. All these changes are produced by the inhibiting of the habitual modes of mental functioning by the continued application of the will. This leads the mind to a point where its transparency becomes sufficient to reflect the pure nature of the Spirit. Ignorance and habit 'naturalise' the mind, while counter-habit and illumination spiritualize it.

The will has to operate at various levels–physical, psychic, and spiritual.[61] The will springs from a certain acceptance and aspiration. This is called *Śraddhā,* 'placing the heart on', explained as 'inner lucidity of the mind' (*cetasaḥ samprasādaḥ*). *Śraddhā* leads to *vīrya* or effort. The practice of yama, niyama, āsanas, prāṇāyāma and pratyāhāra, corresponds to these factors. Aspiration counteracts the force of distracting desire and the resultant effort seeks to inhibit long standing habits, physical and psychic. Moral life arises from spiritual idealism but is in the beginning largely the obedience to certain rules, the cultivation of one set of feelings against another and the resolute effort to abide by them. The practice of āsanas is really an effort at effortless poise. Such a poise is a necessary step in acquiring body-unconsciousness. The theory and practice of prāṇāyāma is a mystery and appears to have undergone a vast development after Patañjali who does not even fully elucidate the nature of *Prāṇa* which is not a distinctive Sāṅkhya category. Patañjali, in fact, thinks of prāṇāyāma essentially as a preliminary to dhāraṇā or concentration at some point, although he mentions its illuminative operation (*Prakāśāvaraṇa Kṣaya*). In its higher development prāṇāyāma is not so much the willed suspension of breath as an application of *Smṛti* or recollection.[62] That is why the Buddhists put it under the practice of *Smṛti Prasthāna*. Even the ordinary prāṇāyāma involving the practice of rhythmic breathing and pause tends to easily induce pratyāhāra or introversion. Dhāraṇā corresponds to *Smṛti* among the 'means' or *Upāyas* mentioned by Patañjali while *Dhyāna* or contemplation is its continuous flow. At this stage consciousness is no longer distracted. *Samādhi* or absorption arises as the logical discursiveness of consciousness also subsides in stages.

Samādhi or Yoga proper is transcendence of the mind (*Asamprajñāta*) following its full illumination (*samprajñāta*).[63] Sometimes a deep and long lasting stage of inconscience supervenes and simulates true transcendence. Some beings are born in such a state when in their previous lives they have attained a stage of desirelessness without transcendental wisdom. The seminal force of active life being thus suspended, their minds remain in a state of latency but are not transcended. True transcendence is possible only through knowledge. Such knowledge arises from that state of yogic absorption where the mind is non-discursively concentrated on an object and even subtle logical constructions are abandoned.[64] Reality is thus revealed in its individuality more freshly and vividly than in sense-perception and more essentially than through logical operations. Intuitive knowledge or *Prajñā* combines essentiality with a higher immediacy. At its highest it is the full revelation of universal Reason (*Mahat* or *Sambodhi*).

When consciousness acquires a sure footing in it i. e., when the individual acquires an inner and constant union with the universal principle of 'Active Reason', the ego-mind is transcended. This is the beginning of true and pure spiritual life. For Patañjali, however, the loneliness of the individual Spirit, its freedom from Nature, is itself the final end of the pilgrimage. If that were so, Kapila himself would not have been able to teach Yoga through a psychic body (*Nirmāṇa-citta*); besides, the spiritual experience of Mahāyāna, Vedānta and Vaiṣṇavism, lying beyond ordinary emancipation, would not be possible.

REFERENCES

1. Cf. *Īśa.*, 1; *Gītā*, 3.12.

2. *e. g.*, *Tai.*, 3.

3. *e. g.*, *Kaṭha*, 2.4.

4. Thus *Īśa.*, 2; *Chā.*, 3.16-17 clearly advocate a life of action. On the other hand, *Bṛ.*, 4.4.22; *Ib.*, 4.5.2 speak clearly of *Pravrajyā*. Upaniṣadic sages, royal and priestly, are not usually mendicants. See my *Śramaṇa Tradition*; also, *Origins of Buddhism*.

5. *Tai.*, 2.7; *Muṇḍa*, 2.2.11; *Kaṭha*, 1.1.26-27.

6. *Śramaṇa Tradition*, pp. 1ff; *Origins of Buddhism*, pp. 258ff. Some unconvincing attempts have been made to derive Śramanism from ritual abstinence etc.

7. Cf. *Bṛ.*, 1.4.17.

8. *Origins of Buddhism*, pp. 322ff.

9. This was acceptable not only to Buddhism but to Sāṅkhya-Yoga and Nyāya-Vaiśeṣika as well—*Sāṅkhya-Kārikā*, 1; *Nyāyavārtika*, p. 2; *Kośa*, IV, pp. 124ff. On early Buddhist views, see *Origins of Buddhism*, pp. 402ff.

10. For the details of such views and their criticism, see my *Sudhakar Chattopadhyaya Memorial Lectures on the Nature of Buddhist Thought*, 1982; also my 'Social Origins of Buddhism', *Bodhi-Rasmi*, New Delhi, 1984.

10a. The very first *Kārikā* of Īśvarakṛṣṇa points out the limitation of empirical means in eradicating suffering.

11. *Origins of Buddhism*, pp. 280ff.

12. Cf. *Āyāraṁga*, 1.5.6 ; *Bṛ.*, 3.26.

13. Cf. *Yoga-sūtra*, 2.13–'*Sati mūle tad vipāko jātyāyur-bhogāḥ*'.

14. See my *R. K. Jain Memorial Lectures on Jainism*, pp. 6-14 ; *Origins of Buddhism*, pp. 428ff ; *Kośa*, 4th chapter ; *Yogasūtras*, 2.12-13 and Vyāsa's comy. on them.

15. See Śīlāṅka's comy. on *Sūyagaḍaṁga*, II.2 ; *Origins of Buddhism*, pp. 358-59.

16. *Lectures on Jainism*, pp. 14ff ; Mrs. Rhys Davids, *Buddhist Psychological Ethics* ; *Kośa*, 5th chapter ; *Madhyamaka*, XVII.

16a. Cf. G. S. P. Misra, *Buddhist Ethics*.

17. Cf. the conception of *Āya-tulā* in *Āyāraṁga*, 1.7 : *Gītā*, 6.32–*ātmaupamya*.

18. Cf. *Bhāratīya Paramparā*, pp. 48ff.

19. Perhaps the best known image of the spiritually liberated person is that given in the *Gītā*, 2.55ff. On Buddha's compassion, see *The Nature of Buddhist Thought*.

20. Cf. *Śramaṇa Tradition*, Lecture II.

21. Mahāvīra's spiritual wanderings are recorded in *Āyāraṁga* II. Buddha's years of wandering in the spiritual quest are recalled at several places in the canon–see *Origins of Buddhism*, pp. 377ff.

22. Cf. *Yogasūtras*, 2.1.2.

23. *e. g.*, Buddhaghoṣa's *Visuddhimaggo*. *Vimuktimārga*, now retranslated from Chinese, is similar. Asaṅga's *Yogācārabhūmiśāstra* is the Mahāyāna classic on the course of spiritual practices.

24. The contrast is common enough in modern literature.

25. For details see *Origins of Buddhism*, pp. 340ff; B.M. Barua, *Pre-Buddhistic Indian Philosophy*; Hoernle, *ERE*, I, A. L. Basham, *History and Doctrines of the Ājīvikas.*

26. *Origins of Buddhism*, pp. 566ff.

27. On the Jain conception of knowledge and reality, see my *Lectures on Jainism*, pp. 33ff. The classical account of Jaina metaphysics may be seen in *Tattvārtha-vārtika.* For the canonical picture, see *Origins of Buddhism,* pp. 355ff.

28. For the Jaina theory of *Karman,* see Glasenapp, *The Theory of Karman in Jaina Philosophy.*

29. See my *Aspects of Jaina Political Thought.*

30. On the nature of *Sambodhi* see my paper on the 'Origin of Mahāyāna', presented at the International Congress of Orientalists held at Delhi, 1964.

31. This is described as *apratiṣṭhita-nirvāṇa* in Hsüan Chuang's *Siddhi.*

32. On the practical and organizational aspect of Buddha's *dharma*, see G. S. P. Misra, *Age of Vinaya.*

33. For a discussion of what constituted the original teachings of the Buddha, see my *Origins of Buddhism.*

34. *Suttanipāta, upasīvamāṇava-pucchā.*

34a. Vide *Origins of Buddhism*, pp. 419-23.

35. See S. N. Dube, *Cross-currents in Early Buddhism.*

36. For this later history of the doctrine see my *Bauddha Dharma Ke Vikāsa Kā Itihāsa.*

37. See my paper 'The origin of Mahāyāna' referred to above; for the historical evolution of Mahāyāna, see my *Bauddha Dharma Ke Vikāsa Kā Itihāsa ;* N. Dutt, *Aspects of Mahāyāna Buddhism and its Relation to Hīnayāna.*

38. Among modern writing on *Sāṅkhya* may be seen—Van Buitenan, *JAOS* vols. 76-77 ; Edgerton, *The Beginnings of Indian Philosophy,* 1965 ; Garbe, *Die Sāṅkhya Philosophie,* Leipzig, 1894 ; Johnston, *Early Sāṅkhya Doctrine* (reprint,

Delhi, 1974) ; Keith, *The Sāṅkhya System,* Calcutta, 1949 ; Larson, *Classical Sāṅkhya,* Delhi, 1969 ; Hulin, *Sāṅkhya Literature,* Wiesbaden, 1978 ; Udayavira Sastri, *Sāṅkhya Darśana Kā Itihāsa ;* Misra, A. P., *Sāṅkhya Darśana Kī Aitihāsika Paramparā*, Allahabad, 1967 ; Chakravarti, *Origin and Development of the Sāṅkhya System of Thought,* Delhi, 1975 (reprint) ; Takakusu, *JRAS*, BEFEO, 1904, p. 58ff. ; Larson & Bhattacharya (ed.), *Encyclopaedia of Ind. Phil.* Vol. IV.

39. Edgerton would make it wholly a way of salvation—*AJP,* 1924, pp. 1-46.

40. See my *Origins of Buddhism,* pp. 305ff ; cf. Garbe, *Die Sāṅkhya Philosophie,* p. 13 ; S. originally non-Brahmanical *i. e.,* Kṣattriya ; Zimmer, *Philosophies of India,* p. 281, S. 'pre-Aryan, indigenous system of thought'.

41. *e. g.,* Hulin, *Sāṅkhya Literature,* pp. 127-36 ; J. A. B. Van Buitenan, *JAOS,* 77, 1957, pp. 88-94 ; E. M. Johnston, *Early Sāṅkhya,* pp. 18-21.

42. Śaṅkara and his commentators regard the author of *Sāṅkhya* as different from the Vedic Kapila—*BS,* 2.1.1. Vācaspati Miśra clearly says—"*Śrutisāmānyamātreṇa bhramaḥ sāṅkhyapraṇetā Kapilaḥ śrauta iti.*"

43. *e. g.,* Oldenberg, *NGWG,* 1918, pp. 218-53 ; Jacobi, Review of the second edition of Garbe's work (Larson, *op. cit.,* pp. 251) ; Keith, *The Sāṅkhya System ;* Johnston, *op. cit. ;* Buitenan, *JAOS,* Vols. 76-77. Frauwallner's account alone takes note of logical and creative factors *History of Indian Philosophy,* Vol. I, pp. 218ff.

44. Takakusu, *JRAS, BEFEO l. c. ;* He relies on an interpretation of the evidence of Kuei-Chi and of Paramārtha's *Life of Vasubandhu.* Cf. Hulin, *op. cit.,* p. 138 ; Larson, *op. cit.,* pp. 154-55. Larson's dating of Īśvarakṛṣṇa depends on Takakusu. Udayavira Shastri represents the other extreme, *op. cit.*

45. Vide M. M. Gopinath Kaviraj, Intr. to *Jayamaṅgalā,* pp. 2-3. Udayavira Shastri's Critique of Kaviraj's view (*op. cit.,* pp. 22ff) is totally unconvincing.

46. *Bhāgavata* III.21. Cf. Baudhāyana, 2.6.30 where Kapila the son of Prahlāda is called an Asura and the creator of the *Āśramas* other than the householder's. Does this explain the name Āsuri for his disciple?

47. Little is known of Āsuri except a quotation ascribed to him in Guṇaratna's comy. on Haribhadra Suri's *Saḍdarśanasamuccaya*—"*Vivikte dṛkpariṇatau buddhau bhogo'sya kathyate/Pratibimbodayaḥ svacche yathā candramaso'mbhasi//*" This view is contrasted with that of *Vindhyavāsa*. On the other hand, Āsuri has been sought to be identified with his namesake in the *Ś. B.*, who was a ritualistic theologian (U. V. Shastri, *op. cit.*). It is not impossible that Āsuri the ritualist was converted by his contact with a mendicant teacher eponymously called Kapila. But in that case the verse quoted above could not be in its present form his creation since stylistically and conceptually it seems to belong to an age of greater sophistication than that of *Ś. B.* It could be a later summary.

48. Some attempts have been made to collect them, *Pañcaśikha Fragmente, Festgruss Von Roth, Stuttgart,* 1893, pp. 77-80; Udayavira Shastri, *op. cit.*

49. Cf. *Majjhima,* III, pp. 404ff.

50. Cf. *Sāṅkhyatattvakaumudī*, p. 159.

51. Cf. Garbe, *op. cit.*, pp. 37-39.

52. *Maṭharavṛtti* mentions Bhārgava, Ulūka, Vālmīki, Hārita and Devala. *Jayamaṅgalā* mentions Garga and Gautama, Gauḍapāda the mental sons of Brahmā. *Yuktidīpikā* has still other names. Cf. K. P. Bhattacharya, *IHQ.* 1932, pp. 510ff.

53. Udayavira Shastri identifies the *Ṣaṣṭhitantra* with the *Sāṅkhyasūtras* unconvincingly.

54. According to the *Sarvopakāriṇī* these twenty-two *Sūtras* were taught by Kapila as the heart of the *Ṣaṣṭhitantra.*

55. U. V. Shastri argues that the *Sāṅkhyasūtras* are the original *Ṣaṣṭhitantra.* Dr. V. S. Agrawal apparently commends the suggestion in his foreword.

55a. Cf. Frauwallner, *op. cit.* I, p. 321. The decline of S. is here attributed to its logical untenability.

56. The earliest extant adumbrations of *Yoga-Śāstra* are found in the *Upaniṣads* (*Kaṭha, Muṇḍaka* and *Śvetāśvatara*) but I have argued elsewhere that these do not represent the *beginning* of yogic science—see my *Studies in the Origins of Buddhism.*

57. It may be recalled how the great modern Indian philosopher, K. C. Bhattacharya declared yoga without *yoga vibhūti* to be a misnomer, *Studies in Philosophy* (2nd ed.), p. 291.

57a. One can see a basic distrust of Yoga proper in Zaehner's writings.

58. Cf. *Vyāsa ad Yoga-Sūtras,* 1.25.

59. *Citta-Vritti-nirodha.* Some degree of concentration or focus is everpresent in the mind. Yoga arises when a habitually recollected mind (*ekāgra-bhumika-citta*) engages in deep concentration. On the role of cortical inhibition in ordinary psychic and parapsychic phenomena cf. Vasiliev, LL., *Mysterious Phenomena of the Human Psyche* (Tr. S. Volochova, New York, 1965).

60. Cf. Kaviraj, C. N., *Aspects of Indian Thought* (Burdwan, 1966), pp. 115ff.; my *M. M. Gopinatha Kaviraj, passim.*

61. Diverse schemes of *Kośas, dehas* and *cakras* attempt to specify them.

62. The full power of Prāṇāyāma is seen in the story of Kāka Bhuṣuṇḍi in the *Yogavāsiṣṭha* or the writings of the Siddhas or in Kuṇḍalini Yoga.

63. Where, to quote the *Prajñāpāramitāsūtras,* 'the mind becomes non-mind' (*Yatra cittamacittaṁ bhavati*).

64. Vide *Yoga-Sūtras,* 1.17, 41-51. The Buddhists also indicate a fourfold classification of contemplative stages which is somewhat similar vide *e. g.,* Buddhaghoṣa's '*Visuddhimaggo*'.

5

CLASSICAL CROSS-CURRENTS: MAHĀYĀNA*

The origin of Mahāyāna presents the students of Buddhist history, philosophy and literature with a variety of problems which are as difficult of solution as they are important. Although many scholars have devoted themselves to the editing, translating and annotating of different Mahāyāna texts and stimulating suggestions about Mahāyānic origins have been made from time to time, a great deal of work admittedly remains to be done. Kimura emphasized the traditional Mahāyāna view of its origin, and, distinguishing between an introspective or ontological and a phenomenological tradition of Buddha's teaching, traced the evolution of Mahāyāna from the former.[1] Despite its depth and value, this suggestion must reckon with the fact that the actual literature of Mahāyāna appears to be historically far removed from the time of Buddha and is thus apocryphal in character. On the other hand, Poussin and Dutt have shed much valuable light on the gradual process by which the various so-called Hīnayāna sets prepared the ground for the emergence of Mahāyāna.[2] It is thus clear that Mahāyānic literature was preceded by a semi-Mahāyānic literature and that several of the tenets of Mahāyāna developed out of the doctrines which were first adumbrated by the Mahāsāṅghikas and the Sarvāstivādins.[3] As this view does not distinguish Hīnayāna from original Buddhism, it tends to make Mahāyāna simply a later stage of Buddha's doctrines, Hīnayāna being the earlier stage. It is as if we were to forget the Upaniṣads and then conclude that the doctrines of Gauḍapāda are simply a derivative of Mahāyāna ! Some other scholars too have commented on the date and place of origin of the Mahāyānasūtras and their language and authorship as well as Mahāyāna art and the systematic phase of Mahāyāna philosophy.[4] Generally, however, the attention of scholars has been directed to the more urgent task of editing and translating original texts.

Much, however, still remains to be done in the investigation of the Mahāyānasūtras, from the point of view of their internal evolution and systematic stratification. The fact that a large number of Mahāyānasūtras are no longer available in their original form, is of course a great stumbling block in all such enquiries. In tracing the genesis of Mahāyānic ideas it is also necessary to avoid assuming that the canonical collections, including Abhidharmic treatises, of the traditional eighteen schools were all completed before the birth of Mahāyāna. It is well known that the so-called Hīnayāna canon had a long and varied development in time as well as space. It contains fragmentary texts of an earlier stage more directly connected with Buddha and now found in the midst of a more usual class of texts which appear to have grown up somewhat later. This idea adumbrated by Mrs. Rhys Davids, has been developed by the present author elsewhere.[5] In the light of an original Buddhism which is thus posited and which is scarcely to be identified with Hīnayāna, it seems desirable to review the question of Mahāyāna origins.[6] At the same time it also seems desirable to consider this question in the light of the wider question of religious origins, to do justice to which the purely historical method needs to be supplemented by a meta-psychological study.[7] It is true that a historian of religion and philosophy cannot afford to limit himself to the asumptions and beliefs of a particular theological or metaphysical system. At the same time this scarcely justifies the usual procedure of confining the historical method to the perspective provided by Positivism. Religion no doubt enters history as a social movement and tradition; nevertheless it seems reasonable to hold that it basically springs from revelation and intuition. The historian of religion, thus, must be prepared to relate the institutions, art and thought of any religious movement with its foundational spiritual experience. It is necessary to consider the genesis of the basic Mahāyāna outlook in the light of original Buddhism, especially the mystical experience of the Founder.[8]

Side by side with the metaphor of Mārga, that of Yāna too

is already found in Upaniṣadic and early Buddhist canonical literature. We thus get the terms 'Devayāna', 'Brahmayāna' and 'Dharmayāna', though not 'Hīnayāna' and 'Mahāyāna'.[8a] But then even in Mahāyānasūtras, the nomenclature of Mahāyāna is not uniform. Vasubandhu in his *Saddharmapuṇḍarīkasūtropadeśa* mentions seventeen names of Mahāyāna.[9] Some of these are quite frequently used viz., Ekayāna, Agrayāna, Bodhisattvayāna and Buddhayāna.[10] The first two, like Mahāyāna itself, are clearly laudatory in their meaning, the last two—Bodhisattvayāna and Buddhayāna are as clearly descriptive and reveal the essential character of Mahāyāna. The contrasted terms Hīnayāna, Śrāvakayāna, and Pratyekabuddhayāna seem to bring out the other side of the distinction.[11] The Mahāyāna was thus essentially the doctrine of the Bodhisattva. The highest spiritual aspiration for a Buddhist must be for Buddhahood itself and since the Buddha was a Bodhisattva in his earlier days, he must act as one. This Bodhisattvayāna was naturally held to be Agrayāna since it led to the perfection of knowledge and compassionate action towards all beings. Since it was basically nothing except following the footsteps of the Master, the 'imitation of Buddha', its emergence or popularity should not really need any explanation. What is surprizing is how any other Yāna obtained currency and how the clear formulation of Mahāyāna was delayed so long.

While Hīnayāna texts are silent about Mahāyāna as such, though not about Mahāyānic ideas,[12] Mahāyāna texts furnish explanations of the prevalence of Hīnayāna and comment on its relation to Mahāyāna.[13] They do not question the authenticity of the sūtras preserved by Hīnayāna.[14] They only question the Hīnayānic interpretation of Buddha's real meaning and claim for themselves a special mystic dispensation.[15] The Mahāyānists also attempt a defence of the authenticity of their own doctrines.[16]

The distinction between Mahāyāna and Hīnayāna rests upon a profound metapsychological principle. At first sight the distinction appears merely one of degree and stage depending on a difference in the level of initial spiritual aspiration. The Hīnayāna is satisfied with the goal of becoming a Disciple (Śrāvaka), Mahāyāna aims at attaining the status of a Teacher (Buddha).[17] There was a view that the 'Inferior' and 'Superior' vehicles are merely the lower and higher courses of a continuous process of spiritual advancement.[18] This, however, was not the general view because it was felt that the Emancipation from the Passions (*Kleśāvaraṇa-kṣaya*) occurs as a watershed between the two courses. At this stage the aspirational impulse of Hīnayāna stops and as no further spontaneous volition is possible, spiritual effort also ceases.[19] Hīnayāna is now like a car which has run out of gas. Mahāyāna, therefore, insists upon starting with what is virtually an infinite potential, the vow to attain Buddhahood and become the saviour of all beings (*Bodhicittapraṇidhāna*).[20] From this it was a natural further step to conclude that the difference in the basic aspirational level should itself be attributed to an innate difference in spiritual potentiality and thus the idea of '*gotrabheda*' came to be propounded.[21]

The example and precepts of the founder are the twin sources of any religion. If the example of Buddha's own spiritual career is by definition Mahāyānic, his precepts as preserved in the Āgamas appear to be of a mixed character. The diversity and even contradiction in the content of these records has been sarcastically commented upon by Brahmanical polemists.[22] Part of the explanation undoubtedly lies in the historically heterogenous character of the early Buddhist canon. The Mahāyānists, however, thought of an ingenious though profound explanation of the diversity of Buddha's precepts. "*Deśanā Lokanāthānaṁ sattvāśayavaśānugā.*"[23] The practice of spiritual life is not a straight-jacket and this has been a commonly recognized principle in India. Any efficient teacher must give to disciples of different abilities and temperaments different practical directions. This would be his 'Skill in means' (upāyakauśalya). It may, however, be contended that although practical directions may vary according to expediency, the basic statement of beliefs or credo must be uniform and all variations must be within a consistent system. While this demand for consistency and system within a doctrine is inevitable from the standpoint of logical thought, it is plainly inadequate for the nature and expression of mystical truth. Buddha's experience was essentially mystical and, as the Mahāyāna contends, truly beyond speech and thought. In this it is fully endorsed by the earliest Buddhist texts which describe the truth (Dharma) discovered by Buddha in Sambodhi and preached later, as *Atarkāvacara* and *Pratyātmavedaniya*.[24] Buddha himself doubted if it could be at all communicated in any way and it was only the inevitable rush of compassion which made him ultimately decide to preach. This beginning of '*Katabasis*' in Buddha's career may be regarded as the spiritual birth of Mahāyāna and is the true meaning of the famous episode of Brahmayācana.[25] It should be noted that though Buddha decided to preach, he observed that different persons have different degree of spiritual aspiration and ability.[26] This coupled with the fact that Truth cannot be stated or communicated in essence, made it inevitable that Buddha should only preach a practical way to the direct realization of the supreme truth and that this way should be relative to the stage and ability of the individual who would tread it. The advice of the spiritual preceptor depends from the previous *Kuśalamūlas* of the disciple and Buddha as the omniscient teacher was able to advise all and adapt his teaching to their specific spiritual constitution and requirements.[27] This practical nature of Buddha's teachings and his impatience with speculative thought and dogma are writ large in the earlier texts.[28] Buddha avoided the 'net of opinions' and steered clear of all categorical formulations on metaphysical questions.[29] In their place he taught the Middle Way which emphasized the relativity of all finite things and conceptions.[30] The inexpressible and infinite nature of truth was clearly pointed out. It is accessible only to a direct experience where the categories and discriminations of finite experience are utterly inapplicable. This was termed Bodhi or Prajñā where Truth stood revealed.[31] The way to this final experience lay essentially through a process of mental purification and detachment. It naturally began with the cultivation of virtue and the avoidance of sin. The mind thus became bright, strong and pliable and next engaged in contemplative detachment from its all habitual finite supports till it was transformed into infinite Radiance or Non-dual Awareness or Being.[32]

It will be obvious from this presentation of original Buddhism that the fundamental doctrines of Madhyamā Pratipad and Prajñā are continued in Mahāyāna from it. Nāgārjuna, the avowed systemizer of Mahāyāna, himself quotes most effectively several ancient texts, such as the *Kātyāyanāvavāda*.[33]

We may now return to another aspect of original Buddhism from which the development of Abhidharmic Hīnayāna can be traced and which thus contributed to the emergence of Mahāyāna in an indirect manner. As Mrs. Rhys Davids has so aptly pointed,

Buddha appears to have encouraged an attitude of analysis towards psychological phenomena.[34] This was intended to help the growth of detachment and discrimination. How Vicāra, Viveka and Vairāgya are causally connected, is well recognized in other systems also. The practice of Vicāra or discriminative thinking is the surest means leading to dispassion. The principal forms of discrimination are between good and evil, transient and eternal, self and non-self.[35] The essential process is to discriminate and reject all that is transient as the non-self. This process is found recommended not only in ancient Buddhism but is also to be found equally in Sāṅkhya and Vedānta. Now since Buddha did not speak of the Self or Truth in positive and categorical terms because of their transcendent and infinite character,[36] the rejection of the ephemeral and the non-self tended to become an entirely negative process which, nevertheless, is not far removed from the practice of Sāṅkhya and Vedānta. On the intellectual plane, however, this negative Vipaśyanā among the early Buddhists led to the growth of that complex system of ethics, psychology and metaphysics which culminated in Abhidharma and formulated the doctrine of Nairātmya in a sense in which the Buddha never intended it. Doubtless a polemical fervour to distinguish Buddhist doctrines from those of other schools encouraged this tendency. Its net result, however, was a spiritual cul-de-sac. Matter and mind, belonging to the realm of the non-self are transient and ultimately valueless but they are nevertheless real possessing intelligible and inalienable essence. On the other hand, the self or a permanent spiritual principle is no more than a name and an illusion, and Nirvāṇa is only the final cessation of the psychophysical process.[37] If this is not materialism or at least the stultification of spiritual aspiration, what is it? Mrs. Rhys Davids was rightly led to the denial of the claim of this doctrine to be the real teaching of Buddha. Even within the Hīnayāna itself, the different sects made attempts to escape the rigorous consequences of their own assumptions and tendeneies, creating for themselves diverse logical difficulties. The Sthaviravādins declared Nirvāṇa to possess an infinite but positive character without apparently realizing that 'determinatio negatio est.'[38] The Sarvāstivādins resuscitated the Sāṅkhya doctrine of the Avyakta under a different guise and by implication relegated time and actuality to the realm of phenomena, with an eternal noumenal world underlying them.[39] From this it was an easy step to conclude that what we know is not real and what is real we do not know, and the step was taken by the Sautrāntikas.[40] The Vātsīputrīyas revived the Self and despite orthodox condemnation, their sub-sects attained great popularity, especially as the Sammitīyas.[41] The Mahāsāṅghikas propounded the reality of matter without defilement and of supernatural personality. The doctrine of 'pure mind' and of the unreality of phenomena were also formulated.

These and other tendencies in sectarian dogmatics really represent the inevitable religious striving after an eternal and infinite or supernatural principle beyond the paralyzing grip of the Abhidharmic tendency which confined reality to transient mental and material states, i.e., made reality wholly temporal, finite and natural. Such a naturalistic point of view has proved very attractive to some modern rationalists and doubtless proved the same to their ancient counterparts. Nevertheless, for the religious consciousness, as the Upaniṣad states, "*Nālpe sukhamasti*". "*Sarvaṃ Duḥkham*" is really a restatement of this very attitude because 'duḥkha' is not basically the sensation of pain but the sense of dissatisfaction with the instability of phenomenal experience.[42] Such an attitude springs from the hope of something beyond commotion and dissatisfaction. This principle was called Artha, Dharma or Nirvāṇa in original Buddhism and its beatific attainment was the goal for which the Buddhists gladly renounced the world.[43] By its reinterpretation of the doctrines of Nairātmya and Paramārtha, Mahāyāna reasserted and further developed the original tendency and indicated a bold departure away from the 'rational metaphysics' of the Abhidharma, fulfilling at the same time several of the partial breaks and returns adumbrated in some of the Hīnayāna sects themselves as indicated above.

Dharmanairātmya is usually considered an extension of *Pudgalanairātmya*. This, however, is to completely mistake the origin, nature and purpose of the doctrine of *Dharmanairātmya* which in effect negates the implication of the *Pudgalanairātmya* and, as indicated above, rescues spiritual aspiration and optimism. According to *Pudgalanairātmya* Mind and Matter are real while the Spirit is not. According to *Dharmanairātmya*, Mind and Matter are certainly illusory while an ineffable and infinite Truth is not denied but often explained as the Non-dual Awareness.[44] This is the doctrine of Śūnyatā or Vijñāna, the two being in the beginning merely the logical and mystical aspects of the same truth.[45] It is a continuation of ideas found in original Buddhism, viz., the ideas of Pratītyasamutpāda, Nirvāṇa, Sambodhi and Vijñāṇa.

In the age of Buddha, Arhat signified a person of the highest spiritual attainments, the most 'Worthy', and there is no reason to suppose that there was at this stage any difference in meaning between Arhat and Buddha.[46] The Jaina usage of Arhat as synonymous with Jina confirms this supposition. Buddha naturally taught the Way that he himself followed and led his disciples towards the same attainment as he had reached. The experience of Sambodhi was apparently the highest development of Samprajñāta Samādhi[47] where the mind not only reflects transcendent Quiescence, but is also capable of illumining any possible object to which it might turn, or alternatively, it illumines the totality of all possible objects.[48] This totality, however, must be sharply distinguished from the world of finite objects as constructed by the intellect. The mind here rests in its natural state, "luminous, ethereal."[49] All finitizing and objectivizing movement of the mind is arrested and the awareness of finitude, if at all, is only as that of an eternally cancelled illusion within the 'synoptic vision' of infinite truth. Or else, the awareness of finitude as illusion and of the truth as the negation of negation is only an intellectual construct seeking to relate the ineffable supernatural experience with the experience of the natural world. Since Buddha's spiritual experience transcended objectivity and the distinction between object and subject knowledge in the ordinary sense is superseded and it is obvious that his 'omniscience' cannot be held to characterize his ultimate experience unless it is interpreted in the sense which, Śaṅkarācārya attributes to it in his commentary on the Kārikās of Gauḍapāda. It is not 'having the knowledge of all' but 'being all-knowledge'.[50] It is comparable to the Sāṅkhya state of Mahat reached in the inverse order where the principle of Egoity is absorbed in its source and the mind becomes infinite light or cosmic Intelligence which in its 'purity', i.e., freedom from all objectivity, already annulled in Ahaṁkāra, and subjectivity which is annulled now, reflects Puruṣa or the Supernatural principle, from which it is only 'a shade removed'.[51] The experiencing mind is still finite and temporal[52] but its content is infinite and eternal and transcends the subject-object relation.

It is natural to suppose that all those wno were awakened to truth at the instance of Buddha were awakened to the same fundamental truth and had a basically identical experience. All the Arhats were freed from Ignorance and craving and might have exclaimed '*anekajātisaṁsāram sandhāvissam punappunam*' etc. Emancipation, Dispassion and Awakening were not distinguished. Nor is there in fact any fundamental distinction between Emancipation and Enlightenment from the point of the truth envisioned or its purely spiritual consequences on the personality of the mystic. On the other hand, the fact cannot be gainsaid that the mind of different seekers have a different degree of natural development depending on the differences of their past actions. This difference persists during and after the experience of awakening or emancipation. As a result, although they share in the vision of an identical supernatural truth, they have different natural attainments and powers. The Buddha and the Arhats of his time were thus alike in spiritual knowledge, different in natural and preternatural power.[53] This difference of power particularly affects the degree to which an emancipated person may act as spiritual teacher, which requires the power of understanding the subtle dispositions and past karman of the disciples and communicating the experience of truth in symbols and terms appropriate to the plane of the disciples' understanding. Thus the "Three Vidyās" were claimed as a normal complement of 'Śrāmaṇyaphala' and hence of Arhathood and Buddhahood. At the same time all felt the extraordinary power of Buddha and no disciple claimed equality with him. This led to the tendency to regard Buddha himself as supernatural and also to attribute his visible greatness to the influence of past good deeds and practice of yoga. Since Buddha occasionally spoke of himself as Buddha, the supernatural Being, and not Gotama, the Man,[54] this tendency is evidenced in the earliest texts, and time and speculation vastly added to it. The result was a veritable apotheosis of the Buddha which increased the distance between him and the Arhat. In this context, the Mahāyāna reversal of the Hīnayāna tendency to regard the Arhat as the normal spiritual ideal must be regarded at once a return to Buddha and a growth of spiritual life and aspiration. On the other hand, the early working out of the four grades of spiritual attainments, the schematic formulation of the Bodhisattva's life, and the distinction between the Pratyeka-Buddha and the Samyaksambuddha are obviously the products of a gradually evolving theology. In this respect, Mahāyāna clearly continues a process which was operative within Hīnayāna and may truly be regarded as a later state of Buddhism following the earlier one of Hīnayāna.

If devotion to the Bodhisattvas was one of the most prominent characteristics of Mahāyāna, its numerous *sūtras* were indisputably another. Mahāyāna relegated the bulk of the old Āgamas to the level of inferior teaching and produced and revered a new and indefinite corpus of sūtras in Sanskrit, often corrupt with Prakritisms.[55] The Prajñāsūtras have been justly considered the earliest of these and placed in the second or first century B.C.[56] They have been connected with the Pūrvaśailīya sect and eastern Deccan.[57] The doctrinal connection between Mahāyāna and the Caitiya schools supports this early tradition about the locality where these sūtras might have originated. The use of Sanskrit and the contact with Sarvāstivāda, on the other hand, suggest a northwestern origin.[58] If the suggestion of a Prakrit original for the early Mahāyānasūtras could be proved,[59] it would be immensely consequential. Unfortunately the suggestion remains hypothetical till we could discover some of these supposed originals. There is, however, no doubt that some of the Mahāyānasūtras draw upon older material in Prakrit. This can be seen most clearly in the *Lalitavistāra* which is a Mahāyānasūtra in its present form. It may also be recalled here that, according to a Hīnayāna tradition, many ancient sūtras of the Āgama got lost.[60] Consequently from the silence of the existing canon on any particular doctrine, it would be unwise to conclude that it was entirely a later invention. The fact is that if we consider the wide variety of tenets presented by the Hīnayāna sects, we find that they have been developed speculatively or dialectically from tendencies already discernible in canonical literature. At the same time Mahāyānasūtras or Vaipulya appear to have continued certain forms of Hīnayāna literature and their tendencies. These do not belong to any single Hīnayāna sect. Nor was Mahāyāna considered a nineteenth sect by the side of the older eighteen. I-Tsing tells us how monks of Hīnayāna and Mahāyāna lived together in the same monasteries and how a Mahāyānist could have a Hīnayānist teacher.[61] We have also to consider the silence of Hīnayāna literature on Mahāyāna in the context of sectarian disputes. Finally, the absence of any distinctive monastic code or Vinaya for the Mahāyāna clearly indicates that the emergence of Mahāyāna was not the emergence of a new sect but that of a clear distinction between two tendencies of a cross-sectarian order. Of these the Mahāyānic tendency harked back to the example and precept of Buddha himself but it developed and found itself only after a phase of sectarian disputes.[62] It is thus that Mahāyāna is at once a continuation of original Buddhism as well as of later so-called Hīnayānic tendencies. This is, of course, not to rule out the possibility that some originally non-Buddhist tendencies did not affect the growth of Mahāyāna. Thus the doctrine of Avatāra in the Gītā is very close to the *Saddharmapuṇḍarika* in its doctrine of Nirmāṇakāya which is conceptually distinct[63] but has the same practical consequences. Although there is no clear doctrine of Bhakti in the Mahāyāna-sūtras, the sentiments and practices appropriate to it are frequently emphasized there.[64] The fact is that although there is no Iśvara-bhakti here, there is clearly Gurubhakti, which again brings us to the heart of Mahāyāna. An individual may through the incessant effort of will gradually withdraw from the whirlpool of life and death. A certain grade of grace or Śaktipāta is required even here and often a Kalyāṇamitra is its medium. Or one may follow a historical tradition of spiritual practice, i.e., the Dharma as embodied in a Śāstra. The help received from a Kalyāṇamitra or Āgama is also ultimately an expression of grace. Nevertheless, the emphasis on individual self-reliance is far greater in this older quest for emancipation than in the Mahāyānic quest for becoming a teacher or saviour. To become a teacher we must rely on the grace of the Universal Teacher. It is thus that Mahāyāna inevitably leads to a kind of Bhakti which nevertheless is not Bhakti in the full sense, for it is essentially Sādhana-bhakti.[65]

In defending its own claim to authenticity and originality, Mahāyāna ultimately appeals to the criterion of 'conformity to Truth' (*Dharmatāṃ ca na vilomayati*).[66] It is doubtless not a historical criterion and yet it must be earnestly pondered over by any student of religion and philosophy.[67] If we believe Buddha to have known and preached the truth, is there any option but to interpret and reconstruct the meaning of his fragmentary sayings in the light of ascertainable spiritual experience and the fruits of a comparative study of mysticism and theology? In proposing the criterion of Dharmatā, Mahāyāna was only relying on an inevitable rational criterion and there are many who would consider its version of Dharmatā as an essentially convincing interpretation of Bodhi. We may sum up the foregoing discussion by saying that although the distinction of Mahāyāna and Hīnayāna has been formulated in the *sūtras* of Mahāyāna several centuries after Buddha, it goes back in its essence to the original experience and teachings of the Buddha in which the spiritual ideal was of Sambadhi and the actual instructions varied according to the spiritual potential of the disciples (*Vineya bhedat desana-bhedah*). The essence of Mahāyāna, thus, was to seek Buddhahood for the sake of universal salvation. The Mahāyānist adopted the vow to follow the path of the *Bodhisattva.* The sublime ideal of the Bodhisattva who puts aside all personal ends including personal salvation in order to save all beings is the hall-mark of the Mahāyānist what motivates him is the search for Enlightenment so that universal compassion may be fulfilled. The Mahāyānic conception of salvation is not simply that of passionlessness (*Kleṣāvarana-mokṣa*) but of enlightened perfection (*Jneyavaraṇa-mokṣa* following *Prajñapāramita*). *Mahāprajñā* and *Mahākarunā* define the Mahāyānic ideal.

For the attainment of this ideal a long and many-stepped course of spiritual discipline has been laid down. It begins with *Bodhicittapranidhāna* and progresses through the cultivation of the *Pāramitās* or Perfections in the various stages or *bhūmis.* According to a version favoured by Candrakirti in the *Madhyamakavatara*, *Danapāramitā* was cultivated in the *Pramuditā bhūmi*, *Śila* in *Vimala*, *Kṣānti* in *Prābhākari*, *Virya* in *Arcismati*, *Dhyāna* in *Sudurjayā*, *Prajñā* in Abhimukhi, *Upayakausala* in *Durangama*, *Pranidhāna* in *Acala*, *Bala* in *Sādhumati*, and *Jñāna* in *Dharmameghā*. The famous six *Paramilasdana*, *Śila*, *Kṣānti*, *Virya*, *dhyāna* and *Prajñā*—are cultivated in the first six *Bhūmis*. *Dāna* or the dedication of oneself totally the good of others is the primary expression of *Karuṇā* or compassion. *Prajñā* or the comprehension of *Śūnyatā* or *Dharmanairālinga* alone makes total selflessness possible. In the remaining stages the Bodhisattva develops the characteristic powers and functions of the Buddha.

The Buddha was conceived not as a historical human being but as the ultimate reality itself which had an inbuilt principle of universal grace, a principle which manifests itself at the cosmic as well as at the human level. As ultimate reality Buddha is the *Dharmakāya*, as self-effulgent grace manifested to the assemblies of the Bodhisattvas etc., at a superhuman level he is the *Sambhoga-kāya*, 'the body of glory' , and as a human manifestation such as the Sakya Gautama he is the *Nirmānakāya*, 'the magical body'. "*Trividhah kayo Buddhanām svabhāviko dharmakāya āsrayaparavrtti-lakṣanah sambhagiko yena parsanmandalesu dharma-sambhogam karoti. Nairmaniko yena nirmaneva sattvartham karoti.*" (*Mahāyāna-sūtra-laṃkāra*, p. 46).

The ideal of the Bodhisattva motivated lay universal com-passion and the virtual apotheosis of the Buddha found a popular echo in the worship of Buddhas and Bodhisattvas in their diverse iconic representations. Mahāyāna, thus, combined a transcenden-tal philosophy with an ethos of universal compassion as well as a popular religion which was akin to the worship of diverse gods and incarnations through appropriate images. One may discern in Mahāyāna a half-turn towards *Vedānta* and *Bhakti*. At the same time it had a most distinctive universality of outlook.

REFERENCES

*It seeks to work out the metapsychological point of view suggested by M.M.G.N. Kaviraj and reconcile it with the histori-cal point of view. Part of it was presented at the Int. Cong. of Orientalists, 1964.

1. Kimura, *JDL*, Vol. XII, pp. 54 ff; Cf. CAF. Rhys Davids, B. S. O. S., IV, 856-7.

2. Poussin, *ERE*, Vol. VIII, pp. 145-46, 328-30, 330-36; *Vijñaptimātratāsiddhi*, la Siddhi de Hiuan Tsang, tr. et ann. par L. de la Vallee Poussin, Vol. II, pp. 721 ff.; N. Dutt, *Aspects of Mahā-yāna Buddhism and its Relation to Hinayāna*, pp. 1-46.

3. Cf. G. G. Pande, *Buddha Dharma Ke Vikāsa Kā Itihāsa*, Lucknow (1963), pp. 322ff.

4. S. C. Vidyabhushana, Mahāyāna and Hīnayāna (*JRAS*, 1900, 29-42); Anesaki, Traces of Pali Texts in Mahāyāna

Treatises (*Museon*, Vol. VII, 34-35, Louvain, 1906); Suzuki, *Outlines of Mahāyāna Buddhism*, (1907); *Studies in the Laṅkāvatāra Sūtra* (1930); Windisch, *Die Komposition des Mahāvastu* (1909); Dr. Schrader, Mahāyāna and Hīnayāna, *ZDMG*, 1910, 341-6; Masson-Oursel: Les Trois Corps du Bouddha, *JA* 1913; Foucher, *The Beginnings of Buddhist Art* (1917); *L'Art Gre'co—bouddhique du Gandhara*, 2 vols (1905-22); McGovern, *Introduction to Mahāyāna Buddhism* (1921-2); Schayer, *Mahāyāna Doctrines of Salvation* (1923); Masuda, *Der Individualistische Idealismus der Yogācāra—Schule* (1926); Abegg : *Dar Messiasglaube in Indien und Iran* (1928); Franwallner's notes on Buddhist logic in *WZRM*, 1929-33; Winternitz, *History of Indian Literature*, Vol. II; *Der Mahāyāna Buddhismus nach Sanskrit und Prakrittexten*, (1930); Bareau, *Les Sectes Bouddhiques du Petit Vehicule*, App. III; Lamotte, *Histoire du Bouddhisme Indien*, Le Traite de la Grande Vertu de Sagesse, 2 vols; Stcherbatsky, *Conception of Buddhist Nirvāṇa*, *Buddhist Logic* (2 vols), Tucci, *On Some Aspects of the Doctrines of Maitreya Nātha and Asaṅga* (1930); Walleser, The Life of Nāgārjuna from Tibetan and Chinese Sources (*Asia Major*, Hirth Anniv. Vol.); Har Dayal *The Bodhisattva Doctrine* (1932); Edgerton, *Buddhist Hybrid Sanskrit Grammar* and *Dictionary* (1953); Conze, *The Prajñāpāramitā Literature*; Japanese Studies on Mahāyāna philosophical schools are noticed by Nakamura in *Acta Asiatica*, I, 56-58; especially noticeable is his own paper, "Historical Studies of the coming into Existence of Mahāyāna Sūtras"; T. R. V. Murty, *Central Philosophy of Buddhism*; A. K. Chatterji, *Buddhist Idealism*.

5. See his *Studies in the Origins of Buddhism* (Allahabad, 1957).

6. Miss I. B. Horner wrote to the author several years back, "Yes, I too wonder if the usual explanation of Hīnayāna and Mahāyāna as earlier and later is really correct. I think you are right in thinking that at all events elements in each hark back to something older and that too, again, perhaps to something some oral tradition, older still." M. M Dr Gopinath Kaviraj has also expressed his belief that it should be possible to trace "the origins of ideas associated with Mahāyānic Buddhism to their first adumbrations in the earlier canonical works in Pāli and the Brāhmaṇas and earlier Upaniṣads in Sanskrit."

7. This was first suggested to the author by M. M. Dr. G. N. Kaviraja long time back.

8. Ch. Up. 4.15.6; Ib. 5-10; Br. Up. 6-2-15-16; SN. (P. T.S. ed), Vol. V, p. 6.

8a. This was suggested by Pt. K. Chaṭṭopādhyāya. Khuddaka (Nalanda ed.), Vo. I, p. 289.

9. Kimura, *J.D.L.*, Vol XII, p. 62.

10. Cf. Kimura, *op. cit.*, pp. 123-25, 146-47.

11. Cf. *ERE*, Vol. VIII, p. 331.

12. Cf. Bareau, *op. cit.*, p. 299. Nevertheless, several of the controversies among the 'Hīnayāna' sects plainly refer to Mahāyānic ideas. Such are the controversies relating to the conception of Buddha and Bodhisattva as supernatural as held by Mahāsāṅghikas and connected sects, vide e.g. Kathāvatthu (Nalanda), pp. 201ff, 208ff, 427ff, 482ff; Masuda, *Asia Major* II, 1925, pp. 18ff; Walleser; *Die Sekten des alten Buddhismus*, pp. 24ff; Mahāvastu I, pp. 159, 167-70; the conceptions of a naturally pure (Prakṛtibhāsvara) or fundamental (mūla) Vijñāna (as especially held by the Mahāsāṅghikas, vide, Walleser, *op. cit.*, p. 27; Poussin, *Siddhi*, I. pp. 178-79); the conception of phenomenal unreality (Prajñapti, Saṁvṛti) as held by the Lokottaravādins, Ekvyāvahārikas and the Prajñaptivādins, vide Bareau, *op.cit.*, pp. 76, 77, 84); and the conception of two Truths (esp. as in the Satyasiddhiśāstra, probably belonging to the Bahuśrutīyas, vide Bareau, *op. cit.*, p. 82). The relationship between the emancipation and ways of Buddha and Śrāvaka or between the three vehicles was already debated in these 'Hīnayāna' sects. The Mahīśāsakas held the Vimukti and Mārga of the Buddha to be identical with those of the Śrāvaka (Bareau, *op. cit.*, p. 186). The Dharmaguptas and the Sarvāstivādins held the Vimukti to be identical but the Mārgas to be different, the Sarvāstivādins holding that the three yānas are distinct. (*Ibid.*, pp. 144, 192).

13. Thus the *Saddharmapuṇḍarika* (Calcutta, 1953, 0.32) has ["Yadā tathāgatāḥ... Kalpakaṣāya votpadyante sattvakaṣāye vā kleśakaṣāye vā dṛṣṭikaṣāye vāyuṣkaṣāya votpadyante. Evaṁrūpeṣu Śāriputra kalpasaṅkṣobhakaṣāyeṣu bahusattveṣu lubdheṣvalpa Kuśalamūleṣu tadā Śāriputra tathāgatāḥ... upāyakauśalyena tadevaikam buddhayānaṁ triyānanirdeśena nirdiśanti"].

Asaṅga points out five points of distinction between Hīnayāna and Mahāyāna (*Sūtrālaṅkāra*, ed. Levi, p. 4).

14. In fact, they quote them occasionally in their own support, e.g., vide Poussin, *Siddhi*, 1, p. 180, where a text from the Ekottarāgama comparable to A. N. II, 131 (P. T. S. ed) "ālayarāmā bhikkhave pajā ālayaratā ālāyasammuditā", is quoted in support of the doctrine of Ālayavijñāna; *Mūlamādhyamikakārikās* (ed. Poussin), pp. 218-19, 237-38, 269-70.

15. Already in the S.N. II, 267 (P.T.S. ed.) there is distinction between the 'suttantā tathāgatabhāsitā gambhīratthā... suññatāpatisaṁyuttā' and the 'suttantā... bāhirakā'. This blossomed into the distinction between Nītārtha and Neyārtha sūtras, which was debated in the early Hīnayāna sects and taken over in the Mahāyānasūtras. On an esoteric Mahāyāna tradition, see Kimura, *op. cit.*, pp. 57-8, Bu-ston (tr. Obermiller) Vol. II, pp. 46-52. On the two or three Dharmacakrapravartanas, Cf. *Saddharmapuṇḍarika*, pp. 44-45, 52-53; *Sandhinirmocanasūtra* quoted and commented upon by Bu-ston, *op. cit.*, pp. 53-54.

16. *Sutrālaṅkāra*, p. 3; cf. *Siddhi*, I, pp. 176-78, esp. Poussin's note on p. 176; *Bodhicaryāvatāra*, (ed. Poussin), pp. 430ff.

17. Cf. G. N. Kaviraja, *Bharatiya Samskṛti Aur Sādhanā* (Patna, 1953), p. 551.

18. e.g. Consider the quotation from *Śrimālāsūtra*, "Śrāvako bhūtvā pratyekabuddho bhavati punaśca buddha iti" found in *Sutrālaṅkāra*, p. 70. This was called Eka-Yāna-naya-vāda, cf. Obermiller, *Analysis of the Abhisamayālaṁkāra*, p. 87fn, Cf. G.N. Kaviraja, *op cit.*, p. 525, cf. Haribhadra, *Abhisamayālaṃkārāloka*, on the Arhats,

19. Cf. Hardayal, *The Bodhisattva Doctrine.*

20. On the stages of *Bodhicittotpāda*, vide *Sutrālaṅkāra*, pp. 14-15, *Bodhicaryāvatāra*, pp. 23-24.

21. *Lankāvatāra*, pp. 63ff; *Sutrālaṅkāra*, gotrādhikāra; *Abhisamayālaṅkāra*, I. 37-40; Cf. Poussin, *Siddh*, II, pp. 721-26; Dutt, *op. cit.*, pp. 84ff.

22. e.g. Śaṅkara ad *Brahmasūtras*, II, 2.19 and 32.

23. Quoted from *Bodhicittavivaraṇa* in *Bhāmati* ad *Brahmasūtras*. II.2.18, *Sarva-darśanasaṅgraha* (Nirnayasagar), p. 18.

24. M.N., suttas, 26 & 28; SN, (P.T.S.) I, p. 136; DN (Nalanda) II, p. 30, etc. Cf. *Lalitavistāra* (ed. Vaidya), p. 286;

Cf. Lamotte, *Le Traitè de la Grande Vertu de Sagesse*, Vol. I, p. 35, fn. 2.

25. Cf. *Origins of Buddhism*, p. 384, Cf. *Mūlamādhyamikakārikās*, 24.12.

26. Cf. M. N. (Nalanda) I, p. 219; Cf. *Lalitavistāra*, p. 292.

27. Cf. *Sphuṭārtha* (Wogihara), p. 5.

28. e.g., in the Aṭṭhaka Vagga of the *Suttanipāta* which is generally accepted as belonging to the most ancient parts of the canon; thus Aṭṭhakavagga, vv, 13, 15-16, 22, 31, 34-35, 37, 60-63, 67-69, 72, 74, 76-78, 117-21, 146 condemn diṭṭhi, saññā, pavitakka, takka, vāda, vivāda, suta, muta, ñāṇa and sammuti and emphasize that spiritual truth is one but infinite, inaccessible to debate and speculative dogmatization. See particularly the comments of the *Mahāprajñāpāramitāśāstra* on these texts—Lamotte, *op. cit.*, I, pp. 39ff.

29. e.g. vide the famous Brahmajālasuttanta of DN.

30. This comes out most clearly in several suttas of the Nidānasaṁyutta of SN—Kaccanagotta, Acelakassapa, Timbaruka, Natuṁha, Aññatarabrāhmaṇa, Jānussoṇi, 8. Lokāyatika; Cf. *Origins of Buddhism*, pp. 415ff, esp. pp. 419-20.

31. Cf. the two famous verses which occur at several places, "*Yadā have pātubhavanti dhammā*..." (Udāna, S.I., Vinaya, mahāvagga), "*Sele yathā pabbatamuddhaniṭṭhito*...." (MN, Ariyapariyesana, Bodhirājakumāra; DN, Mahāpadāna, etc.) Prajñā is here clearly a revelation of truth (Dhammapātubhāva) and provides a perspective for looking at the suffering universe, which leads on to compassion. The second of the two verses is virtually identical, with a 'Paramarṣigāthā" quoted in Vyāsabhāṣya ad *Yogasūtra*. II. 47. Vyāsa's definition of Prajñā as 'simultaneous and vivid illumination of reality' (bhutārthaviṣayaḥ kramānanurodhi sphuṭaprajñālokaḥ) can hardly be improved upon Cf. Nāgārjuna's *Mahāyānaviṁṣaka*, verse 15 where also Pratītyasamutpāda is a perspective for viewing reality.

32. MN (P.T.S.) I. 329 "*Viññaṇam anidassanam anantaṁ sabbatopabhaṃ*". This infinite radiant state of the mind is really its original state—(AN P.T.S.) I. 10. "*Pabhassaram idaṃ cittaṃ tañ ca āgantukehi upakkilesehi upakkiliṭṭham*". Mere dualities and discriminations cease and the lower or discriminative mind ceases to function—DN (Nalanda) I. 190 "*Viññāṇam anidassanaṁ anantaṃ*

sabhatopabham. Ettha āpo ca pathavi tejo vāyo na gādhati. Ettha digham ca rassaṁ ce aṇum thūlam. subhāsubham Ettha nāmam ca rūpaṃ ca asesaṃ uparujjhati Viññṇassa norodhena etthetam uparujhuti". With this may be compared Pārāyaṇavagga, Ajitamaṇavapuccha, v. 6, Mettagū, v. 7, Upasīva, v. 4, 6, 8. The 'astaṅgama' (home-going) of fire or rivers really meant their becoming measureless or indeterminate, not destruction, see *Śvetāśvatara*, I. 13, *Maitrāyaniya Āraṇyaka*, 6.34.1, Kaṭha, 2.5.9, MN (Nalanda) II, 180, Muṇḍaka. 3.2.8, Mbh. Śāntiparva. 21, 42-43. On the ancient meaning of Nirodha, Cf. Praśna, I.10, Cf. Up. 8.6. On the cessation of the dual and emergence of non-dual consciousness, Cf. Br. Up. 5.4. 12-16.

33. MK, XV. 7. Kātyāyanāvavāda is obviously the Kaccānagottasutta of SN. II. 17, Candrakīrti adds "*Idañca sūtraṁ sarvanikāyeṣu paṭhyate*" (MK. p. 269). MK. XI 1 has reference to the Anavaragra or Anamatagga Saṁyutta of SN. MK. XIII.1. has reference to MN. III. 245 (P.T.S.). MK. XVIII, 2 refers to texts like SN (P. T. S. ed.) II. 39-40, AN. II (P. T. S. Ed.) 157-58.

34. This comes out in the emphasis on Smṛti which is part of the Mārga, Indriyas, Balas and Sambodhyaṅgas. Dharmavicaya follows Smṛti in the Sambodhyaṅgas. The importance attached to Yonisomaniśākara may also be mentioned in this context, e.g. see SN. IV (Nalanda), pp. 62-63.

35. The famous three Lakṣaṇas of Duḥkha, Anitya and Anātman indicate the principal directions of discriminative thinking Cf. YS. II. 5. Cf. *Pramāṇavārtikabhāṣya*, pp. 146-47.

36. On the meaning of Buddha's 'silence' see my *Origins of Buddhism*, pp. 505-09.

37. This Abhidharmic point of view has been expressed most lucidly by Stcharbatsky in his Central Conception of Buddhism.

38. Visuddhimaggo, (ed. Kosambi) pp. 355-56.

39. This would be in effect the conclusion of Rosenberg's analysis of Sarvāstivāda Abhidharma in *Die Probleme der buddhistischen Philosophie*. Prof. Sasaki's 'A Study of Abhidharma Philosophy' suggests that Abhidharmic 'realism' is not to be construed as the exclusion of 'idealism'.

40. This followed first from the principle of Bāhyārthānu-

meyatā and next from the sharp distinction erected between Pratyakṣa and Anumāna.

41. This is clear from the evidence of Yuan Chwang.

42. This is the meaning of Saṁskāraduḥkhatā.

43. See Origins of Buddhism, pp. 477-78, fn.

44. MK. XVIII. 6-7; Laṅkāvatāra, II.

45. This is clear enough in texts like *Aṣṭasāhasrikā* and *Laṅkāvatāra* or *Madhyānta-vibhaṅga* and *Sūtrālaṅkāra*, see my *Bauddha Dharma Ke Vikāsa Kā Itihāsa*, pp. 398ff.

46. Cf. Dialogues of the Buddha, II. Introduction to Sutta 14.

47. Cf. YS. I. 48-49 and the Comy. of Vyāsa. Also Cf. Vyāsa ad YS. I—"*Yastvekāgre cetasi sādbhutam artham pradyotayati, kṣiṅoti ca kleśān, karma-bandhanāni ślathayati, nirodham abhimukhikaroti, sa samprajñāto yogaḥ.*"

48. Cf. *Ab. K. V.* pp. 254-55; on the other hand, MN. II (P. T. S.) 127 or *Ib.* p. 121f.

49 "*Bhāsvaram Ākāśakalpam*" as the Vyāsabhāṣya puts it ad YS. I, 36.

50. "Sarvajña iti'.

51. Cf. Vyāsa ad YS. II. 20.

52. Cf. Hariharānanda on YS. 1.2.—"*Rajastu tadā sadṛśapravāharūpam vivekakhyātivikāraṁ janayati.*" Cf. Śaṅkara ad *Brahmasūtras,* II.2.28.—"*Vijñānasyotpattipradhvaṁsānekatvādiviśeṣavattvābhyupagamāt.*" These however are the universal characteristies of Vṛttijñāna and even the '*Ahambrahmāsmityākārikā vṛtti*' must have them.

53. See *Kathāvatthu* (Nalanda), pp. 207ff, *Sphuṭarthā,* pp. 4-5. 640-41. Cf. *Jātakaṭṭhakathā* (ed. Dhammarakkhita) Vol. p. 11 which mentions eight preconditions for the success of the vow to attain Buddhahood.

54. AN. II. 38 (P. T. S.)

55. *Śikṣāsamuccaya* quotes from nearly a hundred sūtras and the *Mahāvyutpatti* has an almost equally extensive list. It is in the Chinese and Tibetan translations, however, that these texts are mostly preserved.

56. Winternitz, *op. cit.*, pp. 314ff, Dutt. *Aspects,* pp. 323ff. Conze, *The Prajñāpāramitā Literature*, p. 26, 50-51.

57. Conze, *op. cit.*, p. 9, Taranatha (Schiefner), p. 58, Cf. *Aṣṭasāhasrikā*, p. 225 Cf. Lamotte, *Le Traite*. I. pp. 24-25; Bareau, *Les sectes*, pp. 297ff.

58. On a double geographical origin, Cf. Bareau, l.c.

59. *ERE*. VIII. 335; Edgerton, *Buddhist Hybrid Sanskrit Grammar and Dictionary*. Cf. N. Dutt (ed.) *Saddharmapuṇḍarika*, pp. XVI-XVII.

60. *Abhidharmakośavyākhyā* quoted by Minayeff, Recherches sur le, Bouddhisme, "tathā hi Ekottarikāgama āśatād dharmanirdeśa āsīd idānīṁ tu ā daśakād dṛsyata iti."

61. I-Tsing (Takakusu), p. 7, 14-15.

62. Cf. Dutt, *Aspects*, pp. 290 ff. *Bodhicaryāvatārapañjikā*, pp. 152-3, 157, 159, mention the following texts as esp. useful for learning the right conduct of a Bodhisattva-*Bodhisattvaprātimokṣa*, *Upalipariprcchā*, *Śriṣambhavavimokṣa*, and *Ratnamegha*.

63. Cf. G. N. Kaviraj in Sarasvati Bhawana Studies, pp. 47ff.

64. e.g., reverence for scriptures and the worship of images, trust and faith in the Buddhas and Budhisattvas, glorification of the Nāma and prayers, are writ large in the *Saddharmapuṇḍarika*. On the glorification of Avalokita's name, also of *Gaṇḍavyūha* (ed. Suzuki and Idyumi) pp. 213-14. Vide Susmitā Pande, '*Bhakti in Mahāyāna*' *Journal, Deptt of Buddh. Study*, Delhi University, 1980.

65. As Madhusūdana Sarasvatī puts it in his celebrated Bhaktirasāyana (1-3), Bhakti is really the unbroken flow of the mind contemplating the Deity with feeling. It relies on Nāma and Rūpa, the twin upādhis of God and passes from an instrumental, often ritualistic, stage to a final self sufficient stage. The result of the earlier stage is to purify the heart and win the grace of God, the later stage is the ecstatic manifestation of divine Love.

66. Cf. *Aṣṭashāsrikā* p. 4; *Abhisamayālaṅkārālokā*, p. 36; *Sūtrālaṇkāra*, pp. 4-5.

67. Cf. "Religious faith often seems able to break through the barriers of space and time, and so to apprehend its object directly". (Burnet, Greek Philosophy, p. 1. 1943 ed.).

6

CLASSICAL CROSS-CURRENTS : VEDĀNTA

As is well known, the *Upaniṣads* constitute the source of the Vedāntic tradition. The *Upaniṣad*s do not propound any system but only record the inspired insights of diverse sages. Doubtless they presume a background of priestly debates or *Brahmodya* as well as debates at the courts of philosophically enlightened kings like Aśvapati, Pravāhaṇa Jaivali, Ajātaśatru and Janaka. Priestly and ascetic trends of thought tended to meet and interact. As a result the *Upaniṣads* which begin with ritualistic symbolism and cosmology end with the rejection of ritual in favour of inward morality and of the pleasures of the world in favour of pure spiritual beatitude. After-life (*samparāya*) and salvation tend to become more important than before. Despite the diversity of ideas and tendencies in Upaniṣadic thought, its focus remains the spiritual principle in man and Nature. Its emphasis, again, is not on distinguishing the Spirit from Nature but in the unity and ultimacy of the spirit. Even if the characterisation of the Upaniṣadic lore as *Brahmātmaikyavijñāna* may be controverted, its description as *Paramātma-vijñāna* or *Brahmadvidyā* is certainly beyond doubt.

The classical *Upaniṣads* may be held to have been already composed by the beginning of the 6th century B.C.[1] In the following centuries which were marked by a strong religious and intellectual ferment, the study of the *Upaniṣads* led to a variety of views seeking to interpret and synthesise their doctrines. This process reached its first culmination in the *Brahmasūtras* or *Vedāntasūtras* of Bādarāyaṇa. When these *sūtras* were composed is uncertain. Jacobi's view placing them in the Gupta period is certainly wrong because Bādarāyaṇa does not seem to be conversant with a state of Buddhism where *Vijñānavāda* and *Śūnyavāda* were well demarcated systems as they were after the second century A.D.[2] Bādarāyaṇa knows the basic ideas of *Sarvāstivāda* and the general Mahāyānic notion of the unreality of the world. The *Vedānta-sūtras,* thus, could not be later than the second century A.D., nor earlier than the second century B.C. Nevertheless, much of the discussion which they sum up about the principles of the *Upaniṣads* should be regarded as the product of the preceding centuries. Pre-Bādarāyaṇa Vedāntic schools and teachers, thus, would belong to the same period during which the different schools of ancient Buddhism arose.

The three main issues for discussion during this period were (1) the nature of creation and the First Cause, (2) the relationship between the supreme spirit and the individual and (3) the role of work and knowledge in relation to salvation.[4] On the first question there were apparently some thinkers who tended to interpret the *Upaniṣadic* First Cause in a Sāṅkhyan manner and Bādarāyaṇa evinces considerable concern in repudiating such an approach. He seeks to establish that a supreme sentient principle is the sole cause of the universe in all its variety. No separate material cause is required for the purpose. Nor is there any inconsistency in supposing that consciousness transforms itself into the inconscience of Nature without loss to itself.

On the second question viz., the relation of the supreme to the individual spirit we learn of a variety of earlier views. Āśmarathya believed that the relationship between the two was one of identity in difference and illustrated it by the example of fire and its sparks. In contrast, Auḍulomi asserted that the two souls are really one only after the soul has become emancipated just as the river becomes one with the sea only when it merges into the latter. While both these teachers saw a certain relative difference between the *Jīva* and *Brahman*, Kāśakṛtsna affirmed their essential identity on the ground that it is *Brahman* alone who presents Himself as the *Jīva*.

On the third question, we gather that Jaimini, presumably the same as the author of the *Pūrvamīmāṁsā*, stressed the necessity of religious works and although Bādarāyaṇa accepted the independent efficacy of knowledge, he too did not regard work as irrelevant to salvation. More, there was a general acceptance of the need for meditation on the Upaniṣadic Vidyās.

The *Vedānta-sūtras* begin the first or *Samanvayādhyāya* by defining *Brahman* as the source, support and end of the world. He is the object of Vedāntic enquiry and an intelligent principle. He is the source of the Vedic revelation and is referred to in the *Upaniṣads* in His diverse aspects, as the golden person, the subtle ether, the vital breath, the light that shines without and within. He is the inner ruler, the Imperishable, the highest person "to be meditated upon with the syllable Om." He is the person in the heart. All these and other descriptions in the *Upaniṣads* are explained to refer to *Brahman*, not to diverse other principles of lower significance.

Bādarāyaṇa then goes on in the second *Avirodhādhyāya* to refute rival philosophies—*Sāṅkhya* and *Vaiśeṣika*, Bauddha and Jaina, *Pāśupata* and *Pāñcarātra*. This gives us a very valuable cross-section of the religious philosophies of India some time before the beginning of the Christian era. Bādarāyaṇa then treats of the fundamental elements of Nature as derived from *Brahman* and seeks to determine the nature of the individual soul. Prof. Thibaut held the opinion that Bādarāyaṇa's views on the subject are nearer those of Rāmānuja than of Śaṅkara.[5] The souls are intelligent and invidual, eternal aspects or parts, *aṁśas* of *Brahman*, endowed with the capacity of will and action. The course of after life is sought to be described and the states of dreaming and dreamless sleep are discussed. The various Upaniṣadic meditations are especially dealt within the third *Adhyāya* which concerns *Sādhanā*. The various meditations in the *Upaniṣads* are discussed with respect to their fundamental unity and occasional differences owing to attributive accidents. It is declared that the vision of the transcendent self is attained through *Saṁrādhana* or devotional meditations.

The need for the mind to dwell repeatedly on the Upaniṣadic ideas arises from the fact that the realization of the ideas as experience is not usually attained at once. This repeated thinking or meditation may be on the meaning of certain symbols (*pratīkopāsanā*) such as in *Daharavidyā* or *Śāṇḍilyavidyā*, or it could be, as *guṇopāsanā*, on the positive attributes of *Brahman* such as bliss, knowledge etc., or on the negative attributes as imperishability, immateriality etc. Finally meditation could be *ahaṁgrahopāsanā* when the *Brahman* is meditated upon as the self.

The last *Adhyāya* of the *Sūtras* deals with the result or the state of emancipation. Liberation implies the absence of rebirth as well as a condition of beatific existence. The liberated soul does not, however, share with God the power of running the universe. While the knowledge of the identity of the self with *Brahman* leads to immediate liberation, meditation on *saguṇa brahman* would lead to a gradual process of liberation (*krama-mukti*). While Bādari held that the released soul has neither body nor mind, Jaimini held the opposite view. Bādarāyaṇa himself held that the two positions were not really contradictory to the liberated soul.

The heart of the Vedāntic view is thus the recognition of a supreme spiritual principle, at once the creator of the universe and the inner self of the individual. The apparently diverse descriptions in the *Upaniṣads* of this reality in terms of natural or biopsychic phenomena all refer really to the selfsame principle. Man's salvation lies in loving devotion to this cosmic spirit who may be described as God in His majesty and as the self in His essential being. There is an obvious tension in this view. On the one hand, it is an intensely religious monotheism and, on the other, an equally intense gnostic monism. On the one hand, it implies the moral relevance of a divinely created order within which the individual has a role to play. On the other hand, it implies that the world of plurality and action is irrelevant from the point of view of true knowledge. This tension came out in the subsequent period in a series of important commentators whose works, again, have been unfortunately lost till at last we reach the great Śaṅkara.

Among the most revered earlier commentators we hear of Upavarṣa and Baudhāyana, who are sometimes identified but were most probably different. The former is quoted by Śaṅkara as Bhagavān Upavarṣa in his commentary on *BS,* 1.3.28 and 3.3.53. Śabara also appears to quote him in his commentary on the *Mīmāṁsāsūtras,* 1.15 as *Vṛttikāra.* In his commentaries on the two *Mīmāṁsās* Upavarṣa appears to have established, inter alia, the theory of the *Pramāṇas,* the reality of the self and the nature of the word as simply a succession of letters. He criticised the Buddhist negation of the external reality as well as of the self. He also rejected the notion of *sphoṭa.* He appears to have relied specially on the doctrines of Yājñavalkya in describing the self as self-luminous or immediately evident and independent of thoughts which are not eternal. He rejected the Buddhist contention that thoughts have forms into which the external objects may be reduced.

Like Upavarṣa, Baudhāyana was another famous commentator. Rāmānuja claims to follow his extensive Vṛtti on the *Brahmasūtras.*[6] Baudhāyana appears to have held that the enquiry into *Brahman* presupposes the practice of Vedic ritual as a preceding condition. He tended to think of the Two Mīmāṁsās as constituting a single system. He appears to have been essentially a theist who did not identify the self with *Brahman. Brahman* is the Lord of all, the inner controlling self of all. He is the Infinity lying beyond the individual soul as its supreme goal.[7]

Apart from Baudhāyana, Rāmānuja mentions several other Vedāntic teachers viz., Bhāruci, Ṭaṅka, Guhadeva, Kapardika and Dramiḍācārya.[8] Little is known of these though the views of a Brahmanandin are quoted in the *Saṅkṣepa-śārīraka* and its commentary by Madhusūdana. These quotations, however, show Brahmanandin to hold that the causal process is a merely pragmatic reality (*Saṁvyavahāramātram*).[9] He thus moves from *Pariṇāma* to *Vivarta*. He appears to have commented on the *Chāndogya Upaniṣad* and was known as *Vākya kāra*. A Dramiḍācārya appears to have commented on these *Vākyas* of Brahmanandin and to have supported the doctrine of *Nirguṇa Brahman*. Both of these—the Vākyakāra and the Bhāṣyakāra—could hardly have been in the tradition which led to Rāmānuja. Dramiḍācārya is stated to have mentioned the parable of the prince who had been brought up by a huntsman from his childhood but came to realize his true identity on being told of it. This was a parable for the soul's self-realization as a recollection or recognition.[10]

Another commentator Brahmadatta supported the monistic doctrine but held that liberation can come only through the combination of *Jñāna* and *Karman*. The *Jīva* is produced from *Brahman* and at the end merges in Him. For this it is necessary to meditate on the *mahāvākyas*. *Śravaṇa*, *Bhāvanā* and *Sākṣātkāra*, this constitutes the invariable order of spiritual effort and vision. For this reason Brahmadatta was called *Dhyāna-niyoga-vādin*.[11]

Just as Dramiḍācārya has been sought to be identified with the Ālvār saint Śaṭhakopa or Vakulābharaṇa, the great Ācārya Sundarapāṇḍya has been surmised to be the same as the Pāṇḍya King who was converted by the Śaiva saint Tirujñāna Sambaṇdhar and found his place in the list of the Nāyanārs.[12] Śaṅkara quotes some verses from him in his commentary on B.S.1.14. Kumārila and Amalānanda quote a few more verses from him. He was certainly an Advaitin who considered the social self of man as 'secondary (*gauṇa*) and the psychophysical self as unreal (*mithyā*). Nevertheless till the supreme knowledge dawns, the validity of the means of knowledge and the relevance of the empirical knower continue. The Absolute, though transcendent, is spoken of through superimposition and negation (*adhyāropāpavādābhyāṁ niṣprapañcaṁ prapañcyate*).

Bhartṛprapañca was another famous Pre-Śaṅkara philosopher whom Śaṅkara especially criticises.[13] He upheld the doctrine of *Brahman* as a unity in difference like a tree with many branches or the sea with its waves or the clay with its forms. He thus believed in *Bhedābheda* as well as *Brahma-pariṇāma.* The same reality is transcendentally one but empirically many, and both these poles are real. The one really transforms itself into the many without losing its oneness. Empirical knowledge which shows the many and revelation which communicates unity are both valid. This is *Pramāṇasamuccayavāda.* As a consequence of these views or rather as their source was the belief that liberation requires a combination of both knowledge and work (*jñāna-karma-samuccaya*).

While the works of all these ancient authors have been lost, the *Māṇḍūkya-kārikās* of Gauḍapāda are still available and since tradition regards him as the teacher of Śaṅkara's teacher Govindapāda, their importance for the development of Advaita can hardly be over-estimated.[14] Some scholars have doubted the historicity of Gauḍapāda as an individual but the scepticism does not appear to be well founded. Nor indeed is the scepticism about the authenticity of the *Māṇḍūkyopaniṣad* itself well founded. As M. M. Vidhushekhar Sastrin has adequately shown, Gauḍapāda's thought is permeated by Mahāyānic influences. To the Upaniṣadic doctrine of the sole reality of the self, he combines the Mahāyānic doctrine of the total unreality of the world. The world is an illusion *ab initio.* It has no real origin. The way out of this lies in the practice of *Aṣparśa-yoga.* The mind must be made quiescent and the illusion will disappear. "Slay the slayer."

The celeberated grammarian Bhartṛhari also pronounced a monistic philosophy which traced the diversity of the world to the original unity of the Word.[15] The Word manifests the world by its inherent power. *"Anādinidhanaṁ brahma śabdatattvaṁ yadakṣaraṁ/Vivartate ṛthabhāvena prakriyā jagato yataḥ//"* This process of creation or manifestation is paralleled by the counter-process of spiritual realization in which one follows the words in the direction of their greater purity and originality till one reaches the creative matrix in the ultimate Logos. Words are not, on this view, merely conventional symbols for pre-existing external things, nor are ideas and words independent. Ideas and objects are aspects of the same reality, which is self-articulating and dynamic. This reality is termed 'word'. Behind the separate letters and sounds and their order lies a unitary entity, the self-same unchanging *sphoṭa,* the matrix of the spoken or heard word. It corresponds to the universal being in which the particular existents share.

It has been argued that Bhartṛhari was earlier than Dignāga and hence not later than the 5th century A.D. Bhartṛhari greatly influenced Maṇḍana Miśra whose separateness from Sureśvara is now generally accepted.[15a] Since Uṁveka, who is quoted by Śāntarakṣita, commented on Maṇḍana, the latter must have lived not later than the seventh century A. D. Maṇḍana proposes a distinctive kind of monism as well as the theory combining knowledge and work as means of salvation.[16] As a learned Mīmāṁsaka he upheld the concept of *Bhāvanā* against the grammarians and explained the meaning of an imperative (*Vidhyartha*) to lie in its "contributoriness to the desired end" (*iṣṭasādhanatva*). On the other hand, he defended the doctrine of *sphoṭa.* He appears to have held that the monistic conception of reality is with reference to positive reality only and does not exclude the admission of another negative reality. This has been described as *Bhāvādvaita* or *Sadadvaita.* Maṇḍana maintains that the negation of the world (*prapañcābhāva*) is a revealed truth, a negative reality which must be accepted.

About the nature of error he defended the view called *Viparītakhyāti* which had been traditionally held by the *Nyāya* school. It looked upon error as a misapprehension and presupposed a plurality of objects. Maṇḍana seems to have minimised the difference between mis-apprehension and the transcendental error about the self which does not go unapprehended and yet which is apprehended differently from what it really is. Maṇḍana's closeness to the school of Kumārila must be the source of his accepting this theory of error. He further held that the *Jīva* is the locus of error while *Brahma* is its object. This position was later followed by the *Bhāmatī* school and was a chief distinction of that school from the *Vivaraṇa* school in Post-Śaṅkara Vedānta.

Maṇḍana preserved his Mīmāṁsaka learning in his view that both *jñāna* and *karman* must be combined for liberation and that although one may obain liberation as a Sannyāsin, a householder will obtain it more easily. He reviews seven earlier theories about the relation of *karman* and *jñāna*—"that all the injunctions in the ritualistic portion of the Veda turn men away from natural activities... ; that all these injunctions are intended to kill desires through a process of enjoyment... ; that the performance of Karman is necessary to discharge the three congenital debts (*ṛṇatraya*) ... ; that the activities prescribed in the *Karmakāṇḍa* have two distinct functions (*Saṁyoga-pṛthaktva*) by conducting to their respective fruits and also to the realisation of Atman; that all *Karma* is intended to purify men and make them fit for *Ātmajñāna* ; that *Ātmajñāna* should be regarded as a purificatory subsidiary to the agent...; and that *Karma* and *jñāna* are fundamentally opposed to each other and have no inter-relation whatever."[17] Of these Maṇḍana rejects all but two. He is favourable to the two views which regard *Karman* as giving fruits and leading to self-realisation (*saṁyoga-pṛthaktvapakṣa*) and as purifying men for *Ātmajñāna* (*saṁskārapakṣa*). Thus the basic contribution of *karman* is to make a person capable of the kind of meditation which alone can lead to supreme knowledge. A *sannyāsin* too may practise meditation and reach the end but he will toil for a long time compared to one who as a house-holder regularly performs the enjoined works. The former will be plodding on feet, the latter galloping on horse-back.[18]

For Maṇḍana the Upaniṣadic *mahāvākyas* need intense meditation before these can lead to immediate knowledge. The meditation was called *Prasaṅkhyāna* and led to *Sākṣātkāra* or *Prajñā*. Since meditation itself is a kind of mental activity, it is easy to see why Maṇḍana regards *karman* as necessary for the attainment of knowledge. Perhaps it could be argued that meditation on the self or the attributeless *Brahman* is more a cessation of activity than activity but then that cessation too seems to require at an earlier stage some kind of volitional effort or direction, at least of bringing the mind back from the world of finite and plural objects towards the self.

With Śaṅkara Vedānta reached its classical position so much so that earlier authors were gradually forgotten and their works lost. Śaṅkara is generally dated from 788 A.D. to 820 A.D. though this date has been questioned.[18a] In any case Śaṅkara lies between Dharmakīrti whom he quotes and Vācaspati Miśra who commented on him, i.e. between the middle of the 7th century and the early 9th century. He refers to a king *Pūrṇavarman*[19] but whether the reference is to a historical *and* contemporary ruler is not clear. Of Śaṅkara's brief career it is clear that it was crowded with preaching, debating, writing, travelling and organising. Although engaged in strenuous activity Śaṅkara denounced *Karma* and upheld the ideal of *Sannyāsa* uncompromisingly.

The original formulation of the Vedānta had been in close relationship to *Mīmāṁsā* but in stark opposition to Sāṅkhya and Buddhism. Jaimini is the author quoted most frequently by Bādarāyaṇa and action and knowledge are not looked upon as contradictory but rather as complementary, finding their natural unity in worshipful meditation. On the other hand, atheism and illusionism are denounced. Among the subsequent Vedāntic teachers Gauḍapāda had taken the extraordinary step of denouncing creation itself and upholding Buddhist illusionism as an essential principle of Vedānta. Śaṅkara accepted this doctrine of the illusive nature of creation while still criticising the Buddhists on the assumption that they propounded only a subjective idealism. On the identity of the *jīva* and *Brahman* various views had been formulated by previous Ācāryas ; Śaṅkara propounded their simple and total identity, explaining their difference as apparent, accidental and illusory. While he condemned the Sāṅkhya for its pluralism and realism, his own conception of the self came perilously near to that of Sāṅkhya. For Śaṅkara *Brahman* is to be understood not as the 'first cause' or the creator of the world, but as the 'self'. And the 'self' is to be understood not as the individual experiencer and agent but as the eternal ground of subjectivity presupposed in experience as such. Such a self is not merely transcendental in the Kantian sense, not a mere logical presupposition, but for Śaṅkara the only reality, though wholly transcendent. To be real, he says is to be eternal, for the real nature of any thing could not be otherwise. Similarly the self must be distinguished from the non-self as light from darkness. The two could never be identical. The self can never be its own object, or any object at all for there can be no object except for the self. The search for the real self must, then, be through the negation of all those elements in self-consciousness which are transient or objects of thought. All thoughts, feelings and volitions are by this criterion excluded from the real self. This method of spiritual search would be identical with that of Sāṅkhya but for the Vedāntic requirement that the search for the self must not be a search for the apparently individual ground of self-consciousness but for the universal ground of apparently individual self-consciousness. The practical difference between the two methods—Sāṅkhyan and Advaitic—apparently rests upon the fact that in the former one merely strips his self-consciousness of the non-self, seeking the pure witnessing consciousness, in the latter one seeks to realize the identity of the individual self with true universal self on the basis of the Upaniṣadic statements. For those who believed in meditation over the Upaniṣadic statements, the difference is obvious. For Śaṅkara who considered meditation unnecessary, the difference must lie in the fact that the Vedāntin continues beyond the so called Sāṅkhyan realisation of the self. If the self is stripped of all the objective and transient elements of empirical self-consciousness, it would seem to realise itself at one stage as the mere witness of nothingness such as happens in the state of dreamless sleep. The Śaivas of the Kaśmīra school later on explained the Sāṅkhyan self-realisation to stop short at this stage. Vedānta, however, seeks the Fourth stage beyond this, which is one of infinite and beatific self-consciousness. If the Sāṅkhya is correct this could only be a delusion. On the other hand, if Śaṅkara is correct, the spiritual method of Sāṅkhya would not be wrong; only its application would appear to stop half way in pursuance of a misleading theory.[19a]

Just as Śaṅkara's 'self' comes dangerously near to the '*Puruṣa*' of Sāṅkhya, similarly his illusionism approaches the Mahāyānic position closely. The Vedic and Upaniṣadic view was clearly theistic and for it the First Cause is a creative, all-wise, all-powerful Spirit. Śaṅkara unfortunately accepted the Sāṅkhyan and Buddhist premises that to act must be to change and hence to be transient. He also accepted their common assumption that whatever is transient must be 'soulless' and 'insentient', subject to the causal law. If *Brahman* is sentient, free and eternal, He must be held free from all action. In other words, the world could not be really created by Him. At the same time, the Sāṅkhyan assertion of an independent in sentient and temporal reality militated against the Upaniṣadic spiritual monism. Śaṅkara was thus logically driven to accept the Mahāyānic position of the unreality of the world which was then explained as a false appearance in a real ground. This acceptance of a unique and spiritual, real and eternal ground for the illusion of the world distinguished Śaṅkara's position from that of Buddhism. He himself raises the apprehension that his position may be misconstrued by the Buddhists as similar to the latter's and states that in contrast to the Advaitic absolute spirit, Buddhist idealism reduces the world to tran sient and particular ideas.[20] It is interesting to note that Śaṅkara's apprehension was well founded, for Santarakṣita declares this mere matter of eternal as opposed to transient idea as a 'minor fault' (*alpāparādha*).[21]

The principal attack of Śaṅkara, however, was delivered against the Mīmāṁsakas and the earlier Vedāntins influenced by them.[21a] He distinguishes between knowledge and work as wholly disparate. Knowledge is determined by the object, work by the subject. The former is subject to logical, the latter (i.e., *karman*) to causal necessity. Consequently, there can be no prescription about the former. Knowledge is not an action. It is neither a cause, nor an effect. It subsists *sub specie aeternitatis*. The means of knowledge such as sensory activities or mental states are only the means of its manifestation or occasioning. Knowledge itself is not a psychological fact. As the revelation of its content it has a purely logical being. Particular contents are only accidental limitations on the inifinite self-revelation of knowledge. The knowledge of the self and the self-revelation of knowledge are not different things. To reach this self-knowledge what is necessary is to move away from the veil of objectivity which a transcendental illusion has produced. Empirical self-consciousness presupposes such an illusion. That is why it shows within it a mutual superimposition of self and non-self. Consciousness and selfhood, on the one hand, and the body and the mind and their relations with other bodies, on the other, are all confused in ordinary self-consciousness. To move away from this illusion we must realise that the true self is pure and universal consciousness. This realisation can only come from hearing the Vedāntic revelation of the identity of *Ātman* and *Brahman*. Ordinarily words communicate only an indirect and relational knowledge and that is why so many previous Vedāntic Ācāryas insisted on the necessity of meditating over the *mahāvākyas*. Śaṅkara however, thinks that since the *Mahāvākyas* have only to evoke an ever-present, non relational self-knowledge, they can lead to direct and intuitive knowledge. Even meditation can do nothing except to remove some psychological barrier to self-knowledge. It can add nothing to the meaning of the *mahāvākyas,* nor furnish any other means for its communication.[22]

It will be noticed that at the empirical level Śaṅkara sharply distinguishes the logical status of knowledge from the merely factual or causal status of psychic events. This enables him to show the irrelevance of all injunctions and prescriptions where knowledge is concerned. At the same time, he relegates all relational knowledge tied to objectivity and duality to the realm of illusion. True knowledge is only the pure and undifferentiated self-revelation of knowledge. Knowledge thus acquires a trans-logical status and becomes identical with the absolute spirit or self-consciousness. This distinction between two levels—empirical and transcendent is crucial to the philosophy of Śaṅkara and has, again, interestingly enough a Buddhist origin. Śaṅkara accepts the claims of common sense and logic at the empirical level but believes that the ultimate truth lies beyond them. This distinction also enables him to accept the validity of the socio-religious order or *dharma* as a preparatory condition for those who have not yet attained to true self-knowledge. All obligations are valid only for those who still labour under the delusion of egoism. Once knowledge is gained, no duties remain to be performed. Nor is the performance of duties an absolute or logical precondition for knowledge, though as things are, most persons will need to pass through the mill of social and moral obligations before their minds are sufficiently disciplined and purified to make them capable of striving after, and attaining to true self-knowledge. It is the same with religion. Worship and ritual are helpful as a beginning but are ultimately replaced by inner enlightenment which comes to constitute true devotion. More concretely, Śaṅkara was not hostile to the *Varṇāśrama-dharma* but rather lamented its imperfect historical conditions. He, however, stressed the importance of *Sannyāsa* as an *āśrama* and thought that it could be adopted whenever one was keen to acquire spiritual knowledge without regard to whether one has passed through other *āśramas* or not. Śaṅkara's contribution to the re-organisation of the Vedic faith is well known. He is said to have instituted an all India monastic order with its four controlling centres in the four corners of the country and is reputed to have left behind general instructions for the heads of these four *pīṭhas* that they must acquire spiritual knowledge and scriptural learning and constantly move about in their area and preach.[23] Such an organisation was earlier known, if at all, only among the Buddhists.

The best known among Śaṅkara's immediate disciples were Sureśvara and Padmapāda. The former was probably known as Viśvarūpa when a householder and was the author of a famous commentary on the *Yājñavalkyasmṛti*. As Sureśvara he wrote a number of celeberated *Vārtikas* of which the one on *Bṛhadāraṇyakopaniṣad* is the best known. His *Naiṣkarmyasiddhi* is another classic. Padmapāda composed a commentary called *Pañcapādikā* on the earlier portion of Śaṅkara's *Śārīrakabhāṣya*. This formed the beginning of a distinct school of interpretation. Vācaspati Miśra's commentary on the *Sārīraka-bhāṣya* known as *Bhāmati* started still another school. Schools in post-Śaṅkara Advaita tended to be divided over the insoluble problems arising in the attempt to explain the precise nature of the empirical self in relation to *Brahman* as well as the original Nescience. Śaṅkara showed his philosophical wisdom in leaving such questions aside.

If the millennium following the Buddha was dominated by Buddhism as the principal philosophical challenge, the millennium after Śaṅkara saw the Advaita in the centre of the debating stage. The various theistic schools attacked Advaita and Vedānta took in a distinctive theistic appearance in these schools. If the period from Buddha to Śaṅkara was dominated by the idea of *Jñāna* and the attempts to reconcile it with the traditional notion of *Karman*, the period after Śaṅkara saw the conflict of the notion of *Jñāna* and *Bhakti* and triumph of the notion of *Bhakti* which had been growing in numerous cults for a long time.

REFERENCES

1. Videha is still a monarchy and Kāśī is independent. Magadha is not mentioned and there is no trace of Buddhism. Nor is the Deccan mentioned. *Saṁsāravāda* is still barely known. Cf. *Origins of Buddhism*, pp. 286ff. Cf. *PHAI*, pp. 33-34 on Kabandhī Kātyāyana, Janaka and Āśvalāyana. Vide my "The *Upanisads* and *Buddhavacana*", in *K. S. Murty Felicitation Vol.*

2. Jacobi, *JAOS*, XXXI, p. 1ff; G. C. Pande, *Baudha Dharma Ke Vikāsa Kā Itihāsa*, p. 402.

3. On the early teachers of Vedānta, M. M. Gopinatha Kaviraj's long introduction published by the Acyuta Granthamālā, Kāśī, is justly famous. Also may be seen Walleser's *Ältere Vedānta*; Belvalkar's *Basu Mallick Lectures*; S. L. Pandey, *Pre-Śaṅkara Vedānta*.

4. On the *Vedāntasūtras* see Thibaut's trans. & intr. in *SBE*; Radhakrishnan's trans. & intr. to the *Vedānta-sūtrās*; R. D. Ranade, *Lectures on Brahmasūtras*.

5. *op. cit.*

6. *Śrībhāṣya,* Vol. I, p. 4—"*Bhagavad-Bodhāyana-Kṛtāṁ vistīrṇāṁ brahmasūtra-vṛttiṁ pūrvācāryāḥ sañcikṣipuḥ tanmatānusāreṇa sūtrākṣarāṇi vyākhyāsyante.*"

7. Cf. Buitenen (ed.), *Vedārthasaṅgraha,* Appendix I.

8. *Ib.,* pp. 18ff; Kuppuswami Sastri, *Proc. Third Oriental Conf.,* Madras, 1924.

9. *Saṅkṣepaśārīraka,* III.218.

10. Cf. Kaviraja, *op. cit.,* pp. 16-17.

11. *Ib.,* pp. 13-15; Hiriyanna in *JOR,* 1928.

12. *Ib.,* pp. 17-19; Kuppuswami Sastri, *J. O. R.,* I, pp. 1-15.

13. Cf. Hiriyanna, 'Fragments of Bhartṛprapañca', *Proc. Third Oriental Conf.,* Madras, 1924.

14. See Vidhushekhar Bhattacharya, *Āgamaśāstram.*

15. Raghunatha Sarma's edition and Comy., on *Vākyapadīya* (pub. Sanskrit University, Varanasi) and Dr. Ayyar's tr. of the work are recent landmarks in Bhartṛhari studies.

15a. Cf. Balasubramaniyam, 'Mandans & Sureśvara'.

16. See his *Brahmasiddhi.*

17. *Brahmasiddhi,* Intr. by Kuppuswami Sastri, p. 33.

18. *Ib.*

18a. Vide Nakamura, *History of the Vedānta,* Vol. I, Baladev Upadhyaya, *Śaṅkaracārya.*

19. Comy. on *BS.*; Kaviraj, *op. cit.*

19a. Cf. my 'A Note on Śaṅkara,' Int. Seminar, New Delhi, Jan. 89.

20. Comy. ad *BS,* 2.2.28.

21. *Tattvasaṅgraha*: *Teṣāmalpāparādhaṁ tu darśanaṁ nityatoktitaḥ* (verse 330); vide my paper "Śaṅkara and Buddhism", International Seminar on Śaṅkara, Adv. Centre in Phil. Madras University, March 1989.

21a. Vide my G. S. P. Misra Memorial Lecture, 'Role of Śaṅkaracarya', Pub. Raj University, Jaipur, Feb. 1989; also my forthcoming work, *Sankara: Life & Thought* (JCHR).

22. Vide K. S. Murty, *Reason and Revelation in Advaita.*

23. For doubts re. this, see ref. cited under 21a.

7

CLASSICAL CROSS-CURRENTS : MONOTHEISTIC TRENDS

The distinction between the mortal and immortal parts of personality came to be made ever more sharply during the later Vedic age. In several of the Upaniṣadic discussions of after life, what survives death individually is something subtle and shadowy, while the immortal essence which attains salvation is conceived as an eternal and universal principle rather than as an individual person. In fact, in contrast to archaic religion, the emphasis of the *Upaniṣads* lay on the universality of the spirit, and all its particular and individual manifestations tended to be looked upon only as transient and non-ultimate aspects. The human being cannot hope for immortality as an individual person. He must detach himself from his life of mind and body and his instinctive sense of a separate being connected with other similar persons in a moral and physical relationship. In the search for immortality the process of spiritualising the human self was carried to the ideal limit where he became the pure, undifferentiable spirit divested of all empirical, historical or human identity.

This process of superhumanization was not without its effect on the conception of the deity. Although conceived as cosmic forces, the gods were always held to respond to human prayer and worship in a personal manner. When in the later Vedic age the unity of the gods came to be stressed and a single cosmic God came to occupy the centre of philosophical discus sion, His nature came to be conceived in an unavoidably paradoxical nature. He was held to be at once transcendent and immanent, beyond all predicates and the subject of them all. Thus conceived *Brahman* in his awsome and sublime majesty was more fitted to be the subject of hushed contemplation than of simple human prayer as was common in the earlier age. While the religion of ritual and prayer addressed to various gods continued as an answer to the human need for a superhuman support within the context of life, a more philosophical and austere gnosticism tended to demand that man must rise above his mortal humanity to gain the vision of Truth and attain to his own essential being or 'self'.

Side by side with the Advaitic gnosticism, the *Upaniṣads* also continued to describe the *Brahman* as Person (*puruṣa*) and Self (*ātman*). They continued to regard Him as the creator and lord of things who is, at the same time, seated in the hearts of men. Only those who are good and pure of heart can hope to see Him. His vision is an ecstatic experience, like the embrace of lovers, an infinitely greater happiness than any other on earth. At some places, such as *kaṭha*, it is said that the vision of God can be attained only by His grace. In the *Śvetāśvatara* it is specifically stated that *bhakti* or devotion is the necessary means for winning God's favour.

The *Upaniṣads* thus express a variety of views and attitudes but, on the whole, the search for Gnosis (*Brahma-jñāna*) tends to be stressed more than the notions of devotion and grace. But then the *Upaniṣads* must not be taken in isolation from the rest of Vedic religion. The pursuit of *Brahma-vidyā* was neither the whole of the Vedic faith nor an independent part of it. The two aspects of the Vedic faith, *karman* and *jñāna*, were dealt with in a theoretical and systematic manner by the two *mīmāṁsās*. The two *mīmāṁsās* were generally considered together till Śaṅkara and his followers sundered them finally. Similarly the older view tended to regard the 'knowledge' of *Brahman* to be nothing except the intuitive vision gained from the loving meditation on *Brahman* in and through a symbol, attribute or manifestation. Thus worship and knowledge were not traditionally sundered in Vedānta till the Advaita of

Śaṅkara distinguished between them radically. Thus there tended to be two streams of Vedāntic interpretation—one seeking to accommodate religious meditation and worship, the other tending towards gnostic purism. But for a long time even the former kept close to *Mīmāṁsā* ritualism. They stressed the prescriptive character of Vedic texts rather the expression of feeling which was actually so important in the Vedic hymns. As a result the theistic and devotional elements of early Vedic religion tended to be underplayed by ritualism as well as gnosticism which became important towards the end of the Vedic age. Devotional theism tended to develop in sects like the *Pāśupata* and the *Pāñcarātra* which claimed independence of the Vedic tradition and it was only after nearly a millennium that the *Purāṇas* gradually wove the multiplex fabric of *Karma, Jñāna* and *Bhakti* where the older opposition of Vedic and non-Vedic became obsolete and forgotten. A series of Ācāryas then formulated a new Orthodoxy and saints and reformers carried it to the common people.

The quest for God and the quest for personal immortality developed as two aspects of the same devotional faith or 'mystical' yearning. The seeking for knowledge tends to move from separate things to their relations and may dialectically tend to a self-sufficient and self-intelligible whole which can be nothing other than self-conscious substance or being identical with knowledge *sub specie aeternitatis*. Thus the seeking for knowledge often tends towards the Absolute. On the other hand, love postulates a personal reality, the reality of free self-conscious beings capable of entering into a personal relationship of loving and being loved. Personality cannot be conceived in the absence of every kind of body and mind nor can love be conceived in the absence of every kind of difference or freedom. The quest for love thus necessarily assumes the personal reality of godhead and the immortality of the human person. Humanity for God and immortality for man are possibilities essential to the religion of love.

The early Vedic faith of cosmic gods and mortal men capable of only a shadowy after-life conceived the relationship of the two in terms of the symbol of sacrifice. In course of time the notions of 'material sacrifice' (*dravya-yajña*) and 'sacrificing to the gods' (*deva-yajana*) were paralleled by the notions of 'inner sacrifice' (*Adhyātma-yajña, antaryāga*) and 'sacrifice to the self' (*ātma-yajana*). In other words, the turning of the mind and heart towards the deity, 'approaching Him' (*Upāsanā*), came to be regarded as the superior form of worship especially for those who were interested in it *per se* rather than for the sake of some wordly end. The nature of this mental contemplation was interpreted in several ways—as symbolic sacrifice originally, as cognitive enquiry by some Vedāntins and as worship by others. The worshippers of Viṣṇu and Rudra, in particular, came to stress the element of devotion or love in worship, marked by surrender on one hand and grace on the other. Mere sacrifice tended to become 'self-sacrifice' with the promise of immortal life in paradise. In this sense, the notion of the devotional relationship of man and god tended to absorb within it the entire development of Vedic religion.

Nevertheless in the form in which these new devotional sects appear in the early post-Vedic period there can be no gainsaying the fact that they did not regard themselves as simply derived from the Vedic tradition nor did Vedic orthodoxy regard them as such at that time. It is obvious that between the Vedic Viṣṇu and Rudra and their worship, on the one hand, and the *Pāñcarātra* and *Pāśupata* cults, on the other, there is a certain interruption or transformation due to the intrusion of non-Vedic influences. Some scholars have argued for the Dravidian or Harappan origin of these cults in which case they ought to be supposed to have gradually interacted with similar Vedic cults till new identities were created, part Vedic and part non-Vedic. In view of the richness of the Vedic tradition in this respect and our ignorance of what constituted the distinctive forms and rites of pre-Vedic or non-Vedic gods and their worship, it is difficult to distinguish the two types of elements in the devotional sects except that their rejection of the Vedas as the sole revelation constituted the crucial difference.

The famous sixteenth chapter of the *Vājasaneyī Saṁhitā* mentions the verses to be used on the occasion of the *Śataru-*

driya homa. Here Rudra is identical with Fire for which the symbolic altar (*agnicayana*) is constructed. Here Rudra the dreaded Archer is conceived to be simultaneously an all-encompassing gracious God. These verses along with others came to form later on the famous *Śatarudrādhyāyī* which is still used as the most important text in Śaiva worship. It is replete with the sense of sin in the worshipper and of an absolving grace in the deity. Philosophically, however, it is the fortieth chapter of the *Yajurvedasaṁhitā* which declares the omnipresence of God in conceptual terms. The *Śvetāśvataropaniṣad* is later still and outlines a philosophical theory of the relationship of God, man and the world. It begins by posing the question which Brahmavādins raise—what is the cause that is *Brahman?* Whence born do we live? Where do we rest? Through whose power do we continue in misery? Various answers are then mentioned only to be rejected. Time, Nature, Destiny, Chance, Matter, Primordial Nature, Spirit, none of these could be the First Cause, singly or together. The non-spiritual causes are to be rejected for they cannot explain human self-consciousness, and the individual spirit is obviously powerless and bound in its own course of experience and suffering. This philosophical setting is reminiscent of the atmosphere of the 6th century B.C. as gleaned from early Buddhist and Jaina texts. The *Śvetāśvatara* answers the basic question thus "Through *Dhyāna-yoga* they saw the Lord's own Power, covered by its 'attributes'. He alone presides over all the causes which function in conjunction with the soul and time." It goes on to describe the world process in terms derived from the ancient Sāṅkhya with one crucial difference—beyond the individual souls is the supreme spirit and *Prakṛti* is His power. "*Prakṛti* should be understood as *Māyā* and Maheśvara as the lord of *Māyā*." "His supreme power is variously known, it is the innate power of knowledge, will and action." Reality is three-fold—mutable but beginningless Nature, immutable and beginningless individual spirit, the supreme spirit which is the ground and lord of the other two and the only one which is free, infinite and ever beyond illusion and suffering. The individual soul is the experiencer (*bhoktā*), nature is the experienced (*bhogya*) and God is the impeller (*preritā*). Only through Knowing God can the individual spirit free itself from illusion, suffering and the cycle of birth and death. Loving devotion (*parābhakti*) and answering grace (*prasāda*) alone can lead to man's salvation. At the same time, the *Śvetāśvatara* definitely emphasised the elements of Yoga and the supernatural powers which it confers.

The *Śvetāśvatara* is clearly a landmark in the evolution of theism and *Bhakti* and the Śaiva sect. At the same time its composition ought to be placed in the age of religious ferment in the early Janapada age. It is clearly eclectic in drawing upon its sources, Vedic as well as Sāṅkhyan. The *Bhagavad-Gītā* would not be far removed in time just as it is not in spirit. Of course the *Gītā* differs in bearing the impress of an individual thinker and a more carefully designed composition. It also differs in emphasising Viṣṇu rather than Śiva and in seeking to reconcile the doctrines of *Karman* and *Sannyāsa*. Again, its focus is ethical rather than cosmological. Whereas the *Upaniṣad* begins with an enquiry after the First Cause, the *Gītā* begins with a moral crisis.

The debt of the *Gītā* to the *Upaniṣads* is as clear as its originality. The *Chāndogya* tells us that Kṛṣṇa Devakīputra was instructed by Ghora Aṅgīrasa and the identification of this Kṛṣṇa with the Kṛṣṇa of the *Gītā* is natural and uncontradicted by any serious evidence.[1] The echoes of the *Īśa* and *Kaṭha* are similarly plain in the *Gītā*. It seems that the principal doctrines derived in the *Gītā* from the *Upaniṣads* relate to the generalized notion of sacrifice which seems to convert all work into worship, and the ideas of *Brahman* and *Ātman*. At the same time the *Gītā* derives from Sāṅkhya the notions of *Saṁsāra* and *mokṣa*, of the actionless *Puruṣa* contrasted with the ever-active *Prakṛti*, and of the renunciation of *Karman*. The Vedic tradition of moral and ritual obligations and the Śramaṇic tradition of asceticism, both find expression in the *Gītā*. At the same time, the *Gītā* begins a new chapter in the history of devotional theism.

The *Gītā* is categorical in affirming that the worship of the personal God is superior to the contemplation of the impersonal absolute. Although those who meditate over the transcendent and eternal principle also reach the highest end, their path is beset with great difficulties. "It is difficult for embodied beings to reach the unmanifest." On the other hand, God holds those dear who are constantly devoted to Him by a supreme faith. Again, it is the human form (*mānuṣaṁ rūpam*) which Arjuṇa prefers to the cosmic form (*viśvamūrti*). The human form of the personal god is the result of incarnation and the doctrine of Incarnation may be described as the principal innovation of the *Gītā*. That the gods may assume an animal or a human form at will and that they may even take birth as a human being as a boon to some devotee, was well known earlier but the doctrine of incarnation in the *Gītā* is something different. The incarnation as *avatāra* is not a casual but a historical manifestation of God. God incarnates Himself in the human race in an age of moral crisis in order to set right the balance of right and wrong. Although ever unborn and unchangeable, the lord of all beings, He takes birth controlling His power of Nature as a divine mystery. But his incarnation in history is not unique. He is born in every age when virtue declines and evil flourishes to protect the virtuous and destroy the evil doers and establish the moral order. His human birth and career are divine miracles which all men are not able to really comprehend. In fact, 'fools may despise God in human form' but those who recognise Him are saved.

This incarnation of God in historical ages, although it reveals His concern with man, has nevertheless the aspect of a moral force re-asserting itself in human affairs when everything appears lost to those treading the path of virtue. For Arjuna certainly Kṛṣṇa was not simply an incarnation, but the object of profound love, a friend, guide and Master. Indeed, he turns away from Kṛṣṇa as the inexorable historical necessity, the force of Time leading upto the dreadful War, historical or perpetual, (*kālosmi loka-kṣayakṛtpravṛddhah*) and though obedient to it, seeks His lovable (*saumya*) human form. It is in this process of personal adoration and love that the full personal nature of God is revealed.

The God of the *Gītā* is more than the Upaniṣadic *Brahman* or the Sāṅkhyan *Puruṣa*. He is the Supreme Person (*Puruṣottama*), other than the individual soul and insentient Nature, controlling them both. Nature is His lower power, the soul is His higher power, a spark from His own being. He is seated in every man's heart as the inner monitor, presiding over his destiny, ready to guide him and respond to the feelings of the heart. He is the one God behind all gods. All worship ultimately goes to Him alone. Those who worship for worldly ends, get their rewards from Him ultimately. Those who love Him for His sake alone, get Him. A story in the *Mahābhārata* illustrates this vividly. Duryodhana and Arjuna both went to Kṛṣṇa to seek His help. The former gladly accepted the gift of Kṛṣṇa's army fighting on his side. The latter chose Kṛṣṇa alone even though he said he will not fight! For God all are alike. He neither likes nor hates. He has no objectives to gain, nothing to work for. And yet those who love Him attain to His nearness. Unwavering and absolute devotion to Him frees a man from the force of sin and as he learns to surrender himself, he ceases to need to worry about himself.

Gītā describes four types of devotees—one who seeks deliverance from suffering (*ārta*), one who enquires into the truth (*jijñāsu*), one who seeks to attain some value or interest (*arthārthī*), and finally, one who knows (*jñānī*).[2] While all of these seek to move towards a higher state, the *jñānī* is described as the very self of the Lord. Devotion tends to move from action and faith towards knowledge and communion. Faith must be unwavering (*avyabhicāriṇī*) and total (*ananya*) The whole soul must be absorbed in seeking to serve God. Social obligations must not be neglected but all work must be performed as a sacrifice to God, as an act of worship. Worshipping God as a person need not be anything except a simple expression of the heart "whoever offers me with devotion a leaf, a flower, a fruit, a little water, I accept that as a token of his sincere effort," The ideal devotee is expected to follow high moral standards. He must not hate anybody but must be the friend of all, compassionate, without egoism, unassuming, equanimous, tolerant, and forbearing. He must be contented, firm and resolute, surrendering his mind and thoughts to God. Neither should he shun society nor should society shun him. He should be free from joy and resentment, fear and agitation. He should want nothing, be pure, skilled in work, passionless and untroubled, renouncing all undertakings. He should be alike to foe and friend, and take praise and blame with equal indifference. Heat and cold, pain and pleasure, they should be the same to him. He should be homeless, firm in mind and devoted to God. Such a person God holds dear.

So far the ideal of the devotee is that of a dutiful, gentle and detached ascetic. He lives in society, though not necessarily so. When his social situation obliges him he meets his obligations and serves God by doing the duties of his station. He is a man of few wants whose heart is not in the world. He renounces the life of acquisitiveness, egoism and aggression. His heart is placed in God of whom he thinks constantly. This sense of a personal relationship with God is what distinguishes devotion from the mere self-abnegation of the ascetic or the contemplation of the gnostic. The *Gītā* makes the other paths of *Karman* and *jñāna* as moments in the development of devotion. "From ripened devotion he comes to know Me, what and how much I really am. Having thus known me in Truth he then dwells in me afterwards." Thus faith and conduct lead to love which through vision leads to an everlasting communion with the Lord

It may be mentioned here that while Śaṅkara distinguishes two phases in the *Bhakti* of the *Gītā*—one characterized by action (*karma-lakṣaṇa*) and the other by knowledge (*jñāna-lakṣaṇa*) Rāmānuja discovers the essence of *Bhakti* to be in the constant remembrance of the Lord (*dhruvānusmṛti*).[2a] Still others consider the surrender of everything to God (*prapatti, śaraṇāgati*) as the essence of the *Bhakti* preached in the *Gītā*.

While Vāsudeva is certainly mentioned as the object of supreme realization, it must be clear that *Gītā* is hardly a sectarian work. It is no more or less Viṣṇuite than the *Śvetāśvatara* is Śivaite. Neither of the two works, in fact, lays much store by any sectarian ritual or symbolism. Both propound a triune unity of God, Nature and man where God alone is the independent, fundamental and controlling reality and the other two but dependent though distinct aspects of Him. God is at once transcendent and immanent, the source and goal of life. The soul is individual, spiritual and immortal, essentially related to God. Its true happiness and destiny lies in the love of God but that presupposes moral conduct, contemplation and wisdom. Faith and works, grace and vision, love and beatific communion, these constitute the ladder of devotion in the *Śvetāśvatara* and the *Gītā*. The principal difference lies in the stress on humanity and love in the *Gītā*.

The teachings of Vāsudeva Kṛṣṇa in the *Bhagavad-Gītā* have an obvious kinship with those learnt by Nārada from Nārāyaṇa as stated in the *Nārāyaṇīya* section of the *Mokṣadharmaparvan*. Even in the *Chāndogya* Nārada is said to have been dissatisfied with merely Vedic learning and approaches Sanatkumāra to be shown the way beyond sorrow. Both Nārada and Sanatkumāra were later recognised as important seers in the *Pāñcarātra* school. Nārāyaṇa is mentioned in the *Śatapatha* performing a *Pañcarātra* sacrifice but it is more than doubtful that Nārāyaṇa should have any historical reference. The *Mahābhārata* mentions *Pāñcarātra* along with Sāṅkhya, Yoga, and Vedic teachings (*Sāṅkhyaṁ yogaṁ pāñcarātraṁ vedāraṇyakamevaca*).[3] The close relationship between the distinct systems was even then obvious. It was, however, explained that while Sāṅkhya and Yoga hold to the plurality of Puruṣas, the alternative systems believed in the unity of the spiritual principle which is the source of all. Between *Pāñcarātra* and Vedic teachings the obvious difference lay in the partial acceptance by the former of the Sāṅkhyan distinction of *Kṣetra* and *Kṣetrajña* and in the mode of worship and conduct. *Pāñcarātra* emphasized *Ahiṁsā*.

Aikāntika bhakti and *mānasa japa* or the remembrance of the Lord's name. The teachings of Nārāyaṇa are explicitly linked with the teachings of the *Bhagavad-Gītā*. The principal difference between the teachings in the *Nārāyaṇīya* and the *Gītā* relates to the doctrine of *Vyūha* which the former mentions and the latter does not. It should also be noted that the *Nārāyaṇīya* does not emphasise Vāsudeva Kṛṣṇa as an *Avatāra*. Nārāyaṇa, the sage Nārada and King Vasu are more prominent here. Their principal agreement is in the conception of a supreme personal God who responds to unswerving and absolute devotion by bestowing His saving and beatific grace.

It seems that the cult of devotional monotheism which emerged among the Sāttvata-Vṛṣṇis in the Mathura region before the 4th or the 5th century B.C. included the contending notions of Kṛṣṇa as *Avatāra*, and the Vṛṣṇi Vīras as *Vyūhas*. It may have had several variations, (an earlier?) one emphasising Nārāyaṇa and Nārada, another Vāsudeva Kṛṣṇa. The several streams, however, gradually coalesced in the Sāttvata-Bhāgavata sect and its principles were systematized in the *Pāñcarātra saṁhitās*. These *saṁhitās* are numerous and have not been fully studied or even fully published. The period of their composition is not certain but some of the earlier *Saṁhitās* are not later than the Gupta period.[4] Since the worship of images in temples is one of their major concerns, these *saṁhitās* could not be much earlier than the Gupta period either.

Along with Buddhism and Jainism, Sāṅkhya, Yoga, and Pāśupata, the Pāñcarātra system was one of the major challenges which the orthodox Vedānta faced when the *Brahmasūtras* were composed. Śaṅkara interprets the *utpattyasaṁbhavādhikaraṇa* to be a refutation of the *Pāñcarātra* system. His summary of the *Bhāgavata* doctrine is interesting. According to him the *Bhāgavatas* believe in the four *Vyūhas—Vāsudeva, Saṅkarṣaṇa, Pradyumna* and *Aniruddha*. Vāsudeva is the ultimately real spiritual principle (*Bhagavānevaikaḥ nirañjana-jñāna-svarūpaḥ Paramārtha-tattvam*) but He divides

Himself into the four *Vyūhas*. This doctrine of One *tattva* and four *vyūhas* may be compared with the Christian doctrine of God as one substance and three persons.[5] Śaṅkara, however, says that Vāsudeva is the substance (*parāprakṛti*) while the other three are resultant modes (*kārya*) so that Saṅkarṣaṇa is the soul, Pradyumna the mind and Aniruddha the *Ahaṅkāra*. Śaṅkara has no objection to God subsisting in many ways but he objects to the creation of the soul which would make it impermanent. He mentions an alternative interpretation of the *vyūhas* which would make all of them fully divine but in that case, he asks, why should we multiply the unitary God. Rāmānuja points out that the *Vyūhas* being divine are not to be identified with the human soul or mind or Egoism.[6] *Vyūhas* are divine in substance, all of them having the 'six qualities' (*ṣāḍguṇya*), viz., *jñāna, aiśvarya, śakti, bala, vīrya, tejas,* but they are distinct in form and function. They share in divine glory but with a difference of emphasis. They may be considered as divine emanations rather than divine persons. Saṅkarṣaṇa, Pradyumna and Aniruddha preside over the souls, minds and egoes taken collectively. God manifests Himself in several grades for the sake of ease of worship. In His *arcā* form He pervades the images which the faithful worship. In His *Vibhava* form as Rāma, Kṛṣṇa, etc., He is available for worship in a fuller manner. Above the *Vibhava* form lies the *Vyūha* form and that leads to the *Sūkṣma* form which is Vāsudeva in His glory.

Śaṅkara mentions that the *Pāñcarātra* mode of worship consists in the 'five practices', viz. *Abhigamana* or worshipfully going to the temple, *Upādāna* or gathering the material for worship, *ijyā* or worship, *svādhyāya* or *japa,* and *yoga* or meditation. The *Pāñcarātra saṁhitās* are full of details about images, *mantras,* temples and specific modes of worship. Compared to the *Gītā* these *saṁhitās* are far more ritualistic and theological. They claim to expound the mysteries of creation and the diverse forms and manifestation of God. It is possible that these *saṁhitās* represent an attempt to collect and systematize a rich variety of cult material found among different votaries of the *Pāñcarātra*.

Among the most important of the doctrines mentioned in the *saṁhitās* is that of distinguishing 'pure' from 'impure' creation. The *vyūhas* or emanations are part of 'pure creation. The notion of a pure creation has far reaching implications. It implies the possibility of supernatural life, a life beyond the evils of this world. Emancipation is not simply a subsidence of life and a 'return' to the unmanifest and transcendent source of life but the gaining of an everlasting life beyond sorrow and ignorance. It implies that spiritual reality is capable of internal differentiation and as constituting a world by its emanations. It is at once consciousness and an infinity of power and potentiality. While continuing to exist in its fullness it can also exist in partial manifestation and a hierarchy of beings. The soul subject to ignorance, passion and evil actions lives within the bounds of the imperfect and transitory natural world but through worship may hope to enter the higher worlds of light. Pure creation, thus, serves also to bridge the gulf between God and man. The doctrine is not peculiar to the *Pāñcarātras* but is also common to the Śaiva and Śākta *Āgamas*. In fact, even some Buddhist sects held the belief in '*Anāsravarūpa*' or 'pure matter', a belief without which the worship of the physical form of the Buddha in an image would not have been possible.[7]

As for the practice of spiritual life, the *Āgamas* emphasize images, temples, formal ritual alongwith *upāsanā,* meditation, devotion and surrender. It is in the Ālvār saints that one may discover devotion in simple, emotional, unconventional piety. The doctrines of the *Āgamas* and the fervour of the Ālvārs together constituted the basis for the philosophical systematization which Nāthamuni, Yāmunācārya and Rāmānuja completed. With these Ācāryas *Pāñcarātra* became a fully and self-consciously orthodox doctrine. Yāmunācārya's *Āgamaprāmāṇya* shows the arguments which had been urged against orthodoxy of *Pāñcarātra* and how these were rebutted. It is interesting to note that one of the arguments urged against the *Pāñcarātra* was that the Sāttvatas were a low caste being professional temple priests who were looked down upon. Since the main critics were the *Mīmāṁsakas* it is obvious that the old Vedic priests with their ancient texts and sacrificial ritual felt hostile to the new ritual of images and temples and the priests and texts which accompanied them. The anger of Bṛhaspati towards Hari mentioned in the *Nārāyaṇīya* section of the *Mahābhārata* may be recalled here.

What the Ālvārs contributed was to popularize *Bhakti* and give expression to it as an intense personal relation and feeling of love. Their songs are imperishable monuments of love divine. The Ālvārs came from diverse castes and the love of God of which they sang carried within it the possibility of a socially levelling and reforming–even revolutionary-doctrine. However, the mildness and quietistic temper of the Ālvārs prevented the realization of such historical possibilities. Orthodox Hindu society always allowed saintly reformers to preach heterodoxy and carve out separate communities of their followers.[8]

The hoary antiquity of Śiva worship is now generally recognised. Sir John Marshall had supposed that the worship of a Śiva-like God was current in Mohenjodaro and he had proposed the identification of a well known figure engraved on a seal from there as that of Paśupati (?).[9] R. G. Bhandarkar and others like Bata Krishna Ghosh have supposed that a non-Aryan influence ought to be seen in the development of Vedic Rudra as a "dreaded" god.[10] The connection between Vedic Rudra and the pre-Vedic 'proto-Śiva', however, remains as obscure as the 'non-Aryan' affiliation of the Vedic god on account of the vagueness which attaches to the epithet 'non-Aryan', which may mean Harappan, or Dravidian or 'primitive'.[11]

Vedic Rudra was an awsome deity presiding over the fearful aspects of nature and life-storm and lightening, misfortune and disease. He is pictured as a mighty hunter with bow and arrows, clad in a skin and with matted hair. He carries a staff and dwells in forests and mountains. In the *Yajurveda* and *Atharvaveda* he is portrayed as a mighty god of sublime aspect. He is a gracious god and the great healer. Suffering comes to man not only because there is a dark aspect to nature but also because as a sinner man incurs the liability of divine wrath and punishment. On both these counts Rudra is feared but he is at the same time placated to be merciful, forgiving and gracious. R. G. Bhandarkar has said that Viṣṇu was the god of love, Śiva the god of fear. Actually it would be more correct to speak of Viṣṇu as Apollonian and Śiva as Dionysian.

As already mentioned, the *Śvetāśvatara* adumbrates a philosophy which seeks to join Sāṅkhya with a Śaivite theism. The thrust of this philosophy is as much against strict monism as against strict dualism. While it distinguishes the soul from God it makes Nature a power of God. It makes salvation depend on grace as well as on the practice of *yoga* and the cultivation of devotion. Here we have the matrix of later Śaiva philosophies.

The *Mahābhārata* refers to the *Pāśupata* system alongwith the *Pāñcarātra* and speaks of *liṅga* worship as a part of the worship of Śiva. The antiquity of *liṅga* worship remains wholly uncertain. The god to be worshipped is generally presumed to have been a fertility god originally. The association of the bull or *nandin* would strength this impression because the bull stood for fertility, virility and power in the Vedic hymns. Thus the personality of Rudra-Śiva appears composite. On the one hand, he is a hunter God ; on the other, a fertility god to be connected with agriculture. His marriage with Umā or Durgā finds mention in the epic and perhaps it was this which converted the lonely hunter into a benign, procreating god. The goddess herself appears to combine many different aspects in her–she is a virgin goddess dwelling in the mountains and riding the wild tiger, she is at the same time a benign mother goddess. Perhaps there was a simultaneous evolution in the conception of both Śiva and Śakti as society changed from a hunting to an agrarian stage. By the time of Patañjali Śiva was certainly worshipped as Bhagavān and images were made of Him but we do not know what the images were like.

It should be remembered, however, that although Śiva and Śakti may have been expressed in symbols drawn from changing modes of social activity, they were not mere images or constructs of such activity. They are really expressions and interpretations of a perennial mode of spiritual experience which may perhaps best be understood with reference to the human experience of Time—the healer, destroyer, progenitor, dovetailed with consciousness, at once Death and Mother.

The first reference to Śaiva philosophy may be discovered in the *Vedānta-sūtras* of Bādarāyaṇa where the *sūtra, 'Patyurasāmañjasyāt'*, criticises the notion of Pati as that of an independent efficient cause only. Śaṅkara refers to three varieties of theism here—Sāṅkhya-yogic, Māheśvara and Vaiśeṣika. By Māhaeśvara he seems to mean the Pāśupatas who believed that God acts independently of *Karman*. Vācaspati Miśra tells us that there were four schools of Māhaśvaras viz., Śaiva, Pāśupata, Kāruṇika-siddhāntins, and Kāpālikas. With some change of nomenclature this fourfold division is referred to in other texts also. Yāmunācārya, thus, mentions Śaiva, Pāśupata, Saumya and Lāguḍa. Not much is known of the doctrines of Saumya or Kāpālika sects except occasional references of a none too edifying character regarding some of their practices which appear to belong to *Vāmācāra*.[12]

The Pāśupatas appear to have been a very ancient sect as mentioned already. There is a tradition that the sect was founded by Śrīkaṇṭha or Lakulīśa or Nakulīśa. Lakulīśa or Nakulīśa is said to have been Śiva Himself who animated the body of a dead person at Kāyārohaṇa in Saurastra and taught four chief disciples. Some historians regard Nakulīśa as a historical person belonging to the second century B.C. M. M. Gopinath Kaviraj, however, thought that Śrīkaṇṭha and Nakulīśa were both divine, not human, persons.[13]

Mādhava's *Sarvadarśana-saṁgraha* gives a summary of the Pāśupata tenets for which the chief authority appears to have been the *Pāśupata-sūtras* and Kauṇḍinya's or Rāśīkara's *Pañcārtha bhāṣya* on it. The *Gaṇa-kārikā* of Bhāsarvajña was another important book on Pāśupata principles.

The Pāśupatas believed in five principles *viz.*, creature (*Kārya*), creator (*Kāraṇa*), esoteric worship (*Yoga*), ritual (*Vidhi*) and salvation (*Duḥkhānta*). *Kārya* is dependent, *Kāraṇa* independent. *Kārya* is threefold–*Vidyā, Kalā* and *Paśu*. *Paśu* or animal indicates the individual souls. *Vidyā* characterises the soul and consists of its cognitive and moral potentialities. The mind is included in *Vidyā*. *Kalā* is insentient but dependent on the sentient and includes the elements in Sāṅkhya from *Buddhi* down to the physical elements. *Kārya* or creation thus includes the souls as well as the world. The creator is the Lord (*Pati*), wholly independent and all powerful, *Yoga* is the union of the soul with God through worship and absorption. *Vidhi* stands for rules of conduct and ritual, some of which appear strange. *Duḥkhānta* is not merely the end of suffering but the acquisition of a God-like independence. The grace of God transforms the human animal into a free spiritual being with superhuman powers.

The most distinctive principle of the Pāśupatas consisted in the absolute freedom of God and the total dependence of the human soul. This is nearer the Semitic conception than the normal Indian view where the doctrine of *Karman* reconciled the freedom of God with the freedom of the soul. The Pāśupatas argued that being the cause of all causes God could not but act in absolute freedom. Such an attitude may appear unreasonable to man's seeking for poetic justice in life but it is a great assurance for the religious man seeking grace. If God were to act in accordance with *Karman,* the hope of grace would be ill-founded indeed.

Nevertheless, the Pāśupatas laid great stress on right conduct, ascetic practices, and meditation culminating in a quiescent state of consciousness (*saṁvid*) and spontaneous living. *Yoga* and *Vidhi,* on one side, and grace or *Prasāda* on the other, are almost equally balanced in this system. *Yoga* means here principally *japa* culminating in *saṁvid*. *Praṇava* is specially recommended and so concentration (*dhāraṇā*) in the heart.

It cannot, however, be gainsaid that our knowledge of the Pāśupata sect remains sketchy on account of the limited extent of the available texts of the school. It is the Śaivism based on the *Āgamas* of which our knowledge is fullest. There are two main streams of Āgamic Śaivism, dualistic and non-dualistic. Of the former, the *Śaiva siddhānta* of the south is the best known while the *Pratyabhijñā* school of Kaśmīra is the best representative of the latter. How many different shades of Śaivism existed originally, is difficult to say because the existing *Āgamas* are only a part of what is reputed to have existed. Even the existing Āgamic literature needs to be studied thoroughly for it is a kind of literature which lends itself easily to corruption.

Southern *Śaiva siddhānta* derives principally from the dualistic *Āgamas,* though the writings of the Tamilian Śaiva saints and the work of Meykaṇḍar and commentarial literature have enjoyed great vogue and prestige among southern Śaivas. Among the twenty-eight Āgamas *Pauṣkara, Mṛgendra* and *Mātanga* are specially notable as they have been extensively commented upon. The Tamilian canon consisting of the writings of the Śaiva saints was redacted by Nambi Aṇḍār Nambi in eleven books called *Tirumurai,* viz., three works of Tirujñāna Sambandar, three of Tiruṇāvukkaraśu or Appar, works of Sundarar, of Māṇikkavāsagar, two sets of miscellaneous writings and Tirumūlar's *Tirumandiram.* The seven works of Sambandar, Appar and Sundarar constitute the *Tevāram.* Meykaṇḍar's *Śivajñāna bodham* was late but influential.[14] It is supposed to be derived from the *Rauravāgama.* The earlier of the saints probably belonged to the seventh century A.D.

The hymns of the saints—Tirumūlar, Appar, Jñāna-sambandar, Sundarar and Mānikkavācagar as those of the Ālvārs are essentially popular and devotional expression of the *Siddhānta* rather than its sources. Some modern enthusiasts have indeed regarded the hymns of the saints as of primary authority and even gone to the extent of regarding the *Āgamas* as themselves derived from Tamil, which can only be described as "a mythical patriotic belief of some Tamil people". This will be clear from the account of Mādhava in *Sarvadarśanasaṅgraha* which appeals to the *Āgamas* and classical Sanskrit writings and altogether ignores the Tamil writings. Mādhava could hardly be accused of ignorance. The Śaivas believe in three ultimate principles viz., *Pati, Paśu* and *Pāśa*. *Pati* or lord is Śiva Himself, *Paśu* is the soul or *jīva* while *Pāśa* stands for the inanimate world which fetters the soul. Of these three only God is independent and truly self-existent. The other two are dependent on Him. God is characterised by five functions—creation, maintenance, and destruction of the universe, projection of *Māyā* and the showering of grace. He is thus called *'pañca-kṛtya-kārī'* and is thus represented in the *Naṭarāja* images from the south.[15] In accordance with these five functions Śiva is imagined to have a primal body consisting of power or *logos* (*śākta, Mantramayatanu*). This too is fivefold so that *Īśāna, Tatpuruṣa, Aghora, Vāmadeva* and *Sadyojāta* are regarded as its parts. The power of Śiva is at once of knowledge and action. It operates on matter which is called *Bindu* in its pure state and *Māyā* in its impure state. There are consequently two levels of creation, pure (*śuddhādhvā*) and impure (*aśuddhādhvā*). The several levels of Pure Creation correspond to the functional manifestations of Śiva. Impure creation is within the limitations of *Māyā* and its Five Sheaths (*Kañcukas*). Impure creation is characterised by Ignorance, dependence, necessity, desire and time. It is the world of suffering. The Śaivas extend the twenty-five *tattvas* of Sāṅkhya to thirty-six by adding to the twenty-five *tattvas* the following additional *tattvas—Śiva, Śakti, Sadāśiva, Īśvara, Sadvidyā, Māyā, Vidyā, Kalā, Rāga, Niyati* and *Kāla*. The first five are the Lord and His functional aspects, the next six the source and limitations of the impure world.

Jīva is sentient and eternal but limited by an innate defilement called *Mala*. To the innate limitation of the soul is added the limitation caused by *Māyā* and its constituents. Thus invested with ignorance, limited power and desire and subject to time and causal necessity, the soul engages in action and accumulates the third layer of obscuration viz., of *Kārma mala* on top of the two earlier ones of *Āṇava mala* and *Māyā mala*. At a certain stage of development and maturity in life the soul becomes fit for receiving the grace of God. This state of ripeness or *mala-pāka* is compared to the maturation of the cataract in the eye when surgical removal becomes possible. This is also a state of equilibrium, between good and evil deeds (*karma-sāmya*). From this point of view the world of suffering becomes a kind of purgatory and the course of life, of action and experience is a slow preparation for emancipation.

When the soul has reached this state of maturity, there is an interaction of divine grace (*śaktipāta*). This takes the form of *dīkṣā* or initiation which pierces through the obscuration of *mala* and awakens the soul towards its true destination. The knowledge of principles, worship and its rituals, *yoga* and prescribed conduct constitute the different aspects of the *sādhanā* of which diverse stages have been formulated by Śaiva scholastics.

According to the Śaiva philosophy *sādhanā* begins as a long period of moral preparation and purgation through suffering. It then goes on to the purification of the soul through the operation of grace. The importance of *mantra-japa* is paramount here. It is through *Nāda* that grace operates. *Nāda* is the divine power of expression and revelation, the Word freed from the impure and discursive elements which beset it in the ordinary human world. The role of devotion is conceived in a dual manner. As worship it is part of the *sādhana,* as pure love it is the end and result of *sādhana* and characterizes the unitive life of the Śaiva saint. The Nāyanmārs illustrated this in their lives.

When the soul is freed from *mala* it begins to reflect the divine nature and participate in divine life. This is the state of union or *sāyujya*. Curiously the Śaiva-siddhāntins describe this as *advaita* or non-duality which they distinguish from difference (*bheda*), non-difference (*abheda*), and unity in difference (*bhedābheda*). Light and darkness illustrate the relation of *bheda* or difference, word and meaning illustrate *bhedābheda* or unity in difference. Gold and ornament illustrate non-difference or *abheda*. None of these apply to the soul and God. They are related like "the body and the soul, eye and the sun, the soul and the eye". They are distinct entities, but the soul has no independent reality. The soul is inseparably related to God and ultimately lives in the vision of God, deriving all its experience through Him but preserving entitative distinctness.

Kāśmīra Śaivism represents the most remarkable system of monistic theism. The system derives from the sixty four monistic *Āgamas* and was given its present shape by a number of Ācāryas between the ninth and eleventh centuries A.D. Vasugupta who wrote the *Śiva-sūtras* claims to have discovered them inscribed on a rock. Kallaṭa's *Spandakārikā* and Somānanda's *Śivadṛṣṭi* distinguished the philosophical position of the school from similar schools among the Vaiyākaraṇas and the *śāktas*. Utpalācārya's *Īśvara-pratyabhijñākārikās* controverted Buddhist views. With Abhinavagupta in the 10th century the system reached its final form. His *Śrītantrāloka* is, like Nāgārjuna's *Mahāprajñāpāramitāśāstra,* a work which bases a systematic philosophy on older Āgamic texts. His *Vimarśinī* can only be described as a peerless work on monistic theism. Two important later works are *Pratyabhijñāhṛdaya* and *Paramārthasāra.*[16]

For this school ultimate reality is nothing except consciousness or *saṁvid.* This is an idealistic view in so far as it regards the objects of consciousness as nothing except consciousness itself. But it does not regard these objects as unreal or illusory. They are real though imperfect self-expressions of consciousness, and are described as *Ābhāsa* or 'partial manifestation'. Consciousness itself is one and universal, eternal and yet essentially creative. It has two inseparable aspects *prakāśa* and *vimarśa.* The former is the aspect in which consciousness is a witnessing or shining of a content, the latter is the self-affirmative aspect of consciousness. Consciousness is both passive and active, registering a content and apperceiving it as self-expression. This conception of consciousness is totally different from that of Sāṅkhya where *Puruṣa* can only witness and *Prakṛti* only act. *Saṁvid* is essentially self-consciousness and infinitely creative, creation being nothing but self-expression.

The Kāśmīra Śaivas accept the thirty-six principles of the *Āgamas* and distinguish between Pure and Impure creation. The school does not, however, regard *Bindu* or *Mahāmāyā* as pure matter. In fact, it regards the whole procession of *tattvas* as an emanation from Śiva in descending order. The principles of the Pure Realm are Śiva Himself with a difference of aspect. Thus Śiva and Śakti are distinguished as *Prakāśa* and *Vimarśa, Sadāśiva* is the subjective moment of the supreme self-consciousness, *Īśvara* is the same self-consciousness affirming the object to be itself, *Sadvidyā* shows subject and object merged equally in knowledge. Neither is *Jīva* different from Śiva nor *mala* an existential or material reality. *Āṇava mala* is free self-delimitation of God and this leads to the emergence of the individual self and *pari passu* of *Māyā* with its Five sheaths which have relevance only for the self subjected to *āṇava.* Thus subjected to *Māyā, Jīva* wanders through *Saṁsāra* and accumulates *Kārma-mala* also. Nevertheless, *Jīva* remains nothing except Śiva and his salvation can come only through the recognition of this identity which is called *Pratyabhijñā.* The highest kind of aspirant needs nothing beyond this Recognition. At a lower level mental cogitation and reflection are helpful. Still lower, one may be helped by taking recourse to *Mantras.* At the lowest level one may seek the aid of purely external ritual in terms of images etc. These are the four methods or *Upāyas*—Absence of method *(Anupāya)*, knowledge as method *(Śāmbhavopāya)*, worship as method *(Śāktopāya)*, and method belonging to the delimited individual *(Āṇavopāya)*. These are comparable to *Sahaja yoga, jñāna yoga,* and *upāsanā* or *kriyāyoga*—subtle and gross.

Śaiva God is virtually an artist who expresses Himself in the form of the world and transforms Himself into a 'character' to play a role but who is free to recall His true nature and enjoy the world as a creative spectator also. No wonder the Śaiva Ācāryas have contributed most significantly to the development of aesthetic and literary theory.[17]

REFERENCES

1. Cf. Raychaudhuri, *Early History of the Vaiṣṇava Sect.*

2. On devotion in the *Gītā,* see Dr. Susmita Pande, *The Birth of Bhakti in Indian Religion.*

2a. Cf. Susmita Pande, *Mediaeval Bhakti Movement.*

3. The *Pāśupata* is also sometimes mentioned in such contexts.

4. See Dr. Susmita Pande, *Birth of Bhakti.* Also, Daniel Smith, *Descriptive Bibliography of the Printed Works of Pāñcarātra Āgama,* Vol. I.

5. Vide Tixeront, *History of Dogmas,* Vol. I, pp. 312-13.

6. *Śrībhāṣya* ad *BS,* 2.2.42.

7. G. C. Pande, *Bauddha Dharma Ke Vikāsa Kā Itihāsa;* Susmita Pande, 'Conceptual Background of the idea of Bhakti in Mahāyāna', *Journal of Buddhist Studies,* Delhi University, 1980.

8. The songs of the Ālvārs are collected in the *Nālāyir Divya Prabandham,* called the Tamil *Veda.* Srinivas Raghavan has translated them into Hindi. The translation is being published by the Visvabharati. Vedāntadeśika recapitulates the most important themes of some of these in his *Dramiḍopaniṣad.* Yāmunācārya's *Āgamaprāmāṇya* defends the *Pāñcarātra.*

9. *Mohenjodaro and The Indus Civilization,* Vol. I.

10. R. G. Bhandarkar, *Vaiṣṇavism, Śaivism and other Minor Religious Systems;* B. K. Ghosh in *Vedic Age.*

11. Finnish and Soviet scholars engaged in deciphering the Indus script support the Dravidian character of Harappan Civilization. S. R. Rao has a contrary theory.

12. Dr. V. S. Pathak has collected interesting epigraphic evidence of the fourfold classification of the Śaiva sects—vide his *History of Śaiva Cults in Northern India.*

13. Dr. Pathak, on the other hand, suggests that Śrīkaṇtha too may have been a human figure *op. cit.*

14. Sekkilar's *Periyapurāṇam* also attained canonical status.

15. Coomaraswamy, *Catalogue of the Indian Collections in the Museum of Fine Arts, Boston, Sculpture* ; Coomaraswamy, *The Dance of Śiva.*

16. Reliable modern interpretations may be seen in J.C. Chatterji's *Kaśmīra Śaivism,* K. C. Pandey's *Abhinavagupta,* Dr. Jaidev Singh's critical translations and expositions of *Pratyabhijñā-hṛdaya, Spandakārikā, Vijñānabhairava* and the *Śivasūtras.* M. M. G. N. Kaviraj's scattered writings and his collected *'Bhāratīya Saṁskṛti aur Sādhanā'* are a most profound and scholarly exposition. The Kashmiri saint Sri Laksmanajoo is the last living representative of the tradition.

17. See K. C. Pandeya, *op. cit.*, Gnoli, *Aesthetics according to Abhinavagupta;* G.C. Pande, *Bharatīya Paramparā Ke Mūla Svara*; Dr. Anupa Pande, 'Concept of Rasa', *Jijñāsā* (pub. Rajasthan University, Jaipur).

8

CLASSICAL CROSS-CURRENTS: SYNTHESIS IN THE SMṚTIS, PURĀṆAS AND TANTRAS

By the early post-Vedic age a number of parallel traditions of spiritual life, orthodox as well as heterodox, had developed in India. Their interaction gradually led to the formulation of a number of systems seeking a synthesis of the different traditional ways. The most ancient Vedic seers seem to have lived with a constant sense of divine presence and vision, a condition which may be compared to that of *Anupāya* as mentioned by the Kaśmīra Śaivas or of *Sahaja* as found among the Siddhas. It was recognised that this condition was not the result of any specific *sādhanā*. It was rather a vision which arose spontaneously and never disappeared, a vision which stayed in the midst of worldly life and transfigured it. The ancient vision was, however, forgotten and transformed into a ritualistic system. *Dhī* and *Ṛta* came to mean ritual action instead of intuitive vision and the eternal Right Order of things. In the Gnostic tradition revived by Buddha *Dhī* and *Ṛta* came to be replaced by the concepts of *Prajñā* and *Dharma* but a gulf was created between eternity and the world of time and hence between spiritual vision and worldly action. Mahāyāna sought to eradicate this dualism and the Buddhist Siddhas even proclaimed the doctrine of *Sahaja*. Nevertheless, the denigration of the world continued as a dogmatic element of the Buddhist creed as ordinarily understood.

On the other hand, within the orthodox Vedic tradition the notion of spiritual vision was replaced by that of Revelation and the Right order was identified with the prescribed Order. The spiritual path, thus, came to mean a religion of trifling obligations, at once social and ritualistic. This was the ancient path of *Karman*, which promised to save man from sin, give him happiness in this life and immortality in heaven. The Mīmāṁsakas were the theoreticians of this path.

As a compensation, side by side with it, a gnostic quest grew up within the Vedic tradition and was called Vedānta. Originally it sought a spiritual knowledge which would take away the sting of death and dissatisfaction, render everything intelligible and confer ever-lasting bliss. Gradually, however, the dichotomy of the Spirit and Nature made its way within this tradition which flowed into two broad streams–Advaitic and theistic. Advaitic Vedānta dismissed the world as unreal and with it the claims, prescriptions and obligations such as were upheld by orthodox Vedism or Mīmāṁsā. The goal of man is emancipation from the world-social and natural–and this can be achieved only by pure spiritual knowledge or *Jñāna*. To reach *Jñāna* one must hear the revealed truth of spiritual unity and reflect over it.

Theistic Vedānta agreed that man's goal is emancipation from the world, because although they held the world to be real they regarded it as a lower order of reality, dependent, insentient and impermanent. For theistic Vedānta, however, emancipation cannot be reached except through the grace of God. For this one must worship Him with faith. *Pāñcarātra* and *Pāśupata* basically agreed.

In the non-Vedic or originally non-Vedic gnostic traditions the world was, again, recognized to be evil and emancipation from it was recognised to be the goal of life. The means for this were held to be primarily spiritual knowledge which revealed the non-selfhood of body and mind, distinguishing them from the individual soul or eternal quiescence. Jainism and Buddhism, Sāṅkhya and Yoga belonged to this tradition.

Thus by the post-Vedic period a number of distinct spiritual paths had been formulated. These may be classified as follows—(1) The path of spontaneous vision and integral life as exemplified by the ancient seers. (2) The path of works (*Karman*) consisting of the performance of duty and the cultivation of virtue. This aimed at moral purification here and felicity hereafter. It was exemplified by Vedic orthodoxy. (3) The path of Gnosis (*jñāna*) aiming at the emancipation of man from the toils of the world. There were several varieties of this. For Advaita Vedānta *Jñāna* meant the realization of the universal spirit. For Buddhism enlightenment was the intuition of eternal quiescence or *Nirvāṇa*. For Jainism, Sāṅkhya and Yoga knowledge meant the intuitive knowledge of the individual spirit in its separateness from the world. In every case, however, the path of knowledge meant the renunciation of worldly life and the acquisition of pure spiritual knowledge, revealing the non-selfhood of body and mind and leading to the cessation of the cycle of birth and death. (4) The path of devotion (*Bhakti*) seeking the grace of a personal God through worship. The *Pāñcarātra* and *Pāśupata* schools illustrated this. At a later stage *Bhakti* came to mean pure love for God and the human ideal changed from that of mere emancipation to that of participation in life divine.

Quite early attempts were made to see the inner connection of these paths and to regard them as moments in a developing spiritual quest or Yoga. The *Kaṭhopaniṣad* and the *Śvetāśvataropaniṣad* contain the first intimations of such synthesis but it is the *Bhagavad-Gītā* which effected a classical synthesis at the end of the Vedic age. This remained the basis for all subsequent attempts. As is well known Śaṅkara interpreted the *Gītā* as an exposition of the *Jñāna-Yoga* but in this context he was compelled to show the connection of *Karman* and *Bhakti* with *Jñāna*. He argued that the desireless performance of duties (*niṣkāma karman*) leads to moral purity and that prepares the mind for spiritual knowledge. *Karman* is, thus, only indirectly relevant to *mokṣa*. He divides *Bhakti* into two parts—*Bhakti* may be the various acts of worship (*Karma-Lakṣaṇa*) or it may be an intimate communion with the ultimate spirit, i. e., the experience of self-realization (*Jñāna-lakṣaṇa bhakti*). Thus *Bhakti* is partly included in *Karman,* partly in *Jñāna.* Madhusudana Sarasvati argues that the first six adhyāyas of the *Gītā* are devoted to *Karma-yoga,* the next six to *Bhakti-yoga* and the last six to *Jñāna-yoga.* He argues that *Karman* and *Jñāna* are mutually exclusive but both are pervaded by *Bhakti-yoga* which unites them as a running thread. *Bhakti* truly takes the form of work when all works are undertaken as the worship of the divine. If man acts selflessly dedicating his works to the Lord, work becomes worship and *Karma-yoga* merely the lower rungs of *Bhakti-yoga.* This active devotion or the combination of 'faith and works' leads to the development of purer devotion or love of God. In his *Bhakti-rasāyana,* Madhusudana explains pure love of God as a *rasa* which is the continuous flow of emotionally tinged thoughts.

Actually the *Gītā* describes itself as a *Yagaśāstra,* i. e. *Karman, Jñāna* and *Bhakti* are to be treated as moments in a developing process of Yoga or spiritual integration. *Karman* begins as the performance of duties and culminates in the sense of serving the divine in all works. Work is not a stage in life or *Yoga.* It is as the *Gītā* says coextensive with life. One cannot live even for a moment without work. Nor should work be abandoned. It sustains the social and ritual order and purifies the soul. Every one must act in accordance with his social station and even though selfless, one ought to work for social good (*loka-saṅgraha*). Although it is implicit in the *Gītā* that right action and the practice of virtue may lead to struggle, it is only the struggle of a moral man with himself that is emphasized. "There is no enemy except within oneself." *Gītā's* social ethics is conservative and it may seem that it does not emphasize the moral struggle against injustice on the social plane. And yet while the *Gītā* holds the moral order to be eternal, it clearly recognizes the fact of social decline and the triumph of injustice in such an age of decline. The task of rectifying the balance of justice and injustice is left to divine incarnation and presumably man's duty must be to fight on the side which God chooses. In fact, as the *Mahābhārata* illustrates, the incarnation of God does not himself fight. He merely guides the principal fighter on the side of righteousness. It was the leader of the unrighteous who chose to accept the gift of the panoply of arms as the contribution of God incarnate to their cause.

Gītā defines Yoga as the art of action. Being inevitably involved in action, man must acquire the skill of so conducting himself that action frees him morally and spiritually instead of binding him, and helping the ideal social order at the same time. Modern commentators like Tilak, Gandhi, Aurobindo and Vinoba have taken pains to bring out the real import of the *Gītā* on the subject of *Karma-Yoga*. The whole tradition of Indian spiritual life shows the strain of the ancient conflict between the way of duty and the way of renunciation. The *Gītā* reconciles the conflict through the notion of disinterested action and goes on to see in right action the art of living and the secret of Yoga.

Jñāna and *Bhakti* recur in *Gītā* at several levels. The practice of Yoga leads to *Jñāna* as an immediate experience of the spirit. Madhusudana Sarasvati points out that Śaṅkara never felt that Yoga as mental control was ever needed for *Jñāna*. Nevertheless, the *Gītā* not only introduces Yoga as the practice of spiritual discrimination along with disinterested action, but goes on to emphasize Yoga as the stilling of the mind which leads to self-knowledge or *Brahman-Jñāna*. This knowledge of the transcendent spirit or *nirguṇa brahman* is not the end. It leads on to a unitive life where the soul is not simply merged in its transcendent nature but a participant in the *līlā* of *Saguṇa brahman*. Thus knowledge occurs at three levels in the *Gītā* viz., as the discriminative knowledge of the soul distinguished from the body, as the intuitive knowledge of the transcendent absolute and as the unitive knowledge of God. *Bhakti,* again, occurs as the worship of the Lord in various ways and finally as self-surrender. The combination of these different means in the *Gītā* is, thus, extremely complex. Arjuna's sorrow or *Viṣāda-yoga* is the beginning. Arjuna then seeks guidance from Kṛṣṇa.

The first lesson given to Arjuna is to distinguish the soul from the body and to do his duty without caring for the result. This is the unity of Sāṅkhya as Discrimination and Yoga as Action. After elaborating both of these and reaffirming their unity, the *Gītā* goes on to point out two alternative ways to direct spiritual knowledge viz., contemplation of the Absolute and devotion to the Personal God. Both of these are ultimately one because the Absolute and God are one. Thus the knowledge of the Absolute and the love of God could differ only in the conceptual and emotional attitudes with which men begin their quest, they could not differ in what they ultimately lead to, like two doors leading to the same room. But the human approaches and their characteristic expressions naturally show differences.

This idea of a diversity of ways and expression for the same Truth was widely accepted in the Indian spiritual tradition. Buddha declared that dogmatic quarrels were like those between the seven blind men who disputed the true nature of the elephant on the basis of touching different parts of it! The Mahāyāna developed the notion of *Vineya-bheda*. Abhinavagupta tried to relate the different spiritual philosophies to different levels of experience. Madhusudana Sarasvati expounded the notion of *Prasthāna-bheda.* Tulsidas assiduously sought to combine Advaita with *Saguṇa bhakti,* though he thought *Jñāna* more difficult and not free from pitfalls. Ram Krishna Paramahaṁsa experimentally verified the efficacy and equality of different spiritual ways and Vivekanand sought to systematize *yoga* in four parts–*Karma-yoga, Rāja-yoga, Jñāna-yoga* and *Bhakti-yoga.*

It was the *Smṛtis* and the *Purāṇas* which wove out of diverse elements a unified fabric of spiritual life for the common people in terms of a concrete way of life, worship and thought. The *Manusmṛti* declares the Vedic *Karma-yoga* to be the most comprehensive and as including within it all the values. It includes *Pravṛtti* as well as *Nivṛtti.* The former leads to happiness and freedom from obligations the latter to spiritual knowledge and emancipation. Even *Nivṛtti* is included in *Karma-yoga* because for Manu the practice of virtues and

Vedic worship in the form of *Japa* and *dhyāna* are never to b abandoned. Those who accept renunciation in accordanc with the *Vedas* still continue in *Karma-yoga*. Nevertheless Manu's Vedic *Karma-yoga* has advanced far beyond mere Vedic ritualism. He places *Japa* above the performance ol sacrifices and places great emphasis on the cultivation of universal virtues, he accepts that the highest and ultimate duty is the cultivation of self-knowledge through the practice of contemplation. At the same time he rejects the notion which even the *Gītā* supports that the *Vedas* are of no use for the knower of *Brahman*. For Manu the *Vedas* must never be abandoned. Manu still continues to see life as a whole as in the older Vedic tradition and although he accepts the institutionalisation of renunciation in one of the *Āśramas* he does not view it as a radical discontinuity. In fact, he calls the gradual procession of the *Āśramas* as a *Karma-yoga* and would prefer a kind of ascetic who instead of being a mendicant stays with his son and cultivates spiritual knowledge without abandoning the *Vedas* but without any involvement in the world. In fact, Manu does not share the extreme ascetical condemnation of desire and the world. Sensuality is undoubtedly evil and self-control good, but desires and actions are the stuff of which the socio-ethical world is constituted. It is through their regulation that virtue is practised and happiness here and hereafter obtained. And it is through the practice of virtue that man is gradually perfected till he obtains spiritual knowledge. In this *Krama-yoga* and Vedic *Karma-yoga* we, thus, have a synthesis of Vedic worship, socio-ethical activism and Vedāntic gnosticism.

This constituted the basic pattern for the synthesis elaborated in the *Purāṇas*. The one important difference which the *Purāṇas* introduce is the great development of new modes of worship following the growth of Āgamic literature and cults. They also seek to evolve a synthetic philosophy out of Sāṅkhya, Yoga and Vedānta. This synthetic philosophy is largely a cosmology and soteriology in terms of incarnations. No radical difference is made between *Saguṇa* and *Nirguṇa*, Action and knowledge. At the same time the notion of

Bhakti is developed greatly. The *Viṣṇu Purāṇa* describes Viṣṇu as the supreme God, transcendent as well as immanent. He creates the universe by assuming the forms of the soul, Nature, manifest and unmanifest, and Time which determines the relationship of the soul and Nature. The divine spirit pervades everything and determines it and yet remains untouched. This is a theistic or Vedāntic transformation of Sāṅkhya, or rather a strengthening of Vedānta on the cosmological side by utilising the principles of Sāṅkhya. The emphasis is clearly laid on the unity of one fundamental divine power underlying the universe. For purposes of worship, however, it is the incarnations of God which are emphasized. "What is your ultimate essence, that no one knows, Gods worship the form in which you incarnate" (4.17). Contemplation of the *saguṇa* form along with *mantra-japa* is the method which *Dhruva* followed. He also joined to it absolute detachment, a burning devotion and severe penances. The legend of Prahlāda shows the concept of *Bhakti* rising to a new peak. Prahlāda prays that he may be blessed with unwavering devotion wherever he is born. Devotion is clearly defined as love. The attachment which the unenlightened have towards sense-objects is turned towards the Lord in the heart of the devotee. Here devotion clearly supersedes the concept of *Mokṣa* and of mere knowledge leading to it.

The legends of Bharata and of Ṛbhu and Nidāgha, on the other hand, preach the doctrine of pure monism, declaring all sense of differences as illusory. In the legend of Aurva and Sagara we get a condensed *Smṛti* detailing right conduct and social duties. The dialogue of Khāṇḍikya Janaka and Keśidhvaja brings the two ideas together. Khāṇḍikya was a famous *Karmayogī* while Keśidhvaja was famed for *Adhyātma-vidyā*. The method for gaining *adhyātma-vidyā* is described in terms of Yoga which is the control of the mind. The mind is the cause of bondage and release and yoga detaches the mind from objects so that it may be attached to the Self. For this purpose the contemplation of the divine form of Viṣṇu is recommended. This contemplation culminates in absorption into the real self devoid of all imagination.

The continuity between the *Gītā* and the *Viṣṇu-purāṇa* can hardly be missed. In both God and the Absolute are identified and regarded as the common ground of the individual soul and Nature. The ideas of *Vibhūti* and *Avatāra* are found in both, and in both Sāṅkhya-Yoga and Vedānta are joined together. In both *Karman, Jñāna* and *Bhakti* are parts of Yoga leading to the supreme realisation. The doctrine of pure *bhakti* in the story of Prahlāda is exceptional but the crucial idea here is found in the *Bhāgavata* at greater length.

The *Bhāgavata* states categorically that there are three and only three ways of spiritual seeking viz., *Karma-yoga, Jñāna-yoga* and *Bhakti-yoga.* There is no contradiction between them. The first is preparatory but essential. The second is also called Sāṅkhya as in the *Gītā* and leads to the same result as the last. *Bhakti-yoga* is declared the best because it is easy and self-sufficient. Those who are involved in worldly desires can begin with *Karma-yoga* only. *Jñāna-yoga* is for those who have abandoned all desires. *Bhakti-yoga* is for all those who are in between as most spiritual aspirants are likely to be. This wide appeal of *Bhakti* is repeatedly stressed. *Karma-yoga* in the sense of the practice of virtue and moral training is emphasized. Ritual obligations and Vedic sacrifices are deprecated as merely attractions offered to the unwise who might be tempted by the prospect of heaven to perform sacrifices. Asceticism including austerities and renunciation is generally held as a necessary part of spiritual life. It is the special virtue of *Bhakti* that it automatically leads to detachment from the world. *Bhakti* also leads to *Jnana.* Contemplating the form of the Lord and rejoicing in His Name and Deeds, practising the ninefold devotion (*navadhā bhakti*), we obtain the grace of God. Ignorance and desire, suffering and rebirth are thus eliminated. Instead one wins communion with God and the bliss of love divine.[1]

This reconciliation of the paths is made possible by an *advaitic* philosophy which does not distinguish between the Absolute and God, *Nirguṇa* and *Saguṇa* and which traces the *Puruṣa* and *Prakṛti* of Sāṅkhya to a common final source in

God. Later commentators have sought to distinguish between *Brahman, Paramātman* and *Bhagavān* and argued that while *Jñāna* leads to the first and Yoga to the second, *Bhakti* alone can lead to the last. They have also argued that *Bhakti* leads beyond mere *Mokṣa* and constitutes an autonomous value. These are undoubtedly later ideas although the *Bhāgavata* takes a big step towards them. In fact, as late as the 12th century Mammaṭa still conceives of *Bhakti* as only a *Bhāva*, not *rasa*. By the 15th century, however, the notion of *Bhakti-rasa* was fully developed.[2]

Tantric Alchemy

The *Tantra* constitutes a fascinating aspect of the Indian tradition and has excited contradictory attitudes and evaluations. It has been condemned as superstitious, magical and immoral by some. Others have exalted it as scientific, esoteric and profoundly spiritual. There can be no doubt that Tantric texts and practices are as diverse as they are but imperfectly understood. To Sir John Woodroffe (Arthur Avalin) must go the credit of seeking to expound for the first time the principles and practices of the Tantra with sympathy and understanding. B. T. Bhattacharya and S. B. Dasgupta sought to expound the principles of Buddhist Tantra while M. M. G. N. Kaviraj has done more than anyone else to explain the meaning and principles of the Śaiva and Śākta Tantras.[3] Even so obscurities continue to plague the history, literature and philosophy of the *Tantras*.

The *Tantras* claim to be a divinely revealed tradition of secret knowledge which ought to be received personally from a qualified teacher and which requires practice to become properly intelligible. The antiquity of the extant texts is uncertain in many cases. The Buddhist Tantric tradition certainly goes back to the Kuṣāṇa period and some of the Śaiva and Śākta tantras are not later than the Gupta period.[4] The impact of the *Tantras* on the overt intellectual and religious tradition of the country was certainly manifest from the end of the Gupta age onwards. Śaiva philosophy and Purānic religion incorporate within themselves some of the basic principles and practices of *Tantra* from the 6th century onwards.[5]

The origin of Tantricism, however, must be deemed prehistoric and universal because in the ultimate analysis Tantricism is nothing except the ritualistic and symbolic aspect of worship considered as a means of communion with a deity. In so far as this ritual is treated as an expression of the will, efficacious by its own innate laws, it may come to have a magical aspect. In so far as it emphasises the will and grace of the deity, it follows the common path of all religions. The magical aspect of *Tantra* is perhaps only an aberration and may merely represent magic mascarading as *Tantra*. This is particularly true of the various rites indicated for gaining worldly ends, moral and immoral. One must admit, however, that even an authoritative text like *Prapañcasāra* mentions them. But this is at par with the tendency of the *Kāmaśāstra* and the *Arthaśāstra* which also mention practices of a morally dubious nature. Even the Vedic texts mention *'abbicāra'*. But then it has to be remembered that none of these *śāstras* recommend or prescribe such practices. They include them for the sake of mentioning what was current so that we may be warned against them.[6]

The conventional religious aspect of *Tantra* is a universal aspect of Purāṇic Hinduism and consists of *pūjopacāra* and may be paralleled with the sacrificial mode of worship in the *Vedas*. *Tantra* thus includes modes of worship current in Vedic and Purāṇic religions but it goes beyond their overt forms to their inner essence.

Just as Yoga is the science of the mind applied to gain intuitive knowledge, *Tantra* is the science of the Word applied to gain communion with the Divine. The essence of Tantra is *mantra* and its result is *Devatāsākṣātkāra*. One could say the same of Vedic religion but the difference lies in the conception and use of *mantra* and in the explicit recognition and formulation of the underlying principles in the Tantra. The Vedic *mantras* are more like *stotras* overlaid with poetry and the practice of *japa* in the later sense is not sufficiently evidenced for the Vedic age. External ritual dominates the main line of Vedic religious tradition, although the spiritualization of such ritual is clear in the *Vidyās* and *Upāsanās*. In the Tantra external ritual is common but the highest position is given to *mantra-japa*.

In the Tantra deity or *devatā* is conceived in three grades. At the gross level (*sthūla*) the deity may be imaged in a specific form. At the subtle level (*sūkṣma*). the deity is nothing except the *mantra*. At the highest level (*para*) the deity is identical with consciousness. Worship at the first level is external. At the second it consists essentially of the repetition of the *mantra*. *Mantra* is a sound or set of sounds and its *Japa* consists in its repeated utterance or uttering inwardly or mere ideation. Sound is not identified with physical vibrations of an audible kind which are called *dhvani*. Nor does the *mantra* consist of a word or sound-symbol with a conventional significance. Behind the physical sound and the conventional linguistic symbol, there lies *nāda* which is said to be like an echo in empty space but the expression of a supramental self-consciousness. It is thus no exaggeration to say that the *Mantra* is the mind oriented towards its own source.[7]

The only way to obtain the *mantra* is through Initiation which requires a Guru who has authority and a disciple who is eligible. Numerous varieties of *dīkṣā* have been mentioned. Practically speaking we may divide them into two classes--*dīkṣā* in accordance with the prescription of the *Śāstra* or the traditions of a family or school by a teacher who has not himself realised the truth but acts on behalf of the tradition; and *dīkṣā* as an act of personal grace by a Realized teacher (*Sadguru*). *Dīkṣā* pierces the veil of *āṇavamala* which may be likened to 'original sin', and thus regenerates the soul which now enters a new spiritual life. The disciple receives a *mantra* which is a 'literal' expression of *Nāda* the first born of God. "From God in the plenitude of His nature and power —His nature consisting of Being, Consciousness and Bliss, arose *Nāda*."[8] The repetition of the *mantra* leads in the first instance to its continuous flow as an idea "*Cittam mantrah*",[9] "*Mantra* is an Idea". The idea is of the divine significance of the *mantra* asociated with the image of sounds constituting its external or literal expression. The sense of significance helps the orientation of the mind towards the superhuman consciousness which is intertwined with the human. The continuity of the sound image leads to the sense of mere reverberation in empty space. As a result the mind is detached from all sensuous images and discursive thoughts. It is still as a listener of a pulsating echo which in time reveals itself as the luminous expression of a superhuman consciousness.

The basic principle on which the *Tantra* is based is that a creative universal consciousness pervades the human consciousness and naturally expresses itself in a rhythm of outgoing and return, as in echoing sound or form in general or self-consciousness. To reach the divine the human mind must catch on to this rhythm and follow it to its source. *Brahman* has been defined as that from which the world emanates, by which it is maintained and to which it returns. *Brahman* as consciousness, thus, has a natural power which expresses itself in the alternation of emanation and resolution. This self-expressive rhythm of *cit-śakti* was called vibration or *spanda* by the Kāśmīra śaivas.[10] The whole universe and every moment of it is only a vibration or pulsation of energy and all particular energies and vibrations are variations of one ultimate Energy and its self-expressive rhythm (*"Ekaiva sā mahāśaktis tayā sarvam idaṁ tatam"*). This ultimate energy is nothing except the inherent nature of consciousness. Just as the moon and moon-light are inalienably one, so are Śiva and Śakti. Consciousness is expressed as much in will as in knowledge. In fact, desire, knowledge and will represent three stages in which consciousness expresses its creativity. Desire itself is an outpouring of bliss which characterizes self-consciousness. Consciousness, thus, in the process of knowing and affirming itself is necessarily creative. In this voluntaristic emphasis *Tantra* differs sharply from gnostic schools like Buddhism, Sāṅkhya and Vedānta. Consequently Tantric *sādhana* also does not merely emphasize the search for the detached witnessing spirit, but seeks to integrate it with the rhythm of the universal mind within which alone witnessing has any meaning. Within the universal spirit witnessing and creating (Prakāśa and Vimarśa, Śiva and Śakti) are merely moments in one inseparable reality. Within the individual mind, however, the subject of knowing is a contentless self, a *focus imaginarius,* which the Vedānta called totally 'non-objective' and 'qualityless' and which the Buddhists proceeded to deny as a mere appearance. The subject of desire, will and action, on the other hand, can only be thought of as the psycho-physical apparatus with a 'qualified' selfhood superimposed upon it. At the level of individual life and experience the Sāṅkhya quite correctly holds that the subject of experience appears characterless and powerless while all power and objective features belong to changing natural forces. *Tantra* is not content with this pessimism and holds that both the subject and the object of individual experience derive from the same divine self-consciousness. The goal of human aspiration is not to reach the haven of pure subjectivity but to reach the divinity that is the inner source of his being.

Mantra is the sound-symbol of the deity, the *Yantra* is the deity's symbol in terms of a geometrical diagram. For example, the *Śrī-Yantra* depicts the process of cosmic emanation and return through a series of triangles emanating from a central point, and enclosed by a many-petalled lotus and surrounding lines. The point is the matrix, the union of Śiva and Śakti. The triangles with apices above represent the Śiva-tattva while the triangles with the apices downward represent the Śakti-tattva. The worship of the *Yantra* too involves a mental seeking for the dynamic source of all phenomena.[11]

Worship itself could take two forms. It could be in terms of inner contemplation in which case the body itself was regarded as the *Śrī-Yantra* with the esoteric plexuses or *cakras* as its constituents. Or worship could be external in terms of external *Yantras* and images. Inner worship was characteristic of *Samayācāra,* external worship of *Kaulācāra.* Some extreme sects of *Kaulācāra* worshipped a living woman as 'Śakti'.[12]

As is well known, the *Tantras* speak of *Vīrācāra* or *Vāmācāra* as a possibility for a type of *Sādhaka*. This kind of '*Ācāra*' used the Five *Makāras*. In particular its use of wine and sex has astonished and repelled people. It has been condemned in older as well as modern writings. It has even been explained away as purely symbolical. While there is no doubt that symbolism was involved, the actual use of the *makāras* was also known.[13] For example, wine symbolised the 'causal bliss' and was called '*Kāraṇa*' but Sri Rama Krishna Parmahaṁsa attested that quite a few just got drunk. On the other hand, Sri Ram Krishna Paramahaṁsa reached ecstasy by merely touching wine !

As a general observation it may be pointed out that the elements of worship generally derive from life but they are used symbolically. Food and drink as part of ritual, for example, are not used to fill the stomach or get drunk but to partake of grace etc. Sex too is a normal element of life and although its ritual use is rarer, it is not unknown. While *Tantra* does not advocate unrestrained indulgence in the instincts, it is certainly not ascetical. It regards the whole world as really divine and the culmination of its worship is in the consecration of the whole of life. Nor does it regard the mere suppression of instincts as ultimately helpful. "*Antarālika-bhāvas te vṛthā vai patanaṁ tathā*". Instincts need to be transmuted. That is the true Alchemy of *Tantra*.

REFERENCES

1. Cf. Dr. Susmita Pande, 'Bhakti in the Bhāgavata', *Journal of Religious Studies*, 1981, Patiala.

2. Cf. Dr. Susmita Pande, *Birth of Bhakti in Indian Religion and Art, Medieval Bhakti Movement.*

3. B. T. Bhattacharya, *An Introduction to Buddhist Esoterism* ; S. B. Dasgupta, *Introduction to Tantric Buddhism;*

G. N. Kaviraj, *Tāntrika Sāhitya Men Śākta Dṛṣṭi, Tāntrika Sāhitya*. For a modern classic in the ancient style see Pratyagātmānanda Sarasvatī, *Japasūtram*.

4. P. C. Bagchi, *Studies in the Tantras* ; Pande, G. C., *Bauddha Dharma Ke Vikāsa Kā Itihāsa*.

5. See, *e. g.*, *Śrītantrāloka* or *Devībhāgavata*.

6. *Śyenayāga* is a typical illustration.

7. This is implicit in Patañjali's statement that *Praṇavajapa* leads to *Pratyakcetanā*. The modern technique of Transcendental Meditation depends on such a conception of *mantra*. This is also clear in Ramana Maharshi's famous instruction to Gaṇapati Muni when his *Puraścaraṇas* had been apparently ineffective.

8. *Śāradātilakam*.

9. *Śivasūtras*, 2.1.

10. See Jaideva Singh's *Spandakārikās*.

11. For modern description of *Yantras*, cf. Tucci, *Theory and Practice of the Maṇḍala*.

12. Cf. Lakṣmīdhara's comy. on *Saundaryalahari*.

13. Cf. *Paraśurāmakalpasūtra*.

9

ADHYĀTMAVIDYĀ AS PHILOSOPHY

"Adhyātmavidyā vidyānām"

Since the Upaniṣadic declaration *Tattvamasi*=that thou are—identifying the individual self with the highest cosmic reality, the concept of the self has remained the most central and challenging concept of Indian philosophy. The Lokāyata and the Buddhists repudiated the very existence of the Self (*Ātman*) as a distinct and independent entity. The various realistic schools like Nyāya and Vaiśeṣika, Mīmāṁsakas and the Jainas, the Rāmānujīyas and the Mādhvas denied the cosmic character of the 'Self', asserting it to be an individual and finite 'spiritual' substance, one object among many others. The Sāṅkhya and Yoga, conceiving the 'Self' as the transcendental subject, were able to advance beyond the 'pan-objectivism' of the realists, but in their turn refused to countenance the cosmic character of the 'Self' which remained for them a featureless spiritual monad.

The controversy over the 'self' thus has been essentially of a metaphysical nature—whether the 'self' is a distinct real, whether its reality is 'substantial' or 'transcendental', individual or cosmic. These are the three main questions over which the philosophers have ranged themselves.

The Lokāyata identified the 'self' with the body and their theory has been called *'Dehātmavāda'*. Even in the *Chāndogya Upaniṣad* we are told that Vairocana was satisfied with regarding the body as the Ātmā. Among Buddha's contemporaries Ajitakesa-Kambali denied that any soul survived the death of the body and Prince Payasi conducted experiments to discover whether any soul escaped the body at death. The *Sarvadarśana-saṁgraha* tells us that the Lokāyata regarded consciousness as a special capacity produced by the organization of material elements into the form of the body just as the power of intoxication arises from fermentation (*caitanyaṁ madaśaktivat*). The Lokāyata, thus, identified the self with the body and considered conscious life as a special kind of bodily behaviour. This doctrine closely resembles that of modern materialism, specially behaviourism. It rested on the assumption that there is only one valid way of knowing viz., sense-perception. If *pratyakṣa* is accepted as the only *pramāṇa*, it would follow that there is no reality going under the name of the Self and transcending the realm of the sensibilia.

The Buddhists were quick to point out that the denial of reasoning as an independent way of knowing the truth, of *anumāna* as *pramāṇa*, is beset with self-contradiction. In the *Nyāya-bindu* Dharmakīrti points out that the statement *'anumāna* is not a *pramāṇa*' is self-contradictory because all negative judgments rest on inference just as all verbal communications becomes intelligible only through inference. Communication precedes statement and inference precedes negation. Thus, the negative judgment under consideration doubly presupposes the validity of firm connections between signs and their significations. In fact, the Lokāyatas themselves admit a weaker kind of inference which they call *śambhāvanā*. In a world of pure contingency there would remain no basis for degrees of probability. The very notion of probability presupposes a notion of law, and contingency acquires meaning only through its contrast with necessity. If one were to abandon the concept of necessity and law, the possibility of scientific knowledge would have to be abandoned. It is obvious, thus, that valid knowledge cannot be restricted to merely empirical knowledge. Human reason must be allowed the capacity of reaching a kind of knowledge which is not wholly limited to sensuous or physical reality. The Buddhists have further pointed out that all mental phenomena are distinguished by the pervasive feature of self-consciousness (*svasam-*

vedana). The possibility of introspection, which the human mind possesses, fixes an unbridgable gulf between subjective and objective being. Mind and matter, *citta* and *rūpa,* are absolutely distinct elements (*dhātus*) and neither can be regarded as a capacity or form of the other.

From these logical and psychological principles upheld by the Buddhists, it follows that the materialistic denial of the *Ātman* is ill-grounded. Since knowledge can not be restricted to mere perception, reality cannot be restricted to the merely physical. And, the mind itself cries aloud to be distinguished from the objects of sense-perception. These considerations establish a realm of psychic and rational realities, a world of intelligibilia, by the side of the physical world, the world of sense-perception.

The Buddhists, nevertheless, denied the reality of the self as a separate spiritual substance, as an independent finite individual that remains identical in the midst of the process of experience. They denied that there is any changeless identical person carrying the burden of the *skandhas.* While the Lokāyata reduced the self to the body on account of their inveterate behaviourism, the Buddhists seemed to reduce the Self to a stream of consciousness on account of their emphasis on psychic introspection. The stock Buddhist argument for denying the Self was—the *Ātman* does not exist because it is never perceived (*nopalabhyate*—here perception includes introspection). One is reminded of Hume when he questioned the reality of any unchanging psychic substance on the ground that looking into one's own mind one can discover only changing states. Another argument which the Buddhists used was of a more general character. There is no changeless self because all reality must be instantaneous. This argument is specially directed against the doctrine of schools like Sāṁkhya and Vedānta. At the same time the Buddhists tried to meet the criticism levelled against them. The notion of a Self which is undoubtedly present in all consciousness is explained as an illusion. Memory is explained through the doctrine of *Vāsanā.* Almost like William James the Buddhists held that each preceding moment of consciousness hands over its own impressions to the next succeeding moment. The validity of the moral law is defended by stating that actions bring about their retribution as an impersonal moral reflex which works so long as one nourishes the illusion of an identical Self. Do we not consider the son entitled to the debts and gifts of his father? The Buddhists further buttressed their conception of man as a mere 'psychic continuum' devoid of any underlying changeless 'self' by analysing the notions of 'existence', 'causality' and 'consciousness' in a new way. Existence is essentially characterised by causal functioning, so that for any thing to be, it must produce some effect. Since to produce a different effect is to be a different thing, it follows that everything that is, must last but for a moment in which to produce its effect and pass away utterly. This makes the universe a ceaseless flux and an 'eternal self' or an identical soul finds no place in it. Consciousness is itself conceived as a series of events or flashes produced by the interaction of 'causes and conditions'.

Unlike the Lokāyata denial of 'self', the Buddhist denial does not repudiate the notion of *Karman* and rebirth. It only repudiates the notions of 'identity', 'permanence' and 'substance'. It replaces these by the notions of 'continuity', 'flux' and 'function'. Without robbing religion of its moral and spiritual validity, Buddhism proposes a metaphysical revolution which is directed as much against the realists as against the materialists.

The realistic views seek to buttress the common sense view of the Self against the physical reductionism of the Lokāyata as well as against the psychic reductionism of the Buddhists. The Soul *has* body and mind; the soul *is* not body or mind. Here the notion of the Self is split up into a changing and accidental part and an unchanging and essential part. The relations of the Self with the body and the mind and through them with the world are accidental, the products of *Karma*, and constitute its experience as well as bondage. The essential nature of the Self which alone continues in the state of liberation is simple and eternal. Liberation permanently divests the soul of the possibility of experiencing the world.

The Naiyāyikas describe *Ātmā* as one of the nine substances where substance (*dravya*) is one of the several categories (*padārtha*) into which reality is divided. The substance has been defined in several alternative ways—as the substratum of qualities or as the substratum of action, or as having the capacity of becoming the inherent cause. In the West, Aristotle had defined the substance as what could only be a subject and never a predicate and medieval scholastics defined the substance in terms of its independence. Although the Nyāya mode of definition is slightly different, the intention and the result are the same. For Nyāya, existence belongs only to *dravya, guṇa* and *karma,* and *guṇa* and *karma* are dependent on the substance. Here, substance alone has independent existence. The *Ātman* as a substance is characterized by the qualities of knowledge, desire, will, effort, sin and virtue, pleasure and pain. In fact, these qualities are the ground on which we can validly infer the existence of the *Ātman.* The qualities imply a substance and these psychic qualities are not to be found in any material substance. Hence, there must be an immaterial substance or *Ātman.* It is a peculiar *Vyatirekī* or negative inference. In all those instances where the Soul is known to be absent the qualities in question are also known to be absent. But, one does not know of any positive instance which may serve as an example because the reason is characteristic of the *sādhya* and is co-extensive with it. This logical difficulty with the inference has led some Naiyāyikas to argue that the soul is known directly in introspection.

The above mentioned qualities of the Soul, however, are manifested only when the soul is in connection with the mind and, hence, the body. The mind is also a substance, atomic and immaterial. Its existence is proved by the fact that we cannot simultaneously know objects through the different senses. It is the contact with the mind that gives the Soul its life of experience and it is disconnection with the mind that gives it liberation, when all the qualities mentioned above cease to operate. Such a soul can be distinguished from matter only by saying that while it had the capacity of experience the material substances are inherently incapable of it.

The Mīmāṁsakas fundamentally agree with the Naiyāyikas in regarding the Soul as a substance. The *Ātman* is the substratum of experience. Whether it is known through self-consciousness as the Prābhākaras hold or through mental perception as the Kaumārilas hold, is a disputed point. But, the Mīmāṁsakas agree in regarding the self as the agent and the experiencer and the Soul as the bearer of sin and virtue. The Soul, thus, comes to have two aspects—a persistent and imperishable aspect and also an aspect of modal change. It is both subject and object. For the Kaumārilas the Self becomes thus sentient as well as insentient, as Madhusūdan Saraswatī puts it (*jaḍo bodhātmakaśceti*). For the Prābhākaras, the Soul is wholly insentient, being not sentience but its substratum.

The Mīmāṁsakas evolve their concept of the Self by working out the metaphysical implications of the reality of action and the validity of Vedic injunctions. There must be a lasting Soul, capable of action and experience, because otherwise Vedic injunctions promising heaven would be rendered nugatory. It is, however, difficult to see how permanence and impermanence, sentience and insentience, can be combined in the same substance without contradiction. On the other hand, the Naiyāyikas, in trying to account for this duality, through the intervention of the mind, bring the Soul perilously near the charge of being insentient.

The Jainas denied that there is any contradiction between being and becoming. The being of the Soul is quâ substance while its becoming is quâ mode or *paryāya*. The true nature of the Soul, however, is to have infinite knowledge, power and bliss. The soul is an infinite spiritual substance, though in the state of bondage it is delimited by the power of *karma* and assumes the size of the body (*madhyama parimāṇa*). In the Jaina conception of *Jīva,* vital, psychic and transcendental categories are rolled into one. The lowliest plants and animals, men and gods, are all links in a chain and the highest possibility, which is also the essence of the *jīva,* is realized in the Siddha or the Kevalī. It presents us with the grand spectacle of a vast spiritual evolution ranging from almost bare possibility to the fullest realization of spiritual being. Nevertheless the metaphysical problem of defending the substance as a viable category and satisfactorily explaining how the transcendent spirit gets into bondage and painfully struggles through it can hardly be said to have been satisfactorily explained. To the reasoning mind the world of natural objects appears to be inexorably subject to the categories of space, time and causality. While human experience is in an obvious sense subject to such determinations, the sole purpose of the belief in *Ātman* is somehow to vindicate a realm of freedom and immortality for the spirit that is in man. If human actions and experiences are part of the natural world, how would the Self be free or immortal and beatific? On the other hand, if the real nature of the Self is infinity and independence, how would it act and experience in the world, subject to law? The theories of a substantial Self place the substance in the world of freedom but its real accidents in the world of bondage. The unity of the substance and its accidents thus becomes wholly unintelligible.

In Sāṅkhya, thus, in order to avoid this difficulty an effort is made to preserve the transcendental character of the Self by refusing to accept any real connection between it and the accidental world of experience. Bondage arises through a radical ignorance. The mind and all its functioning are squarely placed within *Prakṛti.* This explains the heteronomy of human actions and experiences since they are now fully the products of nature. Nevertheless, they point to something beyond them. They would not be possible unless there were an eternal Self as their witness. The Self is the necessary prius of experience. The consciousness of change implies an unchanging consciousness and the Self is the deepest of the transcendental conditions of objectivity.[1] The *Puruṣa* of Sāṅkhya is somewhat like the transcendental Aperception of Kant, only it is not a mere ideal, a focus imaginarius. Nor indeed is it a substance or an agent. These are categories belonging to Nature. The Self is the changeless and non-objective condition of the whole manifested world.

The Sāṅkhya view of the Self attains a singularly remarkable depth in comprehending the paradox of self-consciousness. On the one hand, consciousness is a changing process, a part of the objective world. On the other, it presupposes an eternal and transcendental subject. The Sāṅkhya refused to accept the correlativity of the subject and the object in knowledge. The object depends on the subject for its manifestation. But, the subject has a free and eternal being.[2]

The Sāṅkhya, however, is not wholly able to free itself from the fallacy of regarding the Self as an object, because they continue to attribute plurality to the *Puruṣa*. How is the category of number to be applied to what is wholly transcendental? What is more, how is the unmanifested being of Nature to be understood? If *Prakṛti* in itself does not require the *Puruṣa*, how can it ever require it afterwards? It is strange to be told that the manifestation of *Prakṛti* is only with reference to *Puruṣa* and at the same time that it is essentially independent of the *Puruṣa*. Nature is independent of the spirit and yet functions for it. This appears to be a myth or a mystery rather than a reasoned principle.

The trouble is that the Sāṅkhya does not proceed far enough. Having declared the connection of *Puruṣa* with *Prakṛti* as grounded in illusion, it still continues to regard *Prakṛti* as real. Advaita takes the final step of declaring the whole world of the non-Self to be an illusion.[3] The Self needs no proof because it is self-evident (*svataḥ-siddha*) and undeniable (*anapohya*). The Self is self-luminous (*sva-prakāśa*) and needs no other for its revelation. Being the subject of all change and experience it is itself changeless and non-objective. All plurality falls on the side of the objects and all objects are qua objects mere appearances—unreal because they are objects (*dṛṣyattvāt mṛṣā*). That alone is real which is unalterable (*yat sat tat nityam*). Objects and their experience are part of what is sublated (*bādhita*).

There are not two real worlds, two real natures of the Self, to be somehow connected. There is only one reality which stands eternally above the world of illusion. There are not two natures of the Self but only two levels at which to understand the infinite nature of the Self. At the level of illusion Advaita accepts the apparent reality of the world and in its psychology accepts a good part of Sāṅkhya. This illusory experience, however, is grounded in the transcendent reality of the Self, just as the illusory snake is grounded in the rope. The Self is the transcendent ground of the world and this description itself leaves the nature of the Self untouched. It is a mere *taṭastha lakṣaṇa*. The real nature of the Self is wholly indescribable in relational terms or categories appropriate to finite objects. And yet, the Self does not become, hereby, an X, a wholly unknown entity. For, the Self is not an object. It is the nearest, the most intimate, the self-evident Self of all. By the force of a beginningless ignorance we mistake our true nature and simultaneously enter the toils of an illusory world. Advaita seeks to rescue man from this thraldom.

REFERENCES

1. Vide A. C. Mukherji, *The Nature of Self*.
2. Cf. K. C. Bhattacharya, *The Subject as Freedom*.
3. This may be clearly seen in Śaṅkara's preface to the *Brahmasūtra-bhāṣya* which begins with a Sāṅkhyan dichotomy only to adumbrate illusionism.

10

THE SYNTHESIS OF YOGA IN THE GĪTĀ

Sir R.G. Bhandarkar has suggested that the *Bhagavadgītā* was the product of an age when Vedic ritualism was under fire.[1] In the north-east of India a number of mendicant-orders had arisen and they proclaimed the worthlessness of any rules of conduct taking the form of a mere traditional ritual. The morality which Buddhism and Jainism propounded was essentially spiritual. It assumed the universality and inevitability of the law of *Karma* and emphasized *ahiṁsā* or respect for life as the central principle of the new moral outlook. At the same time the pursuit of secular life was condemned as binding man to the weary round of birth and death. On this view, thus, moral life has two planes—at one level, it is the regulation of instinctive life by the principle of just retribution; at a higher level, it is the renunciation of egoistic claims and the total acceptance of the sacredness of life. Instead of being merely conventional or ritualistic, morality, thus, becomes at successive levels the pursuit of justice and compassion leading ultimately to total resignation and detachment.

The *Bhagavadgītā* takes into account this ascetic, life-denying and universalist point of view which ran counter to the established Vedic tradition. Instead, however, of jettissoning the older outlook, which based morality on the ritual of sacrifice and the traditional duties of caste groups, the *Gītā* reinterpreted the tradition and sought to reconcile it with the force of the doctrines of *jñāna* and *naiṣkarmya*. In this it followed the Upaniṣadic reinterpretation of the idea of sacrifice.

That there is a universal moral principle called *dharma* was accepted universally. The orthodox and the hererodox alike proclaimed that man ought to act by the principle of *dharma*. The great question was—what constitutes the essence of *dharma*? There was the answer in terms of institutional rules which the *Dharmasūtras* were formulating on the basis of the Vedic tradition : the *dharma* of each person is defined by his position in the system of *varṇas* and *āśramas*. The Mīmāṁsakas put forward a formalistic point of view—*dharma* is the value (*artha*) enjoined in the *Vedas* and we discover it as a set of prescriptions and prohibitions.[2] The Buddhists discovered the essence of *dharma* in the disposition of the will[3] and the *Mahābhārata* declared it to lie in the moral reasoning of the heart (*dharmasya tattvaṁ nihitaṁ guhāyām*).[4] In the *Gītā* it is clearly perceived that there are two aspects of *dharma*. On the one hand, we need to know a basic general principle which would guide as in making concrete decisions, and which would enable us to distinguish the essence of a moral action. It is obvious that such a basic principle of moral action must relate to the psyche. It must be some inwardly discerned quality or feature of the will that is the source of all action. On the other hand, the mere formulation of a general principle is not sufficient to give us adequate guidance in moral life. This general principle must acquire concrete and habitual content so that life may not wear the aspect of a perpetual research into what we would continually require to do. The morality which the *Gītā* advocates is neither purely formal nor purely empirical. The *Gītā* not only formulates a general principle and criterion defining moral life ; it also seeks to give the principle practical content.

The central principle which the *Gītā* propounds in this context is the celebrated one of 'desireless action', which seeks to preserve the virtue of action along with that of knowledge. Ideal life is a triple harmony of will (*karman*), reason (*jñāna*) and love (*Bhakti*). At the outset we need to reorient our behaviour, physical and social. Indeed living itself involves ceaseless action and what is true of the individual is equally true of society. Just as the physical body depends on a process of constant exchange between itself and its environment, so does society depend on the exchange of goods and services. We may look upon the whole process of life, individual and social, as one of sacrifice. While necessary for *'śarīra-yātrā'*, *'lokānuvartana'* and *'lokasaṅgraha'*, action is not simply a physical or social necessity. When use and consumption go along with service and sacrifice, life is truly a sacrifice which is paradigmatic of moral action as well as worship.

The *Gītā* takes up the old idea of 'sacrifice' and reinterprets it as a symbol of selfless and dedicated work. The essence of the sacrifice lies not in its mechanical ritual but in its attitude of 'giving up and serving'.

The partisans of pure *jñāna* and *naiṣkarmya,* however. argued that all action—even the socially necessary—is tainted with desire and ignorance. Whether sinful or virtuous, selfish or social, action forges a chain of causal links which in the sequel binds the agent firmly to the process of *saṁsāra.* The wise would, therefore, do well to avoid action in order to avoid the pain of life. 'It is in contemplative reason, *Buddhi,* that man should take refuge; all goal-oriented practical life is narrow and of small account' (*Buddhau śaraṇam anviccha. kṛpaṇāḥ phalahetavaḥ*).[5]

Gītā reinterprets knowledge as it reinterprets action. It refuses to see any contradiction between *theoria* and *Praxis*, *Jñāna* and *Karman.* Knowledge enables one to perceive that the Self is eternally motionless and actionless, free from all seeking and desire; on the other hand, mind and body are parts of Nature, ceaselessly involved in change and determination. This flux of nature cannot be stopped even for a moment. for the forces of nature keep on interacting (*guṇā guṇeṣu vartante*). But this does not worry the wise man who knows himself to be as uninvolved as a disinterested spectator. He knows that in the midst of action, the spirit remains motionless,[6] while even in the so-called inactivity of the mind and body natural processes do go on (*'Karmaṇyakarma yaḥ paśyed akarmaṇi ca karma yaḥ'*). He does not, therefore, vainly seek to stop his body, senses and mind from functioning. That is neither possible nor desirable. Individual and social survival depends on it and so does the possibility of dedicated life, of life as sacrifice. At the same time, the wise man realizes his own inward aloofness in the midst of action. He acts out of duty alone. He does not seek the fulfilment of egoistic ambitions and desires. He universalizes the basis of his action and acts out of love and equality (*Ātmaupamyena sarvatra samaṁ paśyati yorjuna*). He retains perfect equanimity (*sama-duhkha-sukhaḥ*) and an unwavering spiritual serenity (*sthita-prajña*).

Desireless will (*niṣkāma Karman*) grounded on spiritual knowledge (*Prajñā, Buddhi*) is the general principle which the *Gītā* formulates as the guiding principle of moral and religious life. It does not accept the one-sided theories of mere *karman* or mere *Jñāna*. The former fails to realize the transcendent and eternal nature of the spirit, the latter the role of Nature and society in man's liberation.

Nor does the *Gītā* seek to combine *Karman* and *Jñāna* in that mechanical and external manner which the advocates of *Jñāna-Karman-samuccaya* sought. For the *Gītā*, *jñāna* and *Karman* are not external to each other, nor both independent causes of *Mokṣa*. The essential and ultimate unity of knowledge and action is to be seen in God and in his Incarnation where action is only the spontaneous expression of grace. This is the model for the man who seeks liberation or is liberated. He performs duties and renders service without any personal interest. Knowledge constitutes inward being or the eternal nature of the spirit, action is the outward being, the process of Nature. Unlike *Sāṅkhya*, *Gītā* does not create an ultimate dualism between Spirit and Nature. In God both are reconciled. Nature and spirit belong to God, as His lower and higher powers (*aparā prakṛti* and *parā prakṛti*). Reality has an eternal as well as an apparent temporal aspect. Time is merely an image and approach to Eternity. It is this apparent duality of *Puruṣa* and *Prakṛti*, transcended in *Puruṣottama*, which produces the duality of *Jñāna* and *Karman* to be transcended in *Niṣkāma Karman*.

Where *Jñāna* means mental or acquired knowledge and *Karman* virtuous practice, both have relevance to the seeking for ideal life. In this sense there is a truth in *Jñāna-Karma-samuccaya.* But this constitutes only the preparatory thresh-hold of the spiritual journey, *Niṣkāma Karman* virtually the whole of it.

Tilak's interpretation has been called the theory of Jñānottara-Karman, action after knowledge, by Professor R.D. Ranade.[7] This is in contrast to the theory of *Karma-sanyāsa* propounded by Śaṅkara. For Śaṅkara while *Karman* is a duty for the non-liberated, it does not contribute to *Jñāna* or *mokṣa* directly and is impossible after knowledge.[8] For Tilak, the third chapter of the *Gītā* positively establishes that action ought to be continued even by the wise for the sake of society (*loka-saṁgraha*). Besides, rightly performed, action purifies and leads one to liberation. The tenability of Śaṅkara's interpretation rests on restricting the meaning of action to egoistic action grounded in Avidya. For Nature Śaṅkara proposes an uncompromising illusionism and makes creation and regulation of destiny merely an accidental attribute of God. This does not appear to be the obvious meaning of *Gīta,* which Tilak brings out so clearly.

Aurobindo argues that while *Gītā* begins with *Niṣkāma-Karman* it goes beyond it into devotional self-surrender to God at the end (*sarva-dharmān parityajya māmekaṁ śaraṇaṁ vraja*).[9] Sir R. G. Bhandarkar also argued that *Bhakti* is the heart of the *Gītā.* As mentioned above a more usual view is to claim that *Gītā* proclaims *karman* in the first six chapters. *Jñāna* in the next six and *Bhakti* in the last six.[10] This diversity of interpretation partly arises from the different senses in which the crucial terms are used. If *Bhakti* means devotional practice, it cannot be distinguished from *Karman.* If it means participation in the glory of God, or nearness to Him in being or a union with Him, it cannot be distinguished from *Jñāna* in the highest sense. What is knowledge but eternal self-consciousness, which is another name for the highest Love of God.[11] A total surrender to God is possible only in and through the dawn of true knowledge, *'Tato māṁ tattvato jñātvā viśate tadanantaram'.*[12]

While ultimately, *Karman, Jñāna* and *Bhakti* reveal different aspects of the spirit, *Jñāna* is its inner being, *Karman* its outer approach ; *Bhakti* begins as *Karman* and ripens as *Jñāna.*[13] The ethical outlook of the *Gītā* avoids onesidedness and is oriented towards spiritual self-realization. Ethical norms are not simply conventions based on interest, enlightened or otherwise. They are simply the requirements of a spiri tual life. The Spirit is conceived in the *Gītā* as both transcendent and immanent. In its transcendent aspect, it is both the ground and the goal of spiritual quest. In its immanent aspect, it is the self-realizing principle working in time (*'kālenātmani vindati'*). It is this apparent duality in human nature which seems to separate Reason from Will and poses the paradox of *Jñāna* and *Karman. Gītā* resolves it by interpreting each of the terms into their ultimate unity in life divine.

REFERENCES

1. *Vaiṣṇavism, Śaivism and other Miñor Religious Systems.*

The cultural synchronicity of the rise of Buddhism in the north-east and of Bhāgavatism in the north-west is highly plausible. Dating the *BG* in the 2nd cent. B.C. or after is far too late since by that time the cult of Vāsudeva as *deva-deva* had already won adherents even among the Greeks of Taxila. The cult of Vāsudeva Kṛṣṇa is presupposed by Megasthenes and Pāṇini. The *Ch. up.* attests the historicity of Devakīputra Kṛṣṇa who should thus be placed towards the end of the Vedic Age. This accords with tradition placing Kṛṣṇa at the end of *Dvāpara.* His teachings should have formed the kernel of the *BG* which is ideologically close to the *Upaniṣads* and the ascetic movements of the 6th century B.C.

Its monotheism is free from the impact of imperialism, image worship and temples. It does not presuppose classical philosophical systems, orthodox or heterodox.

2. Bühler has placed the *Dharmasūtras* between the 5th Cent. B.C. and the 2nd Cent. B.C.; the *Mīmāṁsāsūtras* are the earliest among the philosophical *sūtras* and presuppose a long tradition which probably began with the *brahmodyas* of the later Vedic age and developed as a system of interpretative rules alongside the *Kalpasūtras*. The *Arthaśāstra* clearly presupposes the *Kalpa* as a *Vedāṅga*.

3. Cf. Nāgārjuna, "*Cetanā cetayityā ca karmoktaṁ paramarṣiṇā*" (*Madhyamaka*). It harks back to an ancient *sūtra*.

4. *Mbh, Vanaparvan.*

5. *Buddhi* may be compared with *theoria*. Cf. Dr. Jaidev Singh's paper on 'The status and role of Buddhi in Kaṭhopaniṣad and Bhagavadgītā', read at the *Indian Philosophical Congress* held at Madras in Dec. 1940.

6. This is the point of view of Sāṅkhya-yoga. The sixth chapter of the *Gītā* elaborates on the practice of stilling the mind. Jñāneśvara's comy. is illuminating from this point of view. "*Na kiñcidapi cintayet*" of the *Gītā* may be compared with *Aṣṭa-sāhasrikā Prajñāpāramitā's "yatra cittam acittaṁ bhavati*".

7. Cf. Dr. Susmita Pande, *op. cit.*, pp. 62-63.

8. For a reinterpretation of Śaṅkara, see Dr. Saral Jhingran's thesis on the *Theory of Action in Śaṅkara* (Rajasthan University Library, Jaipur).

9. *Essays on the Gītā,* Second Series, pp. 417ff; See also Dr. Susmita Pande, *op. cit.*, pp. 61ff.

10. Cf. Madhusūdana Sarasvatī's Comy. on the *BG.*

11. Cf. Spinoza, *Ethics,* V. 33.

12. *Bhagavadgītā,* 18.55.

13. Cf. Śaṅkara's distinction between *Karma-lakṣaṇā* and *jñāna-lakṣaṇā bhakti*—comy. on the *BG.* 18.55.

PART II : SYMBOLISM AND EXPRESSION

11

LANGUAGE AND MYTH

Ancient reflections on the nature of language

Of all the symbolic systems in a culture the deepest is represented by language since without being brought into relationship with it no other symbolic system becomes adequately meaningful. While language claims to symbolize anything and everything, its symbolism is not in fact merely passive or neutral. The meanings of words can hardly be thought of as things in the real world. They are rather constructs of experience and what the words refer to are selectively demarcated fragments of experience and behaviour. Particular words, thus, acquire their meanings in terms of the possible contexts of their use, i. e., in terms of the possible sentences in which they may be used in accordance with the genius of the language. Words, meanings and judgments are concomitant processes and they arise as tools within the process of purposive behaviour.

This conception of the nature of language as an instinctive and constructive activity intrinsically bound up with the exercise of judgmental faculties was elaborated by Buddhist philosophers.[1] The symbolism of language becomes on this view not the realistic representation of an externally given world but the construction of a world of which the deepest principles of construction are subjective but of which the objectivity cannot be falsified by any pragmatic test. The world of language, thus is at once subjective and objective, constructed and yet pragmatically valid.

On this view language also acquires an intrinsically delusive nature.[2] If one seeks a truth which transcends purposive behaviour, the eternal truth of things in themselves, language would prove to be a hinderance. Without language there would be no *Vyavahāra* but *Paramārtha* lies beyond language. "Whence speech retreats along with thought", this view was acceptable not only to the Buddhists but also to Advaita Vedānta. *"Śāntaṁ nirvāṇam"* may be paralleled by *"Upaśāntoyamātmā"*.

It is true that a quite different view may be discerned in Nyāya-Vaiśeṣika for which the ultimate reality is as much knowable as it is 'statable'. God, the souls and the atoms are all eternal and their natures are the subject of logical judgments and linguistic statements. On the other hand, even universals, relations and negations are regarded not as intellectual constructs or linguistic devices but as forms of objective reality. This view of language which regards it as the symbolization of an objectively given world rests on a realistic epistemology which in turn is bound up with a pluralistic metaphysic. It defines the significative power of words to consist in their capacity of presenting meanings or objects before the mind and regards its source to be convention. This significative power is not one of merely stimulating memory but of producing fresh knowledge. In its earlier phase the Nyāya-Vaiśeṣika regarded the will of God to be the original force behind linguistic conventions but this view was given up later on.[3]

If on the Buddhistic view language is at once a source of pragmatic knowledge and transcendental illusion, on the Nyāya-Vaiśeṣika view too it is essentially of the nature of communication and the validity of the knowledge which it conveys depends solely on the reliability of the person who uses it.[4] On both of these views, thus, while it is useful, language is not in itself an original source of truth. On the other hand, the orthodox Vedic view tended to regard the significative power of language to be rooted in its very nature. The word or words are eternal and have an innate power of revealing truth. It is thus that the *Vedas* are an eternally given revelation.[5] This view was later refined in the philosophies of grammar and *Śaivāgama*. These views postulate a necessary connection between words and meanings and also that behind the spoken word there are subtler forms of it. While the words are ephemeral productions with conventional meanings according to the Buddhists and Nyāya-Vaiśeṣika, they are held to be eternal with an inherent significative power according to the Mīmāṁsakas, Vaiyākaraṇas and Kāśmīra Śaivas. The Mīmāṁsakas believed the word to be a sequence of simple but ideal units of sound which could be recognised as such. These are called *Varṇas* and are like the phonemes except that the *Varṇas* are eternal, recognizable identities which are manifested by corresponding sounds. The Grammarians postulated *sphoṭa* instead of the *Varṇas* as the eternal aspect of words.[6] Speech-sounds manifest *sphoṭa* and *sphoṭa* reveals meanings. Ultimately there is an infinite and eternal word which is the source of all speech and meanings. This is *Śabda-brahman* and was identified by Bhartṛhari with the seeing word or Paśyantī.[7] The spoken and audible sound is *Vaikharī* while the mental speech inseparable from the apprehension of meanings is *Madhyamā*. Beyond this lies *Paśyantī*. The Kaśmīra Śaivas differentiated *Parā* from *Paśyantī* and identified the *Parā* with the Reflective Power or *Vimarśa* of God. The ultimate root of language lies in self-consciousness or the self-affirmation of consciousness. This innate self-affirmation or spontaneity of consciousness makes it expressive or creative. The innate symbolism of language is not external and conventional but lies in its expressiveness of self-consciousness.

Nyāya-Vaiśeṣika explains the conventional nature of language. Buddhist philosophy explains the inter-dependence of language and thought. Mīmāṁsakas point out that religious faith postulates an eternal word as the source of revelation. Grammarians and Śaivas trace language to its ultimate root in the very nature of consciousness. Here we have a fundamental insight, language in its deepest aspect is not conventional but natural, natural to consciousness. We have to recognise that linguistic phenomena exist at many corresponding levels. "Behind the pattern of the audible sound waves of speech lie the patterns of articulation and neural activity. Despite the operation of chance in the choice of convention in language and in its actual use, there are discernible in it patterns of a statistical and logical nature. We have here a hierarchy of isomorphic patterns and patterning forces subsisting at various levels—acoustic, articulatory, neural—and soaring upwards to their psychic source which should be accessible only to mystical apprehension. It is the unity of psychic reality which makes communication ultimately possible since it then becomes a process of self-expression and self-recognition."[8] What language symbolizes primarily is not an external, material world but psychic meanings. The world is what we make of our experiences and that making has a necessary reference to the self or consciousness. If language in its ordinary use is a necessary part of *Vyavahāra,* rightly understood it can be a ladder for mystical self-realization. Language is both *prapañca* and *mantra.*

Aspects of Linguistic History

Although the earliest linguistic records in India are supposed to be those left behind by the Indus civilization, they still remain unintelligible so much so that we cannot even decide the kind of language to which they belong.[9] Vedic literature, therefore, remains the earliest linguistic evidence which we have. It has been generally supposed that the Vedic language belonging to the Indo-European or Aryan speech-family must have been introduced into India when the Aryan immigrations occurred, perhaps towards the end of the Indus civilization in the second millennium B.C.[10] The development of the Aryan languages in India, thus, must have been in areas where formerly non-Aryan languages were spoken. These non-Aryan languages have been conveniently grouped into three distinct speech-families, "viz., the Austric (Kol or Munda), the Tibeto-Chinese or Sino-Tibetan, the Dravidian". In course of time the Aryan speech-family largely displaced its rivals in the nuclear areas in north India. Austric and Sino-Tibetan have survived in refuge areas while Dravidian flourishes in the south and part of the Deccan. Owing to natural processes as well as historical changes and contacts the old Indo-Aryan was gradually transformed into Middle Indo-Aryan from about the 6th century B.C. and into Modern Indo-Aryan from about A.D. 1000.

That Vedic Sanskrit was a living and spoken language has not been doubted. When Pāṇini wrote his *Aṣṭādhyāyī* he distinguished the Vedic language as *chandas* from the spoken language or *bhāṣā* for which he produced his grammar. It seems that in the north-west in the fifth century B.C. while Vedic Sanskrit was recognised as archaic in the sense that many of its forms were no longer current, what is now called classical or Pāṇinian Sanskrit was a spoken language or *bhāṣā*. In the north-east in Magadha, however, the situation was somewhat different. Here the spoken language—Māgadhī—had significantly diverged from the old Vedic language not only in its forms but also in its sounds. In the *Vinaya* we hear of the distinction between *Chandas* and *Nirukti*, the former referring as expected to Vedic language, the latter to the spoken dialect.[11] It was the spoken dialect which was adopted by Buddha and Mahāvīra for their preaching and this must have given an impetus to the gradual standardization of new literary languages out of dialects. In the third century B.C. we find Aśoka inscribing his message in different dialects in different regions, presumably because they were current there. Aśoka's inscriptions clearly prove that the dialects in the north-west were much nearer classical Sanskrit than those current in the north-east. In the second century B.C. Patañjali wrote his celebrated *Mahābhāsya* from which it is indubitable that Sanskrit was still a spoken language, although it was the standard language spoken by the educated elite. And this time we have to remember that Patañjali is supposed to belong to the area of Aśoka, not Pāṇini! For long centuries after this Sanskrit continued to be the language of the educated classes while the uneducated spoke diverse dialects called Prākṛtas of which literary standardization also existed.

It must be clearly understood that the original relation of Sanskrit and Prākṛta is that of a standard language and its dialect. Prākṛtas cannot be regarded as different languages even after they were themselves given standard literary forms. Prakrit continues to be a synthetic language, only its grammar simplifies Sanskrit much in the same way as classical Sanskrit simplifies Vedic grammar. "Though simplified, yet the remaining Prakrit grammar is of the same type as Sanskrit grammar. There is a strong tendency to reduce all declensions to one type, that of *a*-stms, and to conjugate all verbs according to one scheme, that of the old A-conjugation."[12] The dative case disappears and so does the distinction between nominative and accusative plurals. Among verbal forms the imperfect, perfect and numerous Aorists disappeared by the time of the Middle Prakrit stage. Nor did the Atmanepada survive in any real sense. This simplification only shows how the spoken tongue tended to avoid subtle differences and complexities. What markedly distinguished Prakrit from Sanskrit was phonetic changes, in particular the tendency of Prakrit to assimilate conjunct consonants. This made words in Prakrit seem different from Sanskrit. Nevertheless the majority of words "could readily suggest a Sanskrit equivalent to anyone with a living colloquial knowledge of the classical language."[13] As a result the Prakrits were mutually intelligible and "A speaker of Sanskrit would readily understand any of the literary Prakrits."[14]

By the 7th Century A.D. the spoken dialects had greatly diverged from the literary Prakrits and Bāṇa tells us of a *Bhāṣā-Kavi*. The colloquial speech now developed as the various *Apabraṁśas* which despite their phonetic changes still retain a synthetic character. By the 12th Century the *Apabhraṁśas* too were standardized for literary purposes. Throughout the period Sanskrit remained the principal language used by the educated classes. Sanskrit drama has a convention by which upper class men speak in Sanskrit while most women characters speak in different Prakrits. This polyglot situation may be regarded as a conventional though not strictly realistic representation of the linguistic reality of ancient India. What it suggests is that educated upper class men were expected to be able to speak in Sanskrit while the men of the lower classes and most women were not expected to have education enough to do so. At the same time the speakers of Sanskrit and Prakrit all belonged to the same social world of communication. Grierson wrote, "In India there is nothing extraordinary in such a polyglot medley. It is paralleled by the conditions of any large house in Bengal at the present day."[15]

Sanskrit is sometimes described as a learned or dead language or even as an artificial language. It is certainly a learned language in the sense that its historically most conspicuous use was by the learned but it was not a learned language in the sense in which Persian and English have been learned languages in India. Sanskrit was rooted in India and its forms and vocabulary were directly connected with those of the spoken dialects. Although standard Sanskrit was regulated by the grammar of Pāṇini, that did not make it artificial. It is of the essence of language to have a structure and to seek to preserve it. Artificial languages are always limited subsets within a natural language such as Sanskrit has been. The notion of a dead language, again, is highly misleading. "We must remember that languages neither live nor die. They are used or cease to be used. Unlike 'death' disuse is a reversible process."[16] The point is amply illustrated by the modern cultivation of Gaelic and Hebrew. The solidarity of human nature and the similarities of the human environment—natural and social—lead to symbolic correspondences in languages. Part of the symbolism of language thus undoubtedly comes to have a transcultural aspect and makes cross-cultural communication possible.

Sanskrit and Indian Culture

At the same time every language is affected by the world-view of the culture in which it grows up. Linguistic symbols and basic cultural concepts are in effect inseparable. Indian culture and the Sanskrit language have been bound together for millennia. Sanskrit, in fact, is the basic articulation of the Indian psyche and some general and distinctive features of Sanskrit tend to reflect the structure of that psyche.

The Sanskrit language has been characterized from very early times by a very well defined phonetic system. It sharply distinguishes the consonants, keeps short and long vowels distinct, and simplifies complicated dipthongs of the Indo-European. It laid great stress on principles of *sandhi* and gradually lost the accent which it had in the Vedic period. It laid the greatest stress on accurate pronunciation and it came to be assumed that there is an eternal and divine system of sounds on which Sanskrit is based. Belief in the magical power of the correctly uttered word and sound came to be a common and persistent belief in India. "Even one word, properly known, fulfils desires here and hereafter."

While Vedic Sanskrit stresses active construction and the use of finite verbs in diverse forms and moods, classical Sanskrit gradually came to prefer the passive construction and finite verbs tended to be replaced by participles and relative clauses were increasingly subsumed in compounds of which the use became more and more prolific. The result was that while Vedic Sanskrit has a strident directness and dramatic quality, classical Sanskrit has a statuesque quality. Perhaps this is a profound reflection of a major change that came over Indian Culture.

The Sanskrit language has a remarkable transparency in its structure and formation, the result of generations of efforts by grammarians and students of language. All forms in the language follow a clearly formulated system of rules and all words are derived from about two thousand verbal roots by the addition of affixes. The language thus represents the form of the cosmos inasmuch as it is a derivation from permanent primary elements. The distinction between *prakṛti* and *vikṛti*, *dhātu* and *rūpa* is clearly exhibited by the language.

The orderliness of Sanskrit, again, reflects another aspect of the Indian psyche. While it was recognised that language is given rather than constructed and rests on convention, still its structure was formulated as a set of rules arising from authoritative prescription. Thus the linguistic order is at once conventional and scientific, given and constructed and in this respect it resembles the structure of *dharma* or social order.

The Sanskrit language is distinguished by its capacity for abstraction as well as ambiguity. It was widely believed that behind the visible, empirical world there is a subtler world of essences. For all logical and conceptual purposes this world of essences was held to be really significant. For every word Sanskrit forms an abstract noun by a simple and uniform rule and the abstract noun can then be used quite easily. It is in philosophical and logical writings that the full potentiality of this feature was realized. Navyanyāya, in fact, is able to develop a logic as abstract and analytical as modern logic with the help of the tool of language.

The ambiguity of Sanskrit arises partly by the fondness for ellipsis and partly by the wealth of synonymns. So long as a continuity of interpretative tradition existed within the school to which the writing belonged, ambiguity was not an obstruction. This was the case with ancient *sūtra* works, for example. Unfortunately, the continuity of such interpretative tradition was often interrupted, with the result that the same *sūtras* in the *Brahmasūtras,* for example, could come to be interpreted quite diversely by later commentators. The growth of synonyms was partly the result of the language losing its contact with actual life and becoming increasingly a language of scholars. As a result even idiom came to lose its force and the language tended to rely more and more on deliberate constructs. This feature of ambiguity and to some extent artificial construction which came to characterise the late classical language, again, reflected a social and cultural process which was taking place at the time.

Myth as Symbol

The modern study of mythology labours under the belief that primitive and archaic thought was essentially irrational. Animism, animatism, fetishism, totemism etc., have been regarded as leading principles of ancient religious thought in the light of which myths are to be understood.[17] Mythology has even been regarded as a disease of language,[18] with which may be compared the modern positivistic diagnosis of metaphysics itself as a disease of language. Modern researchers have discovered and classified a vast amount of data from a comparative study of myths but unfortunately diverse and conflicting principles have been proposed for their interpretation. At the same time most of these theoretical frameworks suffer from a positivistic or Christian bias. Myths are assumed to be irrational fancies arising from diverse social, psychological, linguistic and environmental conditions. Thus studied myths may be expected to throw light on primitive mentality, society and culture. Unfortunately the whole procedure rests on general assumptions which are said to be scientific but are really philosophical and cultural.

What is indisputable is that the myths were regarded in the past as being part of an immemorial sacred lore. They were valued as communications of deep wisdom about the gods, not as the fancies or inventions of poets or story-tellers. Even though the myths have the form of narratives recounting actions from past times, they are more appropriately understood as the symbolic expression of timeless theological truths. Attempts have been made to explain the myth as a specific symbolic form[19] with its own sense of the basic categories. Cassirer envisages "a kind of grammar of symbolic function as such which would encompass and generally help to define its special terms and idioms as we encounter them in language and art, in myth and religion."[20] The task of the historian would be "to penetrate into the sense of all the various symbolic idioms".[21] Behind arbitrary symbols lies the 'natural symbolism' of consciousness i. e. "that representation of consciousness as a whole which is necessarily contained or at least projected in every single moment and fragment of consciousness."[22] This 'natural symbolism' operates differently in different cultural forms. Myth, thus, has its own mode of conceiving and representing objects, their relations and the self. It is characteristic of the myth to "know only immediate existence and immediate efficacy."[23] Myth lacks any dividing line between mere representation and 'real' perception, "between wish and fulfilment, between image and thing."[24] This urgent immediacy of consciousness in the myth makes it the primal image of the destiny of a people. "It is not by its history that the mythology of a nation is determined but conversely, its history is determined by its mythology—or rather, the mythology of a people does not *determine* but *is* its fate, its destiny as decreed from the very beginning. The whole history of the Hindus, Greeks etc., was implicit in their gods."[25]

Cassirer's idealistic historical approach sees in myth the representation of cultural destiny i. e. destiny of a specific historical expression of self-consciousness. This approach brings out the significance of myth as the expression of a specific cultural consciousness in terms of images cohering by a characteristic non-rational logic. It misses, however, the connection of myth with wisdom, a connection to be brought out hermeneutically. This connection of myth with wisdom was recognised in the ancient tradition, western as well as Indian. In seeking to communicate his deepest ideas through the use of myth, Plato was appealing to a traditionally recognised vehicle of wisdom. The *Nirukta* was the Indian counterpart of hermeneutic and found its model in the *Brāhmaṇas*. In the post-Vedic period the *Purāṇas* took over the mythical tradition.[26] What characterizes this tradition is that while it is rooted in intuitive wisdom, it is clothed in imaginative form. While imagination gives to myth a dream-like structure, its symbolic connection with wisdom gives it meaning and value.

Myths relate to the birth and deeds of gods. Thus Ṛ. 1.32.1 begins by saying *"Indrasya nu vīryāṇi pra vocaṁ yāni cakāra prathamāni vajrī"*. The seer announces "Of Indra now I will declare the mighty deeds, those primordial ones accomplished by the bearer of the thunder-bolt". Similarly Ṛ. 10.72.1 begins thus—*"Devānāṁ nu vayam jānā pra vocāma vipanyayā ukthesu śasyamāneṣu yaḥ paśyād uttare yuge."* "Of gods now we would declare the births in adoration so that when (these) hymns are sung even in future ages the gods would know."

The birth of gods is not an event in time; it is the manifestation of the unmanifest unity in specific cosmic forms as the first step in cosmogenesis. "The Lord of the Holy word produced the gods like a smith producing a blaze with bellows (for smelting). Thus in the ancient age of the gods, *sat* arose from *asat*." Then arose the quarters and the earth and *Dakṣa* and *Aditi* mutually produced each other. From *Aditi* arose the gods, kinsmen of immortality. They danced on the formless deep and their feet raised up dust and out of that all the worlds were solidified. The sun hidden in the sea was brought forth. This was the eighth son of Aditi called *Mārtaṇḍa*. With her other seven sons Aditi went to the former age of immortality. *Mārtaṇḍa* was left behind to preside over the birth and death of creatures.[27]

Dakṣa is power or skill, *Aditi* is unboundedness; they are the twin parents of the gods. "But the unmanifest and the manifest lie in the highest heaven in the lap of *Aditi,* the birth place of *Dakṣa*".[28] *Dakṣa* is the skill of acting rightly or ritually. Hence *Dakṣa* was later identified with Prajāpati, the lord of creation and sacrifice.[29] The nature of *Aditi* has been much disputed.[30] It may be suggested that *Aditi* like *Prakṛti* is the original mother being unbounded by existential specificities. Later she was considered the daughter of *Dakṣa*.[31]

The mutual birth of *Dakṣa* and *Aditi* is a paradox which the *Nirukta* explains in terms of the incomprehensible power of the gods *"api vā devadharmenetaretarajanmānau syātāmitare-tara-prakṛti"*.[32] In fact this *māhābhāgya* of the gods explains all the paradoxes about them—they are in essence one though praised in many ways, they may be born of one another, they are self-born and the purpose of their birth is the performance of some cosmic function.[33] This idea of the unity of gods in terms of substance may be traced back to the *Ṛk-saṁhitā*.[34] From this *aikātmya* proceeds plurality (*nānātva*) through infinite power or partibility (*māhābhāgya*).[35] The Ritualists or *Yājñikas* emphasized the plurality of the gods while the Philosophers or *Ātmavidah* emphasized their unity.[36] The Hermeneutists or *Nairuktas* classified the gods into three—terrestrial, atmospheric and celestial. *Agni* is the terrestrial god, *Vāyu* or *Indra* is the atmospheric god, and *Sūrya* is the celestial god. The multiplicity of gods is due to the multiplicity of names, functions and ritualistic injunctions. The unity of thus diversified gods consists in their collocation and cooperation. This unity in diversity is like that of men and society.[37]

Like the question of the Unity and multiplicity of gods was the question of their being sentient or insentient. The *Nirukta* concludes that the gods could be regarded as either or both, again, on account of their *māhābhāgya*.[38] Thus the myths are free to personify the gods or describe them as natural forms. Such modes of description do not exclude the inherent infinity of gods nor their relevance to cosmic functioning or ritualistic worship. The same divine powers which function impersonally at the cosmic level respond as sentient persons to the worship of the human individual.

Agni was first born of Heaven, *'Divaspari prathamaṁ jajñe agniḥ'*.[39] *Śatapatha* explains this to mean that the first birth of Agni was from Prāṇa.[40] For the second time Agni was born of men on earth, *'asmad dvitīyam pari jātavedāḥ'*. His third birth was in the waters, *'tṛtīyam apsu'*. This third birth is supposed to refer to fire as lightening. Fire is even said to have run away from the gods and hid himself in water where the gods and the Bhṛgus discovered him after much search.[41] Agni is the illuminer, literally and metaphorically.[42] He is the celestial wisdom established on earth as the power of worship and vision for man. Hence he is the mediator between men and gods. Men must kindle Agni daily and this takes force. They must tend him with care and nourish him with sacrifice. He would then take up the offering and convey it to the gods. Cosmically Agni is the sun in heaven and the lightening born of atmospheric waters. Hidden in water, he comes down to earth and nourishes plants and trees.[43] Through the friction of wood men produce him in a visible form. As sacrificial fire he points to the path of return to immortality.

The myths of the triple and dual births of Agni and of his hiding and discovery point to the duality latent in human spiritual life which depends on human effort as well as divine grace. What is unborn has to be produced, what is hidden has to be discovered. "Seizing all manliness and frightening the gods, He concealed Himself. The wise heroes find Him here when they chant the *Mantras* carved out of the heart. (It is Agni) who holds aloft the earth and heaven by true *Mantras,* as if unborn. May He, the lord of all creature, though concealed secretly in the cave, protect His dear places and animals. Who knows Agni in concealment and reaches the stream of *Ṛta,* who tends Him and prays to Him, to him does He declare all good things."[44]

If the mythology of Agni is as transparent as his form is visible, the opposite is the case with the principal Vedic god Indra who is located in the atmosphere. He is the most anthropomorphized of Vedic gods but has no visible embodiment in nature. He is said to have been born of *Aditi* and *Dyaus*[45] but is accused of having killed his father.[46] It is said he insisted on being born from the right side of his mother instead of in the usual way. He was born in the house of *Tvaṣṭṛ* and drank huge quantities of *Soma.* Having drunk *Soma* he performed mighty deeds and the chief of these was the slaying of *Vṛtra.*[47] According to Yāska the function of Indra is to provide sap, kill *Vṛtra* and perform all manner of deeds of prowess —*"athāsya karma rasānupradānaṁ vṛtravadho yā ca kā ca balakṛtiḥ indrakarmaiva tat."*[48]

The conflict of Indra and Vṛtra is the most important Vedic example of the theme of *Devāsura-saṁgrāma.* Gods are forces of light and cosmic creativity. Their struggle against the forces of darkness and chaos is original and perennial. The myth refers at once to creation and to salvation, to the subduing of chaos outside and within. The myth of the Indra-Vṛtra conflict has been described at numerous places, e. g., in Ṛ. 212. Here the hymn apparently addresses the people (*janāsaḥ*) and extolls the mighty deeds of Indra.[49] The third stanza says :

Yo hatvā him ariṇāt sapta sindhūn

Yo gā udājad apadhā valasya/

Yo aśmanorantaragniṁ jajāna

Samvṛk samatsu sa janāsa indraḥ//

This may be translated as—'who having killed the Serpent caused the Seven Streams to flow, who drove out the Cows by the setting aside of *vala,* who produced fire between the Rocks, (who is) the victor in battles he O people, is Indra.' We have commented elsewhere on the Seven Streams.[49a] The Serpent or *Vala* is the Prince of Darkness, the Enemy *par excellence. Vala* probably has the sense of one who covers or encloses, which is the sense of *Vṛtra.*[50] The cows are the Rays and alternate with the Streams. The Rocks are the clouds and Fire lightening. The eleventh stanza refers to the myth again: "who in the fortieth autumn found out Śambara dwelling in the mountains; who has slain the serpent as he showed his strength, the son of Dānu, as he lay; he, O men, is Indra" (Macdonell). Dānu is clearly referred to as the mother of Vṛtra—*Ṛ*. 1.32.9. The next stanza speaks of the mighty Sprinkler with seven rays or reins *(sapta-raśmir vṛṣabhaḥ)*, who released the seven streams to flow. From other hymns we learn that the Seers (*aṅgirases*) and the Maruts aid Indra in this conflict after which the sun shines forth. Vṛtra, thus, is not simply the demon of drought and the Indra-Vṛtra myth a fanciful explanation of rain, Vṛtra is also the demon of darkness; the darkness that lies deep inside the cave and prevents the outflow of water. Water, again, is not simply physical water but the powers of healing, purification and creativity. Basically water is the symbol of impulse or desire and hence also of higher impulses which are purifying and creative. The cave has been an age-old symbol of the heart and it is the darkness and inertness in the heart which needs to be eradicated by divine help. The intervention of Indra requires man's own effort in this moral and spiritual struggle. Man must invoke the power of knowledge symbolized by the sun, the power of prayer and the power of the disciplined band of feelings and impulses symbolized by the Maruts. At the same time Vṛtra or Ahi symbolizes the primaeval chaos later represented by waters covered by darkness. *"Nāsadāsīn na sadāsīt tadānīm". "Āpovā idam agra āsan".* The *Purāṇas* describe this state of chaos as *Pralaya* in which Viṣṇu sleeps on the Great Serpent in the 'Waters of non-existence'.[51]

At one level, thus, the myth refers to the atmospheric phenomena of storm, lightening and rain falling from clouds, at another to the victory of the divine spirit over the enemy and the release of creative or spiritual energy. The former is the interpretation of the *Nairuktas,* the latter of the *Ātmavidaḥ.*[52]

The notion of struggle between the gods and the ungodly forces is a common notion in later Vedic literature. The *Brahmaṇas* thus describe the conflict of gods and demons in diverse contexts. Here is an example—*Śatapatha* 9.51.12ff—*"Devāścāsurāścobhayā prājāpatyāḥ prajāpateḥ piturdāyam upeyur vācameva śattyānṛte...te devā utsṛjyānṛtaṁ sattyam anvālebhire'surā u hotsṛjya sattyam anṛtam anvālebhire."*

Devas and Asuras were both the progeny of Prajāpati and both obtained the same paternal legacy, speech which is the same as truth and falsehood. But gods abandoned falsehood and stuck to truth while the demons abandoned truth and chose falsehood. Again, we find in *Śatapatha,* 2.4.2.1-5 that the creatures which Prajāpati made came to him to seek arrangements for their living. To gods he said, "Receive sacrifice as your food, immortality as your life-force, and the sun as your light-sphere." To the *pitṛs* he said, "Receive the funeral offerings of each month as your food, the *svadhā* libation as your mind-swiftness and the moon as your light-sphere." To the race of men, he said, "Night and morning shall you eat, your offspring shall be your death and fire your light-sphere." To animals be said, "Eat as chance allows, how. when and where you will." To the Asuras "he assigned darkness and power. The power of the Asuras does indeed exist." "All those beings, it is true, have perished, but beings continue to live according to the ordinance Prajāpati has given them."[53]

In the *Upaniṣads,* again, Indra as the leader of gods and Vairocana as the leader of the Asuras are contrasted types of humanity. The *asuras* are satisfied with sensuous life and regard the body as the true self devoting their efforts to caring for the body and decking it up. Indra seeks self-knowledge. The *Bhagavad Gītā* distinguishes *daivī sampat* and *āsurī sampat,* and describes Arjuna as characterized by the former. The *Daivī sampat* consists of moral and spiritual qualities, the *āsurī sampat* of egoistic, acquisitive and aggressive traits of character. By implication the Pāṇḍavas and Kauravas exemplify the two groups—*daiva* and *āsura*. As Professor Sukhthankar has said the meaning of the *Mahābhārata* lies in its symbolizing the moral struggle where victory belongs to those who have faith in God.[54] Similarly the *Rāmāyaṇa* with its struggle of Rāma and Rāvaṇa came to be regarded as more than a merely heroic and romantic tale. Rāma and Rāvaṇa have been taken through the ages as the symbols of Right and Wrong. Annual festivals have preserved and popularized the memory of the war of Rāma against Rāvaṇa ever since.

The deeds of the Vedic gods were performed in 'the beginning', before historic time began. The stage for their deeds too was cosmic, not localized on earth. As the doctrine of incarnation came to be formulated, it was held that gods have been born in each human age to destroy ungodly forces and give succour to the righteous man. Appropriate accounts of the birth and deeds of the various incarnations were thus elaborated in the *Purāṇas*. The age when the *Purāṇas* received their final form was an age when plastic art and popular syncretism profoundly affected religious imagination. Vedic ritualistic tradition had declined and along with it a sea-change took place in the popularity and conception of the older gods. Great Vedic gods like Indra and Varuṇa became minor deities. Anthropomorphism and iconographic representation became common. Viṣṇu and Rudra-Śiva became along with the mother-goddess the principal deities. Sūrya undoubtedly remained important but some wholly new gods like Ganeśa emerged. Old myths were modified or newly elaborated.

The very conception of the *Purāṇas* underwent a change. The *Purāṇas* went back in some form to the Vedic age but traditionally they were supposed to deal with five topics—creation, dissolution, genealogies of gods and sages, the legends of kings and royal dynasties and the cosmic cycles (*Manvantaras*).[55] In the Kuṣāṇa and Gupta periods new versions of the *Purāṇas* come to be produced with a much enlarged and miscellaneous scope.[56]

The doctrine of incarnation was specially connected with Viṣṇu who was a minor solar deity in the *Ṛgveda.* The most important myth about him was that he took 'three steps of which the third is invisible.' *"Idaṁ viṣṇur vicakrame Tredhā nidadhe padam."*[57] He was closely connected with Indra but superseded him in course of time. In the later Vedic age he assumes special importance and identification with the sacrifice. Along with his three steps we meet with the idea of his assumption of a dwarf form.[58] The two appear to have come together in course of time and became the basis of the Purāṇic Vāmana incarnation. The *Brāhmaṇas* also contain stories of the connection of sacrifice or creation with Varāha or boar, fish and tortoise.[59] All these became in the *Purāṇas* recognized incarnations of Viṣṇu. However, the most popular of the incarnations of Viṣṇu, Rāma and Kṛṣṇa, appear to have belonged originally to romantic or historical legend, rather than mythology. Kṛṣṇa appears as a historical figure in the *Chāndogya* but was not yet deified. The deification apparently took place in the post-Vedic but pre-Mauryan age. Rāma appears as an adventurous hero in Vālmīki's *Rāmāyaṇa* but was deified before the epic reached its present form. The classical accounts of Rāma and Kṛṣṇa in any case continue to have primarily the aspect of heroic legend and biography, not myth in the ancient sense. Myths are included in these accounts but do not constitute their principal strands—even the portrayal of Hanumān and Rāvaṇa in Vālmīki is more human than supernatural. In any case, that animals and demons should participate in the story is reminiscent of fable and folklore than of mythology. Perhaps the story of Hanumān goes back to some non-Vedic myth.[60]

In the *Ṛksaṁhitā* Rudra appears as the father of the *Maruts,* a fierce god who is implored to be kind. He is described as an archer—*sthiradhanvā, Kṣipreṣu*—and also as one who casts down thunder-bolts and yet was the healer, holding cool medicinal plants in his hands.[61] He was described as *Tryambaka* in the most famous charm against death, which is still in wide use among the Hindus.[62] About the origin of Rudra the most significant myth is related in the *Aitareya*

Brāhmaṇa.[63] Prajāpati consorted with his own daughter whom some identify with the heaven and some with Dawn. The gods were enraged and their fierce aspects came together to form a new and fierce god, Rudra—*"Yā eva ghoratamās tanvā āsanstā ekadhā samabhavan."* For piercing Prajāpati Rudra was given the boon of becoming the "lord of beasts". Prajāpati since then remains the *Mṛgaśiras nakṣattra, Rudra* the *Mṛgavyādha,* Prajāpati's daughter *Rohiṇī* and the arrow of Rudra, *Iṣu Trikāṇḍa.* Rudra, thus, has the divine charge of animals, of instinctive life and is the destroyer of sin especially the basic sin of *Kāma* as represented by the primordial or uninhibited *libido.* He is the embodiment of divine wrath at grievous sin.

In the *Śvetāśvatara* Rudra-Śiva is turned into the supreme god to be placated by Yoga and adoration. According to a Purāṇic myth he was the original pillar of light when the world was not yet manifested. This shaft of light, without beginning or end, was the original Sign or *Liṅga.*[64] The occasional Vedic identification of fire and Rudra and the more frequent identification of fire and the Sun as also the Vedic notion of *Skambha* perhaps contain the seed of the idea of conceiving creative light as a pillar.[65] It may be recalled that the pillar was a primal element in all kinds of constructional contexts.[66] In the cosmic context it easily stood for the central axis or support.[67] How the *liṅga* came to be connected with the male organ of generation is not exactly known since the Vedic evidence is almost silent on the question.[68] Vedic thought certainly interpreted the creativity and strength of gods in terms of maleness. How they represented the idea is not known. In the post-Vedic period Śiva is clearly represented by *liṅga* understood in a phallic sense. This feature is sometimes traced back to the Indus civilization but the identification of the so-called phallic stones has been too lightly assumed.

Of the myths centring on Śiva the one which relates his marriage to Pārvatī has been told most immortally by Kālidāsa in the *Kumārasambhava.* Śiva is unborn and aloof, immersed in Yoga but the gods have been defeated by the *asura* Tāraka and need a saviour. A part of Śiva must be born to become the leader of the divine host. Pārvatī, the daughter of the Himālaya, must be married to Śiva so that a son may be born. As the efforts of Eros fail since he is burnt down by Śiva, Pārvatī proceeds to win Śiva by the force of penance and at last succeeds. The union of Śiva and Pārvatī has to be understood as the union of two halves of an integral unity, of eternal consciousness and its infinite though mysterious power.

The antiquity of the mother-goddess is undoubted and may go back to prehistoric times. The Indus civilization shows female figurines and ring-stones which have been connected with the mother-goddess. Early Vedic literature knows of several mother-goddesses—*Aditi, Pṛthvī, Sarasvatī, Vāk, Āpaḥ, Uṣas, Śraddhā*. Umā Haimavatī occurs in the later Vedic literature.[69] The independent worship of the mother-goddess in classical times tended to look upon the goddess as *Parā Prakṛti* and interpreted her nature in terms of the power of consciousness. Already this can be seen in the *Śvetāśvatara* where *Prakṛti* and *Māyā* are identified and the triple power of the Lord is referred to.[70]

Among the most influential myths connected with the mother-goddess in the *Purāṇas* may be mentioned that of Durgā and her three forms—*Mahākālī, Mahālakṣmī* and *Mahāsarasvatī*. This account in Seven Hundred Verses in the *Mārkaṇḍeya Purāṇa* is still recited or heard by large numbers all over the country especially in Bengal. The great *Navarātra* festival centres round the worship of Durgā and the recitation of the *Saptaśatī*.

In the *Ṛ*. we have *"Indro māyābhiḥ puru-rūpa īyate"*.[71] *Māyā* is the magical power of Indra by which he assumes diverse forms. It is at once creative and delusive. The *Upaniṣads* call it the will of the Lord, which expresses Him but hides Him. That same power in view of its inherent divinity is called here *Mahāmāyā*. The account begins with the predicament of a prince and a merchant who have been driven out of their kingdom and family respectively but still cannot forget them. They both repair to a hermitage where a sage explains that their helplessness is due to the power of *Mahāmāyā* which makes the force of irrational instincts greater than that of merely intellectual reason. The spririt is initially bound by *Mahāmāyā* as *tamas* or inertia and in this form she is symbolised as *Mahākālī*. As *Mahālakṣmī* she is the light of all the gods aggregated as a supergoddess and destroys the demons Caṇḍa and Muṇḍa. As *Mahāsarasvatī* she kills the demons Śumbha and Niśumbha. Through the worship of *Mahāmāyā* one gains success in this world as well as emancipation hereafter.

Vedic ritual fundamentally symbolized the act of creation. It constituted an act of worship since to worship was to attune oneself to the gods. In the later Vedic literature the symbolism of creation was elaborately worked out in the construction of special altars or *agnicayana*.[72] In a diluted measure sacrifice was part of the sacramental ritual which pervaded the course of individual life. In Vedic ritual solar symbolism played a large part. The sun stood for light and life. He was identified with the source of wisdom and knowledge and also *prāṇa*. The identity of all the luminaries was realized and the sun was held to be the source of them all. The fire was the same power on earth as the lightening was in the atmosphere and the sun in the heavens. The sun through its changing position was the source of the seasons, of heat and the rains, and the regulator of the year. The sun, thus, was held to be the power of Time. Not only did He preside over human mortality but through Him lay the way to Immortality. The sun, in short, symbolized the *Saguṇa Brahman* but while the sun was a natural symbol, the ritual symbolized the sun in diverse ways.

In the Pravargya rite, for example, the pot called *Mahāvīra* stands for the sun and the milk heated in it is the divine energy which falls to the share of the sacrificer. In the *Aśvamedha* the horse itself symbolizes the sun.

The counterpart of the sun and the fire was the *soma*, the divine substance on which the cosmic energy was fed. Energy and matter, *Prāṇa* and *Rayi*, constitute a dyad. Creation is the transformation of energy and matter. The fire in the *Vedi* into which *soma* is sacrificed, symbolizes this creative process. In contrast to the sun the *soma* came to be latterly identified with the moon and just as the sun was the cosmic source of *Prāṇa, soma* came to be regarded as the cosmic source of the *manas* or mind. The sacrifice of the *soma* was, thus, the merging of the mind into cosmic *Prāṇa*. Even the animal sacrifices contained the notion of self-sacrifice and redemption for the animal was a substitute for man. "The oblation is verily the initiate– (*havir vai dikṣitaḥ*)". In Purāṇic ritual we find a sea-change. Worship now is homage paid to personal gods. The forms of homage are modelled on social practice. The gods are invited, seated, offered water, eatables, clothes, sandal paste etc. It is, however, realized that these offerings are being made to Gods who do not need them. The real offering consists only in recalling the majesty of the gods.

Purāṇic and Tāntric rites are by and large continuous though a distinction may be made between the external worship or *pūjā* with diverse *upacāras* or means and internal worship which is essentially symbolic. Tantric worship in esoteric *maṇḍalas* could be inspired by *Vāmācāra,* in which case it used wine and sex symbolically. The basic symbolism in such cases was that of the Union of Śiva and Śakti and the creative joy of such union symbolized by Wine called *'Kāraṇa* or cause'. As far back as the *Śatapatha* one can trace the idea of the divine couple and the joy of their union. The use of the *Yantras* or diagrams was another symbolic device used in Tāntric worship. These used geometric symbols like triangles, circles etc. Perhaps the most famous of the *Yantras* is *Śrī-yantra*. Its core consists of nine triangles emerging from a central point. Five have their vertices downwards and are called female, five point upwards and are called male. Creation and dissolution, time and eternity, becoming and being, *Śakti* and *Śiva* are here locked in an "uninterrupted series of lightening flashes." "This composition summarizes in a single moment the whole sense of the Hindu world of myth and symbol."[73] Among its most moving commemorations in verse may be mentioned the *Saundaryalaharī* of Śaṅkarācārya.

The cycle of festivals included popular elements. In classical times *Kaumudī-mahotsava* on the day of *Śaratpūrṇimā, Yakṣarātri* which later on came to be called *Dīpamālikā, Vasanta* and *Madana-mahotsava* constituted the principal annual festivals. Of these the second and the fourth have fully survived with transformations as *Diwali* and *Holi.* The former was originally a kind of winter All Souls festival of which parallels can be found in mediaeval Europe. It celebrated the 'night of the Yakṣas'.[74] The connection of the lord of the Yakṣas, Kuvera, with Lakṣmī tended to make it gradually an Apollonian instead of a Dionysian festival and the lighting of lamps became more important than the invocation of spirits of the dark.[75] *Madana-mahotsava,* again, was probably a harvest festival and had elements of fertility rite. It was the festival of the god of love (Eros) celebrated with great eclat and was essentially a mixed festival.[76] Incourse of time, however, this festival came to be considerably vulgarized. The place of *Kaumudī mahotsava* was gradually taken up by the *Navarātra* and *Dashera* festival.

REFERENCES

1. *Vide* my *Apohasiddhi.*

2. Cf. Candrakīrti ad *Madhyamaka,* pp. 68ff.

3. *Nyāyamuktāvalī,* p. 266. *"Navyāstu īśvarecchā na śaktiḥ, Kiṅtvicchaiva",* Cf. Badarinatha, Sukla, in *Bhāratīya Bhāṣā—Śāstrīya Cintana* (ed. V. N. Misra), p. 70.

4. But contra Badarinatha Sukla, *op. cit.,* p. 64. *Śābda pramā* may be a unique type of cognition but can its validity be decided without examining the credentials of the speakers ?

5. Cf. *Sarvadarśanasaṅgraha,* pp. 101ff; *Brahmasūtras.* 1.3.29.

6. Cf. Śaṅkara's critique of *sphoṭa* in *Śārīraka-bhāṣya,* pp. 124ff.

7. Cf. Hārāṇacandra Bhaṭṭacharya, '*Vāktattvavimarśa*' in *Sarasvatī Bhavan Studies,* Vol. X, pp. 124-32.

8. G. C. Pande, 'The Life and Death of Language', *Diogenes,* 51, pp. 193-94.

9. The protagonists of Dravidian are more numerous among scholars.

10. Cf. *The Vedic Age,* p. 210. If the reference in the Boghaz koi records of treaties is to Vedic gods, Aryan immigration should be placed in the first half of the 2nd mill. B. C. But the whole concept of 'Aryan immigration' in historical times is supposititious.

11. Cf. S. K. Chatterjee, *Bhāratīya Ārya Bhāṣā Aur Hindi,* pp. 64-65.

12. A. C. Woolner, *Introduction to Prākrit* (3rd. ed.), pp. 7-8.

13-14. *Ib.,* p. 9.

15. Quoted, Woolner, *op. cit.,* p. 91.

16. G. C. Pande, *op. cit.,* p. 206.

17. Such is the assumption, for example, in Macdonell, *Vedic Mythology ;* Cf. Keith's critique of the current theories of the origin of religion, *RPV* Vol. I, pp. 42ff.

18. Such is the view which was adumbrated by Karl Otfried Müller, *Prolegomena zu einer wissenschaftlichen Mythologie,* 1825. Max Müller sought to trace the influence of reified metaphor in the development of Vedic mythology.

19. Cassirer, *Philosophy of Symbolic Forms,* 3 vols.

20. *Ib.,* Vol. I, p. 86.

21. *Ib.,* Vol. I, p. 177.

22. *Ib.,* Vol. I, p. 105.

23. *Ib.,* Vol. II, p. 63.

24. *Ib.,* Vol. II, p. 36.

25. *Ib.,* Vol. II, p. 5.

26. Cf. "*Aitareya-taittirīya-Kāṭhakādi-Śākhā-sūktāni Hariścandra-Nāciketādyupākhyānāni dharma-brahmāvabodha-yuktāni*

teṣu teṣvitihāsa-grantheṣu spaṣṭīkṛtāni Upaniṣaduktāḥ sṛṣṭisthiti-layādayo 'pi Brāhma-Pādma-Vaiṣṇavādi-purāṇeṣu spaṣṭīkṛtāḥ." Sāyaṇa's comy. ad *Ṛ.*, Vol. I, pp. 21-22.

27. *Ṛ.*, 10.72.2-9.

28. *Ṛ.*, 10.5.7 : *Asacca sacca parame vyoman dakṣasya janmannaditer upasthe.*

29. *Śatapatha*, 2.4.4.1-2.

30. See Macdonell, *Vedic Mythology*, 41.

31. "*Yadaitihāsikā āhuh Aditir dākṣāyaṇīti*"—Durga on *Nirukta* (ed. Bhandarkar), Vol. II, p. 1066.

32. *Ib.*, p. 1064.

33. "*māhābhāgyād devatāyā eka ātma bahudhā stūyate ekasyātmano'nye devāh pratyaṅgāni bhavanti api ca...prakṛtisārvanāmnyāccetaretara-janmāno bhavantiitaretaraprakṛtayaḥ Karmajanmāna ātmajanmānaḥ...*" (*Nirukta*—ed. *Ānandāśrama* ed., Vol. II, p. 625).

34. *Ṛ.*, 1.164.46.

35. Coomaraswamy renders *māhābhāgya* as 'great partibility'.

36. Durga on *Nirukta* (*Ānandāśrama* ed.), Vol. II, pp. 636ff.

37. "*Tatraitan nara-rāṣṭramiva*", *Nirukta*, Vol. II, p. 636.

38. Cf. Durga, *op. cit.*, p. 655.

39. *Ṛ.*, 10.45.1.

40. *Śatapatha*, 6.7.4.3., quoted by Sāyaṇa.

41. *Ṛ.*, 10.46.2 ; *Ib.*, 1.65.

42. "*Athāsya Karma vahanaṁ ca haviṣām āvahanaṁ ca devatānāṁ yacca Kiñcid darṣṭi-viṣayikam agnikarmaiva tad.*" *Nirukta*, Vol. II, p. 656.

43. Cf. Bergaigne, *op. cit.*

44. *Ṛ.* 1.67.4-7.

45. Macdonell, *op. cit.*

46. *Ṛ.* 4.18.12.

47. *e. g., Ib.* 1.32.

48. *Nirukta,* Vol. II, p. 653.

49. According to the tradition of the *Nirukta* Gṛtsamada is here addressing the demons who have mistaken him for Indra ! (Durga on *Nirukta, daivata-kāṇḍa,* 10.1.10) ; so *Bṛhaddevatā* and the *Mbh.*—see Sāyaṇa on Ṛ. 2.12).

49a. Vide my *Aspects of Indian Culture & Civilization* (1985).

50. Cf. *"Vṛtro ha va idaṁ sarvaṁ vṛtvā śiśye, yadidamantareṇa ayāvāpṛthivī tasmādvṛtronāma"* (*Śatapatha,* Vol. I, pp. 8-9).

51. Vide Zimmer, *Myths and Symbols in Indian Art and Civilization,* pp. 35ff.

52. *Nirukta,* 7.3.3—*"asya karma rasānupradānam Vṛtravadho..."* Sāyaṇa tends to follow this—comy. ad Ṛ. 2.12.3 ; Cf. Anirvan ; *Veda mīmāṁsā,* Vol. III, pp. 618ff; Cf. Madhu sudana Ojha, *Indravijaya,* II, pp. 102-103 where the struggle of Indra with Vṛtra and Sambara is construed as a kind of history. Modern interpretations support the interpretation of the myth in terms of natural phenomena—e. g. Keith, *op. cit.,* Vol. I, pp. 126-27.

53. Panikkar, *Mantramañjarī,* pp. 383-84.

54. *The Meaning of the Mahābhārata.*

55. *Amarakośa.* The *Purāṇas* had been composed out of old tales (*ākhyānas*), anecdotes (*upākhyānas*), songs (*gāthās*) and immemorial lore (*Kalpajokti*)—Hazra, *Purāṇic Records,* pp. 4-5.

56. Hazra, *op. cit.,* pp. 188-89.

57. Ṛ. 1.22.17. Yāska comments on it and mentions several interpretations—*Nirukta, daivata-kāṇḍa,* 6.2.

58. *Śatapatha,* Vol. I, pp. 28ff: the gods and *asuras* wished to divide the earth and the *asuras* agreed to give up as much as may be covered by Viṣṇu lying down. Now Viṣṇu was dwarfish—*"Vāmano ha Viṣṇur āsa".*

59. Cf. Keith, *op. cit.,* pp. 111-12.

60. The only Vedic source would be *Vṛṣākapi* of which

the interpretation is doubtful. There is no clarity about any Dravidian derivation.

61. *e. g., Ṛ.* 7.46.

62. This is the *mahāmṛtyuñjaya mantra.* Modern scholars diversely debate the meaning of *Tryambaka*—e. g., see Keith, *op. cit.,* Vol. I, p. 143.

63. *AB,* Vol. I, pp. 375ff.

64. Cf. S. N. Roy, *Historical and Cultural Studies in the Purāṇas,* pp. 263ff.

65. This goes against an originally phallic meaning of *liṅga* such as is argued by Gopinath Rao, *Elements of Hindu Iconography,* Vol. II, Pt. I., pp. 56-58.

66. Cf. *Harṣacarita,* 1.1; *'Trailokya-nagarārambha-mūlastambhāya śambhave.'* Cf. *"Nagarārambhe hi mūlastambho bhavati. Tatra ca paṭṭa bandhādivodutprekṣanānantaram unnate pṛṣṭhadeśe candratulyaṁ śvetaṁ cāmaraṁ kriyata itisthitiḥ"* (Śaṅkara's comy.).

67. Coomarswamy—*liṅga* as *axis mundi* f.n. to Zimmer, *op. cit.*

68. For the story of the Dāruvana, *Vāmana Purāṇa.*

69. *Kenopaniṣad.*

70. *'Māyāṁ tu prakṛtiṁ vidyān māyinaṁ tu maheśvaram'.*

71. Cf. "*Māyā* is precisely the maker's power or art. Magic in Jacob Boehme's sense", Coomarswamy, in Zimmer, *op. cit.,* p. 24 f.n.

72. *Śatapatha,* 10.5.4.10ff. "The Year indeed is this fire which has been piled up. Its nights are the *parisrit* which are three hundred and sixty even as are the nights. The days are the *Yajuṣmatī* bricks... These are the twin foundations: gold and lotus leaf, waters and the solar orb, two ladles, two arms, they are Indra and Agni; the two *svayamātṛṇṇā* bricks are the earth and the atmosphere; the three *Viśvajyotis* bricks are the gods Agni, Vāyu, and Āditya...".

Ib. 10.5.2ff. *yad etan maṇḍalam tapati-saiṣā trayyeva vidyā tapati...athādhiyajnaṁ-yadetan mandalaṁ tapatyayam sa rukmah adhyātmam-yadetan mandalam tapati...sa yoyam daksine ksan purusah...sa esa evendrah...atheyam indrāni... tau hrdayasyākāśam pratyetya mithunībhavatah...atha haitat purusah'ḥ svapiti...daivam hyetan mithụnam paramohyeṣa ānandah...".*

73. Zimmer, *op. cit.*, p. 140.

74. Cf. Yaśodhara's Comy. on the *Kāmasūtras.*

75. Cf. P. K. Gode, *Studies,* 3 vols. for the history of festivals.

76. Cf. Harṣa's *Ratnāvalī* for an early description.

12

FORMS OF RATIONAL KNOWLEDGE

Knowledge patterns data in the search for value. The data are given by experience, reason discovers or constructs patterns and 'faith' or intuition gives the sense of values. Overemphasis on any one of these elements tends to distort the quest for knowledge, which may degenerate into empirical common sense or abstract speculation or dogmatism and superstition. The tradition of knowledge in India began with emphasis on intuition in the Vedic age, flowered into the philosophies and sciences of the classical age, and then sank into scholasticism and superstition in the mediaeval period.

The seers of the early Vedic age believed that natural phenomena worked by invisible powers in accordance with a pattern laid up in Heaven. This recognition of the concept of cosmic law and of phenomena as regulated by it was obviously reached by both observation as well as intuitive speculative thought which was called *Dhī*. The highest honour was to acquire the status of a seer which one did through the illumination of *Dhī*; that was the highest prayer—the prayer for light. The search for truth and order led to the development of phonetics and metrics, grammar and hermeneutics, astronomy and ritual. The development of these six branches of Vedic learning rested as much on accurate, patient observation as on a generalising discovery of hidden patterns. Four of these were connected with language and showed the imporance which the Indian mind attached to the investigation of linguistic phenomena. In fact, grammar came to occupy in the structure of Indian learning the same position which geometry did in Greek learning. Astronomy sought to connect the regularities of time and seasons with astral changes while ritual being the primary symbolic science was the queen of sciences in the Vedic age.

The tendency to regard the elements of order in the visible world as suggestive or symbolical of the higher order, unrestrained by empirical procedures and verifications, naturally tended to push Vedic thought far in the direction of speculation. Nevertheless, the linguistic and astronomical sciences developed on a very firm empirical basis.

By the later Vedic age the scope of learning and sciences had ramified immensely as is revealed in the *Chāndogya*. Nārada mentions not only the four *Vedas* but *Itihāsa-Purāṇa* as the fifth, and a large number of other scientific disciplines. Vedic education was carried on in different schools specialising in different parts of the Vedic tradition. We do not know whether there were separate schools for other sciences or they were studied alongwith the scriptures. The sciences included grammar, the *Veda* of the Vedas, *Bhūtavidyā,* science of material elements or of beings, *rāśi* or arithmetic, *Daiva* (Divination ?), *nidhi* 'treasures', *Vākovākyam* (Dialectics or logic), *Ekāyana* 'the sole path', *Daiva vidyā* (theology), *Brahma vidyā* (philosophy), *pitr-vidyā* (the lore of the departed ancestors) *Kshatra vidyā* (science of rulership), *Nakṣattra vidyā* (astronomy), *Sarpa vidyā,* (lore of serpents), *Daivajana Vidyā,* the lore of supernatural beings. The nature of many of these is not clear. Some of these could have been magical or superstitious ; nevertheless, we have here a wide spectrum of specialisation ranging from grammar and logic to arithmetic and astronomy, medicine, politics, ritual and theology. Reality, however, was not yet fragmented to the extent of being divided into incommensurable areas and orders to be studied by mutually unconnected disciplines. The sense of unity was palpable in the concepts of *Brahman* and *Dharma.* All phenomena arise from a common matrix and are governed by a common universal law and this fact of their unity and order is reflected in all the realms of human experience.

The Unity of being implies that the highest knowledge must be the essential knowledge of all phenomena. Such a knowledge must obviously be distinguished from empirical knowledge which varies from object to object. The knowledge of the highest essence or ground as *parāvidyā* is distinguished from empirical or phenomenal knowledge which is called *aparā vidyā*. All the sciences including the scriptures which Nārada had studied fall under *aparā vidyā*. They are all 'words' i.e. discursive. They relate only to Name and Form, the concept and sensation of objects. The Upaniṣadic distinction between Higher and Lower knowledge is not, contrary to the Greek distinction between *episteme* and *doxa*, a distinction between conceptual and sensuous knowledge but between spiritual and intellectual knowledge. The latter was regarded as practically useful while the former was valued because it led to liberation. This distinction between a spiritually liberating transcendent knowledge and a practically useful intellectual knowledge has remained a permanently accepted distinction within the Indian tradition.

All the *Śāstras* or *Vidyās*, systems and sciences, belong to the Lower knowledge. The truth which they aim at is pragmatic or *Vyāvahārika* as distinguished from the absolute truth of reality (*Paramārtha*). The latter never undergoes any change or correction and radically alters man's self-consciousness. The former enables one to realize a purpose by indicating the nature and existential conditions of the object sought. Such 'pragmatic' knowledge is relational and corrigible. It is of the nature of an intellectual construct of which the validity is based on proof and evidence.

The two *vidyās* differred not only in their aim and nature but also in their method. Although both depended on the personal contact of the teacher and the disciple and required study and practice over a period, the role of the *Ācārya* and the meaning of *Brahmacarya* in the two cases differed. In the case of *aparā vidyā* the *Ācārya* gave information and trained the student to acquire and assimilate it. Studentship too stressed the rules of social behaviour as much as those of ethics. In the case of *parā vidyā* the role of the *Ācārya* was that of communicating an imponderable truth and the preparation for it was moral and spiritual.

Of the numerous Vedic schools and the vast and varied literature which they produced little is known except in terms of the canonical literature which has survived. Even so this literature is vaster than any which has survived from such antiquity.

Of the many different recensions of the Vedic *saṁhitās* only a few survive. Patañjali tells us that the *Sāmaveda* had a thousand branches. Scarcely a few have survived. Of Vedic music with which *Sāmaveda* was intimately connected, little survives except some technical terms and enigmas. The *Atharvaveda* included hymns connected with healing but we do not know much about Vedic medicine any longer. We can only recall that in the age of Buddha there were famous physicians like Jīvaka who belonged to the school of Taxila. It is said that Jīvaka could not discover a non-medicinal herb around Taxila even after industrious search. So vast was the pharmacopoeia which had developed during the preceding Vedic age.

Vedic astronomy was conceived primarily in connection with the calendar and our knowledge of it is derived from references in the *Brāhmaṇas* and a brief text on *Vedāṅga Jyotiṣa.* It is in the field of Grammar that the greatest achievement lay. The *Aṣṭādhyāyī* of Pāṇini, generally placed in the 5th Cent. B.C., is easily the most important single work in the intellectual tradition of India. Pāṇini was preceded by many other grammarians and the virtue of his work lies not in the discovery of grammatical regularities or their description; the unique achievement of Pāṇini lies in presenting grammar as a deductive system. Beginning with primitive elements, definitions and rules Pāṇini develops a coherent and complete set of formulae from which any grammatical form of the language could be derived. The level of abstraction and formalization at which the grammar of Pāṇini is written hardly permits of any improvement even after 2500 years. The system of Pāṇini remained the ideal and despair of all other *Śāstrakāras*.

The concept of the *Śāstra* was that of a system of rules with its own techniques and concepts. It was required to define itself with respect to its subject matter, purpose, relevance and the class of enquirers who were eligible for its study. These were called the *anubandha-catuṣṭaya.* Generally it began by stating the object of enquiry and went on to list its categories or peculiar concepts, so as to divide and classify the phenomena. Each class or category was then explained and defined, and alternative concepts examined in the light of the evidence. The principles of evidence and proof too were generally discussed and formulated. The views of earlier authors and of rival systems were carefully examined and where necessary the older tradition was amended and refined. The tradition of the *Śāstra* was not static ; it grew through debate and controversy.

Between the 6th Cent. B.C. and the 2nd Cent. A.D. were completed the major classical formulations of the various *śāstras* in *sūtra* form. Afterwards their growth took the form of commentaries which introduced new ideas in the guise of explaining old ones. Different *śāstras,* however, did not all develop at the same time or pace. The great period of grammatical creativity was thus from the 5th Cent. B.C. to the 2nd Cent. B.C. while for astronomy it was from the 5th Cent. A.D. to the 9th Cent. A.D. It is only in the realm of philosophy that creativity was uninterrupted throughout.

Vidyā or Science reached the status of a formal system or *śāstra* after the model of Pāṇini. The *vidyās* came to be classified into a standard four-fold viz., *ānvīkṣikī, trayī, vārtā* and *daṇḍanīti. Trayī* stood for Vedic learning. According to the *Arthśāstra* it included not only *Sāman, Ṛk, Yajus* but also *Atharva Veda* and *Itihāsa Veda.* It further included the six *Aṅgas* viz., *Śikṣā, Kalpa, Vyākaraṇa, Nirukta, Chandas* and *Jyotiṣa.* In the *Kāmandakīya-nīti-sāra* to these are added *Mīmāṁsā, Nyāya, Dharmaśāstra* and *Purāṇa.* It should however, be remembered that the *Kalpa* included *sūtra* texts dealing with *Dharma* and the *Itihāsa-Veda* could not exclude the *Purāṇas. Mīmāṁsā,* too, is continuous with the systematisation attempted by the *Śrauta-sūtras* or the discussion in the *Upaniṣads,* the *mīmāṁsās* being the systematisations of ritual or philosophical principles respectively. The inclusion of *Nyāya* in *Trayī* as of *Mīmāṁsā* as a distinct item, shows the development of philosophical systems within the Vedic tradition.

Ānvīkṣikī or philosophy was counted as a distinct science and was held to provide light to all the sciences. Methodology or logic was an important if not the predominant part of *ānvīkṣikī.* Elsewhere we are told that *Ānvīkṣikī* included *nyāya* and *adhyātma vidyā* i. e. logic and metaphysics. The *Arthaśāstra* counts within *Ānvīkṣikī* the system of *Sāṅkhya, Yoga* and *Lokāyata. Sāṅkhya* could have meant the *Sāṅkhya* system or more generally any gnostic philosophy. *Yoga* could have meant the Yoga philosophy or any spiritual philosophy stressing the need for action (*Kriyāvāda*) or a philosophy like the *Vaiśeṣika* seeking to explain the universe as compounded out of simpler original elements.[1] If we put together the *Mīmāṁsās* and *Nyāya* included under *Trayī* alongwith *Sāṅkhya* and *Yoga* we virtually get the major classical systems of philosophy. *Lokāyata* probably stood for materialistic philosophy and perhaps signified more generally secular social philosophy as well. Of these systems the ancient literature has all vanished except for the *sūtras* of *Mīmāṁsā, Nyāya* and *Vedānta.*

Vārtā and *Daṇḍanīti* together constituted the *Arthaśāstra* which included a comprehensive study of the social, economic, administrative, legal and military phenomena as parts of one complex system. If the *Dharmaśāstra* studied the whole of society from an ethical and religious point of view, the *Arthaśāstra* studied it in an equally comprehensive manner from a utilitarian point of view as a kind of applied science. The two together constituted the science and philosophy of man, moral and material. Science or *Vidyā* was, in fact, defined as the knowledge of values. "*Vidyābhirābhir nipuṇaṁ Caturvargam udāradhīḥ/ Vidyāt tadāsāṁ vidyātvaṁ'vid' jñāne nigadyate//*[2]

The concept of *Vidyā* was thus not entirely that of a positive science. Nor was it simply normative. As *Trayī* including the *Dharmaśāstra* it formulated a system of Right and sought to lay down norms. As *Arthaśāstra* it sought to describe social phenomena concretely and indicate policies based on the principle of public utility. The serious pursuit of knowledge in the age of the First Magadha empire had principally a human concern. It was the science and philosophy of man that was sought and the seeking was humanistic on one side and gnostic on the other. The rise of Śramaṇic movements like Buddhism, Jainism and Sāṅkhya emphasized the gnostic and ascetic attitudes. This linked up with one aspect of the Upaniṣadic tradition. For it true knowledge was purely transcendent, super-human and super-natural. The tradition of such a knowledge was sought to be preserved in hermitages and monasteries. On the other hand, the knowledge of man in society was pursued within the various sciences mentioned above.

The sciences of nature as distinct from the philosophies of nature, apparently did not receive as much attention as the humanistic and formal sciences. Nevertheless we can infer considerable development in several directions, though actual scientific texts of such an early age have not unfortunately survived. *Āyurveda,* thus, was one of the *Upavedas* attached to the *Ṛgveda.* Its study required a special initiation or *upanayana.* The *Milindapañho* mentions many ancient teachers of the science viz., Nārada, Dhanvantari, Āṅgyārasa, Kapila, Kandarāgnisvāmī, Atula and Pūrṇa-Kātyāyana.[3] According to the *Caraksaṁhitā, Āyurveda* was first taught by Prajāpati to the *Aśvins* who taught it to Indra who in turn taught Bharadvāja. Then followed a long line of sages who learnt from Bharadvāja. Agniveśa, Bhela, Jatūkarṇa, Parāśara, Hārīta and Kshārapāṇi acquired the science from Ātreya and composed their own systems of *Saṁhitā.*[4] All these ancient works have been lost. Texts called *Bhela Saṁhitā, Kāśyapa Saṁhitā* and *Hārīta Saṁhitā* still exist, but their authenticity is debatable.[5] The present *Carakasaṁhitā,* however, is held to be a modified form of the Agniveśa Tantra. It may be remembered that Tantra is a systematized form of *Saṁhitā*. It seems that ancient traditions were first collected as *Saṁhitās* and then re-classified and systematized as *Tantra*.

Just as the *Carakasaṁhitā* recalls the traditions of Ātreya and Agniveśa, the *Suśrutasaṁhitā* claims to go back to the traditions of Dhanvantari and Divodāsa. Both Caraka and Suśruta appear to have undergone several revisions. Their present form appears to go back to the Sātavāhana and Kuṣāṇa periods but they recall an ancient tradition which approached disease systematically seeking to diagnose it in the first place and then suggesting a course of treatment as well as indicating a prognosis. It presupposed the categories of Sāṅkhya and Vaiśeṣika and regarded disease as basically an imbalance of the three guṇas viz., *Sattva, rajas* and *tamas* in the forms of *Pitta, Vāta* and *Kapha*. For the treatment of diseases it used drugs as well as surgery and laid much stress on prevention by the proper regulation of diet and regimen. *Āyurveda* was the science of health and longevity rather than a morbid science of disease. How extensive was the development of medical science in the early post-Vedic times may be inferred from the fact that quotations and references to more than sixty lost *saṁhitās* still survive. The analytical and diagnostic approach of *Āyurveda* inspired the growing spiritual philosophy of the times to adopt the four categories (*Catvāri arthapadāni*) in its analysis of suffering on the model of Illness.

The Vedic tradition of astronomy was based on the observation of the heavens and the seasons. The earth was believed to be round and held in position by the sun. It was realized that the sun does not really rise or set. Some scholars have suggested that the motion of the earth was known. The ecliptic was known as the annual course of the sun and was divided into twelve parts. Later Vedic *saṁhitās* explicitly refer to the twenty-seven *nakṣattras*. Eclipses were observed and the Attris claimed to be able to predict the duration of a solar eclipse.[6] The Vedic calendar had a solar year and lunar months. The two were adjusted in a five year luni-solar cycle and the years were named *Saṁvatsara, Parivatsara, Idāvatsara, Udvatsara* and *Idvatsara*. "At the end of each cycle of five years the conjunction of the moon with the sun and the fixed stars was taken to repeat in the same order."

The cardinal directions were determined by the gnomon. The day on which the sun rose or set exactly in the east or the west was taken to be the day of the equinox. Similarly the solstices were determined by noticing when the sun seemed to rise from the northernmost or the southernmost point of the horizon for a number of days. The solstices were relevant to the commencement of some of the seasonal sacrifices. The *Vedāṅgas* state that the solstices occur in the middle of Aśleṣā and at the beginning of *Dhaniṣṭhā* or *Śraviṣṭhā.* It has been argued that this would be true of the period about 1200 B.C.[7]

Just as ritualistic requirements prompted the rise of astronomical observation so did they lead to the development of geometrical constructions. The construction of the altars of various shapes and sizes and the problems involved in their transformation led to a special body of literature called the *Śulba-sūtras* which are the earliest extant geometrical literature of the late Vedic and early post-Vedic times. The *Śulba-sūtras* were well aware of the substance of the so called Pythagorean theorem and developed methods of dealing with squares equal to the sum of a number of other squares. Thus they dealt by geometrical methods with problems involving surds, simultaneous equations and indeterminate equations and laid the foundations of later Indian algebra.[8]

In the sphere of arithmetic Vedic literature gives evidence of numerals named after the decimal system and names are given for very large numbers. Even and odd numbers are distinguished and several kinds of series of numbers are mentioned and summed up. The basic operations as well as fractions were known.

If grammar and logic evince the development of knowledge as a formal system dealing with abstractions, the *Arthaśāstra* with its vast data about the natural resources of the country and their management furnishes ample evidence about the growth of empirical observation and its systematic recording. The *Vāstuśāstra* or the science of building and town planning was evidently well developed. Mining and metallurgy constituted a distinct science called *Śulbadhātuśāstra*. Agriculture, horticulture and forestry were subjects of specialized study. Kṛṣitantra is traditionally said to have been found by Parāśara while *Agniveśa* is said to have founded *Vṛkṣāyurveda*.[9] Śulba has been interpreted as water-divining. *Aśvāyurveda* and *Hastyāyurveda* seem to have already existed.

The Kuṣāṇa, Sātavāhana and Gupta periods were the classical age of Indian science and philosophy. The science of grammar appears to have undergone a decline for some time after the great work of Patañjali. Perhaps the Sātavāhana patronage of Prākṛta had something to do with it. Attempts were made to create grammatical systems of Sanskrit and Prākṛta independent of Pāṇini. Towards the end of the Gupta age, however, a revival of the Paninean tradition took place. The *Mahābhāṣya* was recovered from oblivion and Bhartṛhari expounded the philosophy of grammar in its classical form. The Buddhists too contributed their share and the *Kāśikā* and the *Nyāsa* were memorable productions.

In medicine the *Saṁhitās* of Caraka and Suśruta received their classical form and have been used as authoritative texts ever since. Medical science was developed in eight distinct specializations–*Kāyatantra* or medicine, *Śalyatantra* or surgery, *Śālakyatantra* or the treatment of ear, nose and throat, *Bhūtavidyā* or psychotherapy (?). *Kaumārabhṛtya* or pediatrics. *Agadatantra* or toxicology, *Rasāyanatantra* or the science and art of restoring health in old age, and *Vājīkarma* or rejuvenation. Unfortunately only the first branch appears to survive in practice in modern times.

In medicine a new development in the classical period was the increasing interest in the preparation of medicines from minerals especially mercury. The search for elixir vitae and perpetual motion inflamed the imagination and inspired scientific experimentation. The *Bṛhatkathā* imagines flying machines and Nāgārjuna was credited with the discovery of the elixir of life. A great period for the development of Chemistry and Physics thus commenced. Atomic theory was developed in various versions and the principles of the conservation of matter and energy were formulated. The problem of change was assiduously studied. The concept of Nature as a common matrix of energy was debated along with its notion as a system of ultimate elements.[10] The propagation of sound and the formation of echoes, the acoustics of music, the reflection of light and the process of visual perception, the properties and process of heat, the problems of gravity, weight, viscosity and fluidity, motion, inertia and acceleration were discussed in the light of observation and speculation. The preparation of chemical extracts, essences and compounds, on the other hand, involved much experimentation involving mixtures and solutions, distillations and precipitation, oxidation and calcination etc.[11] The properties of different substances were carefully observed especially in the context of healing. Plants, animal products, minerals and chemical compounds were systematically classified and their properties recorded. A vast pharmacopoeia was thus gradually developed. It should be noted that while the problems and principles of physics were discussed in the context of natural philosophy, the development of chemistry was largely inspired by the search for medically useful chemical compounds. No record remains of the efforts made towards building 'flying machines' or producing perpetual motion except in the mythico-magical speculations of early mediaeval alchemy.

For a time much progress was made in surgery. Suśruta recommends the dissection of dead bodies for anatomical knowledge. The circulation of blood was clearly understood.[12] Several diseases were held to be due to microbes and transmissible through contact, water or air. Amputation, laparatomy, lithotomy and the trephining of the skull were practised. The Caesarian section was well known and particular success was attained in plastic surgery especially to undo the amputations of noses and ears.[13]

In the sphere of astronomy *Vedāṅga Jyotiṣa* was followed by the period of the Five *Siddhāntas* viz., *Sūryasiddhānta*, Pauliśa, *Romak°*, *Vasiṣṭha°* and *Paitāmaha°*. Varāhamihira's

Pañcasiddhāntikā gives an account of the *Siddhāntas* and comments: "The *Siddhānta* made by Pauliśa is accurate; near to it stands the *Siddhānta* proclaimed by Romaka; more accurate is the Sāvitra (Saura), the two remaining ones are far from the truth." The *Paitāmaha Siddhānta* describes a luni-solar calendar similar to that of *Vedāṅga Jyotiṣa* and does not treat of any other planets except the sun and the moon. The *Vāsiṣṭha* is much more advanced. Its luni-solar constructs are more accurate and it gives the motion of the five planets. It has been suggested that this *Siddhānta* was indebted to Babylonian astronomy.[14] The *Pauliśa Siddhānta* calculates the length of the day by the methods of spherical astronomy and gives rough rules for the calculation of the lunar and solar eclipses. Foreign influence has been held to be the source of this *Siddhānta*.

Romaka "distinctly bears a Greak name and represents perhaps the sum total of Greek astronomy transmitted to India". It is obviously "a most fragmentary and incomplete transmission of Greek astronomy". The *Sūryasiddhānta*[15] had two stages of development since the older tradition was revised after Āryabhaṭa who has been described as the founder of scientific Indian astronomy.[16] His system is based on the epicyclic theory but his constants at least are original. The planets were held to move in circles round the earth but their centres did not coincide with the centre of the earth. Varāhamihira was not original in astronomy but brought the *Sūryasiddhānta* upto date by borrowing from Āryabhaṭa. Brahmagupta corrected the inaccuracies left in Āryabhaṭa's work. The highest water mark of this astronomical tradition was reached in the works of Bhāskarācārya in the 12th century. Mathematics too reached its climax in his works. Carrying forward the tradition of Mahāvīra and Śrīdhara, Bhāskara shows a remarkable development of algebra. Numericals with place value system as well as zero were already in use. Rules for operating with rational and irrational numbers had been formulated. Bhāskara points out that division with zero is inadmissible and virtually reaches the notions of limits and differential co-efficient. Simultaneous equations, quadratics, permutations and combinations, areas and volumes were competently worked out. In arithmetic problems of time and distance, simple and compound interest and profit and loss were solved.[17]

It is philosophy, however, which was the queen of the sciences in ancient India. While the Age of the First Magadha Empire had seen the emergence of diverse systems of spiritual philosophy as soteriologies, the period from the Kuṣāṇa to the Gupta empires saw the development of abstruse metaphysical systems and a lively debate between them. The six orthodox systems of philosophy, the major systems of Buddhist philosophy, Mahāyāna and Hīnayāna, and the Jaina metaphysical system, all received their classical formulation in this period. Their mutual debate led to the need of the formulation of common logical principles and from the 5th Century onwards we see a remarkable development of logic as a formal science. Vasubandhu and Dignāga laid the foundations of Buddhist logic. Vātsyāyana and Uddyotakara criticised them and were criticised in turn by Dharmakīrti. A lively debate on logic involved the Buddhists, the Jainas, the *Nyāya* and *Mīmāṁsā*. Between the tenth and the twelfth centuries a yet higher degree of abstraction was reached in the language of logic in the works of Udayana and Gaṅgeśa. The work of the latter tended to replace all earlier work and became the basis of mediaeval scholastic logic.[18]

In the 11th century Alberuni complained of Indian complacence. It seems that having been the intellectual leaders of the ancient world after the fall of Alexandria, Indian thinkers gradually ceased to have enough intellectual contacts or ceased to profit from them in the period subsequent to circa 900 A.D. The result was that although science continued to be cultivated for a few centuries in the Deccan and the south, the north-west was the first to lose its ancient high culture. Perhaps it was a gradual process begun by Hun conquerers and completed by the Turks. In the east the monasteries were the centres of education and they were dramatically destroyed by the Turks. The growth of superstition doubtless aided this process of the erosion of rationalism and science.

The Indian intellectual tradition presents a dialectic of two interacting streams, the orthodox and the heterodox. The former stressed authority and tended to be conservative while the latter relied on reason and experience alone. In the course of their interaction the orthodox stream sought to reconcile tradition with reason and introduced modifications through commentarial interpretations and even interpolations. Unfortunately the heterodox tradition gradually declined and was finally cut off by the Turkish destruction of Buddhist monasteries. As a result the orthodox tradition tended to become scholastic in the mediaeval period.

Another feature of this tradition was that the intellectuals were largely recruited from the class of priests and monks and their theorizing in the realm of physical sciences was not accompanied adequately with the experience of practical work in the mechanical arts and manufacture. *Śilpasthānavidyā* was recognised as an academic discipline till the 7th Century A.D. and the important social position of the guilds ensured a certain connection of the head with the hand. But later on the position changed and the guilds themselves were depressed socially. This increasing distance of the head and the hand exaggerated the scholastic character of theory and the mere empiricism of the mechanical arts and crafts. In Philosophy, however, the connection of theory with spiritual experience continued but the broad experience of secular life became increasingly unavailable to it in the mediaeval times.

Characteristics of the Indian Rational Tradition

The knowledge which the *śāstras* embody is discursive, rational and practical. Being discursive it is different from intuitive spiritual wisdom which is timeless and unchanging. Its rational and practical aspects are complementary. Reason is not conceived here as an independent source of knowledge. It is integrally connected with experience and faith but differs from these in being self-critical and indirect. Its classic form is the syllogism which is itself a paradigm of the union of different epistemic principles (*pramāṇa-samavāyaḥ*). "*Pratijñā* illustrates *āgama, hetu anumāna, udāharaṇa pratyakṣa, upanayana upamāna. Nigamana* illustrates the mutual co-operation of all these towards the establishment of one end."[19] Reason examines a principle given in tradition in terms of its logical ground, empirical evidence and analogy. If reason were unguided by tradition it would lead to endlessly changing conclusions. Although it is admitted that doubt requires reasoning and reasoning proceeds till one reaches a contradiction, it was realized that merely hypothetical reasoning or *tarka* can only have a subordinate role within the broader sweep of syllogistic reasoning or *anumāna*.[19a]

By its working within the framework of tradition this conception of reason tends to be scholastic and conservative but by its working within a context of practical enquiry and experience, it has a pragmatic or *vyāvahārika* character. Rational knowledge, thus, implies the preservation and development of tradition through critical validation and practical employment. The process of reasoning begins with the determination of the object of enquiry not merely in terms of purpose which is ultimately nothing but the liberation of the spirit, but in terms of foundational categories—*padārthas* or *tattvas*. Then comes their critical examination through the ascertainment of definition and proof, *lakṣaṇa* and *pramāṇa*. The ultimately transcendent purpose of the Śāstraic enquiry is the reason why it keeps close to tradition and seeks absolute certitude rather than merely a furtherance of corrigible knowledge. As Vācaspati Miśra has said, corrigible and probable knowledge is satisfactory only in the realm of empirical purposes.[20] If one makes a mistake in agricultural science, for example, one can correct it by noting practical results. One cannot, however, undertake such a correction about a belief of which the consequences would be apparent only after death. It is this search for absolute certitude which necessitates the grounding of the *śāstras* in a tradition coming down from seers and sages. Even the sciences like Medicine and Astronomy are held to be connected with the realization of a transcendent purpose, the former by helping true health and longevity, the latter by helping the determination of calendrical phenomena for the proper observance of ritual. Modern science, on the other hand, claims to be motivated by disinterested curiosity and at the same time to develop a social tool for the fulfilment of secular ends. Modern science is necessarily involved in change and progress and is oriented towards the future betterment of society. It is also naturalistic in its philosophical presuppositions. The ancient *śāstras* differ in all these respects. They seek to express perennial wisdom and are oriented towards man's realization of eternity. They have, thus, a dual status. On the one hand, they constitute a body of logical and practical knowledge. On the other hand, this knowledge traces its roots to an original and unchanging vision and seeks to help the salvation of man indirectly. It encourages enquiry and debate so that the truth may be grasped more firmly and immediately but it does not look upon truth as a utopia conceived in relation to the future of society.

The character of *Śāstraic* knowledge, thus, is quite different from the modern forms of rational knowledge. The radical distinction which modern thought draws between religious faith, philosophical speculation, moral wisdom and science does not obtain in ancient thought where the fundamental distinction is between mystical intuition and discursive knowledge, the latter comprising all forms of rational knowledge in a hierarchical unity and synthesizing within it the diverse strands of faith and experience in a single web of reasoning. Thus conceived and structured knowledge had a distinctive aspect and should not be regarded as a merely confused matrix out of which several elements may be looked upon as archaic steps in the evolution of modern sciences and philosophies. *Āyurveda,* thus, is not an empirical and superstitious system of which the genuine elements have been incorporated in the evolution of modern medicine. It is an autonomous system with its own essential principles and methods viz., of *Tridoṣa,* of vital and healing powers, and of symptomatic diagnosis. Like the three *guṇas* of *Sāṅkhya* the three *doṣas* are not a primitive classification of observed phenomena but a holistic insight into the human constitution. The *doṣas* may be discerned when specially manifested in specific physiological and biochemical phenomena but cannot be identified with them. The manifestations are discernible in terms of sense-perceptible qualities but the triply functioning life-force, healthy in balance, diseased in imbalance, is not so discernible. Its state can only be judged symptomatically. Modern medicine, on the other hand, rejects the whole notion of life-force because the tendency of modern science is to discard transcendent entities and this is rooted in a philosophical perspective of empiricism and analysis. Modern medicine consequently seeks to reduce the art of healing to the physico-chemical manipulation of the body as directly as possible. The *Āyurveda* did not possess such knowledge of the mechanical, chemical and physiological structures and processes of the body nor the mechanical means to observe them or reach them directly. It relied on the intuitive grasp of the invisible but holistic state of the psychophysically conditioned human being through its symptomatic manifestations. For curing the imbalances of the human system, it relied largely on rules of health in terms of regulated exercise, rest, food etc. and on drugs prepared from herbs and minerals in peculiar ways and combination. It can hardly accept the view that the healing power of organic substances found in nature is wholly reducible to their physico-chemical action. If such reduction were valid the Āyurvedic methods of preparing their medicines would have to be deemed full of superstition and ignorance. The potency of Āyurvedic medicines prepared according to traditional as distinguished from modern methods is, however, undoubted.

It should, however, be understood that this overall contrast of Śāstraic knowledge with modern knowledge such as illustrated by the case of *Āyurveda* does not mean that the two are different in all respects. A good deal of the *śāstras* contains scientific and philosophical discourses which can be abstracted and adapted into modern systems. It is possible to regard ancient medicine, astronomy, mathematics and logic as simply elementary parts of, or archaic stages in the development of these sciences which have now reached greater accuracy, sophistication and power. Nevertheless, this partial overlap does not furnish any real ground for identifying ancient *śāstras* and modern sciences or for subsuming the former under the latter. The overlap really relates to practically applicable results and methods, not to theory. Now knowledge-systems are systems of theory i. e., logical systems of concepts claiming to explain the nature or necessity of the data of experience. They are systems of reasons which would show the necessity of empirically attested facts and rules. It is with respect to this theoretical structure that the *śāstras* differ from modern sciences. They may be conceived as alternative perspectives on the facts of experience. Modern science is relevant to a machine-using society. It is difficult to think of modern astronomy without the telescope or of modern medicine without the microscope. In this quest the methods of introspection and intuition are rejected and spiritual reality missed. The *śāstras,* on the other hand, see no need of endlessly exploring the possibilities of sense-bound experience through mechanical inventions and experiments. They, however, do include a knowledge intended to help society in dealing with the practical problems of a pre-machine age though not to convert it into a self-transforming machine-age. In this empirical or *vyāvahārika* aspect the knowledge of the *śāstras* shows a partial overlap with modern scientific knowledge, but as a logical or rational structure it has a distinctive character.

The concept of *padārtha* or *tattva* is the concept of an ultimate category within the context of the particular *śāstra.* In the *śāstras* which deal with reality in the most general manner these categories become ultimate classifications of the world of experience. The *Sāṅkhya,* thus, lists twenty-five *tattvas.* The *Vaiśeṣika* lists seven *padārthas.* The Buddhist *abhidharma* lists numerous ultimate elements or *dharmas.* The *Jainas* give their own list of basic elements. In the special sciences *Āyurveda* relies on *Sāṅkhya* and *Vaiśeṣika.* While mathematical and astronomical works deal with the use of numbers, measurement, spatial relations and motion, the conceptual discussion of such objects finds a place in *Nyāyavaiśeṣika.* Philosophical conceptions of knowledge and reality thus underlie the different forms of rational knowledge which the *śāstras* exhibit.

Perhaps the most general tendency in the conception of *padārtha* or category is 'phenomenological' in the sense that the ultimate principles are generally conceived as distinct intuitable essences. The principles are conceived in terms of *lakṣaṇas* or distinctive characters. Whether informing physical or spiritual reality the principles carry their separate marks (*lakṣaṇas*) which are intelligible essences and can be grasped as such. The intellectual intuition of principles is admitted by the Buddhists even though they are nominalists. The same is implied in the Jaina notion of *Kevalajñāna.* The Nyāya-Vaiśeṣika theory of *sannikarṣa* especially *alaukika saṁnikarṣa* goes far in the same direction. The enquiry into principles (*tattva-jijñāsā*) searches the intelligible forms which constitute the permanent essences of the objects of experience. Its objective, *tattvajñāna,* is contemplative or theoretical in the original sense. Its method is the discrimination of *lakṣaṇas* and their ascertainment by *pramāṇa.* In common usage *pramāṇa* has the sense of measure or standard and the search for *pramāṇa* in philosophy may be said to be the search for the validity or authenticity of cognition. *Pramāṇa,* thus, is generally defined as the 'means to right knowledge' and although a wide variety of opinions exists about the number and nature of *Pramāṇas,* it would not be too bold to say that *Pratyakṣa, anumāna* and *Āgama* were generally recognised as the three principal *pramāṇas. Pratyakṣa* was believed not to be limited to sense-perception but to include introspection, intuition of spiritual or purely intelligible verities, and self-consciousness. It, thus, encompassed the whole range of experience from common perception and introspection to intellectual and mystical intuition. This conception of *Pratyakṣa* distinguishes the Indian tradition from western empiricism which is sense-bound.

Anumāna or inference provides an indirect knowledge. Here one cognition acts as the reason for believing in another. This process of reasoning presupposes knowledge given by experience or tradition. Traditional Indian logic does not attach any significance to mere formal validity divorced from all material truth nor is much importance attached to merely hypothetical reasoning or merely assumed or a *priori* premises. What is discussed is the basic nature of reasoning, not the diversity of forms and figures.

Although Indian logic developed a high degree of abstraction it was always conceived as an aid to the discovery of truth, not a merely formal or symbolic system. The truth which it searches is held to be characterised by the invariance of the cognition and its object, the object being real. The usual form of reasoning consisted in beginning with some basic concepts and rules and proceeding to build a system on that basis. This procedure is not purely axiomatic as it appeals to factual data or principles where necessary. Thus in the paradigmatic case of grammar linguistic data are admitted. Astronomy uses observations. Mathematics rests on the facts of counting or measuring by natural numbers. Logic presupposes philosophical principles. So does *Āyurveda.*

Of *Prameya,* the Buddhists have emphasized negation and indeterminability, the Jainas infinity and multiplicity, the Vedāntins eternity and unity, Sāṅkhya-yoga infinite transformability, Nyāya-Vaiśeṣika the multiplicity of substances and intelligible entities entering in them directly and indirectly. The most widely accepted feature of temporal reality which includes knowledge is, however, accepted to be its pervasive causal order. The very notions of *lakṣaṇa* and *pramāṇa* rest on the principle of causality.

The concept of causality in Indian philosophy

THE HISTORICAL ORIGIN OF THE PROBLEM

Already in the early Vedic period the question was raised 'who fashioned the world? What was the material out of which the world was fashioned?' The gods or a special god *Prajāpati* were invoked as creators and the sacrifice was described as symbolising the act of creation. Causation is here conceived in the cosmic setting and on the analogy of 'making or 'creating'. In the *Upanisads* the creator is the *Brahman* or *Ātman,* 'one without a second'. The Self creates the world out of itself and remains immanent in it. An alternative view already existed and held that the world has evolved out of a primordial chaos or non-being. In a way the Sāṅkhya doctrine of *Prakṛti-Pariṇāmavāda* is a development of the *Asat-Kāraṇavāda* mentioned in the *Upaniṣads.*

These cosmological speculations were challenged in the Age of Buddha by the rise of Naturalism (*Svabhāvavāda*), materialism (*Lokāyata*), and Agnosticism (*Ajñānavāda*) as well as by the emergence of the doctrine of *Karman.* If the world is a natural or material process, no god is needed to explain it. If human life is wholly governed by the force of *Karman,* no god is needed to explain it. In either case, thus, God seems unnecessary to understand the material world or human life. The formulation of such views led to a prolonged controversy between theists and atheists over what governs and explains the world process or the process of human destiny. Out of this controversy arose the philosophical debates concerning the validity and nature of causality and its relation to freedom.

VALIDITY OF THE PRINCIPLE OF CAUSALITY

There were some who doubted or rejected the very principle of universal causality. The Buddhists describe this as the doctrine of Chance Happening (*Adhītyasamutpāda*). The *Lokāyata* argued that necessary or universal connections (*Sarvopasaṁhāravatī Vyāpti*) cannot be securely established because it is impossible to know all possible instances which range in endless space and time. Nor can we rule out the possibility of an accidental connection (*upādhi*) between 'cause' and 'effect' in the observed instances. There can be no secure knowledge of causality because there cannot be a sufficient basis for empirical generalization. All such generalisation (*vyāpti*) on which practical activity depends gives us only a probabilistic knowledge (*Sambhāvanā*). These doubts and negations are reminiscent of Hume. Starting from a basic empiricism, this attitude doubts the validity of universal laws and hence of causality. Since apparently regular and apparently casual connections are equally observed in nature and the possibility of a casual connection in any given instance cannot be absolutely excluded, the belief in a connection as 'regular' can only remain problematic.

In the west Kant had sought to answer Hume's scepticism by proposing to regard causality as a 'necessary' category of thought. Kant puts forward a 'transcendental proof'—although the principle of causality is not empirically discoverable, it is necessarily presupposed in theoretical knowledge. In a partly similar manner, the Buddhists, the Naiyāyikas and the Jainas argue that the principle of causality must be accepted because its denial will stultify knowledge and make life impossible (*Vyavahāroccheda-prasaṅga*). It is not that the denial of causality is self-contradictory but that the implications of its denial would not be acceptable to any rational person. Even the Lokāyaṭa and the Yadṛcchāvādins act as if they believed in causal connections, though they describe their belief as merely one of expecting what is probable but not certain. *Tarka* or *reductio ad absurdum* is used to establish the general validity of the principle of causality.

Dignāga came nearest to Kant by holding that causality is not a datum in experience but something imputed in judgment. For Dignāga, events alone are perceived, substances and relations are constructed in judgment (*Vikalpa*). "*Na sambandha indriyaṇa gṛhyate.*" The world that is directly perceived is only a flux of instantaneous events, but the world that is constructed by rational knowledge is an ordered whole of substances and relations. All regular relations are either based on identity or existential unity (*svabhāva*), or on causality. If two things are different entities, they can have a regular relation only in terms of causality. The constructed world is superimposed on the perceptual world as its relevant description in verbal conceptual terms and this 'systematic' or 'transcendental' illusion is the basis of all thought and action. In this view causality is traced to the nature of the mind as an *anādi vāsanā* or *vikalpa* and justified on the ground of its indispensability. It may, however, be objected that even if we accept the denial of the principle of causality as stultifying rational thought, we still need a criterion by which to ascertain the validity of any specific causal law. The relation between two events may be causal or accidental. To establish the necessity of their relation we must go beyond the mere observation of their concomittance. The Buddhists point out that the belief in necessity follows from the joint operation of observation and inference based on non-observation under specified conditions (*Pratyakṣānupalambha*). It is like Mill's Joint Method of Agreement and Difference. The Naiyāyikas also agree that *Anvaya* and *Vyatireka* enable us to establish a valid universal connection. While the relation between two events is suggested to us by their observed association, our belief in the necessity of the relation arises from not discovering their dissociation (*avyabhicāra*), a condition which removes the suspicion of an accidental relation (*upādhi*). As Bain has stated in a different context, "If two things have been incessantly conjoined in our experience, they are inseparably associated, and we believe that the one will be followed by the other, but the inseparable association follows the number of repetitions, the belief follows the absence of contradiction".

While this combination of empiricism and rationalism seeks to validate the principle of causality against the scepticism arising from pure empiricism it does not take care of the attack mounted by Dialecticians—Mādhyamika and Advaitin. If the effect exists prior to its causation, it does not need to be caused; if it does not so exist, it cannot be caused. If the effect is identical with the cause, it precedes its own causation; if it is different, it becomes essentially independent of the cause. If the cause changes or ceases to be before producing the effect, it ceases to be the cause before causation; if the cause remains unchanged, no causation ensues. These and similar arguments have been advanced by the dialecticians. The arguments, however, rest on assumptions which are very general in scope. Their acceptance questions the very possibility of change and relation, of any combination of identity and difference.

There are three possible ways of meeting these difficulties—(a) one may stick to one's trust in common sense knowledge and language and seek to rebut the dialectical charge by seeking to show that a careful use of ordinary language is perfectly consistent with what common sense understands to be real or plausible and urge that the dialectical difficulties are either spurious or against common-sense. This is the general manner in which the Naiyāyikas attempt to deal with these objections. It leads them, however, to an interminable analysis of common terms and ideas and to sophistications so curious and rare that common sense would blush to be quoted as their remote progenitor. (b) One may, on the other hand, consider reality itself to be dialectical and like the Jainas declare it to have an infinity of aspects. Thus contradictions can be resolved by turning them into limited affirmations and negations. This approach has a certain resemblance to the Hegelian dialectic and rests on the rejection of identities and differences as absolute. It also tends to make relations objective and internal and thus to resolve reality into an infinite whole with internal differentiations. At this stage, it would seem that the contradictions in describing reality emerge from the inadequacy of human language which seems to be made to deal with things piecemeal and has an inveterate tendency to first divide up what is integral and then seek to join them into artificial unities. Here then, it is not reality that is dialectical but language! (c) And this is the Sautrāntika Buddhist point of view which regards concepts and judgments as not having a one-to-one correspondence with the elements of reality. Words signify through contrast and every time we use a word we create a dichotomy, in such a way that while the real reference of the word is a pair of contrasted sets of evanescent elements, they are represented to us as quasi-objects in terms of concepts. Words neither present nor represent reals but they enable us to deal with them in a practical manner by guiding us into neglecting what is irrelevant. From this point of view the validity of concepts is limited to the pragmatic world, which is accepted by the Mādhyamikas as well as Advaitins. If we were to regard the principle of causality as established in the very nature of ultimate reality, we would certainly be faced with the unanswerable arguments of dialectic. But we do not need to fear the validity of the causal principle in relation to that world of finite objects which has a practical reality for discursive thought.

THE NATURE OF CAUSALITY

Assuming then the validity of the causal principle at least in relation to the empirical world, let us proceed to examine the nature of causality more closely. For the Naiyāyikas to cause is to make and its type-instance is the activity of the potter. Some agency producing some entity by acting on some thing else as its material—this is causation. The agent is *Nimitta-Kāraṇa* or efficient cause, the material is *Samavāyi-Kāraṇa,* the joining of the material and similar indirect contributive factors are called *Asamavāyi-Kāraṇa.* The cause is held to be radically different from the effect which is regarded as a new emergent. This is the *Ārambhavāda* or *Asatkārya-vāda* of Nyāya. The effect is supposed to reside in the material cause by the relation of *Samavāya* or inherence which is the Nyāya equivalent of 'unity in difference', more strictly, a relation between entities which cannot exist in separation. With this analysis of the process and factors of causation, Nyāya defines the cause as the 'regular antecedent (*Niyata-pūrvavartin*) which is not required by anything other than the effect (*ananyathā-siddha*)'.

The most obvious difficulty with the Nyāya theory is its account of the material cause and its relation to the effect. Even when the effect is produced, the cause persists as that in which the effect inheres. The effect is quite different and wholly new and yet it has a mysterious and essential dependence on the cause. If the effect can emerge out of nothing, why does it have to be preceded by the cause? How can any changes in the cause charm the effect out of its beginningless repose in non-existence? The Nyāya appears to look at causality in too mechanical a fashion and fails to see the continuity between cause and effect. Causation is really a process of the transformation of one thing into other. If we look at the organic world, this would become at once plain. The Sāṅkhya therefore replaced the Nyāya notion of emergence or

Ārambha by that of *Pariṇāma* or transformation and asserted that the effect already pre-exists its creation in a latent form (*Satkārya-vāda*). Causation is really manifestation. Nature is not a collection of disparate atoms which are mechanically moved and combined by the will of God into the diverse objects of the worlds, as the Naiyāyikas believe, but an amorphous stuff in ceaseless change, containing within itself infinite possibilities and revealing them by a kind of blind instinct for the bondage as well as the self-realization of the Spirit.

Almost as serious difficulties beset the Sāṅkhya view as have been mentioned for the Nyāya. In fact the famous Kārikā '*Asadakaraṇāt*' etc., has been simply reversed point by point for its refutation. If the prior non-existence of the effect makes it impossible, its prior existence makes it unnecessary. The Buddhists replace this antinomy by replacing the contrasts of identity and difference, change and persistence, by the category of continuity in a flux. The cause should not be conceived as producing the effect out of itself or conjuring it out of nothing by some special exertion. The cause should not be conceived dynamically at all, for that is only a veiled anthropomorphism. Nor is there any persistent material cause in which the effect might inhere. There are only momentary events which show certain uniformities in their sequence. This alone is the causal relation, 'this being, that becomes, this ceasing that ceases', called 'contingent genesis' or *Pratītya-samutpāda*. The cause is simply the antecedent set of circumstances, *Hetu-pratyaya-sāmagrī*. There is neither an agent nor a material. There is only a process with evanescent elements. And this process applies to the realm of the mind as much as to that of matter. The Buddhist view of causality makes it a wholly impersonal and objective process marked by sequential regularities.

This old Buddhist view, however, appears to be only a half-turn to the truth. It is hard to conceive of reals which arise and perish in the same moment, which arise because another moment has already wholly perished and which perish out of their own nature. How, again, is it to be decided whether a moment belongs to one sequence rather than to another?

How, for instance, is the dream sequence to be distinguished from the waking sequence? How do we decide whether we have awakened or not? Indeed, the early Buddhist view inexorably presses forward to the Mahāyānic view where all substances finally disappear into phenomena and causality becomes merely a regularity in appearances. For the Vijñānavādins, all things are mere manifestations of the mind, mere ideas, and the original seed and form of causality lie in the mind. The force of *Vāsanā* arising out of desire and past experience is the ultimate cause which underlies the procession of ideas. The Mādhyamikas negate even the reality of the mind and deny causality in the realm of the ultimately real.

Advaita Vedānta had begun by regarding *Brahman* as the real cause of the world, both efficient (*Nimitta*) and material (*Upādāna*). Latterly, however, it was felt that a *real* cause would be involved in *real* change and *Brahman* would become something like *Prakṛti*. The Advaita thus developed its celebrated theory of *Vivarta* as distinguished from *Pariṇāma*. *Vivarta* is illusory transformation such as is undergone by the rope when it appears as a snake. In effect, it is a refusal to apply the category of causality to the ground of all phenomena. The problem of causality thus underwent a full circle. It had begun with interest in the cosmological problem of creation and after passing through diverse sophistications seemed to return to a basic denial of any real creation. The Nyāya-Vaiśeṣika appears to attend to the mechanistic realm primarily and explains causation as the production of new entities through the assembling of separate material particles. In the organic realm causation appears as a continuous evolution and is so defined by the Sāṅkhya. The Buddhists concentrating on the psychic realm explain causality as the regularity of a series of vanishing functions (*saṁskāras*) or point-instants (*kṣaṇas*). Considering, finally, the unalterable eternity of the Spirit, the Advaitins came to feel that the category of causality cannot truly be applied to it.

CAUSALITY AND FREEDOM

It seems, then, that man finds himself in the heteronomous

world of Nature but is impelled to seek freedom from it in the eternity of the Spirit. That man is in bondage (*bandha*) within *Saṁsāra* and that he must seek liberation (*mokṣa*), is a position which is acceptable to all schools of Indian philosophy except the Lokāyata. The bondage of man is his subjection to suffering which arises from *Karman*. The basic causal principle operating in human life is the force of past actions producing consequences for experience. What is causally determined is the situation and the experience of pleasure and pain, not the will or the act. Rather, what is predetermined is the situation and experience, not action. The freedom of the will (*Puruṣa-kāra*) is zealously guarded in most schools of Indian thought. What determines a man's action is the force of his own character and self-identification. His character, impulses and beliefs are the product of his own past actions and experiences. Man remains free in his *Karman* though his *Karman* determines his *Bhoga*. Naiyāyikas and Buddhists, Mīmāṁsakas and Vedāntins, Sāṅkhya and Yoga, all lay down that man is free to act but that his experiences are determined by his own actions. The causal nexus between action and experience is both natural and moral. In fact, from the point of view of the empirical self the law of *Karman* is not one of heteronomy but of autonomy. A man finds himself in situations and experiences for which his own past actions are responsible. Actions and consequences form invariances and exemplify causality, but in so far as the actions belong to the person he binds himself autonomously. His real bondage, however, consists in his involvement in the process of actions leading to experiences. It is only through the ignorant identification of the self with a part of Nature that man gets involved in action—a causal process. Even the Buddhists who did not accept any real self, argued that it was the illusion of a permanent, finite self which led to action and its consequential bondage.

The problem of causality in relation to human freedom was thus conceived somewhat differently in India than in the west. Here it was not a question of securing a place for the freedom of the will against the force of external circumstances, since the natural and moral orders were not regarded as indifferent or hostile to each other. The real question in India was to vindicate the possibility of man's spiritual freedom. Being within the natural-moral order and its causal law, how is man to win the freedom of transcending it ? Human bondage lies ultimately in *Karman* itself and human freedom in transcendence. Causality is not the source of bondage but merely its form. Bondage arises from the involvement of the self with the finite reals which are necessarily part of a causal process. If one enters the stream, one is bound to be carried in its direction. One need not, however, enter the stream or choose to remain in it. The possibility of freedom rests on the spiritual nature of the self. The causal world with its laws and order has meaning if the self stands at its centre with its freedom. Deeper than the principle of causality, thus, is the principle of being for the self.

REFERENCES

1. Cf. Phanibhushan Tarkavāgīśa, Bengali tr. and comy. on the *Nyāyasūtras.*

2. *Kāmandaka,* 2.3.17.

3. *Milindapañho,* 4.7.69.

4. *Carakasaṁhitā,* Vol. I, pp. 8ff.

5. Cf. Priyavrata Sharma, *Āyurveda Kā Vaijñānika Itihāsa,* pp. 48ff.

6. Cf. Bose, Sen, Subbarayappa, *Concise History of Science in India,* p. 60.

7. Gorakh Prasad, *Bhāratīya Jyotiṣa Kā Itihāsa,* p. 45.

8. See B. Datta, *The Science of Śulba.*

9. See G. P. Majumdar, *Vanaspati.*

10. See B. N. Seal, *Positive Sciences of the Ancient Hindus.*

11. See P. C. Ray, *History of Hindu Chemistry,* 2 Vols.

12. Priyavrata Sharma, *op. cit.,* pp. 492ff.

13. See G. N. Mukhopadhyaya, *Surgical Instruments of the Hindus,* 3 Vols.

14. Cf. Bose, Sen, Subharayappa, *op. cit.,* pp. 130ff; G. R. Kaye, *Hindu Astronomy.*

15. See *Sūryaśiddhānta* with the excellent commentary of M. P. Srivastav.

16. See P. C. Sengupta (Tr.), *Āryabhaṭīya.*

17. See B. Datta and A. N. Singh, *History of Hindu Mathematics,* 2 parts.

18. See Stcherbatsky, *Buddhist Logic,* 2 Vols.; S. C. Vidyabhushan, *History of Indian Logic.*

19. *Nyāyabhāṣya* ad *Nyāyasūtras,* 1.1.1

19a. Cf. S. Bagchi, *Inductive Reasoning—A Study of Tarka and its Role in Indian Logic.*

20. *Nyāyavārtikatātparyaṭika.*

APPENDIX

HETERODOX PHILOSOPHIES AND SCIENTIFIC DEVELOPMENT

PHILOSOPHICAL TRENDS AND THE HISTORY OF SCIENCE IN INDIA—HETERODOX TRENDS

Author's paper reprinted from the Indian Journal of History of Science, Vol. 4, Nos. 1 & 2, 1969

[In anctent India, though the philosophical systems intersected with science in their treatment of certain common problems such as of a logical or methodological nature, the two developed in essential independence.

The three principal heterodox systems of philosophy, viz. the Lokāyata, Buddhism and Jainism, developed as critical philosophical movements. They rejected the authority of Vedic revelation as a valid source of knowledge and emphasized the testimony of human experience and reason.

The Lokāyata emphasis on observation and their explanation of general laws as merely probabilistic could both have helped in the progress of scientific inquiry but the only thing we know for a fact is that it acted as a corrective to the emphasis on speculations of a transcendental nature.

The Buddhists emphasize causal processes and have a pragmatic view of truth. The Buddhist causal law pictured a world in terms of an ordered flux of instantaneous synergies. For this they refined the notions of 'element' and 'cause', 'existence' and 'truth' but such concepts and theories were far in advance of what the science of those days was capable of measuring, calculating and constructing. However, in the sphere of psychology the Buddhists had a continuous and extensive scientific interest.

Jainism seeks to preserve the truth of common sense along with the truth of philosophy and religion. The sturdy common sense of Jainism establishes a probabi listic dialectic. The Jaina doctrine of *syādvāda* is a remarkable theory of relativity. The Jainas not only reached considerable precision and elaboration in their measures of space and time but also put forward an elaborate atomic theory.

Thus, these philosophies have nothing definitely obstructive of scientific progress. In fact the period of these synchronized with a period of growth and development in many branches of science. In those days the intellectuals tended to be essentially philosophers and scholars, not technicians or practical inventors. It naturally limited the progress of strictly scientific thought by restricting the progress of mechanical development and technology. Medicine and astronomy alone attained the status of prestige disciplines and in these spheres the progress on the whole was as extensive as in those times elsewhere.]

The present paper is concerned with delineating and evaluating the philosophical tendencies of the ancient heterodox systems from the standpoint of their relevance and helpfulness to scientific progress. It is not concerned with describing specifically scientific works of which the authors might have been Buddhists or Jainas.

Before seeking to correlate philosophical trends with the history of science, it would be helpful to define the relationship between philosophy and science. In the history of Western culture, philosophy and science have developed in close connection. Among the Greeks the two rose together as a kind of natural philosophy.[1] This conception, after its definite formulation by Aristotle,[2] continued to rule for centuries.[3] The Greeks, however, considered all true knowledge to be purely rational and Aristotle thus defined science (*episteme*) as apodeictic or demonstrative,[4] a view which was supported by the great rationalist philosophers of the seventeenth and eighteenth centuries. It was the gradual adoption of the experimental method in the natural sciences since the seventeenth and eighteenth centuries which revealed the sharp gulf between philosophy and the sciences. Since then, the tendency in Western philosophy has been to emphasize this distinction. In his *Critique of Pure Reason* Kant asserted the impossibility of a rational metaphysics and sought to limit philosophy to transcendental considerations. Recent philosophy has been at great pains to emphasize that philosophy is concerned with principles or concepts or forms of experience or judgement, not facts or things. Philosophical assertions do not purport to describe the natural world. They are rather concerned with the principles involved in human reasoning, valuing, or experiencing in the most general sense. That is why the history of philosophical ideas is closely bound up with the vicissitudes of cultural attitudes—religious, moral, aesthetic, logical and scientific. Science is one of the cultural variables on which the function of philosophizing depends. It is true that the various cultural variables have a certain interdependence or *Zusammenhang*. Yet, it is also true to say that while within the cultural *ensemble* science and philosophy influence each other to a certain extent, they are, on the whole, influenced far more by certain other proximate variables which form largely different sets. Thus, the progress of science has depended more continuously and closely on the changing patterns of felt social need realizable in terms of the control of factors constituting the natural environment than on the remoter philosophical, moral or religious beliefs about human nature and destiny. Necessity is indeed the mother of invention. The conditions of practical crafts and industries, commerce and agriculture, mining and war have directly and indirectly raised the questions which scientific thinking has been geared to answer from time to time. It seems to be a grave misconception to believe that science is an extension of philosophical principles and attitudes or *vice versa*. Although the aspiration after an *a priori* rational system is ingrained in the human mind, science remains essentially empirical and *a posteriori*, the universality and necessity of its laws representing merely an idealized expression of what *qua knowledge* is only approximate and tentative.[5] It is the giving up of the large-scale speculative bias of philosophy which helped the emergence of the methods of scientific research in the seventeenth and later centuries. It is a pity, however, that some recent philosophy has sought to imitate the method of the so-called piecemeal research in a sphere where it has little relevance. The historian, in any case, must note the distinction between science and philosophy and yet place developments in both within the common and larger stream of *Kulturgeschichte*. While the working of the inner dialectic of ideas gives an autonomous character to the histories of science and philosophy, the emergence of the basic concepts in either must be connected with that changing social experience which is part of general history.[6]

In the Indian tradition philosophy is considered to comprise the twin disciplines of *adhyātma-vidyā* and *ānvīkṣikī* or *nyāya-vidyā*.[7] The former of the two may be generally rendered as metaphysics, the latter as logic. Metaphysics included the account of cosmology and of all the essential constitutive principles of the universe. Thus, a part of it came to be a kind of natural philosophy and has relevance for the history of science. Similarly, logic studying the methodology and criteriology of knowledge has an evident significance for scientific development. It may, however, be remarked that interest in natural philosophy tended to decline with the progress of philosophical systems. Interest in logical questions, however, tended to increase. This is a general feature which the history of philosophy in India evinces. The reason is that philosophy began as cosmological speculation in the *Vedas* and the earlier *Upaniṣads* but, as it developed, it concerned itself more and more with the inner *psyche* of man and the very possibility and limits of philosophical knowledge. Philosophy became increasingly an effort at self-knowledge.

As is well known, the need for defining the calendar, building altars and the simple problems of evaluation involved in the exchange of goods led to the growth of Vedic arithmetic, geometry and astronomy such as may be found in the *Vedāṅgas*. Interest in the medicinal properties of herbs and the need to understand sickness, injury, etc., constituted another direction of the growth of scientific knowledge. The increasing use of metal and the alchemy of fire constituted a yet third direction which led to the growth of scientific know ledge. In the age of Buddha, apart from the precious metals and copper, iron was used widely for plough-shares, arrow-heads, etc. Takṣaśilā was a famous centre for the study of medicine. Trade and commerce were well developed and organized in guilds.[8] Philosophical speculation and logical disputation had become subjects of specialization.[9] It was in these conditions of a growing urban civilization that the three principal heterodox systems of philosophy, viz. Lokāyata, Buddhism and Jainism, took their rise in India.

These heterodox systems rejected the authority of Vedic revelation as a valid source of knowledge. On the contrary, they emphasized the testimony of human experience and reasoning. The Lokāyata[10] regarded sense-perception as the principal source of knowledge. They confined the role of reasoning to the drawing of probabilistic inferences from perceived facts. Reason for them is not an independent source of knowledge. It is not possible to gain certitude in terms of a purely rational knowledge. This emphasis of the Lokāyata on perception has often suffered a crude misrepresentation. They do admit probable knowledge or *sambhāvanā* beyond the direct evidence of the senses. What they do not admit is the possibility of establishing a necessary and universal connection (*vyāpti*) between two things or facts. Experience shows connections between particular things and facts. Observed connections are always parts of a given situation. When we generalize such connections, we cannot do so with certainty. We can only say that under similar circumstances we hopefully believe to observe similar phenomena, but conditions never are in fact absolutely similar. Consequently, the entire structure of rational knowledge is only probabilistic and tentative. From a scientific point of view, this theory, with its emphasis on direct observation and on the approximating nature of reasoning, can hardly be regarded as unhelpful or obstructive of progressive knowledge. Perhaps it does not sufficiently emphasize the role of creative imagination and deductive reasoning in the growth of knowledge. Yet, it is a sober corrective to the emphasis, then current, on transcendent causes and on the innate powers of the human mind to reach truth.

In conformity with their logic and epistemology, the Lokāyata formulated a materialistic metaphysics. Earth, water, fire and air were regarded as the four elements constituting the whole universe. Life and mind were explained as emergent functions (*madaśaktivat*) developing from a special combination of these elements. We have to remember that however positivistic or materialistic the Lokāyata may be, it is still primarily a philosophy, not a science. It is not its purpose to analyse the nature and qualities of the physical elements or to discover the laws of their motion and functioning. In speaking of earth, water, fire and air, the Lokāyata did not formulate any original view ; it merely took over a current enumeration of physical elements and for the purposes of its philosophy these four are simply illustrative. They are illustrative of natural entities perceivable by the senses. The complex nature of elements and their capacity of producing life and mind seems to have interested them only in terms of a philosophical possibility, not as sources of a possible practical knowledge which would give power over them. The Lokāyata, in fact, is to be understood as a philosophical movement with a critical bias. Its intention was to question and deny certain current philosophical tendencies. In fact, it was this excessive interest in mere criticism which seems to have led to the failure of the Lokāyata to evolve any detailed philosophical system. Their role in the history of philosophy has been of voicing a certain type of scepticism and criticism which any idealistic or religious philosophy must face. This position has always been accorded to them with great seriousness by all the other systems of Indian philosophy.

That the Lokāyata had some definite influence on the growth of a school of political thinking is undoubted. That they sharpened the dialectic of the other philosophical systems is also certain. Whether they, in point of fact, advanced or hindered the growth of scientific knowledge is quite uncertain. We hear of a prince who performed many experiments to find out whether the soul could ever be perceived escaping the body, but in vain.[11] The fact is that materialism could not develop in ancient India any special relevance to the growth of even medicine and biological science for the simple reason that the non-materialistic views themselves often conceded that life and mind are natural rather than spiritual entities. The great Śaṅkarācārya, for example, says that the mind is material and depends on the interaction between the body and its environment.[12] Sāṅkhya, Yoga, Vedānta—all strictly distinguish the mind from the soul and cheerfully abandon the mind to the realm of nature. Under the circumstnces a materialistic philosophy did not have to free biological inquiry from the unpredictable incursions of transcendent spiritual substances.

If we could speak of a scientific religion, Buddhism would be the one to qualify for the appellation. Buddhism banishes transcendent substances and also the futile quest for understanding phenomena in terms of rational essences. It is interested in the phenomenal nature of things, in their objectivity, specific characteristics, transformations and order.[13] Buddha laid down not a list of metaphysical substances but the general characteristics of phenomena and the law of their motion. Mind and matter were placed at the same level of objectivity. The soul was banished from the mind and the metaphysical substances from nature. Here is a banishment as complete as one might find in any positivist. Phenomena are called *dharma* or *saṃskāra*. *Dharma* is defined as *nissattva-nirjīva,* i. e. lacking a soul.[14] In other words, naturalness is made the defining feature of phenomena. The existence of a phenomenon is constituted not by its instancing or manifesting some essence but by its functioning. Thus, the Buddhist definition of existence is *artha-kriyā-kāritvaṃ sattvam,* i. e. existence is causal efficiency. To be is to function. From this rigorously follows the instantaneous character of being.[15] In the light of this doctrine of instantaneous phenomena arising and perishing in the causal nexus of a natural flux, the whole picture of the world as constructed by common sense or eternalist transcendent philosophies undergoes a sea-change. We look at the world with a microscope, as it were, and existent things become merely sets of point-instants (*kṣaṇa-saṁghāta*). The familiar identities of everyday life are merely the continuities (*santāna*) of instantaneous functioning.[16] Things are thus constructed, as it were, through the integration of infinitesimal causal functioning. The causal law is called *pratītyasamutpāda*. The Buddhist theory of causation is an extremely sophisticated doctrine.[17] Causation is not to be conceived anthropomorphically as some kind of activity in things distinct from their nature, nor is the concept of any dynamical force to be introduced. Neither an anthropomorphic or animistic, nor a dynamical or mechanical model is adequate for the understanding of causality. The essence of causality lies in the definiteness of the order in which natural processes occur. Each point-instant arises, functions and ceases spontaneously and simultaneously but in discernible sequences. There is only a fixed order in which the process develops. The Buddhist view of causality is simply a highly abstract description of ordered functioning.

In the sphere of logic, Buddhism accepted in its classical phase only two valid sources of knowledge–perception and inference. They pointed out that perception itself depends in its developed form on complicated apperception. The prior state of our knowledge inevitably colours the formation of perceptual judgements which do not, therefore, reveal to us nature in itself. The perceptual world is also a phenomenal world and the truth of perceptual judgements is only pragmatic. Inference and inferential judgements were broadly classified into three types, viz. analytical, synthetic and negative.[18] The first type refers to pure deduction or formal implication, the second to inferences based on causal connection, the third to the diverse conditions under which a negative judgement may validly arise. The reference of the inferential judgement to the outside world is mediated through possible perception. The truth of an idea depends on the invariable concomitance (*avyabhicāra*) of what the idea refers to with the thought which refers. This invariance of correlation arises from a natural psycho-physical process of causation. The Buddhist theory of truth, thus, has to be essentially pragmatic. That is true which does not deceive (*avisaṁvādin*) in practice.

Some of the Buddhist schools developed a theory of material elements and atoms.[19] They, however, completely transformed the meaning of the familiar terms–earth, water, fire and air.[20] The common meaning of these terms has hardly anything to do with their technical significance. The four elements are forces rather than substances. They are ever co-present, 'always in equal proportion. There is as much element of heat in a blazing flame as there is in wood or in water and *vice versa,* the difference is only in their intensity'.[21] The elements of 'earth', 'water', 'fire' and 'air' are characterized solely by resistance, cohesion, heat and motion. The four co-present atoms of these primary forms of matter constitute the basic unit of the material world. For becoming manifest in the experienceable world, this basic unit needs many other additions and it is only the resultant 'molecules' (*saṁhata-paramāṇu*) which may be regarded as the effective units of material phenomena. The idealistic schools of Buddhism, however, severely criticize this atomic theory.[22] They pointed out the difficulties in the concept of an actual infinitesimal. If matter were to be regarded as infinitely divisible, atomicity will not be actually realizable. On the other hand, it is certainly odd to conceive a finite atom which should be in principle indivisible. It was also pointed out that if the atom were to be imagined as a geometrical point, no finite collection of such points would acquire finite dimension.

Buddhist philosophical concepts and theories, thus, have a remarkable appropriateness for the synthesis of a world-picture based on scientific knowledge as it has developed in modern times. The Buddhist concepts of *dharma* or *dhātu* (element), *pratītyasamutpāda* (functional dependence), *nairātmya* (phenomenality), *kṣaṇa* (point instant), *saṃghāta* (aggregate), *saṁskāra* (force), *kāritra* (function), *sattva* (existence) and *pramāṇa* (valid knowledge) constitute a great departure from traditional thinking. The Buddhists pictured a world in terms of an ordered flux of instantaneous synergies. For this they refined the notions of 'element' and 'cause', 'existence' and 'truth'. Such concepts and theories were far in advance of what the science of those days was capable of measuring, calculating and constructing. The Buddhist thinkers themselves were philosophers, not scientists. They were interested in reaching a conceptual position, not in the practical application of the concepts in the course of everyday life. For example, they developed the notion of causality through an acute dialectic but they were not interested as philosophers in discovering the causal laws of the physical world. In one sphere, however, they did have a continuous scientific interest and that was in the realm of psychology. Buddhist psychology constitutes an extensive body of knowledge which evolved through centuries although modern scholarship has taken a very insufficient notice of it.[23] Buddhist psychology does not miss the mind for the body as much of modern psychological research working under the shadow of some kind of behaviourism appears to do. Psychic phenomena are undeniable and yet irreducible to physical phenomena. The Buddhist psychologists were not interested in controlling the outward behaviour of human beings in pursuance of some scheme of social planning. They were interested in discovering the laws along which the mind can acquire freedom from the tribulations of everyday life. It is possible for the human psyche to reach by its own efforts a superior level of knowledge and being. This attitude is scientific in so far as it studies the mind and its laws impersonally and objectively, and the validity of the Buddhist science of psychology is verifiable in terms of its techniques of meditation and contemplation[24] which do not in any sense depend on faith in transcendent entities. It is also worth noting that the asceticism or other-worldliness of the Buddhists did not prevent them from organizing educational institutions such as the *mahāvihāra* at Nalanda where secular learning was also pursued.[25] The Mahāyānic doctrine of *upāyakauśalya* easily resolved this contradiction.

Jainism seeks to preserve the truth of common sense along with the truth of philosophy and religion. It does not deny either the reality of the sensible world or that of the supersensible world. At the same time, Jainism emphasizes the central place of action in any scheme for understanding the world. So, the early Jainas called themselves 'believers in the spirit, believers in the world, believers in action' (*āyāvāī*, *loyāvāī, kiriyāvāī*).[26] A real soul acting in a real world—this is the Jaina picture. Action is meaningful only in the context of change, though not a change such as the Buddhists conceived. In the Buddhist flux all entities lose their identity. For the Jainas, change means modal transformation with substantial persistence. In seeking to defend the common-sense notion of change against dialectical antinomies the Jainas were led to the formulation of a new and extraordinary dialectic. Jaina dialectic is not negative like the Buddhist. It is nearer the Hegelian dialectic.[27] For it considers each of the different alternative predications of a subject to have a certain relative validity. The Jaina doctrine of *syādvāda* is essentially a theory of relativity. The nature of things is infinitely complex (*anantadharmātmakaṁ vastu*).[28] Consequently, no simple characterization of reality can be absolutely true. Any particular characterization has truth relative to some expressed and unexpressed condition. Measurements and direction in space, the colour and appearance of things, the application of abstract concepts like existence or identity—all these are examples of only relatively meaningful descriptions. In the realm of philosophy this doctrine helps the creation of comprehensive syntheses of points of view.

The Jainas reached considerable precision and elaboration in their measures of space and time. They attempt to give measurements at various levels suited to the atomic or the cosmic dimensions.[29] They also have an elaborate atomic theory.[30] The nature of the inter-atomic bond (*bandha*) is explained as the union of dissimilars where a critical role is played by the level of intensity or degree. Atoms are credited with moving at variable speeds. Their slowest motion just suffices for them to move from one point to the next. On the other hand, their fastest motion will carry them across the universe in a single instant of time. The diameter of the universe is defined as 14 *rajjus,* one *rajju* being a distance which has been variously calculated. Mathematics (*Gaṇitānuyoga*) is one of the four principal branches of Jaina literature and in the Jaina canonical works occur some of the earliest references to the different branches in which mathematics developed in ancient times.[31] Some of the later great mathematicians are also definitely known to have been Jainas.[32]

The Jainas claim that their doctrine of *Karman* is fully scientific. They regard *Karman* to be a kind of fine matter. It is the relationship of *Karman* to the soul which in its various modes determines the range of knowledge as well as the emergence of the passions in the soul and also provides the network of occasions for the realization of the individual's destiny. In short, *Karman* is a subtle material force which determines psychic functioning and events. It is claimed that by suitable psycho-physical askesis the soul can acquire the power of perceiving the subtle manifestations and working of *Karman*.

From this survey of the three principal heterodox systems of philosophy it would be clear that as philosophies they could have been held in different ways consistently with scientific progress. The Lokāyata emphasis on observation and their explanation of general laws as merely probabilistic could both have helped in the progress of scientific inquiry. Similarly, the Buddhist emphasis on causal processes and their pragmatic view of truth could both be similarly useful. The sturdy common sense of Jainism, along with its relativistic dialectic, and also its attention to systems of measurement could be parts of a growing science. There is nothing essential in these philosophies which should have been definitely obstructive of scientific progress. In fact, the period when these philosophies flourished was a period when medicine, metallurgy, mathematics and astronomy certainly grew and developed. It must, however, be remembered that in those days the intellectuals tended to be essentially scholars and philosophers, not technicians or practical inventors. As a result, the progress of strictly scientific thought tended to be doubly limited—by the predominantly philosophical inclination of the intellectuals and again by the relatively slow development of mechanical inventions and technology. Medicine and astronomy alone attained the status of prestige disciplines, and during this period, at least, their progress on the whole was as extensive as in contemporary times elsewhere.

REFERENCES AND NOTES

1. Farrington, B., *Greek Science, its Meaning for us*, pp. 29ff. Cf. Burnet, *Greek Philosophy*, pp. 11-12, where the stress is laid on the distinction between philosophy and science.

2. Ross, W. D., *Aristotle*, pp. 62ff.

3. Newton's *magnum opus* in the seventeenth century was still entitled *Philosophiae Naturalis Principia Mathematica.*

4. Ross, *op. cit.*, pp. 216ff.

5. Alexandrov, Kolmogorow, Lavrentev (Ed.), *Mathematics, its Content, Methods and Meaning* (M.I.T., 1965), Vol. I, p. 17. 'This...is one of the fundamental laws of formation of mathematical concepts : They are brought into being by a series of successive abstractions and generalization, each resting on a combination of experience with preceding abstract concepts'. *Ibid.*, Vol. II, p. 47–'The ultimate criterion of the truth of the result is thus practical experience only.'

6. Wilder, *Introduction to the Foundations of Mathematics*, pp. 264ff. ; Spengler, O., *The Decline of the West*, Vol. I, Chapter II.

7. Vātsyāyana's *Nyāyabhāṣya, Nyāyasūtras*, 1.1.1.

8. Rhys Davids, *Buddhist India*.

9. Pande, G. C., *Studies in the Origins of Buddhism*.

10. Lokāyata views have to be gleaned from their presentation and refutation by their opponents through the ages or through such compendia as Mādhavācārya, *Sarvadarśanasaṁgraha.* Among modern works one may mention, Tucci, *A Sketch of Indian Materialism* ; Shastri, D., *Short History of Indian Materialism*.

11. *Dīghanikāya* : *Pāyāsī Sūtta*.

12. Commentary on the *Chāndogya-upaniṣad*, 7.26.

13. Rosenberg *Die Probleme der buddhistischen Philosophie.*

14. On the Buddhist concept of Dharma, see Rosenberg, *op. cit.*, Stcherbatsky, *Central Conception of Buddhism.*

15. See texts like *Tattvasaṁgraha* or *Kṣaṇabhaṅgasiddhi.*

16. Stcherbatsky, *Buddhist Logic,* Vol. I, pt. II.

17. Pande, G. C., *op. cit.*, pp. 407ff.

18. Dharmakīrti's *Nyāyabindu,* 2.11.

19. Vasubandhu, *Abhidharmakośa,* 2.22.

20. Stcherbatsky, *Central Conception of Buddhism,* pp. 11-12.

21. *Loc. cit.*

22. Vasubandhu's *Vijñaptimātratāsiddhi* (*Viṁśikā*), vv 11-15.

23. The work of Mrs. Rhys Davids, *The Birth of Indian Psychology and its Development in Early Buddhism* may be mentioned.

24. See Buddhaghoṣa, *Visuddhimaggo.*

25. Mookerji, R. K., *Ancient Indian Education,* pp. 528ff.

26. *Āyāraṅga,* I.

27. Pande, G. C., *op. cit.*, p. 544.

28. *Syādvādamañjarī* with Hemacandra's commentary, ad. v. 22ff.

29. Nathmal, *Jain Darśana ke Maulik Tattva,* Vol. II, pp. 192.

30. *Ibid.*, pp. 195ff.; Seal, B. N., *Positive Sciences of the Ancient Hindus,* pp. 93ff.

31. Nathmal, *op. cit.,* Vol. I, p. 224.

32. Shankar Balkrishna Dikshit, *Bhāratīya Jyotiṣa* (Pub. Hindi Samiti), p. 317.

13

LITERATURE

Ancient Sanskrit literature is much vaster than ancient Greek, Latin or Hebrew literatures. In its extent and variety, quality and quantity Sanskrit literature is an unparalleled heritage moulding the life and thought of India through the millennia. Like a golden thread it binds together the diverse modern language and literatures of India and its production has not ceased still. But the value of Sanskrit literature is more than national. It constitutes a distinct and permanent achievement of the human spirit, a part of the universal heritage of man. It is a pity, however, that very few adequate modern translations from Sanskrit exist.

At the outset it is necessary to remember a certain general difference between ancient and modern literatures. Modern literature is agnostic and secular and its social awareness is historical. It is also individualistic in the sense that it regards the expression of the individual psyche in its particularity as a value. From the point of view of ancient tradition modern literature is replete with the particular and the ephemeral. On the other hand, ancient literature can hardly satisfy the modern taste for subjectivity, democracy and naturalism. It is necessary to mention this because several modern writers on Sanskrit have tended to disparage it in terms drawn from the critique of classicism by the Romantics.[1] Sanskrit literature is neither classical like Graeco-Roman literature nor Classicist like 17th and 18th century English or French literatures. This is not to say that Sanskrit literature has to be judged solely by its own standards or criteria.[2] While it presupposes a distinctive cultural background and taste, Sanskrit literature lays claim for universality and permanence and must be judged by appropriate standards which must not, however, be confused with particular conventions of form and taste. Thus 'tragedy' and 'comedy' do not represent distinct forms in Sanskrit; nor is there any reason why they should. Literary forms are conventions, not natural species. And yet one may legitimately expect any great literature to give adequate expression to the experience of suffering as well as happiness and must be judged by the depth and breadth and height of such expression.

Thus in approaching Sanskrit literature one must avoid three types of errors. One must not think of it as a literature which ought to have been modelled on Graeco-Roman literature, a mistake which Professor Keith commits implicitly.[3] Nor should we think of Sanskrit literature as one which ought to have been an anticipation of modern forms and trends, a mistake which is implicit in Prof. Dasgupta and De's *History of Sanskrit Literature*. Finally, we must not think of Sanskrit literature as entitled only to the opinions of its own ancient critics according to traditional standards, a point of view which Professor Warder has adopted in his *History of Kāvya Literature*.

Literature seeks to communicate primarily felt and intuited values and does it principally through the representation of experience in a suitable form. We value literature for the insight it gives us into values, for the imaginative experience which moves us and in which we seem to think that we are seeing things in perspective and are grateful for the flood of magical light which sweeps us along and makes us feel wiser for the moment at least. As the ancient tradition tells us, this imponderable and felt experience of value constitutes the real 'meaning' of a literary work.[4] All other meanings, literal and figurative, and words are only the medium for the revelation of *Rasa*. *Rasa*, mistranslated sentiment, is manifested in terms of experience but is really a quality belonging to the spirit.[5] The intuition of *rasa* is nothing except a self-realisation in terms of imaginative experience (*bhāvāvacchinna-cidāvaraṇa-*

bhaṅga).[6] Since it is an empirical self-realisation in *imagination, rasa* may present itself as the essence of the most diverse characters, situations and responses. It is unfortunate that the attempts at classifying *rasa* and *bhāva* in later theory had the effect of encouraging the search for creating and recognising stereotypes and of encouraging sentimentality. But then critical theory always does have this unfortunate effect on the lesser minds. The great work of art is a law unto itself and in course of time what the critics unravel of its structure and technique becomes standardized as a model for the lesser writers who in any case deserve oblivion. The classification of *rasas* and *bhāvas* is, however, significant as an analysis of the basic cultural ideas and attitudes with which the critics believed the literary tradition to concern itself. The diverse *rasas* and *bhāvas* are not descriptions of aesthetic experience, nor recipes of literary creation. Nor are they standards of literary judgments, nor yet permanent elements of human psychology. It does not need to be pointed out that the experience of a literary work is not the same as the experience of the life situations described in it. Nor indeed are life situations experienced in the raw since they are apperceived socially. Again, literary creations must be original and literary judgment cannot be based simply on generalized contents. For this reason, *rasas* and *bhāvas* in their differentiated forms represented merely the broad themes with which literature concerned itself according to ancient critics.

We have to remember that this classification is first found in a standardized form in the *Nāṭyaśāstra*. Already a long and rich history of literary creation existed before this and with respect to it the classification mentioned by Bharata could only have been descriptive, not normative. It was really an attempt at a broad thematic classification. Unfortunately it came to be regarded as an integral part of the theory of *Rasa* without any attempt being made to connect the classification with the general theory systematically. The fact is that the *Nāṭyaśāstra* (6th chapter) mentions the *rasas* and *bhāvas* as known in the Nāṭya tradition and then goes on to suggest a general theory of *rasa*. Thus it says *"Śṛṅgāra-hāsya-karuṇa-*

raudra- vīra-bhayānakāḥ/ Bībhatsādbhutasañjñau cetyaṣṭau nāṭye rasāḥ smṛtāḥ// (6.16.) "Romance, humour, pathos, fierceness, heroism, terror, disgust and wonder, these eight are known as *rasas* in drama." This is not a description of what exists in nature but what is traditionally recognized in drama. Commenting on this further, Bharata traces the eight *rasas* to four fundamental *rasas*. *"Śṛṅgārādhi bhaved hāsyo raudrācca karuṇo rasaḥ/ Vīrāccaivādbhutotpattir bibhatsāccabhayānakaḥ//"* (6.40). *Śṛṅgāra, Raudra, Vīra* and *Bībhatsa* give rise to humour, *pathos,* wonder and terror respectively. *Raudra* here becomes the attitude corresponding to Greek tragedy, beginning in violence and ending in pity. Along with the classification of *rasa,* Bharata also gives a theory of *rasa* as such. The famous *sūtra* runs—*"Tatra vibhāvānubhāva-vyabhicāri-saṁyogād rasa-niṣpattiḥ"* (*Nāṭyaśāstra,* p. 93). This is not a description gleaned from literary works, nor is it properly an empirical psychological formula, for *rasa* is not simply a psychological fact. It is inseparable from a judgmental process.

The full implications of this theory were discussed by generations of scholars. For some time many felt that this theory referred only to drama and did not apply to poetry for which rival theories of *alaṅkāra, rīti* and *guṇa* were put forward. In the eighth century Ānandavardhana propounded the theory of *dhvani* and brought all literature within the compass of *rasa.* In the ninth century Abhinavagupta's commentaries on the *Nāṭyaśāstra* and the *Dhvanyāloka* formed the capping stone on the development of the theory of *rasa. Rasa* was now clearly understood in the context of the spiritual metaphysics of Kaśmīra Śaivism.

The *rasa-sūtra* of Bharata means *Rasa* is accomplished through the combination of *Vibhāva, Anubhāva* and *Vyabhicāri-bhāva* (*with-sthāyi-bhāva*). The primary material of *rasa* is *sthāyi-bhāva* or one of the instinctive attitudes like love. When such an attitude finds a suitable objective correlate, a person and a situation, we get the combination of *bhāva* with *vibhāva.* This combination develops through the emergence of transient feelings (*vyabhicāribhāva*) and emotional bodily expressions. The result of this process is *rasa.* Bharata explains that *rasa* is so called because it is enjoyable. "*Rasa iti kaḥ padārthaḥ ucyate āsvādyatvāt.*" Just as out of different ingredients a tasty dish may be produced so *rasas* are produced out of *bhāvas* in drama. "*Bhāvebhyo rasānām abhinirvṛttiḥ*".

It will be obvious that this exposition of Bharata is neither clear nor complete. It does not clarify whether it is describing the arousal of emotions in real life or the enjoyment of their dramatic depiction on the stage by the spectators. The meaning of the crucial term *niṣpatti* is not clear. Does it refer to actual causation or to imitation on the stage or to evocation by dramatic means? On the other hand, Bharata's reference to the tasting of a dish can only be regarded as highly misleading. It seems to compare *rasa* with hedonic enjoyment, with *aesthesis*, and its literal sensuousness. It is for this reason that for long the critics of the more intellectual literary arts which depended on the word rather than on visible representations, appealed to *rhetoric* as against the mere aesthetic of *rasa*.

Among these who sought to clarify the aesthetic of *rasa* the most important were Bhaṭṭa Lollaṭa, Śaṅkuka, Bhaṭṭanāyaka and Abhinavagupta. Bhaṭṭa Lollaṭa represented the earliest tradition of interpretation. "*Cirantanānām ayameva pakṣah*". On this view *niṣpatti* simply means production or causation. *Rasa* is primarily nothing but the arousal and continuity of some basic emotional attitude in real life. Thus Duṣyanta is the primary locus of love and Śakuntalā in the woodland the primary *vibhāva*. The overt indications of love in their behaviour include *anubhāva*. The diverse feelings through which their love develops are the *vyabhicāribhāvas*. The actors represent this life situation on the stage and the spectators imaginatively identify the enactment with reality and reach an intuitive awareness of the emotional procession belonging to the latter.[7] This view came to be criticised because of its inability to sufficiently emphasize the distinctiveness of aesthetic experience. There is an undoubted connection between life and literature but to identify literary appreciation with the emotional experience of real life appears to be a simplification. Śaṅkuka, therefore, suggested that *rasa* should be regarded as the spectator's inferential awareness of the feelings imitated by the actors.[8] *Niṣpatti,* thus, becomes *anumiti.* Inference, however, is not understood here in a strictly logical sense. The knowledge which the spectator acquires is not an emotionally neutral cognition, valid or invalid. The knowledge of the spectator is an experience (*pratīti,*[9] *anubhava*) which is neither true nor false nor a mere doubt.[10] Its inferential character only means that the enactment on the stage is the means which lead the spectator to a distinctive experience. The mediation of 'imitation' and 'inference' appears to transform the material of life into the distinctive aesthetic experience. Śaṅkuka's *anumiti* seems to grope towards a notion of empathy.

Both Lollaṭa and Śaṅkuka agree in regarding aesthetic experience as the immediate awareness of *rasa,* as an emotional process which is given objectively. Lollaṭa regards this process to belong to real life and its immediate awareness to be perceptual but influenced by an assumed belief or imagination. Śaṅkuka regards the awareness to be a peculiar inference to which the question of the ontic status of its object is irrelevant. Both regard drama as an imitation of life but while Lollaṭa thinks that the spectator under the influence of imagination is charmed by the imitated spectacle of life surcharged with emotion, Śaṅkuka thinks that the charm lies in the very nature of the experience which the spectator undergoes.

Whether quasi-perceptual or quasi-inferential the spectator's awareness is clearly of a different order than that in life. Even with this recognition both these views are essentially misled about the nature of *rasa* since they conceive it as the *object* of some kind of cognition, perception or inference. Real *rasa* is made to belong to a real subject and dramatic *rasa* is the same or its imitation becoming somehow the object of the spectator's awareness.

Bhattanāyaka declared that *rasa* is neither cognized, nor produced nor manifested—"*raso na pratīyate notpadyate nābhivyajyate.*[11] *Rasa* cannot be cognized by the spectator either as belonging to another or as belonging to himself. Besides if such cognition be indirect it will fail to move the spectator. If it is direct it will cause him embarrassment and revulson. If *rasa* were produced, i. e., if it were regarded as a natural psychological effect, it will still need to be cognized by the spectator and the same difficulties will arise as mentioned above. Nor can *rasa* be thought of as a pre-existing fact or state which is manifested because we would then have to admit many degrees in *rasa*. Besides, the difficulties in the case of a cognition will still persist. Thus rejecting the earlier views Bhaṭṭanāyaka clearly extends the *rasa*-theory beyond drama to poetry too and holds that there is a function of words or dramatic presentations which creates a state of universalized or de-individualized subjectivity in the spectator or reader and then there is another function of withdrawal into the inner consciousness along with the enjoyment of its bliss which is similar to beatific experience.[12] The generalizing power of words and representations and their power to awaken the capacity of the psyche to reach and enjoy its own tranquillity, these account for *rasa*. *Rasa,* thus, has several roots—feelings, generalizing effect of representations, inward tranquillity. What art does is to transfigure feelings so that the self is enabled to turn inwards.

Bhaṭṭanāyaka has certainly seized on the essential moments of aesthetic experience viz., its impersonal character and its tranquillity. Nevertheless, he does not give any systematic account of the whole. His conception of the two capacities appears inadequately reasoned and if he discards both causation and expression with reference to *rasa,* he traps himself in a blind alley.

Abhinavagupta, therefore, joins the notion of *rasa* with that of *dhvani*. *Rasa* is simply a meaning expressed by a literary work to a properly sensitive reader or spectator.[13] This power of expression is something which the words have in addition to their power of denotation or of metaphor. It is the power of suggestion or evocation.[14] Thus grasped the meaning is a felt whole in an act of mental intuition, *"mānasī sākṣātkārātmikā pratītir upajāyate."*[15] *Rasa* is, thus, an undistracted, intuitive awareness. *"Sācāvighnā saṁvic camat-*

kāraḥ."[16] 'Wonderment, enjoyment, absorption, withdrawal', are all different ways of referring to *Rasa*. Abhinava mentions seven distractions (*Vighnas*).[17] The first of these is the lack of plausibility of the presentation so that the reader's disbelief cannot remain suspended. The second is the identification of the presentation with self or other or with specific times and places. Such identifications tend to produce distracting reactions characteristic of real life. The third distraction is by one's own personal feelings of pleasure, pain etc. The fourth distraction arises from an inadequacy of means enabling one to cognize the meaning sought to be expressed. The fifth is the lack of vividness, the sixth is lack of focus, the seventh, doubt about the meaning.

Abhinava distinguishes *bhāva* from *rasa*.[18] *Bhāvas* are innate tendencies while *rasa* is the self-enjoyment of consciousness. *Bhāva* is not *produced* as a psychic *fact* as far as literary appreciation is concerned. It is only *expressed* as a *meaning*. *Vibhāva*, therefore, is not a real cause but a representation of it.[19] Thus, words present the images of the objective correlates of instinctive attitudes, and their recognition evokes feelings. When this felt experience is impersonal but a vivid and coherent intuition, the innate self-enjoyment of consciousness is manifested. This is *Rasa*, and it is neither an object nor a cognition. It is essentially a self-revelation of consciousness.[20]

Pandit Raj Jagannātha says that on this view *Rasa* is the name given to *Bhāva* when it is immediately apprehended by the consciousness without veils. The absorption of consciousness in a world of felt images produces as in a dream a state of immediacy in which consciousness and feelings both stand revealed in an integral moment. What happens in such a moment is that the self reveals itself in and through the limitation of feelings. The self-revelation of consciousness assimilates *rasa* to spiritual ecstasy but the presence of feelings and images distinguishes it. *Rasa*, in short, is the moment of self-revelation within a process of felt, imaginative experience evoked by words or representations. "*Ratyādyavacchinnā bhagnāvaraṇā cideva rasaḥ*."[21]

The connection of the classification of *rasas* with this general theory of *rasa* is tenuous. It is true that Abhinavagupta tries to give a systematic account of the diversity of *rasas* by an appeal to empirical psychology, and that Bhoja seeks to give a meta-physical derivation, but the fact remains that the different *rasas* really represent socially recognised attitudes or sentiments. That is why their enumeration has varied in the course of ages. At first, as mentioned before, only eight *rasas* were recognised.[22]

Gradually *śānta* was added as a ninth *rasa*. Ānandavardhana, in fact, held that *Mahābhārata* belonged to *Śānta rasa*. Even in the twelfth century *bhakti* was treated only as a transient *bhāva*.[23] In the sixteenth century Vedāntic authors like Madhusūdana held that *bhakti* was a *rasa*.[24]

According to classical theory the three principal *rasas* are *Vīra, Śṛṅgāra* and *Śānta*. If we turn to the history of Indian literature we can see that its earliest phase of Vedic poetry or Upaniṣadic prose and verse is characterized by the revelation of heroism, wonder, or tranquillity based on spiritual enlightenment. In modern terminology we could say that Vedic religious and philosophic poetry is characterized by the sublimity of an overarching, cosmic or spiritual vision. In the early post-Vedic phase we find the tradition of *Śānta rasa* emerging in ascetic poetry, Brahmanical, Buddhist and Jaina, as the poetry of this age is characterized by the sense of *Weltschmerz,* resignation and quiescence rather than by that of activism, joy and harmony, characteristic of the Vedic age. By the side of this religio-philosophical poetry we have the great heroic poetry of the epics which also depict a delicate sense of the romantic. In the classical age the heroic idea persisted but gradually degenerated in the same way as the aristocracy did. Romance was the other major theme of classical poetry. Here too gradually erotic sensuousness tended to predominate in *Śṛṅgāra*. The classical age with its emphasis on *Vīra* and *Śṛṅgāra* may, in fact, be divided into two distinct phases. The earlier one to which Kālidāsa and Bhavabhūti belong, treat of heroism and romance within an integral and balanced view of life. It was an age when society was prosperous and flexible and when an attempt was being made to synthesize *pravṛtti* and *nivṛtti*. The age after the 8th century A.D. showed a growth of rigidity and growing imbalance in society and religion. The literature of the age also tends to show a one-sided exaggeration. It culminates in Śrī Harṣa.

Vedic hymns are traditionally regarded as *śāstra* rather than *kāvya* but then that does not alter the structure of words and meanings in the *Veda* which are undoubtedly poetic. There is no reason why revealed poetry speaking with authority should cease to be regarded as poetry. It is just unfortunate that the study of Vedic hynms was for long left to the ritualists. The Vedic seers themselves regarded their work as poetry and that should be sufficient to dispose of any doubt on the subject.

"Never was poetry held in higher esteem and its nature and purpose conceived more exaltedly than in the early Vedic age. Poetry, vision and wisdom were held to be identical. When clothed in rhythm and skillfully composed, the words could attract divine grace and become inspired visions. The human poet was a counterpart of the divine. Vision, creativity, form and rhythm, these really belong to the divine mind. God is called Poet, Seer, Creator, Fashioner of Forms.[25] Man can only imitate God and become a poet only when inspired, a creator in the realm of words. But what the poet creates must, being inspired, have authority. This authority of the poet's word was turned into a kind of literal and legalistic authority by the Mīmāṁsakas"[26] but even they had to admit that a distinction must be made between *vidhi* and *arthavāda !*

The vision of Vedic poetry is that of the inherent value and sublimity of being. Joy, peace and harmony underlie the universe. The cosmos is the manifestation of a divine order, an expression of divine forces. Vedic poetry gives expression to the delight of cosmic existence, its harmonious order, the play of its luminous powers. Poetry never reached such sublimity, nor such rhythm and cadence touching 'over mind' heights.[27]

The Vedic poet is the priest seated by the altar, engaged in worship, his compositions are invocations and prayers addressed to the gods and in these the fact and metaphor of ritual play a leading part. The ritual is the earthly counterpart of the *Ṛta* in the highest heaven and the altar is the 'nave of the whole cosmos'. The imagination of the Vedic poet thus ranges over all life and nature and sees in them the working of the gods in accordance with the laws and pattern of *Ṛta*. Gods are not 'things' or 'beings' but 'essences' and 'values', forms of the indwelling creative and determining mind or spirit in all cosmos.[28] Despite their setting and vocabulary the hymns to the gods do not belong to some mythical world apart but represent the experience of nature in its mythical understanding. The hymns to Agni speak of the flaming resplendence of the god, his golden hair and beard, the crunching of his jaws and at the same time they speak of his wisdom and poetry. He is the poet and singer among the gods, the patron of human poets and singers. He is the Father, the lord of the house, guide and protector. Agni is the visible god on earth linking men with gods. "If modern man does not follow what has been said, let him wait until winter and evening, kindle the hearth and simply gaze at the live coals, and he will surely understand that the Lord is he who breaks his isolation without breaking his solitude."[29] Even after death it is Agni that takes man through the Path of Smoke to the world of his ancestors. The hymns to Agni are hymns not only to the presiding spirit of the home and the hearth but also to the spirit of prayer and poetry.[30] In fact, the concern with the Word and the creative process is one of the central concerns of the Vedic poets.

Another important concern of the Vedic seers is the phenomenon of governance, the exercise of righteous and wise authority. Indra, Varuṇa and Mitra are the symbols of authority. Their writ runs over the universe. Of these Indra is not only the mighty ruler but also the leader of the hosts, a mighty warrior. The hymns to Indra represent war and conflict, might and victory, heroism and exhileration. The hymns to Varuṇa and Mitra express the solemn and sublime grandeur of cosmic law and sovereignty. If lightening and thunder symbolize the striking might of Indra, the star-studded night-sky symbolizes the eternal vigilance of law.[31]

If Agni and Indra correspond to *Brahman* and *Kṣattra,* to prayer and governance, the Maruts correspond to the *Viśaḥ,* the common people. The gods of wind and storm are a multitude, a throng of warriors in gleaming armour following Indra and showing their prowess in battle. The atmospheric phenomenon of rain attracted the poets as much as the celestial phenomenon of daily illumination. The glory of dawn was sung as that of a beauteous maiden, waking up early and prompting all living beings to go to work. She is the model of all earthly maidens.[32]

Centred in the experience of nature and society as the expression of *ṛta,* Vedic poetry represents kings and warriors, priests and poets, maidens and mothers. It dwells on fields and forests, the procession of Night and Dawn, the fertilising shower of rain and clouds. It portrays domestic and wild animals in their strength and speed. It presents meditations over the mystery of creation, of the cosmos and of the Word. It contains sombre farewells to the dead and also light-hearted ditties on the occasion of soma-pressing. There is a hymn celebrating ploughing; another giving a gambler's lament.[33]

Among the hymns of the *Ṛgveda* best known for their poetic excellence may be mentioned the hymns to Dawn. Ṛ. 4.51, for example, begins by welcoming the pathmaking light emerging from darkness in the east. The brilliant dawns are said to stand up like decorated sacrificial posts and to travel round the world in their chariot drawn by Ṛta-yoked horses. Doubtless there have been older and younger dawns but they all appear alike, unaging. They are luminous with grace (*abhiṣṭi-dyumnaḥ*) and "true with the truth that springs from holy Order" (*ṛta-jāta-satyāḥ*). Here and elsewhere it is not simply the brilliance and hues of the light of dawn which attract the poet; what attracts him specially is the regularity with which they appear and prompt men to action. They are part of an order in which darkness and light are divided. They do not age but men do. The hymns to Dawn are not hymns to sensuous beauty. They are reflections of man's encounter with the occurrence of illumination in time. Given to rise early for the activities of the day Vedic man never failed to wonder at the passing of the night and the dawning of a fresh day. He saw the event not only in its natural setting but in its relationship to the life of worship. Light comes to men by its own fixed order, awakening them and calling them. Even while men work their day passes. Light remains the same, unaging immortal.

The Vedic perception of beauteous form is not a minute, visualizing perception such as one might find in Kālidāsa or Dante. The Vedic perception is an insight into the luminous force which creates forms and transcends them. The freedom of beauty from mere sensuous plasticity also enables the Vedic poets to see the continuity of beauty and goodness. And this perception joins with that of natural being in the perception of a cosmic harmony. "For the pious the breezes are honeyed, the streams flow with honey. May plants be honeyed for us. So night and dawn and the earthly firmament. May our father, Heaven, be honeyed. May the woods and the sun and the cows be full of honey for us." (Ṛ. 1.90-6-8). This sense of harmonious unity is reflected in the notion of *Ṛta* as well as *Brahman* where being, and knowledge and value are unified. "If this sky were not blissful who would have breathed and lived?" (*Tai-upa*). "This is the best of all worlds" (*Viśvamidaṁ Variṣṭham—Muṇḍaka*).

The mystery of time is an important theme of Vedic poetry and with it is bound up the mystery of creation. The famous Asyavāmīya hymn of Dīrghatamas (Ṛ. 1.164) says, "Seven to the one-wheeled chariot yoke the courser; bearing seven names the single courser draws it.

Three-naved the wheel is sound and undecaying, whereon are resting all these worlds of being...

....

Upon this five-spoked wheel revolving ever all living creatures rest and are dependent. Its axle heavy-laden is not heated, the nave from ancient time remains unbroken."[34]

Despite its obscure symbolism this hymn is replete with a sense of mystery of how time is dovetailed with eternity, separate parts of an order which is nothing but one. The sun was the most appropriate symbol of Time as well as Eternity.

Water similarly symbolized the unmanifest source of creation. The famous *Nāsadīya sūkta* (Ṛ. 10.12a) begins by saying "Neither non-being, nor being then obtained. Neither was the atmosphere, nor that sky beyond. What covered and where? What was the shelter? Was water there, impassable and deep?"

What enables the Vedic poet to sing of beauty and harmony, to probe the mystery of time and creation? His own answer was that it is Vāk, Speech, or rather seeing speech, the faculty of intuition and expression—"*Uta tvaḥ paśyan na dadurśa vācam uta tvaḥ śṛṇvan na śṛnotyenā/ Uto tvasmai tanvaṁ visasre jāyeva patyā uśatī suvāsāḥ.*"[35]

If Vedic poetry seeks to express the sense of cosmic delight, the sense of cosmic suffering and pain, of *Weltschmerz*, is expressed by the ascetic poetry of the *Mahābhārata*, and of the Buddhists and the Jains. Just as *rasa* or *ānanda* should not be confused with sensuous pleasure or gratification, similarly *duḥkha* in this context should not be confused with the sensation of pain. *Duḥkha* is subtle and comprehensive enough to include all experience. *Duḥkha* is not accidental, arising for some specific situation in which the psyche finds itself. It is on the contrary, an existential sorrow belonging to the psyche and arising from the very conditions from which experience arises just as heat arises along with light in the burning wick. Ancient Śramaṇism supplied the philosophical background of this notion of sorrow and it has remained a continuing strand within the complex web of Indian sensibility.

The Buddhists held that to realize the universal nature of suffering is to realize the sublime truth of suffering. Every one remembers the pangs of pain but few the transitoriness of pleasures. Few remember that we must grow old.

"You are like a yellow leaf, death is at hand."[36] "Sickness and palsied tottering Eld,

Yea, Death itself, these eyes beheld."[37]

To remember old age and death is bound to lead to distaste for life. "Where is laughter, where joy when everything is burning constantly?"[38] One must remember that death carries away life as a nocturnal flood the village.[39]

This sorrow arising from the impermanence of all things is *Pariṇāma-duḥkhatā*. After gaining victory over the Kauravas, Yudhiṣṭhira was assailed by the sudden realization of Impermanence and wanted to quit. In the *Strīparvan* we have the lamentation of women over the dead. In the *Śāntiparvan* we find the expression of Yudhiṣṭhira's regret over the war and reflections over impermenence. The celebrated Dialogue between the Jackal and the Scavenger Bird presents two contrasted attitudes towards death most forcefully.[40]

With ascetic poetry in the Buddhist and Jaina canon we find a new poetic form, the single or 'free verse', sometimes combined into strings of a few verses. These verses are distinguished by their mood and theme and easily form collections. The *Theragāthās* and *Therīgāthās* are the earliest examples of such collections where the short poems are of definite and known authorship. More than a millennium later came the *Vairāgya-śataka* of Bhartṛhari.

The sense of impermanence and of the inevitability of death led to a revulsion from pleasures and desires which were felt as snares. Women and carnal beauty being the most powerful of the objects of instinctive passions came in for condemnation. The whole of worldly life was felt to be a bondage and one longed for freedom and solitude and peace. The gamut of ascetic experiences began with the sense of suffering and ended with the sense of peace and liberation.

Some examples would illustrate the diverse feelings which constituted the experience of *Weltschmerz*. A song of a Buddhist monk thus renders the sense of impermanence:

"Days and nights go speeding fast;
Life itself doth pass away;
As the river rushing fast,
Men hasten by, and may not stay!
Though they would its sting ignore,
Fools the doom of sin endure:
Retribution cometh sure!"

(*Thera*° 145, tr. Saunders, *op. cit.*, p. 36)

The *Chāndogya Upaniṣad* relates that seeing his mirror-image the prince of the Asuras felt satisfied that the body is really the soul, deserving all care and devotion. A Buddhist poet on the contrary says:

"The barber came to dress my hair.
I took the mirror from his hand,
And in it all my body scanned.
And whilst I gazed, lo! then and there
I knew the vileness of the flesh;
So broke I through the clinging mesh
Of Ignorance, and cast aside
the unclean garment of my pride.
Now stript of Vanity I go;
No more shall I be born to woe!"

(*Thera*° 160, tr. Saunders, *op. cit.*, p. 34)

Here is an expression of the sense of solitude:

"Blind and alone my way I wind,
The desert sand before, behind,
Shunning the haunts of evil men,
Here let me die, alone and blind."

(*Ib.*, 95, tr. Saunders, *op. cit.*, p. 35)

Solitude is also freedom:

"Alone dwell I in dreadful cave,
The rain pours gurgling ceaselessly;
These things for me no terrors have;
Heeding them not, my mind is free."

(Saunders, *op. cit.*, p. 40)

So is contentment:

"Cold and dark is the winter's night;
It chops the skin; it freezes thought!
Where shall the shivering bhikkhu lie?
Into safe barns the harvest's brought;
The Magadhans rejoice; and I
Rejoice with them. I'll sleep, all right.
In good warm straw this winter's night."

(*Ib.*, p. 41)

Abandoning the fetters of home life is a foretaste of greater freedom. A nun exclaims "O free, indeed! O gloriously free Am I in freedom from three crooked things: From quern, from mortar, from my Crookback'd lord." (I. B. Horner, *Early Buddhist Poetry*, p. 61).

Realizing the vanity of domestic and worldly life the monk turns to solitary meditation. The meditating monk is deeply aware of the quiet beauty of nature—"White against the dark storm-cloud/Homeward fly the frightened cranes;/ The cave they seek is hid by rains;/The toads awakened croak aloud/Here where the streamlets rush in spate/Beneath dark trees I'll meditate".[41] Here is another example of nature seen through meditative eyes, reminding one of later Zen poetry—"Big with rains is the stormy sky;/The crested peacock calls his mate;/The earth gleams fresh with greenery;/A fitting time to meditate."[42]

Meditation meant not only silent contemplation but also intellectual analysis and comprehension. The nun Vajirā thus analyses the human personality into a fleeting compound of parts even as a chariot is. "For just as, when the parts are rightly set, The word 'chariot' ariseth (in our minds) /So doth, our usage covenants to say : /A 'being' when the aggregates are there."[43]

The end of the journey is beyond Speech and thought—"Just as the bourn of a blazing spark of fire/Struck from the anvil, gradually fading.

Cannot be known..."[44]

Quite distinct from ascetic poetry is the tradition of heroic poetry. It has been argued that the *Mahābhārata* and the *Rāmāyaṇa* were originally epics with the predominance of *Vīra-rasa.*[45] In their revised forms, however, the *Mahābhārata* now has a predominant *Śānta rasa* and the *Rāmāyaṇa* the *Karuṇa rasa.* This trasformation is attributable chiefly to the additions made after the end of the description of war in each case.

If we read the *Mahābhārata* without its episodic sections often introduced with *Atrāpyudāharantīmamitihāsaṁ purātanam* and appropriately trim the *Ādi°* and *Vana°* and leave out of account the *Bhagavadgītā* and *Śāntiparvan,* we would reach fairly near an epic in the Homeric sense. We would have a tale beginning with the humilitation of the *Sabhā parvan* and ending with gory destruction and revenge. Such an epic, however, would still lack the dramatic unity and concentration of the *Iliad* and in any case such a reconstruction of the *Mahābhārata* would be without any authority and yet most modern discussions seem to assume just such a reconstruction.[46] They think of the *Mahābhārata* as a bardic tale of war and horror which was embellished by the gradual additions of episodic material and moral and religious discussions with the result that it tended to become amorphous and encyclopaedic. Such a view errs on the side of excessive reconstruction and an unproved hypothesis. Bardic ballads and tales of war possibly existed before the *Mahābhārata* and might have been utilized in it just as heroic tales and legends of diverse kinds existing by the side of the *Mahābhārata* might have been interpolated in it in the process of recitation to elaborate a point. But the basic structure, characters and mood of the *Mahābhārata* reflect too strong a unity to be attributed to the process of fortuitous interpolation from time to time. It is difficult to think of the *Mahābhārata* without the *Gītā,* of Arjuna without Kṛṣṇa, of Yudhiṣṭhira without the moral doubts raised in the *Śāntiparvan*. If Karṇa and Bhīma in their implacable search for revenge belong to the level of the *Iliad,* Arjuna and Yudhiṣṭhira belong to a much more rarified and elevated plane. The heroism of the *Mahābhārata* too is inconceivable without its moral and spiritual dimensions. In the *Rāmāyaṇa* the moral dimension is plain enough.[47]

Heroism in the Indian epics may be discerned at two levels.[48] At one level the hero is a mighty warrior with immense physical powers and skill in arms, proud of his birth and reputation, keen to keep his word and loyalty, friend of friend and foe of foe, quick to take offence and determined in seeking revenge to defend his honour. He is ever engaged in hunting, fighting and gallantry. At the same time the hero is a just and virtuous person who can be magnanimous even to a foe and is expected to be generous to all in need. He fights but he fights in accordance with *Dharma*. Nor is he an illiterate warrior. He is commonly expected to be educated and to take counsel from the learned and the wise. While drinking and gambling were common among them, these were also recognised as faults. The moral element in the character and deeds of the heroes is too pervasive to be brushed aside. The epics, in fact, contrast the true heroes from the false ones and the struggles which they describe partake of a moral character with the result that they do not constitute ultimate tragedies. There is immense pathos in the deaths of *Karṇa* and *Duryodhana* but one cannot think of them as tragedies in the same sense in which the death of Abhimanyu was.

Tagore described the epics as 'eternal history'.[49] They represent the fundamental patterns of human life as seen from the point of view of moral idealism. The characters of the *Mahābhārata* and *Rāmāyaṇa* have been more real and vivid through the ages in Indian imagination than any historical characters. The ironic vicissitudes of fate which dogged Nala, and the undying love of Sāvitrī are household words. The generosity of Karṇa and the rectitude of Yudhiṣṭhira, the firmness of Bhīṣma and the wickedness of Duḥśāsana still stand out vividly. Nor should it be supposed that such moral or immoral characters must be 'flat' characters and the narrative itself an unconvincing partition of virtue and vice. Of the impressiveness of the characters and the effectiveness of the narrative there can be no doubt. But the epics are not realistic histories but imaginative stories and its figures are characters, neither types nor individuals since the former belong to convention, the latter to actuality. The epic world is neither conventional, nor realistic. It is the essential world of idealities.[50]

Vālmīki was the last of the seer-poets. After him begins the 'classical' age of Sanskrit literature. Its principal concern is now humanistic and aesthetic. The glory and enjoyment of human life, the endless seeking of love and the fascination of beauty, these now occupy the poets and authors. Vedic, epic and Buddhist poetry was essentially transparent and in appearance at least unselfconscious. Classical poetry is self-conscious and its transparency is like that of stained glass. Its principal interest is aesthetic, in the discovery and expression of beauty, the sensuous beauty of nature and of the feminine form, the beauty of words and rhythms. The poets are like sculptors and in no other poetry has plastic imagination found such perfect expression.[51]

The *Nāṭyaśāstra* of Bharata mentions ten types of drama and more numerous types of musical 'Operas'. The theory of *rasa* as the essence of the dramatic is formally propounded. A modern theorist and critic has with great insight identified *rasa* with the 'total impression' of the play.[52] Although drama was held to be an 'imitation' or 'representation' of human situations, its essence was to organize and focus the feelings into a climactic experience. The nature of poetry too was ultimately conceived to be similar. At first its formal qualities were emphasized and its excellence was sought to be judged in terms of its composition and style, and figures of speech. Gradually, however, it was realized as mentioned above that the essence of poetry is the dramatic intimation of a felt impression or *rasa*. The analysis of meaning also led in the same direction. It was realized that the real and effective meaning in poetry is neither what is stated nor what is implied as a fact or even as form. Its real meaning is a felt imponderability. Thus the theories of *rasa* and *dhvani* came together and became central and the theories of *guṇa, rīti* and *alaṅkāra* became ancillary to them. The result of this grand synthesis was that the different literary forms, drama, epic, lyric, prose, novels, stories, came to be regarded as exterior and formal rather than essential. In fact most of these forms had already evolved before Bharata or Kālidāsa and as forms they were treated as stereotypes in later times and tended to be regarded as mere pegs on which the poet might hang his delicately woven fabric. The poets attended to more important things than the requirement of ancient form.[53] In the case of drama, to its detriment, these ancient requirements tended to be observed quite faithfully.

Kālidāsa, "the teacher of all poets", stands at the head of the classical tradition. When and where he lived is not certain. A popular opinion makes him the contemporary of the Gupta emperor Candragupta II Vikramāditya but competent scholars have argued for a much earlier date.[54] He claims to follow in the footsteps of Vālmīki. This is more a homage than any indication of indebtedness, for Kālidāsa never really borrows any significant poetic image or phrasing from Vālmīki.[55] Since pre-Kālidasian classical poetry has almost completely vanished, we do not know any other sources for Kālidāsa either, though the name of Aśvaghoṣa is sometimes suggested.[56] He stands as the most original poet in Sanskrit to whom all others are indebted. "No other poet walked the earth with such sensitiveness to the beauty of nature" or of the feminine form and no other poet had so vivid an imagination. He discovered the genre of describing the cycle of seasons in his *Ṛtusaṁhāra* and his *Meghadūta* started the tradition of *dūtakāvyas* of which dozens were composed later on.

Attempts have naturally been made to connect Kālidāsa with the spirit of the Gupta age. The story of the rain of gold in the *Raghuvaṁśa* (5.29) is said to be symbolic of the gold which poured into India in that age. The story of Raghu's *digvijaya*, again, has been connected with the *digvijaya* of Samudragupta. Along with opulence came a new aesthetic polish and an attempt to synthesize sensuousness with spiritual serenity. This new synthesis was reflected in the plastic art of the age, and Kālidāsa was its literary representative. Whether Kālidāsa belonged to the Gupta age or not, one can certainly discern in him a spirit of synthesis and balance, polish and perfection.[57]

The opening verse of the *Śākuntala* celebrates the presence of God in the visible forms of nature. It has even been suggested that Kālidāsa was moved by the philosophy of Kaśmīra *Śaivism*. Kālidāsa certainly believed in the spiritual unity of all things manifested in nature. At the same time his monism does not deny the reality of the world, nor is he a sectarian. His personal inclination perhaps was more towards Śiva, but he pays unstinted homage to Viṣṇu, and his incarnations. Between the enjoyment of the world and ascetic withdrawal from it, Kālidāsa maintains a balance. Each is right in its own time and place.

Perhaps the search for a personal faith or a philosophy of life in Kālidāsa can never be satisfactorily concluded. The art of Kālidāsa is like that of Shakespeare, "a mirror unto nature". Kālidāsa was struck by the wonder of things, each in its distinctive character, and never tired of representing them in vivid images revealing the marvel latent in every-day life. It is as if his eyes had been touched by the grace of Nandinī, enabling him to see what lay hidden before. And his poetry has the same effect on the reader.

Traditionally Kālidāsa has been admired for his *Vaidarbhī rīti,* his skill in the use of *Upamā* and his mastery in the art of *dhvani* and *rasa*. *Rīti* may be roughly translated as style. It has been conceived as the way in which an author used words. "*Viśiṣṭapada-racanā rītiḥ*.[58] This texture or manner of composition was sought to be defined in terms of *guṇas* and then broadly classified into two or three or even more styles. *Guṇa* is a characteristic of words or meanings contributing to literary excellence. Daṇḍin enumerated ten *guṇas* viz., *"Śleṣaḥ prasādaḥ Samatā Mādhuryaṁ sukumāratā/ Arthavyaktir udāratvam ojaḥ kāntisamādhayaḥ//"*[59] Compactness, simplicity, delicacy, clarity of meaning, vibrantness,[60] power, brightness and figurativeness, these are the *guṇas*. There were many opinions about the exact number and nature of these 'qualities'. Gradually the consensus came to be that there are three main 'qualities', viz., *Prasāda, Mādhurya* and *Ojas*. The first of these, i. e., simplicity or transparency, is a necessary element of all poetry. *Mādhurya* is what causes the heart to melt while *Ojas* is what causes it to burn or expand.[61] These qualities now came to be defined primarily in psychic terms. They belong to words only in relation to their function with respect to the communication of meaning except to the extent to which their sounds and stresses may be conceived to have an evocative effect. Now originally the *Rītis* were divided into two, *Vaidarbhī* and *Gauḍī*. This is the position in Bhāmaha and Daṇḍin.[62] In Vāmana we find three *Rītis* viz., *Vaidarbhī, Gauḍī* and *Pāñcālī*. This became standard but Bhoja mentioned six, adding *Avantikā, Lāṭī* and *Māgadhī*. Despite regional names, it was recognised that this distinction of styles was really based on formal characteristics. The principal distinction was between *Vaidarbhī* and *Gauḍī*. The former was characterized by simplicity and balance, the latter by its vibrant power which tended towards excess and used compounds frequently. Kālidāsa is the acknowledged master of *Vaidarbhī*. Here the complete adequacy of word and meaning leads to a transparency which we can only marvel at. Like the union of Śiva and Śakti, this union of word and meaning created an infinite world of *rasa*. The data of experience and the principles of interpretation are here fused into a seamless but transparent world of images. Kālidāsa avoids display of all kinds. As with a great magician his art is so unnoticeable as to appear non-existent. Only the marvel of images stands forth as if moved by their own autonomous spontaneity.

One example, often given in old critical texts, would suffice to illustrate this—

"Gāhantām mahiṣā nipāna-salilaṁ śṛṅgairmuhus tāḍitam/ chāyābaddhakadambakaṁ mṛgakulaṁ romantham abhyas yatu/ Visrabdhaṁ kurutāṁ varāhavitatir mustākṣatiṁ palvale viśrāntiṁ labhatām idaṁ ca śithilajyābandham asmaddhanuḥ."//
The verse is from the second act of *Sākuntala*. The king had been hunting earlier but since his encounter with Śakuntalā he has lost interest in the strenuous pursuit. He says he would let his bow relax and so may the beasts of the woodland—the buffaloes wallowing in the ponds and striking the water with their horns, the herds of deer chewing and resting in the shade of trees, the boars digging undisturbed wild roots near the ponds. From being the hunter of beasts in the woodland, the king is transformed into what he really should have been, their protector. And the transformation is wrought by love. But all this is implicit in the words as a mere suggestion. Ostensibly we have a series of images of the woodland centering paradoxically in the hunter's bow. The nearby buffaloes, the deer further on, and boars still further off are resting, each in its way, and the woodland is quiet. The hunter's bow is relaxed. The description is simple but suggestive.

This simplicity and suggestiveness was characteristic of Kālidāsa and remained the ideal of classical poetry. The notion of simplicity, however, should not be misunderstood to mean that the images should always be direct representations of reality as here. Here we have at one level what is called a *svabhāvokti* i. e. a direct expression of what obtains in nature. The vividness of the images is obtained not by comparison and superimposition but by introducing associated background images and at the same time focussing on a detail, the word *'mahiṣāḥ'* is thus placed between *'gāhantām'* and *'nipāna-salilam'* and then comes the sharply focussed detail of "horns repeatedly beating on the water" (i. e., the buffaloes seek to ward off the flies). An alternative way of giving vividness to images is the impressionistic one of comparison or superimposition, i. e., of figurative representation. Kālidāsa is specially famed for his skill in the use of such figurative representation called *Upamā*. "*Upamā Kālidāsasya*". A very famous example of Kālidāsa's use of *Upamā* may be seen in *Raghuvaṁśa* (6.67) : *Sañcāriṇī dīpaśikheva rātrau yaṁyaṁ vyatīyāya patiṁvarā sā/ Narendra-mārgāṭṭa iva prapede vivarṇabhāvaṁ sa sa bhūmipālaḥ//* During her *svayaṁvara* Indumatī passes by the seated and anxiously waiting kings who gathered from far and near to win her favour. As she passes particular rulers without showing her interest, the rulers are downcast. To illustrate this situation the poet brings up a simile—when at night the light of a moving lamp passes a mansion on the royal highway, it is lit up for a moment but then fades. Critics have written a lot on this, which it is unnecessary to repeat here.[63] The virtue of such an image is that although its immediate tie with the context is abstract and limited, it is endlessly suggestive and evocative and illustrates in a way the Coleridgean conception of imagination. The poet's image is not a mere representation but a pregnant comment.

Ṛtusaṁhāra describes the seasons and "is perhaps the first poem in any literature written with the express object of describing Nature."[64] The cycle of seasons has been of perennial interest in India. The work opens with the oppressive heat of summer and ends with the joy of spring. The hot wind of summer "crackles with shrill shoutings in the dry bamboo reaches" : *sphuṭati paṭuninādaiḥ suṣkavaṁśasthalīṣu.* The rainy season and its stately clouds are the saviours of the oppressed—"*Santaptānāṁ tvamasi śaraṇam*". The *Meghadūta* captures the spirit of the rains and the varied moods of nature which one can feel in it. Kālidāsa gives us the aerial survey of the ever-changing landscape of India more than once. One can only wish that while travelling with the clouds in a modern *Puṣpaka,* one could be endowed with the divine eyes of the poet and hear his golden voice ! The second half of the *Megha* soars beyond the heat and monsoon showers of the Indian plains with their rivers and towns, fields and hills, to the lofty Himalayas beyond which lies the city of Alaka ever-illumined by the moonlight streaming from the moon on Śiva's forhead. In this distant and divine city lies the home and the beloved of the forlorn Yakṣa. He hopes, however, that destiny will turn and better days come.

The sense of present loss owing to some past sin and the hope and yearning for future redemption through suffering and sacrifice is a recurrent theme in Kālidāsa. If the *Meghadūta* shows it in the personal sphere, *Raghuvaṁśa* exhibits it in the public sphere.

The *Raghuvaṁśa* is a great political epic, representing the ideal of ancient kings and probing the decline of kingship. Tagore points out how the epic breathes the despondency of political decline but still hopes for a bright future. The *Kumārasambhava,* then, would be a natural sequel. As Aurobindo points out, here we have an epic with a profound theme, in mythical form. For the birth of Kumāra who would lead the divine host, Śiva and Śakti must come together and for that to be possible 'śakti' must purify herself through *tapas.*

The theme of true love forged through suffering is taken up, again, on a human plane in the *Śākuntala.* Beginning in the midst of chase in an earthly forest the love of the King for Śakuntalā has to pass through the pain of separation and remorse, till it is finally fulfilled in the heavenly hermitage beyond violence and evil.

While Kumāradāsa in his *Jānakiharaṇa* followed the model of Kālidāsa, Bhāravi's *Kirātārjunīya* cuts out an entirely distinct path. Here the *mahākāvya* has a much shorter but much more elaborated narrative. In fact, the narrative is only a means for revealing the characters, emotions, situations and descriptions. In the *Śiśupālavadha* of Māgha and the *Naiṣadhīya* of Śrī Harṣa the narrative is only a minor device in the progressive revelation of the poet's imagination. It is, as Tagore remarked, of no more consequence than the words of a song in the progression of a *rāga* in classical Indian music.

Bhāravi, generally placed in the sixth century, represents, thus, a departure in the history of the Sanskrit *mahākāvya.* Henceforth the story of the mahākāvya is a mere fragment of some traditional epic story. The poets believed what Ānandavardhana later formulated that the poet achieves no success by merely narrating history.[65] A concentrated treatment can make even a 'short story' alive with *rasa.* Mallinātha praised Bhāravi for the moving quality of his poetry concealed behind a hard exterior. Bhāravi himself appears to strive after a clarity which is consistent with the depth of meaning. *"Sphuṭatā na padair apākṛtā na ca na svīkṛtam artha-gauravam."*[66] That he succeeded in this ideal is generally accepted by critics. His expression has a distinct rhetorical organization and his mea ning has an element of intellectual construction even though it rises on the wing of imagination. He is clearly a poet of what Sri Aurobindo calls 'Poetic Intelligence'. His verse has often a self-conscious, dancing or swaggering, rhythm which draws attention to itself and pleases. The *vaṁśastha* in the first and fourth cantos and the *Pramitākṣarā* in the sixth canto are examples of this. Praise has been recently showered on "the balance, proportion and harmony found in the poem and in all its structural elements."[67]

As is well known Māgha, probably belonging to the 7th or 8th century, sought to excel Bhāravi and in the opinion of traditional scholarship largely succeeded in doing so although modern opinion is distinctly unfavourable.[68] Actually the comparison with Bhāravi serves to obscure the fact that Māgha has a divine person as his hero while Bhāravi's hero is only a human person. The poem of Māgha has a distinct though subdued undertone of devotional adoration. Again, what has attracted the attention of most critics is the learning and rhetoric of Māgha rather than his imagination which is always unusual and quite often quaint, even bizarre. *"Nārikela-phala-sammitaṁ vacaḥ"* would be a more appropriate description of Māgha than of Bhāravi.

Śrī Harṣa belonged to the court of Jayacandra of Kannauj and was as great a philosopher as a poet. His reputation in traditional circles is unrivalled. But a modern critic describes his masterpiece, *Naiṣadhacarita,* as a mere 'counterfeit'.[69] His imagination has been accused of being "phantasmagoric and devoid of visualisation".[70] This criticism is really the result of a wrong perspective. Śrī Harṣa does not follow the model of Kālidāsa. He is far more musical than picturesque, to borrow from Coleridge about Milton. This is the real import of the adage *"Naiṣadhe padalālityam"*. The reference is not merely to the mellifluousness of Śrī Harṣa's verse, but is a much deeper characterization of its rhythm and lyricism. Further, he does not 'see' things as much as 'reflect' over them in an ironical and witty manner. As a dialectician he was convinced of the unreality and inconsequentiality of things. He describes their beauty, not with imaginative passion, but with an amused twinkle, a subtle and devastating turn of fancy. Any attempt to construe his imagery as a vivid representation of things belonging to the natural world would create disappointment just as any attempt to read the poem as a dramatically tense and structured epic would do.[71]

Imagination may be to boost the original subject or to replace it largely, as in a conceit. It is of the nature of the image, for example in *atiśayokti* to subsume the subject by superimposing another object on it. The bond between the original and the image may be abstract and tenuous but the image often has a great suggestiveness and autonomy of its own. The suggestion, again, does not need to be in terms of the feelings of the *dramatis personae* of the story at the moment but may be of wit or irony coming from the author as a commentator. When Damayantī's waist, for example, is compared with the border between two rival states, the comment really is political, not romantic.[72] It does not on that account lose its charm. Wit and music, *Vaidagdhya* and *lālitya,* characterise the verse and imagination of Śrī Harṣa.

The origin of the Sanskrit drama has been much debated, some scholars have traced it to *Saṁvāda-sūktas* of *Ṛg Veda* postulating a kind of ritual drama, others have imagined a popular play with song, dance, mime and dialogue as the basis of the ritual drama itself. Puppet play has also been suggested as the original of the drama. Greek influence is another explanation put forward. All these hypotheses have been duly criticised. There is no doubt that actors as a class existed in the later Vedic age. By the time of Pāṇini in the 5th century B.C. specialised treatises on the art of the actor already existed. We thus hear of the *Naṭa-sūtras* of *Śilālin* and *Kṛśāś-*

va. In the *Arthaśāstra* in the 4th century B.C., we hear of wandering troops of actors. If Subandhu and his *Vāsavdattā nāṭyadhārā* are to be placed in this age, drama was obviously very highly developed and sophisticated. In the 2nd century B.C. Patañjali refers to actors enacting plays like *Bali bandhana.* On one view Kālidāsa himself belonged to this age. From the 1st Century A.D. we have the plays of Aśvaghoṣa. The *Nāṭya Śāstra* itself ought to be placed in the Śaka-Kuṣāṇa age.[72a] In other words the origin and development of Sanskrit drama may be placed as a gradual development taking place from the later Vedic to the Kuṣāṇa-age. All the types and technicalities of drama were evolved in this period. The *Nāṭyaśāstra* declares that the *Nāṭyaveda* was created by Brahmā at the beginning of the *Tretāyuga* as a fifth Veda so that wisdom may reach all, whether high or low. Unlike the other *Vedas Nāṭyaveda* was accessible to the *śūdras* also.[73] At the same time it is called *Itihāsa. "Itihāso mayā sṛṣṭaḥ."*[74] We may note that *Itihāsa* too has been called the fifth *Veda.*[75] *Nāṭya,* thus, has a high and moral purpose but a universal appeal. At the same time it relies on narratives refering to the past, whether myths, legends or histories. Theoretically it is conceived as the essential representation of the human world in its diverse moods and conditions.[76] It communicates wisdom and at the same time entertains.[77] As in the Aristotelian theory, drama is believed here too to be an imitation (*anukaraṇa*) but it may be argued that while Greek drama imitated action, Indian drama imitated the inner reality of the felt idea (*bhāva*). Action and idea are present in both but there is a difference in emphasis.

Ten principal dramatic types or *rūpakas* are mentioned in Bharata. The most important of these were the *nāṭaka* and the *Prakaraṇa.* The *nāṭaka* was an aristocratic and traditional play. Its hero had nobility of character (*dhīrodātta*). It has at least five acts and its usual themes were romantic or heroic. *Śākuntala* could be an example of this kind. The *Prakraṇa* may be described as a buorgeois play.[78] It has an invented story. The hero may be a Brāhmaṇa, minister or merchant. Love is the principal theme and the acts may be from five to ten. The *Nāṭikā* was a lighter version of the *Nāṭaka* in four acts. *Ḍima* and *Īhāmṛga* too had four acts. The former emphasized *adbhuta, bībhatsa* or *vīra*. *Īhāmṛga* avoided *hāsya* and *śṛṅgāra*. *Samavakāra* had three acts but a wholly mythical theme with gods and demons as the *dramatis personae*. The remaining five varieties viz., *Aṅka, Vyāyoga, Bhāṇa, Vīthi* and *Prahasana,* all had only one act each. *Aṅka* had *Karuṇa* only, *Prahasana* only *hāsya*. These two come nearest to the pure tragic and pure comic plays of Greece as far as form is concerned but there is a vast difference in spirit.

The principal elements of drama are three—plot (*vastu*), hero (*netā*), and *rasa*. The plot is a structured story (*itivṛtta*). The structure has five *sandhis*. The first is *Mukhasandhi* in which a seed-situation (*bīja*) leads to the commencement of the hero's efforts in a definite direction (*Prārambha*). The efforts of the hero (*Prayatna*) constitute the second, *Pratimukha sandhi*. Some hope (*prāptyāśā*) as well as difficulties and search mark the *Garbhasandhi*. The *Vimarśasandhi* generally contains a reversal but at the same time leads to an assurance (*niyatāpti*). The *Nirvahaṇasandhi* brings about the conclusion (*phalāgama*) in a surprising way.

The structure of the plot is such that it has multiple strands in the beginning but becomes like the cow's tail simplified at the end. It begins with uncertainty and hope but passes through a crisis of reversal before revealing a marvellous fulfilment. It is not an artificial or onesided structure of pure tragedy or pure comedy. Suffering and effort, moral responsibility and ultimate hope these characterize the pattern of life and so of drama.

Sanskrit drama has a quite different flavour from that of classical Greek drama where tragedy and comedy were kept strictly apart and in its earlier phase love had no part in either. Love, on the other hand, was the chief theme in Sanskrit drama and tragic endings were avoided. But both joy and sorrow were depicted generally at the penultimate stage.[79] Some of the most famous plays are the *Svapnavāsavadattā* of Bhāsa,[80] the *Mṛcchakaṭika* of *Śūdraka,*[81] the *Mudrārākṣasa* of

Viśākhadatta,[82] the *Ratnāvalī* of Harṣa and the *Uttararāma-carita* of Bhavabhūti. The play of Śūdraka has received high praise among western critics. Ryder says its characters have a universality which goes beyond merely Indian conventions and taste.[83] In fact, a character like Vasantasenā will be hard to match anywhere in literature. Although a professional *hetaira*, her love for Cārudatta is remarkable for its sublime selflessness and constancy. The scene of walking in the rain is as remarkable for its poetry as for its tenderness. The political intrigue is skillfully woven into the tale of love and the vicissitudes of fate are brought out most effectively.

Bhavabhūti claimed to be the best and resented his apparent neglect by his critics. He had an unusual turn of mind which was exceptionally sensitive to the "tears of things". He declared that the only basic feeling which man could entertain was that of sorrow and pity. The love which he depicts between Rāma and Sītā is remarkable for its tenderness, affection and pathos. At the same time, Bhavabhūti is a master of words and proudly proclaims it. Of nature he is able to see the more forbidding side. Bhavabhūti may be described as the poet of sublimity rather than that of beauty.[84]

It has sometimes been said that Sanskrit drama represents characters as types rather than individuals. Perhaps this criticism has arisen from a misunderstanding of the role of classifying heroes in dramaturgy. If a hero is called *dhīrodātta* or *dhīroddhata*, that is only a general classification, not a full characterisation. Of course, in lesser plays the characters will not be so effectively portrayed but the heroes and heroines of Bhāsa and Kālidāsa, Śūdraka and Viśākhadatta or Bhavabhūti are certainly no mere types. No greater individuals have ever been portrayed than Vasantasenā or Śakuntalā, Duṣyanta or Cārudatta.

The Prākṛta *gāthās* of Hāla[85] are a treasury of love poetry largely drawn from the life of the village folk. The poems are as remarkable for their revelation of the moods of love as of the ways of life of the people and the rural landscape in its diverse aspects. The *Muktakas* of Amaru and the *Śatakas* of

Bhartṛhari are more sophisticated and abstract but have the same power and vividness. The erotic interest in this lyrical tradition is unmistakable. If its origins lay in folk-songs they have been left far behind. The *muktakas* are the product of a sophisticated sensibility and polished craftsmanship. They present brilliant vignettes of love-life in its domestic setting. Despite their compactness they have often a dramatic quality which is what makes them expressive of *rasa*.

The growth of fiction was apparently connected with the growth of city life, trade and mercantile class. The *Jātakas* are not available in their original form but the commentary recounts ancient tradition. The *Jātakas* represented the most ancient collection of tales gathered from diverse popular sources but geared to Buddhist purposes. In this process folk tales received artistic form and moral embellishment. The *Jātakas* enable us to see common life from the uncommon angle of vision of the Bodhisattva. The *Bṛhatkathā* of Guṇāḍhya, written in Paiśācī in the Sātavāhana age, revolutionized story telling, and its importance in Indian literature is almost comparable to that of the *Mahābhārata*. The spirit of adventure, the broad humanism, the variety of characters and situations, the sense of the marvellous, the capacity for irony and humour which distinguish this extraordinary work—which, alas no longer exists in its original form[86]—are without a parallel in the whole range of Indian literature. The *Bṛhatkathā* is the very embodiment of *Kautuka-rasa*. Daṇḍin's *Daśakumāracarita,* probably of the 6th century, has the same spirit of adventure and humanism but a remarkably powerful and chaste prose style. Story-telling and its *Kautuka-rasa* are now sought to be joined to the poet's power of description and the dramatist's sense of form and plot, to *rasa* and its evocative technique in short.

In Bāṇa story has receded into the background and the spirit of poetry has taken over. But what poetry, and what power in the prose! The whole cosmos is compressed in a book which is truly like a mirror unto nature. The power of words, the beauty of descriptions, the tenderness of love, the elegance of wit and the complexity of the plot, all make

Kādambarī a unique work in Sanskrit. It is a pity that some scholars with insufficient Sanskrit or insufficient learning have disparaged Bāṇa as an obscure Indian jungle where one must hack out one's way with great difficulties ! What would they say of James Joyce !

Humorous and satirical writings in Sanskrit have not drawn as much attention as they deserve. Perhaps it is partly due to the fact that satirical wit and humour tend to date quickly and much scholarly annotation is necessary before one can appreciate ancient jokes and witticisms. Nevertheless, works like the *Pañcatantra* where humour is combined with the shrewd observation of human nature are universal. The same is true of some of the *Prahasanas* and *Bhāṇas*. The *Caturbhāṇi*, the *Bhagavadajjukīya*, the *Mattavilāsa* are typical and yet highly original and display great imaginative power. Philosophical humour may, also, be discerned in many religious writings like the *Purāṇas*.

For a long time *Bhakti* or love of God was not recognised as a *rasa* by rhetoricians but after the *Bhāgavata* such a title could not justly be denied to *Bhakti*. The *Gītagovinda* of Jayadeva is a perfect blending of *bhakti* and *śṛṅgāra* and has been praised most highly for its lyricism. Here are a series of songs depicting the various stages of love between Rādhā and Kṛṣṇa. The felicity of expression, the sweetness of words, the haunting rhythms and the perfect matching of sense and sound make Jayadeva's verse unique.

The *stotra* literature must also be mentioned in this context. The *Śivamahimnastotra*, the *Saundaryalaharī* attributed to Śaṅkara, the *stotras* of Abhinavagupta, the *Sūryaśataka* are some examples of *stotras* where religious feeling and poetry mingle spontaneously.

REFERENCES

1. *e. g.*, Dasgupta and De, *History of Sanskrit Literature*, pp. 27ff.

2. A mistake often made, see my review of Warder's *History of Kāvya Literature*, 3 vols. in *History & Archaeology*, I, 1-2.

3. *History of Sanskrit Literature ; Sanskrit Drama.*

4. *Dhvanyāloka*, esp. Uddyota I, establishes elaborately that the real meaning of poetry lies in the evocation of feeling.

5. Vide my *Bhāratīya Paramparā Ke Mūla svara, anubhūti aur abhivyakti*; Anupa Pande, *Historical & Cultural Study of the Natyaśastra of Bharata* (Kusumanjali Prakashan).

6. Jagannatha Panditaraja, *Rasagaṅgādhara*, pp. 26-27.

7. *"Tena sthāyyeva...rasaḥ...mukhyayā vṛttyā Rāmādāvanukārye anukartari ca naṭe Rāmādirūpatānusandhānabalād iti."* (Abhinavagupta, ad *rasa-sūtra* of Bharata) ; *"Mukhyatayā Duṣyantādigata eva rasaḥ ratyādiḥ kamanīyavibhāvādyabhinaya-pradarśana-kovide Duṣyantādyanukartari naṭe samāropya sākṣātkriyate."* (*Rasagaṅgādhara*, p. 33).

8. *"anukartṛsthatvena liṅgabalataḥ pratīyamānaḥ sthāyibhāvaḥ sthāyibhāvaḥ mukhya-Rāmādigatasthāyyanukaraṇarūpah. Anukaraṇatvādeva ca nāmāntareṇa vyapadiṣṭo rasaḥ."* (*Abhinava-bhārati*, p. 446).

9. *"Samyaṅ-mithyā-saṁśaya-sādṛśya-pratītibhyo vilakṣaṇā citra-turaga-nyāyena...pratītirastiti."* (*Ib.*, p. 449).

10. Cf. *"Yuktyā paryanuyujyeta sphurannanubhavaḥ Katham."* (*Ib.*, p. 450).

11. *Ib.*, p. 462.

12. *"Evaṁ ca trayoṁśāḥ kāvyasya-abhidhā, bhāvanā caiva tadbhāgīkṛtireva ca."* (*Rasagaṅgādhara*, p. 29) *Bhāvanā is sādhāraṇīkaraṇa. "Bhogastu vyaktiḥ. Bhogakṛttvaṁ tu vyañjanād aviśiṣṭam."* (*Ib., l. c.*)

13. *'Tatkāvyārtho rasaḥ'* (*Abhinavabhāratī*, p. 470).

14. Cf. *Dhvanyāloka*, 1.4 which compares the suggested or expressed meaning to the overall impression of beauty in a woman. On the *Dhvani*—theory see Ṣuresa Candra Pandeya, *Dhvani-siddhānta, virodhī sampradāya unkī mānyatāyen* ; B. Bhattacharya, *Dhvanyāloka of Ānandavardhana* (Uddyota.I).

15. *Abhinavabhāratī, l. c.*

16. *Ib.*, p. 471.

17. *Ib.*, pp. 474ff.

18. *"Sthāyi-vilakṣaṇa eva rasaḥ"*, *Ib.*, p. 483.

19. Cf. *"Apūrvaṁ yad vastu prathayati vinā kāraṇa-kalām"*, (*Dhvanyāloka, locana*, p. 1).

20. Among modern treatments of *rasa* the following deserve special mention—Gnoli, *the Aesthetic Experience according to Abhinavagupta*; Visnupad Bhaṭtacharya, *Sāhitya-mīmāṁsā*; N. D. Parekh, *Abhinavaka rasa-vivecana* (Hindi tr.); Hiriyanna, *Art Experience*; Panchapagesa Shastri, *The Philosophy of Aesthetic Pleasure*; Anupa Pande, *op. cit.*

21. *Rasagaṅgādhara*, p. 27.

22. Cf. V. Raghavan, *The Number of Rasas.*

23. *e. g.*, Mammaṭa, *Kāvyaprakāśa.*

24. *Bhagavad bhakti-rasāyana.*

25. Cf. *"Kavirmanīṣī paribhūḥ svayaṁbhūḥ yāthātathyatorthān vyadadhāc Chāśvatībhyaḥ samābhyaḥ."*

26. *Bhāratīya Paramparā*, p. 108.

27. *Ib.*, *l. c.*, cf. Sri Aurobinda, *The Future Poetry, Letters* (Third Series).

28. *Bhāratīya Paramparā, l. c.*

29. Panikkar, *Vedic Experience.*

30. *Bhāratīya Paramparā*, p. 109.

31. *Ib.*, *l. c.*

32. *Ib.*, p. 110.

33. *Ib.*, p. 110.

34. Griffith's trans. For the interpretation of the hymn see V. S. Agrawal, *Vision in Long Darkness.*

35. *Ṛ.* 10.71.4.

36. *Dhp.*, 235.

37. *Thera*, 72 (tr. Saunders in *The Heart of Buddhism*, p. 21).

38. *Dhp.*, 146.

39. *Ib.*

40. Cf. *Bhāratiya Paramparā*, p. 114.

41. Saunders, *op. cit.*, p. 33=*Theragāthā*, 307.

42. *Ib.*, *l. c.*=*Thera°*, 211.

43. I. B. Horner, *op. cit.*, p. 54 (from *Saṁyutta nikāya*).

44. *Ib.*, p. 80 (from *Saṁyutta nipāta*).

45. *Bhāratīya Paramparā*, p. 111.

46. *Ib.*, *l. c.*

47. Cf. Aurobindo, *Kālidāsa*, p.

48. *Bhāratiya Paramparā*, p. 112.

49. *Ib.*, *l. c.*

50. *Ib.*, *l. c.*

51. *Bhāratīya Paramparā*, p. 116.

52. Nicoll, *Theory of Drama*, *World Drama*.

53. See Tagore's revealing essay, *Kādambarī-citra*.

54. *e. g.*, see Mirashi, *Kālidāsa*; K. Chattopadhyaya: *Date of Kālidāsa*; B. S. Upadhyaya, *Kālidāsa Aur Unkā Yuga*.

55. My friend Prof. Lakshmi Kant Dikshit, Retd. Professor of Sanskrit, University of Allahabad; is quite emphatic on this.

56. This is the opinion of those who place him in the Gupta age.

57. As mentioned above considerable literature and controversy exist on the date of Kālidāsa, In this context his relationship to Aśvaghoṣa is crucial. To the present author Aśvaghoṣa appears to borrow from Kālidāsa, an opinion which Prof. K. Chattopadhyaya had formulated.

58. Vāmana, *Kāvyālaṅkārasūtravṛtti*, 1.2.7.

59. Daṇḍin, *Kāvyādarśa*, 1.41.

60. Vāmana's def. '*Vikaṭatvam udāratā*', *op. cit.*, 3.1.2.3.

61. Mammaṭa, *Kāvyaprakāśa*, eighth *ullāsa*.

62. Daṇḍin, *op. cit.*, 1.40-42 ; Bhāmaha, *Kāvyālaṅkāra*, 1.32-35. Bhāmaha disputes the division–cf. S. C. Pandeya, *Kavi Aur Kāvyaśāstra*, pp. 29-30. To place Daṇḍin in the 4th century is a new departure not yet accepted.

63. Cf. Suresa Chandra Pandeya, *Kavi Aur Kāvyaśāstra*, pp. 8-9.

64. Aurobindo, *Kālidāsa*, p. 32.

65. *Dhvanyāloka.*

66. *Kirātārjunīyam*, 2.27.

67. Prof. Renou quoted by Warder, *History of Sanskrit Literature*, Vol. III.

68. *e. g.*, Keith, *History of Sanskrit Literature*, pp. 126-27.

69. Dasgupta and De, *op. cit.*, p. 325.

70. *Ib.*, p. 329. But contra Winternitz, *op. cit.*, Vol. III, p. 76, where it is said that Śrī Harṣa, *"in Naturschilderungen manche gute Einfalle hat."*

71. Cf. Chandika Prasad Shukla, *Naiṣadha-pariśīlana.*

72. *Naiṣadha*, 7.81.

72a. Vide Anupa Pande, *op. cit.*

73. *"Vedaṁ pañcamaṁ sārvavarṇikam"*, *Nāṭyaśāstra*, 1.12.

74. *Ib.*, 1.19.

75. Cf. *Arthaśāstra*, 1.5.

76. *Nānābhāvopasampannaṁ nānāvasthāntarātmakam / Lokavṛttānukaraṇaṁ nāṭyam etan mayā kṛtam //* *Ib.*, 1.112.

77. *Ib.*, 1.114-120.

78. Cf. Abhinavagupta, *"Evaṁ sakalapuruṣārthaviṣayā vyutpattiḥ nāṭakena pradhānasya rājaprāyasya kriyate prakaraṇe ca madhyamaprāyasya apūrvakutūhalavataḥ."* (*Nāṭyaśāstra*, Vol. II, p. 1482).

79. Abhinavagupta points out that serious drama represents value-seeking activity while the evocation of mere tears or laughter is enjoyed only by the uneducated.

80. The date and authenticity of the plays of Bhāsa have been much disputed. Cf. Warder, *op. cit.*, Vol. II, p. 265.

81. Perhaps to be placed in the 3rd cent. A.D. Warder, *op. cit.*, Vol. III.

82. 6th Cent. A.D., the times of Avantivarman.

83. Introduction to Ryder's tr. of *Mṛcchakaṭika* in *HOS*.

84. Dwijendra Lal Thakur's comparative study of Kālidāsa and Bhavabhūti in Bengali remains a masterpiece. Satyanarain Kaviratna's Hindi tr. of *Uttararāmacarita* is equally a masterpiece.

85. Hāla is supposed to have been a Sātavāhana ruler. His work is an anthology.

86. *Bṛhatkathāśloka-saṅgraha* is an incomplete later Sanskrit version. *Kathāsaritsāgara* retells the tales in Sanskrit at a much later date.

14

ART

Music

Abhinavagupta has said that out of *Sāman* arose *Gāndharva* and out of *Gāndharva* arose *Gāna,* thus tracing classical music to Vedic chanting.[1] These three may be held to represent the three principal stages in the development of music in Ancient India. Jaimini has defined *Sāman* as a song based on a *ṛc.*[2] The verses from the *Ṛk-Saṁhitā* were set to music in different melodies and sung in different parts in many different ways. The first part of the *Sāma-Veda* consists of lines from the *Ṛgveda* as a kind of index of melodies. This was the *Pūrvārcika.* The *Uttarārcika* consisted of groups of verses which constituted the body of *Sāman* singing. The singing itself was of various kinds. There were songs for the villages, songs to be sung in the forests and songs called *ūha* and *ūhya.* For example the line—*agna āyāhi vītaye* formed the subject matter of different musical compositions such as the *Parka* or 'mixture of Gautama', or 'the *Barhiṣa* of Kāśyapa'.

To the words of the *ṛc Sāman* singers added *svara* or musical notes and modifications called *bhakti* and *vikāra.* The original *svaras* were presumably developed from the three pitch accents, which are a common feature of the Vedic language.[3] In *Sāman* these pitches must have been made definitely musical, and possibly standardized with the help of string instruments. We may recall that Bharata attributes the origin of *Gāndharva* to the lute and the flute.[4] We must remember that in a ceremony such as that of the *Mahāvrata* dance, singing and instrumental music were combined. The development of the full octave of notes must have come about from the original three *svaras* through the discovery of natural harmonics with the help of string instruments in particular. The *Bāṇa* was, for example, a hundred-stringed lute. In the later Vedic literature the different notes on the octave are clearly mentioned, and the parallel between the god-made and the man-made *Vīṇās* is clearly drawn.[5] This parallel between the human body and the wooden *Vīṇā* became a common place in later times, when *śārīrī* and *dāravī* were juxtaposed.

The singing of the *Sāman* was divided into a number of parts which were taken up by a number of singers. These parts were called *bhakti*. These were counted as five or seven. The five were *prastāva, udgītha, pratihāra, upadrava* and *nidhana*.[6] While the different parts of the *Sāman* were being sung there was also continuous musical humming of *upagāna* to serve as their standard linkage.

The *Sāman* singers did not much care for the intelligibility of the song and freely distorted the sounds. This distortion was called *vikāra*. Simple *vikāra* could substitute *ognāyi* for *agna*. *Viśleṣaṇa* could separate the syllables of the words, *Vikarṣaṇa* could change the quantity of the *mātrās*. *Abhyāsa* was repetition. *Virāma* was stopping in the middle of the word. *Stobha* consisted in the addition of new syllables and was something like the *ālāpa* in later music.[7]

The bridge between the notes used in Vedic music and later times is now held to be provided by *Nāradīya śikṣā*, which says that the first note of the *Sāman* singers is the *madhyama* of the flute. Their second is *gandhāra*, the third is *ṛṣabha*, the fourth is *ṣaḍja*, the fifth is *dhaivata*, the sixth *niṣāda* and the seventh is *pañcama*.[8] Thus the Sāmic octave consisting of *Kruṣṭa, prathama, dvitīya, tṛtīya, caturtha, pañcama* or *mandra* and *antya* or *atimandra*, corresponds to *ma, ga, ri, sa, dha, ni* and *pa*. It is curious that the octave mentions the notes in a descending order. It is important to note that in this ancient music the *ṣaḍja* did not constitute a necessarily fixed beginning. The *Vīṇā* could be tuned in different ways and as a result the octave could be taken to consist of different actual notes. Instead of imagining a universal octave which gave rise to different sets of notes differing from the notes of the fixed octave, the system at this time was to fix the octave in different ways. Now-a-days out of a fixed octave different combinations are specified as *thats* from each of which different melodies arise. In the most ancient system the *śrutis* were taken at different points to constitute the different ways in which the *grāma* could be constituted out of the *śrutis*. These were called the *Ṣaḍja grāma,* the *gandhāra grāma* and the *madhyama grāma.* Of these the *gandhāra grāma* went out of use quite early.[9] The *ṣaḍja* and *madhyama grāmas* were used in *Gāndharva.*

The word *Gāndharva* sometime stood for music in general but also had the technical sense of a particular system of music. *Gāndharva* music had four principal elements *Pada, Svara, tāla* and *avadhāna.*[10] *Pada* meant the words of the song, but it could even consist of nonsense syllables though this must have been a later development. The *svaras* were aggregated in *jāti, mūrchanas,* and *tānas.* A *jāti* was a succession of notes beginning from different notes of the octave. Their classical number was eighteen, and they constituted the fundamental melodies in the *gāndharva.*[11] They were regarded as the matrices of later *rāgas* or rather *rāgamelāpakas,* but the number and arrangement of the notes was rigidly regulated in *gāndharva.* However, the most distinctive feature of *gāndharva* was its elaborate patterns of *tāla.*[12] Even the unit for measuring time consisted of not less than five short *mātrās.* The movement of the music must have been exceedingly slow, sombre, complex and rigid. Compared to it the most elaborate *dhrupad* must appear simple. The meaning of *avadhāna* and the appreciation of its role appear to have been lost in later times. Apparently *avadhāna* stood originally for a meditative idea, a certain psychic concentration and attitude which were required for the proper singing of *gāndharva.*

By the time of Bharata a more popular and flexible kind of music had gained ground. This was called *gāna* and included *rāga, bhāṣā* and *vibhāṣā.* While *gāndharva* was used in the *pūrva raṅga* of the theatre, *gāna* was used for the *dhruvās*. The principal criterion of admissibility into the new melodic compositions was the effect on the audience. *Gāndharva* was essentially the musician's music while the new music of the *rāgas* as the name itself announces, is governed by the pleasure it gives to the audience. Thus freed from traditional and ritualistic restrictions *grāmarāgas* developed into a great variety. A distinction now came to be clearly made between *mārga* and *deśī*,[13] which may be roughly rendered as classical and popular. The distinction was relative and hence the confusing use of the terms in Mataṅga and Śārṅgadeva.[14] Compared to *gāndharva* the *gāna* system appeared relatively popular, but within it also a distinction was made between regulated and standardized singing, on the one hand, and free improvization, on the other.

As the names of the melodies show folk tunes current in different regions and communities played a great part in their development through standardization. Till about the 13th century when Śārṅgadeva wrote his *Saṅgītaratnākara* Indian music grew through a continuous process of popularization and standardization. There was a continuous effort to retain ancient conventions but also to bring *lakṣaṇa* and *lakṣya* together. Although the lute and the flute along with *mṛdaṅga* and '*khartala*' were the principal musical instruments,[15] it is the human voice that occupied the centre of the musical system. Its great rival was, of course, the *Vīṇā* in its innumerable varieties. There was a firm belief that musical sound originates in that great sound (*Nāda*) which creates the universe.[16] Music properly performed was regarded not merely as entertainment but as meditation and worship.[17] It was also believed that musical notes have inherent evocative power, and thus music came to be connected with *rasa* and was brought in line with general aesthetic theory.[18]

Dancing

Vedic hymns sometimes address the gods as 'dancers'—*Nṛtū*,[19] which shows the high esteem in which dancing must have been held. A later Vedic text says that *Śilpa* is triple consisting of *gīta*, *vāditra* and *nṛtya*.[20] It is also said that *Śilpa* is really a refinement of the self, *ātmasaṁskṛti*.[21] At the same time some other later Vedic texts treat of actors, dancers and acrobats as a distinct group held in scant respect. This duality which esteemed dance and acting but looked down upon dancers and actors as a professional class continued in later times. By the time of Pāṇini the art of dancing and acting had already been codified in *sūtras* and we hear of the *Naṭasūtras* of Śilālin. The *Nāṭyaśāstra* of Bharata, however, is the first systematic treatise on the subject which has survived.

Dance with music by nymphs. Alambushā, Miśrakeśī and Padmāvatī on Prasenajita pillar, Bharhut, 2nd century B.C.

Dancing had two main varieties—*nṛtta* and *nṛtya*.[22] The former was pure dancing in accordance with rhythm and tempo. The latter involved the expression of feeling, a silent enactment of some theme. The art of dancing included stylized bodily movement and stances, gestures and acting. The position of the body was fixed with reference to a number of vertical and horizontal axes and the movement of each part of the body was defined with reference to these axes. A series of movements leading to some characteristic stance or total impression of fluidity ending in a cadence of momentary motionlessness constituted a dynamic composition or *Karaṇa* of which 108 were defined in the *Nāṭyaśāstra*.[23] Another important type of composition was *Piṇḍībandha* which was a group composition.[23a] Of gestures those with the eyes and hands were the most elaborate and significant. The gestures of hand in particular constituted an elaborate language.

For Indian dancing space is not an endless expanse to be filled by leaping and flying as in the ballet, but a limited location in which movements never depart very far from the governing axes. The purpose of movement and gesture is above all to express an inner state or feeling. Dance had an inevitable sacred aspect since it was Śiva and Pārvatī who started the *tāṇḍava* and *lāsya*. It was also a constant inspiration to the sculptor seeking to render human figures in motion or rest.

Art and Architecture

The vast changes introduced by the birth of civilization did not mean a total interruption in the continuation of earlier social and cultural traditions. It has been suggested that in India several of the surviving crafts go back to at least the neolithic times.[24] Cave paintings of broadly similar types have continued in India in refuge areas from the prehistoric to the early historic times.[25] Social traditions of the family and the clan, of magic and ritual, of myth and religion have similarly continued with transformations. One simple instance of this might suffice. The worship of Śiva in historical times has included the aspect of the Great Hunter (*Kirāta*), the Master of the Beasts (Paśupati), the spouse of the goddess of fertility and creation. Here we have a fierce hunter dwelling in the caves, on mountain tops, in the forests and the wastes, a god appropriate to a hunting community. We also have here a god who tames animals and protects them, appropriate to a pastoral life. The same god is wedded to the goddess of fertility and becomes appropriate to a rural agricultural community. He is also an abstract god symbolised aniconically, appropriate to the invisible forces controlling urban life. Śiva again is the great personal god performing the five-fold functions, presiding over the empire of the universe. In the diverse aspects of Śiva, thus, we can discover a syncopated *kulturgeschichte*. We can discover a similar variety of aspects in the idea of the Mother Goddess whose worship has continued down the millennia and whose myth and image are a veritable palimpsest of social and cultural history. This remarkable continuity from the remote past of which the articulations had been long lost but gathered up in symbols of diverse degrees of obscurity or transparency, has been made possible by that tolerant ethos which enabled tribal *pallis,* pastoral *ghoṣas,* and agrarian *grāmas* to coexist alongwith growing cities and empires. Different phases and varieties of social and cultural life have contributed to the ever-richer mosaic of Indian culture and art. Behind Indian art, thus, lies the most complex and ancient world of meanings and traditions, which transcends any narrow explanations in terms of specifically determined socio-economic conditions. The figure of the elephant or the *pipal* tree, for example, are common motifs but they are enriched by a history of more than four millennia.

It would thus be obvious that the beginnings of Indian art like that of Indian culture antedate the birth of civilisation. Prehistoric cave paintings and tool forms, ceramic forms and designs and modellings of figurines from neolithic villages are some of the meagre material remains of those lost ages.[26] It is from the Harappan civilisation that we get our first extensive material remains of art though without any decipherable articulation. From the Vedic age on the other hand we meet with a wealth of ideas and symbols though without any material representation. Taken together the Harappan and the Vedic give us as it were the matrix of Indian art both as image and idea though without any clear or historical connection between them. It would perhaps be reasonable to trace the beginnings of the Indian art tradition to both the Harappan and Vedic cultures. It is true that no continuity of tradition can yet be firmly demonstrated from the Harappan and, as mentioned, no art finds date from the Vedic period. Nevertheless, religious and cultural continuity from the Harappan has been postulated by successive generations of archaeologists from Marshall to Wheeler.[27] The continuity of art motifs is equally undeniable, whether one looks to animal motifs or motifs drawn from the plant world or geometrical designs or human figures. Some composite animal figures are sometimes referred to West Asiatic mythology but identifications in terms of Indian mythology have hardly been given a full trial. On the other hand, the stylistic connection between animal modelling and motifs on Harappan seals with those on some punch marked coins and Aśokan sculptures is too striking to be ignored.[28] Then, again, elements of social architecture show continuity which may be seen in the basic house plan, the idea of town planning, the importance attached to the ceremonial tanks and the construction of the ramparts. Similarly it is not unreasonable to suppose that the tradition of some of the basic crafts such as stone-cutting, clay-modelling, brick-laying, construction of corbelled arches, ceramics, work on bronze and copper, shell work or gem-cutting were not wholly interrupted in the subsequent age. Vedic literature is not ignorant of the *pur's* or *iṣṭakās* and mentions numerous crafts.

In fact Harappan art shows some of the most general characteristics of Indian art quite clearly. It clearly maintains the wide-spread ancient feature of continuity between art and craft and between the sacred and the secular. It also shows the most characteristic motif of Indian art, namely the figure of the seated Yogi. The Yogi is not simply a human being, he is the self-realized spirit which is expressed through the human form but essentially transcends it. Later Indian tradition clearly makes the Yogi a being apart, as much above gods as men of the world.[29] Again we notice in Harappan art the contrast of representing animals naturalistically but emphasising *Cetanā* or *prāṇa* rather than musculature as far as the human figure is concerned.[30] Animals are represented with loving observation and sympathy but as fixed natural forms whereas the human form is felt to be expressive of inner psychic energy.[30a] Again, the plastic representation of the rhythm of dancing is a theme which proved of abiding interest in the later history of Indian art. In architecture we already find that despite the skilled use of bricks, the basis of construction is always trabeate with the addition of corbelled arches where necessary. There is no attempt to use the true arch, a tradition which was faithfully maintained in later times.

Although no art remains date from the Vedic period there can be no doubt that ideas, forms and symbols developed during this period acted as seed and mould for the succeeding ages. For example, the elements and forms evolved for the construction of houses in terms of the fragile materials of this rural phase were utilized when stone began to be used for monumental architecture with the growth of cities and empires. These 'wooden origins' of the later stone architectural forms have often been commented upon. Similarly the influence of carving and engraving in wood or precious and semiprecious materials like gold and silver, gems and ivory is unmistakable on the work of early stone carvers and sculptors. The influence of the cosmic symbolism developed in the 'fire altars' and the *Yūpa* has been traced by scholars on later architectural forms. Vedic mythology, again, formed the basis of Purāṇic mythology and thus constituted the imaginative world on which the classical visual art rested. The world as caught in the struggle between the forces of Light and Darkness, and as constituted by a hierarchy of types of beings—*devas* and *yakṣas, sādhyas* and *ṛṣis, gandharvas* and *apsarases, pitṛs* and men, *Nāgas* and *Suparṇas, asuras* and *rākṣases*—this image of the world goes back to the Vedic age. Classical art copies these diverse forms of the mythical-natural world but these in turn were held to be not ultimate but merely expressive of a greater and hidden reality. *Sarvaṁ khalvidaṁ brahma. Rūpaṁ rūpaṁ pratirūpo babhūva.* The Vedic vision of a spiritual unity expressing itself in the diversity of phenomenal forms gave the imagination of the artists an inward and meditative turn which, however, was not ascetic in the sense of spurning the world. Nature and men were felt to be united by an underlying bond. An ecstatic rhythm pervaded the whole universe. *Yadyeṣa ākāśa ānando na syāt. Viśvamidaṁ variṣṭham.* The Vedic vision favoured the goodness and sacredness of life and love, though it stressed the need for *askesis,* favoured the appreciation and enjoyment of life but at the same time realised that immortality lay beyond it. This clear realisation made a tremendous difference for Indian art. It did not attempt to assist the magical and ritual search for constructing permanent monumental structures out of perishable materials as was only too often attempted in the ancient civilizations and which is implicity decried as *āsuric* in the *Upaniṣads.* Nor did Vedic society seek to express the majesty of law in terms of the exaltation of the royal person or the magnificence of his palaces. There is no place in the Vedic view for seeking monumental permanence in the dwellings of the king, alive or dead. Similarly the identification of the human self with *Brahman* prevented any special exaltation of the human form. It is the great forms of nature which were held to be the visible and permanent embodiments of Deity. *Pratyakṣābhis tanubhirvatu vastābhir aṣṭābhirīśaḥ.* This philosophy which discouraged tombs, imperial monuments and anthropomorphism gave a distinctive character to the aesthetic inspiration of Vedicism.

As inspired by the Vedic view Indian art became the visual expression of the sacred joy of life. The Vedic *Madhuvidyā,* the concepts of *Śilpa* and *Rūpa, Rasa* and *Ānanda, Prāṇa* and *Chanda,* all these are part of the Vedic legacy to the art as were the symbols and motifs of Vedic philosophy and mythology. The Vedic tradition of India encouraged the creative imagination to search for the unity of the transcendent with the phenomenal, a search which followed from *Brahma-vidyā* itself. Although, as mentioned above, ancient art was never sundered from craft, its basis was profoundly philosophical and meditational for the simple reason that the social and cultural ethos of the community itself was such. Art provided universally understood and visual symbols mediating between the abstract understanding of the seers and philosophers on one hand, and the day to day practical living of the common man on the other. At first, in the Vedic age itself, when the community still possessed the unbroken integrity of archaic faith and a living continuity of the sacred and spoken languages, this task of mediation was accomplished by a pervasive system of rituals which drew the attention of its participants to the primal archetypes underlying human actions and phenomena. Increasingly, however, in the post-Vedic period the need for visual representations must have been felt especially as the ambit of society and state expanded to include untutored tribes and peoples living on a receding horizon. In classical times, thus, the old myths and rituals were modified into their Purāṇic and Āgamic forms and were buttressed and popularised by the visual language of art, just as this task was performed by wandering saints and singers in a still later age when monumental sacred architecture and representational art were not favoured by the power of the State at Delhi.

In the age of the *Mahājanapadas* a number of changes provided a transition from the older Vedic tradition. The Śramaṇic point of view of *nivṛtti* introduced a contradiction and tension within the prevailing *weltanschauung,* the distance between men and gods tended to be bridged by the doctrine of *saṁsāra,* the idea of Perfected Men (*buddha, siddha*) and Incarnations or Emanations (*avatāra, vyūha*) tended to make the human figure of supreme value and interest, the rise of cities and empires changed the social scene and commerce and war brought the country into closer contact with other civilizations. The tension between the spiritual and the sensuous and the urge to overcome it became a characteristic feature of the classical tradition and expressed itself in art in diverse ways, for example in the sombre simplicity of the *stūpa* structure contrasted with the sculptured richness of the *Vedikās* and *toraṇas*. The doctrine of *saṁsāra* conceived the gods as *Jīvas* in certain transient stations and basically continuous with men and beasts. Gods, thus, came to be conceived anthropomorphically rather than in terms of natural phenomena. The *Yakṣas* were already conceived as human figures and the new conception of gods brought the *devas* and *yakṣas* nearer. This is clear enough in the position assigned to some of the great Vedic gods in Buddhist and Jaina thought. The notion of the enlightened or perfected One envisaged a being human in appearance but transcendent in reality. Buddha denied to the Brāhmaṇa Doṇa that he could be looked upon as *deva, gandharva, yakṣa* or man. He was just Buddha.[31] The incarnation similarly complained that fools deprecated Him in human form and failed to understand the divine essence.[32] The problem for the artist then became to render the human form transparent for superhuman reality. In this task he was assisted by a symbology which came to be plastically interpreted in terms of iconography in due course.

Growing royal power and pomp and the contact with western neighbours made palaces and forts increasingly important just as growing commerce made coins and writing of more moment. It was a time when the invisible earthly power of the state sought to express itself in visible monuments, architecture, coinage, writing. On the other hand, the wandering *śramaṇas* preached to the common man in his own language and used stories and parables frequently. These could easily be translated into visual representations and became a perennial source of art. All these new tendencies and forces reached a climax in the Mauryan empire.

If we consider only the materially surviving monuments of art we would have to regard the Mauryan or rather the Aśokan period as the earliest period of Indian art. Remains of cities from earlier date undoubtedly survive but they do not furnish any significant data for art history. Thus stone walls from Rajgir, brick ramparts from Kauśāmbī, the figure of the Mother goddess or a gold leaf from Lauriya Nandangarh, carved designs in earlier medallians from a number of sites, carved and engraved materials including crystal vases from the Piprahwa *stūpa,* are some examples dating from the Pre-Mauryan period. Udayana's palace from Kauśāmbī would have been of great significance, if only its authenticity were not in heavy dispute. Thus although archaeological remains combined with literary evidence make it abundantly clear that palaces and monasteries were being built in the Pre-Mauryan period and that numerous craft guilds flourished in the cities of those times, and served the need of their wealthy patrons, the use of stone on a large scale for artistic purposes was not common.

The sudden efflorescence of stone sculpture in Aśokan times has been the subject of much speculation. Persian and Hellenistic influences have been surmised and it has been said that the perfection of animal sculptures on Aśokan capitals could not have been achieved except by Hellenistic artists.[33] Actually the use of stone and the craft of the stone-cutter began much earlier than Aśokan times and the art of carving on wood and ivory too was an undoubtedly ancient one Carved wooden columns with much symbolism were known from Vedic times and even stone pillars antedated Aśoka on his own evidence. Under the circumstances there are no convincing reasons for seeking any decisive foreign influence on Aśokan art. The rise of towns, especially capital towns in the *Mahājanapada* age with their need of defence walls, monumental structures and craft specialization must have been a factor in the adoption of stone for certain constructional purposes. City architecture, however, continued to be largely wooden. Even the famous royal palace at Palibothra despite its slender stone columns was essentially made of wood.

The Sarnath pillar is the most impressive of Aśokan monuments.[34] The free standing column goes back, on the one hand, to the idea of the cosmic tree through the sacrificial *Yūpa.* On the other hand, it recalls the principal post on which the construction of the Vedic house rested. The pillar thus had a symbolic sacred-cum-architectural function in the planning of the cities. It was as it were the support of the city, linking it with its heavenly prototype. Bāṇa, thus, calls

PLATE XVIII

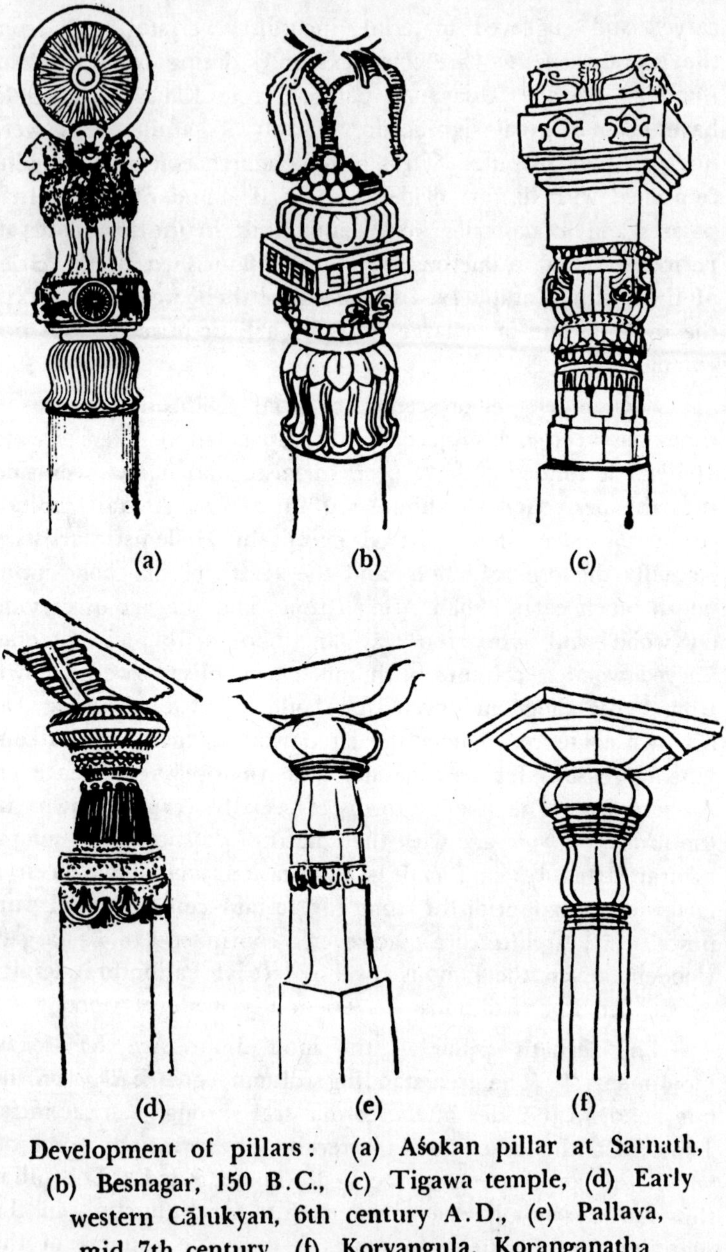

Development of pillars: (a) Aśokan pillar at Sarnath, (b) Besnagar, 150 B.C., (c) Tigawa temple, (d) Early western Cālukyan, 6th century A.D., (e) Pallava, mid 7th century, (f) Korvangula, Koranganatha Temple, early 10th century.

Sambhu Himself as the original Pillar of the cosmic city.[35] In Aśokan art, however, the pillar is adapted to a Buddhist purpose. It serves to bear aloft the wheel which suggests at once the universality of *Dharma* as well as of imperial sway. The couchant lions which prop up the wheel suggest the *Dhārmika cakravartī, Śākya siṁha.* The frieze with animals is suggestive of the four quarters and the wheel in between apparently indicates the *Cāturdiśa saṁgha.* The inverted lotus has been explained as lotus leaves drooping from the *Pūrṇa kumbha.* On the other hand, it may be suggested that *Puṣkarapalāśa* was used as a foundation in the construction of the *suparṇa-citi.* In fact, if we conceive of the slender shaft of the pillar as the long underwater stem of the lotus, it would then be the proper foundation for a world created above it.

The general sacred and Buddhist significance of the Aśokan columns is evident though the degree and detail of symbolism must always remain speculative and uncertain. The beauty of these capitals is, however, essentially formal, not symbolic. The wheel standing for the solar disk, the animals like lion, elephant and bull, birds like the *haṁsa* and lotus are forms drawn from nature and have an instinctive appeal for the human heart. The rendering of these forms has a smoothness of finish and a sureness of modelling which is most attractive. The mouldings, again, seek a self-conscious effect. This is not to say that the cultural symbolism of these columns does not add to their significance and expressiveness. Buddhist and imperial aspirations after universality fuse in Aśokan art just as traditional symbolism fuses with the new urge for permanence through stone appropriate to the new imperial achievement.

The Aśokan *stūpas* were enlarged, elaborated and carved in the Śuṅga and Sātavāhana times. Of these the great Stūpa at Sāñchī is the most magnificent. It has been argued that the *stūpa* shows a cosmic symbolism. If so, it must also be conceded that the Buddhists have adapted an ancient symbol to a new use because there is no doubt whatever that the Buddhist *stūpa* is above all the symbol of Nirvāṇa. The very simplicity and solidity of the hemispherical form is suggestive of the finality of the Great Decease. The Enlightened One has gone for ever and only a tumulus with a handful of bones has remained.

The Buddha did not think much of his physical body and wished to be remembered only in his *dharma*-body. His followers, however, gradually developed a veritable religion of relic-worship. And the desire to worship and venerate brought in the tendency to elaborate and decorate. As the worship must have caught on and pilgrims came from far and near, the place developed into a huge monastic complex with the great *stūpa* towering in the centre. The railing at the base of the *stūpa,* of which the form was imitated from ancient bamboo railings, was pierced by four ornamental gateways or *toraṇas* which, again, are an imitation in stone of originally wooden forms. There is a path for perambulation around the *stūpa* and from the top colourful parasols fluttered in the breeze beckoning the faithful. The severity of the solid hemisphere is contrasted with the carvings of the railings and the *toraṇas*. Much has been written on these sculptures. Their technique of modelling has moved far from primitive frontality and shows a competent and free movement of planes. It has been said that the spirit of religious quiet is aided by the style of modelling where figures quietly blend in the composition and are neither static nor ambeant with motion.[36] The theme of the sculptures is taken from the *Jātakas* or from the life of Buddha. The representation of three dimensional space in the panels depicting *Jātaka* scenes follows what has been called a kind of 'vertical' perspective. It does not follow a naturalistic, geometrical perspective, which is not so much a matter of technical backwardness as of aesthetic tradition and choice. These sculptures are veritable sermons in stone. The Buddha is still represented only symbolically.

The *stūpa* remained a favourite architectural object with the Buddhists. In the north-west in Gandhāra it tended to become elongated and was constructed in several stories to resemble a kind of tower. The sculpture was much influenced

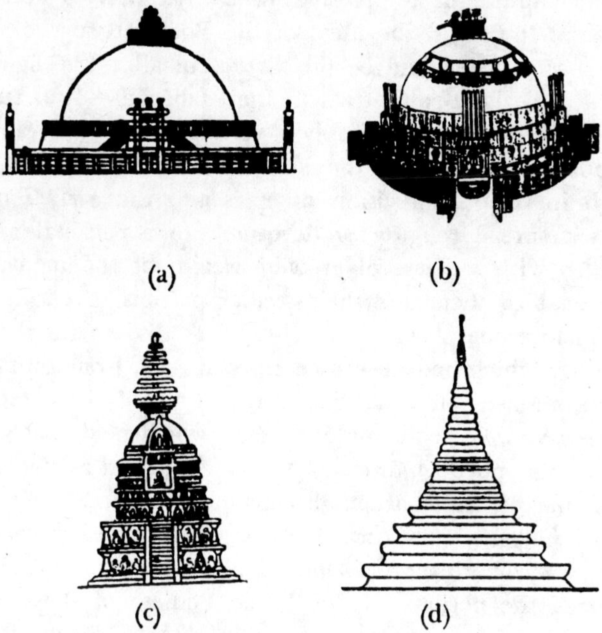

Development of stūpa : (a) Great stūpa at Sāñchī, (b) Stūpa at Amarāvatī (reconstructed), (c) Stūpa at Takht-i-Bahi, (d) Tawyagyaung stūpa, Mandalay.

by Hellenistic and Roman motifs, and most important of all, the Buddha was represented in a human figure. In the Deccan, thanks to the Sātavāhana empire and the trade-routes, Buddhism and art travelled to the western and eastern ghats. The great *stūpa* at Amarāvatī represented the high water-mark of this art. The sculpture of Amarāvatī was marked by a remarkable sense of fluidity and *joie de vivre*. The artist delights in representing dynamic stances and expressing exuberant and ecstatic religious emotion.

The most revolutionary change which came over Indian art between the 1st cent. B.C. and 1st cent. A.D. was the emergence of the Buddha image. This was the period when Mahāyāna made its appearance as a powerful religious movement. Mahāyāna sought to devise a universal spiritual appeal. It harked back to the central experience of Buddha himself and the impulse of compassion which led him to become a preacher. It upheld the ideal of the Bodhisattva who would develop compassion and be the saviour of all. The figures of Buddha and the Bodhisattvas in the Mahāyāna sūtras such as the *Saddharmapuṇḍarīka* imply a veritable apotheosis and the undoubted emergence of the idea of *Bhakti*.[37] This is clear enough in the final revision of epics and the early *Purāṇas*. This widespread religion of devotion to a personal saviour coincided with a phase of growing wealth of the monasteries which enabled them and their secular patrons to encourage a more picturesque phase of art. Buddha's disdain for the physical body which had prevented his followers from commemorating the Master in a material icon had already been replaced by a new view in some Buddhist sects which held that matter could also be pure (*anāsrava-rūpa*) and function as the expression of the principle of enlightenment and grace.[38] The doctrine of *śūnyatā* now turned matter into mere appearance—*rūpaṁ śūnyatā śūnyatā rūpam*. The Mahāyāna, in fact, now developed the notion of the Three Bodies of the Buddha. *Dharmakāya* stood for the Absolute, *Sambhogakāya* for the body of Glory, *Nirmāṇakāya* for the body projected on earth.[39] In this hierarchy of bodies even the lowest or physical body came to be regarded as spritually expressive. It is this transformation of thought and sentiment which led to the emergence of the Buddha image.[40] The form of the Buddha had always been an object of loving meditation (*Buddhānusmṛti*). There was now no theological barrier in expressing this mental image externally in plastic form.

The iconography of the Buddha image was based on the thirtytwo *Mahāpuruṣalakṣaṇas* which were part of an ancient physiognomic tradition about the *Cakravartī*. The Bodhisattvas were clearly represented as princely figures. Foucher's attempt to derive the *lakṣaṇas* from the accidents of sculpture is unconvincing.[41] While the influence of Hellenistic-Roman art on the Gāndhāra images is undeniable, the influence is limited to plastic externals and was soon adapted to the deeper purpose of rendering an image of enlightenment.[42] This process of discovering an adequate expression for the idea of

(a) (b) (c) (d)

(a) Bodhisattva, Sarnath, year 3 of Kaniṣka (b) Bodhisattva on railing pillar, Kuṣāṇa, Mathura (c) Bodhisattva Maitreya, Mathura (d) Buddha, Mathura, Gupta period.

enlightenment reached its climax in the famous Saranatha image of Buddha from the Gupta period. Here the material aspect of the image is wholly subordinated to the expression of an ineffable and radiant peace. It is one of the central mysteries of art that a masterpiece never fully lets out its secret. A thousand imitations of the Saranatha Buddha have been made, but the original remains as unapproachable as the smile of Mona Lisa or the aspect of *Banī Ṭhanī*. All the descriptions of the objective features of the image correspond to what is fully imitable. No description, therefore, is adequate to the inimitable integrity of the whole.[43]

Bodhisattva, Katra, Mathura—Kuṣāṇa period.

If the Buddha image sought to perfect the expression of silence and stillness, the expression of force and motion was rendered in its perfection by the image of the Naṭarāja.[44] Here in the Cola bronzes the best icons have been achieved where Śiva is represented as a dancing figure.[45] The *ḍamaru* signifies creation, the fire destruction, the hand half pulled down signifies *tirodhāna*, and grace is showered by the raised palm.[46] The stance of the whole shows the stillness which

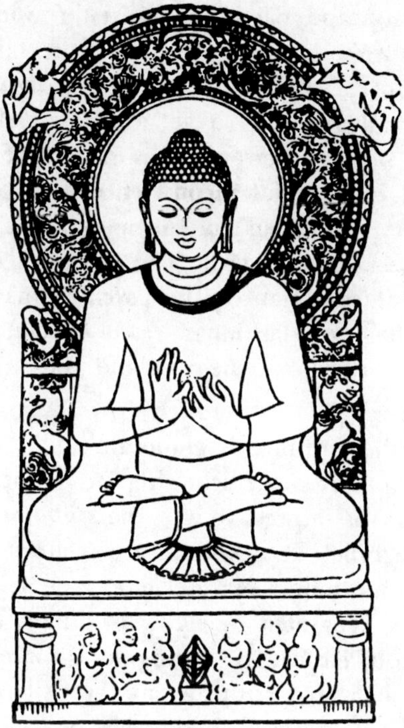

Buddha, Gupta period–Sarnath.

can exist only within the perfect rhythm of motion.[17] The Buddha and the Naṭarāja between them render Being as well as Becoming. The symbolism of Indian art suggests to many the numerous conventions which necessarily enter into iconography. In fact, this symbolism is deeper, since it seeks to create a form appropriate to an abstract idea. Icons immediately seek to image ideas with the help of conventions but created with the artist's genius they acquire an innate though imponderable expressiveness.

The earliest Buddhist cave temples belong to the Maurya period. With the passage of time Buddhist cave temples and monasteries became more elaborate and the great cave temples at Karle may be said to represent the best. The cave temple is more a work of sculpture than architecture in the sense that it is not bothered by exactly the same problem of creating a structure able to support the weight of the covering and pro vide for openings and partitions as in the usual case of structural architecture. At the same time the uncovering of the temple form out of the rock-mass had to be tackled by the excavator who also had to have adequate engineering skill. The essential process, however, was one of recovering a form or idea latent in material inconscience or *avyakta*. The cave was the archetypal symbol of the meditator's heart where he withdrew to seek inner light. The 'home' (*gaha*) symbolised in early Buddhist parlance the psychic matrix of bondage. Desire was the home-fashioner (*gaha-kāraka*) *par excellence*. The monk left the home behind and retreated within, from *gaha* to *guhā*.

At Karle the entrance is elaborate and the great fan window not only provides a fascinating front but lighting within. The central hall is impressive and the *stūpa* at the apsidal end with light reaching it from the top frontal opening would provide a sublime object for the monks meditating in the hall. The aisles were separated by a row of pillars, the top of which formed a sculptured frieze. Here was a place with an attractive entrance and bold sculpture and yet silent, spacious, with just enough light to serve those who worshipped and meditated.

The greatest development of excavated architecture may be seen in the great Kailāśa temple at Ellora. Here is a Hindu temple of the 8th century which has been wholly carved out of the mountain side to resemble a fullfledged structural temple. The standing marvel which the temple presents defies description. As Sri M. N. Deshpande who spent years looking after the Western Circle has remarked, perhaps the best description of the temple may be found in a couplet of the saint Gyaneswara : space was created out of a 'tamarind leaf', (i. e. nothing) and the construction laid down the pinnacle first and the foundations last ! Percy Brown has remarked that the siting of the temple suffers from the grave fault of being in an excavated hole. It seems as if the temple has been erected inside an empty tank and is thus robbed of proper perspective.[48] This, however, totally fails to appreciate the whole idea of the temple. The temple has been excavated from the mountain and remains attached to it. It is a cave and a temple in one. The mountain side itself provides the perspective for the temple.

Kailāśanātha temple, Ellora, Eighth century.

The structural temple appears to have been originally just a platform for some rude image under a tree with some kind of a fencing. These early images were probably of the Yakṣas.[49] The worship of the Śivaliṅga in the centuries immediately preceding the Christian era by the sect of Śiva Bhāgavatas is well known. The Pāśupatas following Lakulīśa added to the popularity of Śiva worship. At the same time the Bhāgavatas were popularising the worship of Vāsudeva. We know of Greeks who were converted to the Bhāgavata cult and some Kuṣāṇa rulers professed to be Śaiva. The development of these Bhāgavata and Śaiva sects between the 2nd Cent. B.C. and 2nd Cent. A.D. led to the transformation of the images as well as the temples needed to house them. The *Saṁhitās* and the *Purāṇas* contain the literature where we can find the prescriptions for these. It is in the Gupta period that the temple structure attained its classical form.[50] The Hindu temple unlike the Muslim mosque or the Christian church is not a mere place for the faithful to gather but a veritable dwelling of the god. The image itself is not a likeness because Śiva and Viṣṇu are not in their essence anthropomorphic figures. A human form is iconographically endowed with symbolic significance and then ritually consecrated. It is this last act which makes the image fit for worship since it ensures the presence of the deity. The image is housed in the *garbha-gṛha* or the sanctum sanctorum. Around the *garbha-gṛha* lay the *pradakṣiṇā-patha*. In front of the *garbha-gṛha* lay a small anteroom called *maṇḍapa* which could even be an open porch. In the Gupta temples the *Garbha-gṛha* has a flat roof, though in some instances a smaller construction appears above the roof of the *garbha-gṛha*. The *pradakṣiṇā-patha* is covered by a wall or lattice. The door to the *maṇḍapa* is elaborately carved with the figures of Gaṅgā and Yamunā on either side of the jambs. The whole construction is on the basis of posts and beams without any arches. There is a delicate balance between the religious function, the architectural construction and the sculptural decoration. The Gupta temples are not monumentally imposing but at once serviceable and beautiful.

The post-Gupta period is the great period of temple construction. It is also the period of the flowering of Tāntric cults and literature and of the proliferation of ritual and iconography. The older extant *śilpaśāstras* too seem to go back to this period.[51] They defined three major styles of temple architecture, *Nāgara, Vesara* and *Drāviḍa*.[52] The *Nāgara* style which has also been called the northern or Indo-Aryan style has a number of regional varieties. The temples of Orissa, Bundelkhand, Abu and Gujrat constitute its provincial variations. The most important feature of this style is its high, towering *śikhara*. The origin of the *śikhara* has been attributed to the multiplication and compression of stories on top of the *garbha-gṛha* till ultimately they came to be stylized towers of diverse designs. The dimensions of the temples increased considerably since the Gupta period and they came to be imposing monuments dominating the landscape by their height as well as their chiselled and definitive form.[53]

The greatest of the Orissan temples was undoubtedly the unfinished sun temple at *Koṇārka*. Why the temple was left unfinished is a mystery. Possibly the temple was conceived on such a colossal scale that as its height went up it was discovered that the weight of the top could not be supported by the structure specially in view of the nature of the ground which is near the sandy seashore. There is of course an alternative view that one temple had been completed but part of it fell down. Part of it undoubtedly fell down, but the temple perhaps had never been completed either. The temple breathes the spirit of a colossus. The life-like carving of its sculpture and its more than life-like proportions still amaze the spectator. The fiery horses of the sun might be expected any moment to move the giant wheels of the chariot which the temple represents. Fantastic animals, situations and scenes of fluid motion and stress, delicate and bold erotic scenes on the frieze at different levels all give to the temple an extraordinary aspect. The temple of *Liṅgarāja* in Bhuvaneshwar, the temples of *Khajuraho,* the delicate marble temples of Mount Abu all belong to the centuries between the 8th and the 11th.

One aspect of the sculpture of these temples has received particular attention. They depict erotic scenes of such frankness as to revolt a conventional taste. Attempts have been made to discover diverse explanations for this eroticism. The

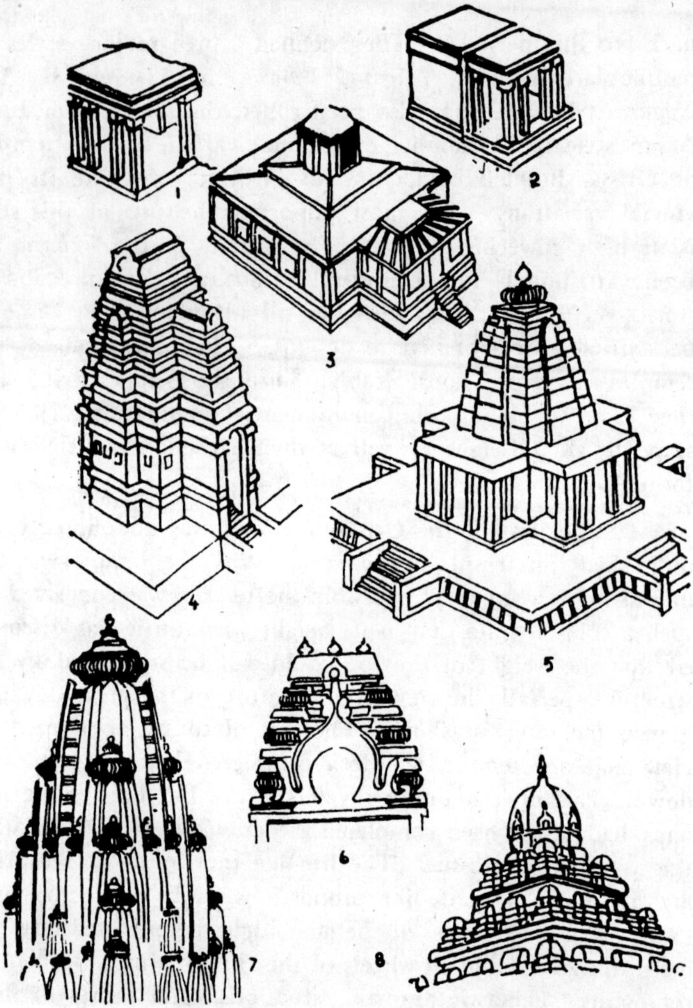

Development of the temple : (1) Cave temple with maṇḍapa, Udaigiri, 400 A.D., (2) Temple no. 19, Sāñchī, 415 A.D., (3) Lad Khan temple, Aihole, 450 A.D., (4) Brick temple of Bhitargaon, c. 400 A.D., (5) Daśāvatāra temple at Deogarh, c. 500 A.D., (6) Vaital Deul, c. 850 A.D., Orissa, (7) Upper part of Kandariyā Mahādeva temple, Khajuraho, (8) Dharmarāja temple, Mahābalipuram. (After Percy Brown).

tantra has been called in, and some have laid the responsibility on the debased taste of a feudal age. All this seems to be unnecessary. The representation of female beauty, of auspicious couples (*mithuna*) and of erotic play was as widespread in literature as in art in ancient times and the Indians were never very squeamish about it. The artist felt an added fascination in representing emotions and contortions and the general public seems to have granted him this license with as little difficulty as is felt to-day with respect to some of the films produced in the West. More important than the eroticism of the sculpture is its mastery of motion.

Although *Vesara* is sometimes identified with the Orissan architecture, it might more plausibly be taken to be the same as the *Cālukyan-Hoysala* style. From the interaction of *Nāgara* and *Drāviḍa* styles in the Cālukya and Hoysala domains, a distinctive style gradually emerged and flowered in the Hoysala age climaxing in the peerless temple of Hoysaleśvara at Halebid. Several features of this style of architecture have been noticed.[54] Its *śikhara* seemed to combine features of the *Nāgara* and *Drāviḍa śikharas*. The plan of the temples is often hexagonal. The pillars were elaborately divided and carved out of a single stone. The walls were almost completely covered by sculptures in multiple rows. The patterns of the rows were conventionally fixed but the boldness and crowding of figures in this broad frieze almost destroyed it as a wall.

The Draviḍian style began with the Pallavas. The shore temples of Mamallapuram are among the earlier masterpieces of this style. It is the sculpture that is remarkable rather than the architecture. Even today one can still see by the roadside a rock suddenly looming high with the most marvellous carvings. The scene of the *gaṅgāvataraṇa* is justly famous. Along with the sublime, the artist has not forgotten his sense of sly humour. Nor is the warlike sentiment neglected as may be seen in the panel depicting the *Mahiṣamardinī*. It is in the *Cola* period that the Draviḍian style reached its climax. The *śikhara* came to be domical in shape. It is described in texts as octagonal in plan. Whereas the *nāgara śikhara* is tall and curvilinear, the Draviḍian *śikhara* gives a squat appearance. An important feature of the Draviḍian temple was the elaborate and ornamental outer gateway called the *gopuram*. The *Bṛhadīśvara* temple at Tanjore is the most remarkable example of this kind and belongs to the time of Rājarāja the Great. In course of time the Draviḍian temple came to acquire numerous corridors, courtyards and gardens. The

Mahiṣāsuramardinī—Pallava, Mahābalipuram

temple developed into a virtual complex of structures, a miniature 'holy city'.

Of ancient paintings the only examples left are the murals of a religious character in some caves of which the Ajanta and the Bagh caves are the best known.[55] Apart from these some underlying paintings have been discovered on the walls of some south Indian temples and we have some miniatures in manuscripts from Gujrat and Bengal towards the end of the ancient period. This gives through large omissions a somewhat one-sided notion of ancient Indian paintings. The paintings at Ajanta represent a particular style of painting which wielded great influence in central Asia and the far East. But there were many other kinds of purely secular paintings which unfortunately have been lost altogether. Ancient literature, for example, bears testimony to both portraiture as well as landscape painting. The famous Purāṇic story about *Uṣā* and Aniruddha turns on a portrait. Kālidāsa describes in the *Śākuntalam* a landscape of the River *Mālinī*. Bhavabhūti mentions a picture gallery (*citra-vīthī*) in the palace in *Uttararāmacarita*. Some of the scenes from plays or perhaps legends even find a place in the cave paintings.

A royal hunting scene identified with Duṣyanta Śakuntalā story—Rānigumphā, Udaigiri hills, Orissa, Ist century B.C.

The theorists of painting mention six features of a painting. *"Rūpabhedaḥ Pramāṇāni Bhāvalāvṇyayojanam Sādṛśyaṁ varṇikābhaṅga iti citraṁ ṣaḍaṅgakam//"*.[56] *Rūpabheda* meant the distinctiveness of form. It included typal as well as individual differences. Pramāṇa meant measure and stood for a canon of proportions. *Bhāvalāvaṇyayojana* was the infusion of feeling and beauty. *Sādṛśya* or likeness suggested verisimilitude where the archetype could be drawn from the natural or the ideal world. *Varṇikābhaṅga* was the manner of using brush and colour. It was further held that the masters praise a painting for its expressive lines while the common folk admire the richness of colours. The paintings at Ajanta fully illustrate the preeminence of line and expression. These paintings belong largely to the Gupta period and a large proportion of the original work has already been eroded by time especially since the caves were discovered and opened up. The theme of the paintings is drawn from the *Jātakas* and the life of the Buddha. The surface of the walls was specially prepared with a plaster of lime and while it was still wet the paintings were first drawn in bold outline in ochre red, corrections being made in black. Colours used were drawn from vegetable and mineral sources but even today they remain bright and fast. The scenes are composed in panels which are easily distinguished by the change of focus from one to the other. The perspective is not naturalistic but a development of the 'vertical' perspective mentioned above in connection with the reliefs of Sāñchī.

The most remarkable thing about the paintings of Ajanta is the expressiveness of the bold and sweeping lines and the almost perfect synthesis which we find here between sensuousness and spirituality. Hegel had said that beauty is the Absolute shining through the veil of the senses. If so, beauty must be said to have found itself at Ajanta in the most perfect measure.

This tradition of representing beauty cast its spell far and wide in Asia. During the Kuṣāṇa and Gupta periods conquering armies and trading caravans plied along the great overland routes connecting India through Afghanistan and Central Asia to the borders of China. Buddhist pilgrims and preachers followed the same routes or routes leading from Kashmir to Central Asia. Non-Buddhist preachers especially those belonging to the theistic cults too followed these routes to Central Asia. Numerous sites from Bamian and Kashgar to Turfan and Tun Huang contain the remains of now vanished faiths especially Buddhism. Buddhist monasteries and *Stūpas* with sculptures and paintings were once the pride of numerous Central Asian realms as noticed by Chinese pilgrims and confirmed by modern archaeology. While the spread of Islam ended these Buddhist cultures of Central Asia, Buddhism made a second entry into Central Asia through Tibet in the post-Gupta period. Apart from the introduction of Buddhist motifs and themes which naturally passed with Buddhism, the most abiding influence of Indian art was in terms of the characteristic flowing line of Ajanta and its idealized drawing of the human figures. Tun Huang was the furthest outpast of this influence. In China itself Buddhist influences gradually waned after the T'ang period. The Ch'an school founded by Bodhidharma introduced a new philosophy which proved of abiding influence on Chinese painting and later as Zen on Japanese painting. Here the spirit of *dhyāna* in Buddhism found a new pictorial embodiment. The inexpressible identity of *Śūnyatā* and *Rūpa,* of *Citta* and *acitta,* of *Karma* with *nirvikalpa* and *Sahaja,* strain to find their expression in the art inspired by Zen, whether in *Theragāthā,* the *Laṅkāvatāra Sūtra* or Chinese and Japanese painting.

The opening of maritime trade in the Kuṣāṇa and Gupta periods led to the expansion of Indian culture into South-east Asia where in due course a distinctive civilization flowered in which Indian ideas, symbols, institutions and languages were joined with different regional cultures. In some ways the artistic creations in this civilization represent the climax of the Indian art tradition. The paintings at Sigirya in Ceylon, the great *Stūpa* of Borobudur in Java,[57] the temple complex of Angkor Wat in Cambodia leap to the mind as peerless examples. The stimulating meeting of minds and cultural diversities in an atmosphere of peace and affluence, tolerance and devotion helped this final efflorescence of the Indian art tradition outside India.

Aesthetic theory in the Indian tradition

The word nearest to art in the *Ṛgvedasaṁhitā* is *Kāvya.*

Kavi is one endowed with vision or wisdom and *kāvya* is his work. Both the words were used for men as well as gods and for their creations. *Kāvya* is what is made by a seer, an embodiment of vision. Thus *Kavi* is often used of Agni e. g., Ṛ. 1.12.6: *Kavir gṛhapatir yuvā, Ib.* 1.31.2.: *Kavir devānām*, *Ib.* 1.71.10: *Kaviḥ san.* In the first two cases Sāyaṇa explains *Kavi* as wise, *medhāvin*; in the third case he explains *Kavi* as transcendental seer or *Krāntadarśī.* Other gods too are sometimes called *Kavi.* For example Maruts are called *Kavayaḥ* in Ṛ. 1.31.1. Now Agni has brought down the perennial *Kāvyas* of the creator—*ni Kāvyā vedhasaḥ śaśvataskaḥ* (*Ib.* 1.72.1), i. e., what is perennial in heaven is revealed to man on earth. This could refer to wisdom enshrined in words or to all the created things as the expression of the eternal wisdom of the creator. In Ṛ. 2.5.3 Agni is said to encompass all the *Kāvyas* just as the rim encompasses the spokes. Here the *Kāvyas* are the same as *brahmāṇi*, i. e. holy words. But in Ṛ. 10.55.5 we have *'Devasya paśya Kāvyam'*, 'see the *Kāvya* of the god'. Here *Kāvya* has the sense of a miracle or marvel. At many places it has clearly the sense of man-made verse as, for example, in Ṛ. 5.39.5 or *Ib.* 9.97.7. Thus while *Kāvya* often has the sense of a human poetical creation, it has also the sense of the divine miracle of creation or revelation. There is an eternal truth in heaven belonging to divine vision. Creation or revelation is its manifestation on earth. Poetry is the expression of this truth[58] in words.

Word or *Vāk* is what mediates between the highest heaven and the earth, i. e between the transcendental and the manifested worlds. *"Gaurīr mimāya salilāni takṣati...sahasrākṣarā parame vyoman"* (Ṛ. 1.164.41).[59] Speech measures and fashions forms out of the unmanifest like a carpenter. Infinite in the highest heaven, she becomes limited and numbered. She is fourfold, but three of her forms are hidden.[60] Only the fourth form is what men use in speech. *Vāk,* thus, alternating with *dhī,* is the power of making by wisdom and truth, creating, fashioning of forms. This creative power is superior to particular created forms, which not only reveal but also conceal.

Thus we are told that in assuming many forms, Indra uses magical power : *"Indro māyābhiḥ puru-rūpa īyate"*.

The earliest Indian conception of art is, thus, that of creating forms with due measure which reveal and conceal the vision of perennial truth. In the later Vedic literature we get the word *śilpa.* Sāyaṇa explains *śilpa* to mean a marvellous work. A famous passage in the *Aitareya Brāhmaṇa* (30th chap.) says human arts are in imitation of the divine arts— *"devaśilpāni eteṣāṁ vai śilpānāmanukṛtīha śilpam adhigamyate hastī kaṁso vāso hiraṇyam aśvatarīrathaḥ śilpam iti"*.[61] It then goes on to say that the arts are nothing but the ritual purification or renovation of the self—*"ātma-saṁskṛtirvāva śilpāni"*.[62] Art is, thus, an imitation of divine archetypes and a re-making of the self. In both respects it is parallel to ritual. "This is the 'imitation of Nature in her manner of operation', and, like the first creation, the imitation of an intelligible, not a perceptible model."[63]

Early Buddhist literature recognizes four sources of poetry—*cintā* or reflection, *suta* or learning, *attha* or moral wisdom and *paṭibhāṇa* or inspiration.[64] It recognizes *sippa* as a specialized craft requiring training.[65] This conception of the arts and crafts traces them to human invention and skill. This skill could be used to entertain people or could be used to lead them to seek wisdom. Words and forms have no inherent power to reveal truth but their skilled use could make men find the truth within themselves, a truth which is beyond words and images. Buddha's teaching is the greatest miracle, the supreme example of skill in means. All art which subserves truth is like the finger which points to the moon, a marvellously suggestive means created by skill.

The classical conception of art and creativity contains elements of both these notions, Vedic and non-Vedic, but they were subjected to an 'aesthetic' transformation. The ritualistic association of literature and the arts continued[66] but tended to become a formality. The notion of imitation tended to be interpreted semi-realistically.[67] The mysterious power of words was recognized[68] and so the symbolic significance of forms.[69] It was, however, believed that the age of seers had passed away and a sharp distinction was drawn between *śāstra* and *kāvya*. In the revealed *śāstras* the word was more important than the meaning. In the scientific *śāstras* the meaning was more important than the word. In *Kāvya* the two stood balanced so that the word needed to be understood in all its meanings but remained irreplaceable.[70] The creative process thus retained its imponderability but its revelatory character was interpreted as expressiveness and that was connected with feelings rather than with vision. The wisdom of the poet was understood as arising from learning and experience rather than spiritual intuition. Poetry at once instructs and delights and is rooted in genius, cultivation of the mind, and practice.[71] There was an increasing tendency to conceive expression as emotional expression, skill as the art of decoration and symbolism as convention. Thus the ancient notion of art as the creation of a form which reveals ideal truth through some mysterious correspondence or symbolism tended to be replaced by the notion of art as the creation of a pleasing form with conventional significance but the capacity to evoke an emotional experience. The theory, however, persisted that what was needed of the artist was contemplation so that in a state of absorption he would be able to spontaneously express the idea in its intuitive immediacy or imponderable vividness.[72]

The Vedic vision of reality was not mediated by mentally constructed or artificial images. The notion of form or *rūpa* was there. "All *rūpas* are of *Tvaṣṭā* (the divine fashioner)". *Tvaṣṭā* inherited them from Agni[73] or, as *Aitareya* has it, *Tvaṣṭā* is nothing but speech. In other words, all forms are originally contained in divine wisdom, the ultimate illuminer. It is from there that the artificing and fashioning mind derives them. Reality is conceived as a luminous power which creates things or forms out of itself. The human mind is capable of responding to the Light and apperceiving the forms in which it expresses itself. The forms which man perceives, thus, are not phantasms produced by the senses or the mind but created things rooted in reality. That is why although Vedic poets use images from nature as transparent expressions of divine majesty and splendour, they do not conceive gods iconically. They rely on the power of seeing–*dhī* and the truth which it seeks–*dharmāṇi*. They do not use imagination to weave dreams or paint the lily. They, however, do use forms as symbols for what cannot be seen. *Rūpa* is, thus, often used for a symbol in the *Brāhmaṇas*.[74]

In the *Upaniṣads,* however, we can see a tendency which Buddhism carried further. Words and forms, *Nāman* and *Rūpa,* are run down as merely the limitation under which manifestation takes place.[75] Truth is transcendent and cannot be represented by sensuous images or mental constructs. Buddhism elaborated the further idea that all representations contain the working of imagination and that imagination is innately bound up with desire and instinct.[76] If in Vedic thought creation is rooted in divine will and a manifestation of perennial truth, Buddhist thought makes Ignorant Desire the delusive creatrix of the world of images in which human life is lived. Idea as vision (*Prajñā*) or true form (*dharma, lakṣaṇa*) is thus sundered from the image as mental construct (*Vikalpa*) or sensuous presentation (*pratibhāsa*). The deceiving nature of imagination, however, has a redeeming feature. There is such a thing as a useful deception, *avisaṁvādi-bhrama.* The image may not represent reality but it may be non-discrepant in the sense that it may help in the course of successful action. The visual image of the moon or a map are not like the reality they claim to represent but they are nevertheless useful to the navigator.

If this view clips the truth-claims of imagination, it simultaneously clips the claims of the intellect by recognizing the inevitability of imagination in the cognitive process. If the world of imagination is not the world of truth, let it be recognized that what is commonly called the real world is itself a world of images.[77] If the truth of this world is pragmatic, so can the truth of the declaredly imaginative world be. But the praxis is not the same in the two cases. The common man slaves after ephemeral things at the biddings of desire but the philosopher seeks an eternal truth by dialectically negating the world of contradictions. The poet and the artist may similarly represent the world of images for what they are, restless constructions covering the face of eternal peace like clouds covering the sky or smoke covering the brightness of the lamp.[78]

In the classical age a distinction was made between the cognitive and aesthetic modes of awareness.[79] Cognitive awareness is wholly object-determined and relevant for action. Aesthetic awareness is connected wholly with an immanent object or image and unconnected with any real subject or his practical life. It is thus contemplative in character and its imaginative content is referred not to the real world but to that of ideal essences.[80] The distinction between *lakṣaṇa* and *lakṣya* is well known in aesthetic theory. *Lakṣaṇas* are defined in the *śāstras* but what exactly is *lakṣya?* Since the *lakṣaṇas* have only a partial connection with empirical reality, the *lakṣya* cannot be identified with the latter. *Lakṣya* can only be regarded as an ideal or essential reality which is imperfectly encountered in actual experience and is sought to be defined by traditional conceptions or *lakṣaṇas.* The presentations which are constituent of art, thus, are significant images, immediate and sensuous but recognizably exhibiting ideas or *lakṣaṇas* and pregnant with a sense of significance. The image seeks to realize an imponderable idea which serves as a standard of excellence or perfection.[81] Thus even though *śrutis, svaras* and *rāgas* are patently sensuous presentations, they are at the same time characteristically recognizable and ideal just as phonemes (*varṇas*), words and meanings are. Neither musical notes nor words are merely physical sounds. The critical recognition of their distinctness and patterns requires them to evoke and fuse with memory–images to be matched with expectations of standards. Even in painting the representational character of form is only one aspect of it and the representation too is more or less idealized to correspond to some mental idea or impression. The painter does not draw from nature but from within.[82]

The image may be defined as the immediate object of a vivid apprehension.[83] In art its ontic status remains as undetermined as the epistemic status of its apprehension.[84]

Nevertheless, the image appears to belong to a coherent whole and is characterized by an imponderable expressiveness. It also invites judgment with reference to ideal standards. The image-world of art is autonomous but not arbitrary.[85] It has a sensuous vividness but an ideal expressiveness. The experiential process which the image furthers tends to attain to a non-discursive but intelligibly structured intuition. The images belong to art not merely as means but ends. They contribute to aesthetic value *per se* and also as signs. This makes aesthetic experience at once intuitive and critical.

Different constituents of art are differently emphasized in its different forms. Image and symbol are obvious in the visual arts. Meaning and idea are equally unmistakeable in literature. Form and expressiveness constitute the substance of music. Despite this diversity of aspects a basic duality is noticeable in all the arts, the duality of image and idea. It is least noticeable in music and most noticeable in the literary arts. In music the wholeness of the sensible form seems to be the whole sense. In literature the sense clearly lies beyond the sensuous signs.

The question of meaning arises most clearly in the case of literature. There were several ancient views on the subject. On one view words constitute literature, on another, words and meanings together constitute literature.[86] Both the views regard words as irreplaceable. The former, however, does not regard a logically coherent meaning as indispensable. This is undoubtedly the deeper view whether we illustrate it by the verse *'Ayaṁ vandhyāsuto yāti Khapuṣpa-kṛta-śekharaḥ/'* or by *Finnegans Wake*. The dispensability of meaning is not the dispensability of meaning as such but only of logically coherent meaning. Words cannot be substituted by non-sense syllables though the words used may almost give that appearance. Words not only have meanings but they have multiple meanings and the original way in which the words are combined in literary creations leads to unusual patterns of meaning which are not always logically coherent. In fact, full logical coherence will imply continuity with the rest of our knowledge and experience, in which case the literary meaning will be a part of common-sense and science and the words expressing it would be replaceable. Meaning may be logical, non-logical or illogical. The main emphasis in ancient theory was on a combination of logical and non-logical meanings.[87] The logical meanings may be factual in the sense that they may be adequately communicable by designation, description or definition. The power by which words function in this multifarious logical context has been called *Abhidhā*.[88] Closely allied with this is the oblique use of words which may be seen in their idiomatic or metaphorical use. This is called *Lakṣaṇā*. The former power enables the words to state a meaning literally, the latter to communicate it by a kind of implication. It is an apparent inconsistency in the stated meaning which leads to the operation of *Lakṣaṇā*. In *Abhidhā* words are used literally, in *Lakṣaṇā*, non-literally. These two types of signification literal and non-literal or figurative, were generally accepted. Some poeticians went beyond these and postulated a further power of the words called *vyañjanā* or *Dhvani*.[89] This refers generally to the suggestive or evocative use of words. It is through this kind of use that words are able to convey a felt meaning. To convey a feeling or an experience in its vividness, neither is statement adequate, nor a mere oblique use of language. It is only through evoking the psychic associations of words, meanings and the situations represented through them, that language can communicate meanings as aspects of subjectivity. This is the revelatory use of words and the meaning ultimately revealed is the self-awareness of the subject in so far as it is mediated by feelings and images. The symbolism of words is thus, not simply conventional, nor its ultimate meaning simply objective.

If symbolism is understood as expressiveness (*vyañjakatva*) dependent on obscure associations which do not need to be perceived for being effective, and if meaning is understood as a subjective condition, these two terms—symbol (*vyañjaka*) and meaning (*vyaṅgya*)—would then pervade all the arts. *Svara* and *rāga*, *śabda* and *rasa*, *rūpa* and *bhāvalāvaṇya* represent the *vyañjaka* and the *vyaṅgya* in music, literature and painting respectively.

As a consequence of this duality beauty or aesthetic experience too has a dual aspect. It is a peculiar combination of the value exhibited by signs and images in their expressive use and the value expressed as an intuitive experience.[90] The proportion of these two can vary greatly. In pure or formal art value seems to be wholly immanent in the immediate aspect of the signs and images and the skill of their use. This kind of art may be purely ornamental (*citra*) or its overt impression may be more powerful than its suggested sense (*guṇībhūta-Vyaṅgya*).[91] Formal music divorced from any integral cultural context, tends to illustrate this kind of pure aesthetic value or beauty. So does decorative painting or rhetorical poetry. On the other hand, where art apparently subserves a religious or social value transcendent or humanistic, aesthetic value or beauty is realized in terms of a revelatory or intuitive experience of which the ideational and emotional content is constituted by the specific cultural value in question. When a devotee loves God, the devotee and his love are both subordinated to the idea of God. In devotional poetry the idea of God only serves to evoke the image of love in such a manner that it becomes the immediate object of an unhindered appreciation or enjoyment. Beauty thus consists, on one hand, of the fascination exercised by the perfection of sensuous form and the appreciation of the skill underlying its creation, and on the other, of a revelation of value in some basic human situation. Beauty thus, exists at two levels viz., at the level of the perception of form and at the level of the intuitive experience of value. The appreciation of the flawlessness or perfection of form may be within an immediate sensuous experience but is quite distinct from sensuous enjoyment (*bhoga*). Aesthetic appreciation of form is always implicitly or explicitly critical and involves imaginative reproduction and synthesis.[92] It also involves a detachment of the spectator from his habitual practical concerns and specific ego-identity.[93] Music and natural beauty have a sublimating effect on the percipient who not only receives pleasing sensations but refers them to an objective form. The perception of beauteous form, thus, is the apprehension of a spectacle where actuality is transmuted into an image. It was natural, therefore, to seek to define ideal forms, visual or acoustic, so that the proportions of beauty itself could be formulated. Both in the *saṅgītaśāstra* and the *śilpaśāstra* thus, *lakṣaṇas* and *pramāṇas* were elaborated.

Deeper theory, however, realized that flawlessness (*adoṣatva*) or propriety (*aucitya*) is nothing except the transparency of form or its harmony with the inner experience of value called *rasa*. The beauty of art does not lie in mere lines and colours, notes and rhythms, words and acting but in their revelation of an ideal and imponderable significance. Like all value beauty pleases and invites critical approval.

In the Vedic conception beauty was inseparable from goodness and the vision of truth. The hymns to Dawn reveal the reverence with which the seers approached beauty which was to them the expression of divine glory, conformity with divine law. The *Upaniṣads* identify beauty with *rasa,* the beatific aspect of the spirit.[94] In Buddhist literature beauty is what gives rest and lucidity to the mind, else it is nothing but a snare and a delusion.[95] With image worship and contemplation in classical times there evolved the notion of form as symbolic of psychic or supernatural realities. Idealized form[96] as the symbol of psychic or spiritual verities ultimately as expressive of *rasa,* may be said to define the basic conception of beauty in classical thought.[97]

REFERENCES

1. *"Gāndharvaṁ hi sāmabhyastasmādbhavaṁ gānaṁ"* Abhinava ad. *Nāṭyaśāstra,* 28.9-10.

2. Cf. Sāyaṇa *"Sāmaśabdavācyasya gānasya svarūpaṁ ṛgakṣareṣu Kruṣṭādibhiḥ saptabhiḥ svarair akṣara-vikārādibhiścaniṣpādyate".*

3. Cf. Paranjape, *Bhāratīya Saṁgīta Kā Itihāsa,* pp. 82ff.

4. *Nāṭyaśāstra,* 28.10: *"Asya yonir bhaved gānaṁ vīṇā vaṁśas tathaivaca".*

5. *Sāmavidhāna Brāhmaṇa*, 1.3; *Saṁhitopaniṣad Brāhmaṇa*; *Taittirīya Prātiśākhya*, 23.15.

6. *Ādyaḥ prastāra udgīthaḥ pratihārastataḥ param|*
Upadravo'tha nidhanaṁ hiṅkāroṅkārakau tathā||
Iti sapta samācaṣṭa sāmāṅgāni pitāmahaḥ|
(*Saṅgītaratnākara*).

7. Cf. Jaimini, *Mīmāṁsāsūtras*, 9.2.39.

8. *Nāradīya śikṣā*, 1.5.1-2 "*Yaḥ sāmagānāṁ prathamaḥ sa Veṇormadhyamaḥ smṛtaḥ Yo dvitīyaḥ sa gandhāraḥ tṛtīyastvṛṣabhaḥ smṛtaḥ caturthaḥ ṣaḍja ityāhuḥ. Pañcamodhaivato bhavet. Ṣaṣṭho niṣādo vijñeyaḥ saptamaḥ pañcamaḥ smṛtaḥ*".

9. *Nāradīya śikṣā* already says "*svargān nānyatra gāndhāro*"; Abhinava explains that *Gāndhāra* became obsolete because it included too high and too low notes and unmelodic intervals—"*atitārātimandratvāt vaisvarayān nopadarśitaḥ*".

10. Lat, *A Study of Dattilam*, p. 192. Lat carefully distinguishes the nature of *gāndharva* from *gāna—Ib.*, pp. 80ff. *Nāṭyaśāstra* mentions only *Pada*, *Svara* and *Tāla*—28.11.

11. *Nāṭyaśāstra*, 28.41; Anupa Pande, *op. cit.*

12. Bṛhaspati, *Bharata Kā Saṅgīta siddhānta*, pp. 233ff; Lat, *op. cit.*, pp. 313ff.

13. *Saṅgītaratnākara*, 1.1.22-24.

14. *Bṛhaddeśī*, 13-15; Lat, *op. cit.*, pp. 168-69.

15. For plastic representations, see Kapila Vatsyayan, *Classical Indian Dance in Literature and the Arts.*

16. Cf. Sanyal, *Prachīna Bhāratiya Saṅgīta Cintā*, pp. 54-55.

17. "*Dhana-nirapekṣaṁ cedaṁ devānāṁ yajanam*" (*Abhinavabhāratī*, ch. 28.9).

18. Bṛhaspati, *op. cit.*, pp. 266ff.

19. *Ṛ.*, 8.92.3.

20. *Kauṣītakī Brāhmaṇa*, 29.5.

21. *Aitareya-Brāhmaṇa,* Vol. II, p. 764ff (Ānandāśrama ed.).

22. Kapila Vatsyayana, *op. cit.,* pp. 29ff.

23. *Nāṭyaśāstra,* Chap. 4; Kapila Vatsyayana, *op. cit.,* pp. 106ff, where a comparison is made with sculptural representations.

23a. Vide Anupa Pande, '*Pindibandha*', *Purātattva.*

24. Allchins, *The Birth of Indian Civilization,* Middle-Sex, 1968.

25. Sankalia, *Pre-Historic Art in India,* New Delhi, 1978; V. N. Misra and Y. Mathpal, 'Rock Art of Bhimbetka Region, Central India', *Man and Environment,* Vol. III, 1979, pp. 27-33.

26. Cf. Fairservis, *The Roots of Ancient India,* pp. 122ff.

27. Marshall, *MIC*; Wheeler, *The Indus Civilization*; Stella Kramrisch, *Indian Sculpture,* pp. 6-7; S. K. Saraswati, *A Survey of Indian Sculpture,* pp. 21-22; V. S. Agrawal, *Bhāratīya Kalā,* p. 50; B. Rowland, *The Art and Architecture of India,* p. 48. *Contra,* S. P. Gupta, *Roots of Indian Art,* p. 4.

28. Cf. Durga Prasad, *Observations on the Silver Punch-marked Coins of Ancient India and their Age,* Banaras, 1931.

29. Cf. *Aṅguttara,* (Nalanda) II. pp. 40-41.

30. G. C. Pande, *Bauddha Dharma Ke Vikāsa Kā Itihāsa,* pp. 203-4; Stella Kramrisch, *op. cit.,* p. 15; Rowland, *op. cit.,* p. 15. Cf. Coomaraswamy, *History of Indian and Indonesian Art,* pp. 87-88.

30a. The *Śrisūkta* speaks of *Paśūnām rūpam.*

31. *Aṅguttara* quoted above.

32. *Gītā*: '*Avajānanti māṁ mūḍhā mānuṣīṁ tanum āśritam.*'

33. Marshall, *CHI,* Vol. I, pp. 273ff. The best recent discussion of date and hypothesis may be seen in S. P. Gupta, *Roots of Indian Art.*

34. An excellent account in V. S. Agrawal, *Cakradhvaja.*

35. *Harṣacarita,* 1.1.

36. The best account may be seen in Marshall and Fou-

cher, *The Monuments of Sāñchī*, 3 vols.

37. Vide Susmita Pande's paper in *Journal of Buddhist Studies*, Delhi University, 1980.

38. See my *Bauddha Dharma Ke Vikāsa Kā Itihāsa*, p. 344.

39. Cf. M. M. G. N. Kaviraja's article on *Nirmāṇa-citta* in *Saraswatī Bhavan Studies*.

40. Cf. Coomaraswamy, *Figures of Speech or Figure of Thought* (London, 1946) ; S. K. Gupta, *Indian Art Motifs* (unpub. thesis, Rajasthan University), pp. 98ff.

41. Foucher, *Beginning of Buddhist Art* (1917). For a detailed critique of the foreign origins of the *Lakṣaṇas,* see S. K. Gupta, *op. cit*., pp. 126ff. For older views see V. Smith, *History of fine Art in India and Ceylon*, Grünwedel, *Buddhist Art in India,* Lohuizen de Leeuw, *The Scythian Period.* These views about Gandhāran Buddhist art were criticized and modified by Coomaraswamy and V. S. Agrawal, see Coomaraswamy, 'Indian Origin of the Buddha Image', *JAOS,* 1926, also in *The Art Bulletin*, 1927 ; V. S. Agrawala, *Indian Art,* Vol. I.

42. Cf. N. R. Ray, *Idea and Image in Indian Art*.

43. On Buddhist aesthetics, see my 'Early Buddhist Notion of Beauty' (*Rajasthan University Studies,* 1964), 'Reflections on Aesthetics from a Buddhist Point of View', (*Journal of Buddhist Studies, Delhi University*, 1978).

44. Cf. Coomaraswamy, *History of Indian and Indonesian Art*, p. 127 :

> "The Naṭarāja type is...a perfect visual image of Becoming, adequate complement and contrast to the Buddha type of pure being."

45. Cf. The Tiruvālaṇgādu figure in the Madras Museum. The Naṭarāja temple at Chidambaram sculptures 108 types of dance by Śiva corresponding to descriptions in the *Nāṭyaśāstra*—see *Madras Epigraphist's Annual Report* for 1913-14.

Of these the *Śaivāgamas* emphasize nine types of which the *bhujaṅgatrāsa* is common in *Naṭarāja* figures—Gopinatha Rao, *Elements of Hindu Iconography*, Vol. II, part I, p. 229.

46. This corresponds to the form of the Lord as *Pañcakṛtyakārin.* In the older theistic thought God performed three functions—creation, maintenance and destruction. In Āgamic thought He is also the Absolute and the Saviour, hence the source of Illusion as well as Grace, both immanent in the flow of Time. The eternity of Form and the fluidity of Time are merely two aspects of the integrity of the Absolute.

47. On the symbolism of *Naṭarāja,* see Coomaraswamy, *The Dance of Śiva ;* Gopinatha Rao, *op. cit.*, pp. 231ff.

18. Percy Brown, *History of Indian Architecture (Buddhist and Hindu)*, p. 86. But he goes on to remark, "Standing within its precincts and surrounded by its grey and hoary pavilions, one seems to be looking through into another world, not a world of time and space, but one of intense spiritual devotion expressed by such an amazing artistic creation hewn out of the earth itself." (p. 87).

49. On the Yakṣas, see Coomaraswamy, *Yakṣas.*

50. Soundara Rajan's *Indian Temple Styles* attempts a correlation between actual temples and the prescriptions in the *śāstras.*

51. Cf. L. M. Dubey, *Socio-Cultural Study of the Aparājitapṛcchā* (Unpub. thesis, Allahabad University), Introduction.

52. e. g., *Mayamatam,* 19.35-38—

"Nāgaraṁ drāviḍaṁ caiva vesaraṁ ca tridhā matam/
Caturaśrāyatāgraṁ yan nāgaraṁ parikīrtitam//
Aṣṭāśraṁ ca ṣaḍaśraṁ ca tattadāyāmameva ca/
Saudhaṁ drāviḍam ityuktaṁ vesaraṁ tu prakathyate//
Grīvāt prabhṛti vṛttaṁ yad vesaraṁ tadudāhṛtam//"

According to Soundara Rajan the basic distinction was between *prāsāda* and *vimāna* (*op. cit.*, pp. 16ff).

53. On temple forms and their diversity, cf. L. M. Dubey, *op. cit.*, pp. 317-83.

54. Cf. Cousens, *Chalukyan Architecture.*

55. Griffiths, *Paintings in the Buddhist Cave Temples of Ajanta,* 2 vols., Herringham & others, *Ajanta Frescoes;* Yazdani, *Ajanta,* 3 vols.; Dey, *My Pilgrimage to Ajanta and Bagh.*

56. Abanindra Nath Thakur, 'Bharata Śilpa Ke Ṣaḍaṅga' (Hindi tr.)–*Sammelan Patrika, Kalā Aṅka,* pp. 400ff.

57. Coomaraswamy doubts if the monument was originally intended to be a *Stūpa, History of Indian and Indonesian Art,* p. 205.

58. Cf. Coomaraswamy, *Selected Papers,* Vol. I, p. 243 fn.

59. *Salilāni* may be compared to *ambhaḥ* in the *Nāsadīya.* Water may be said to be archetypal of the formless which can assume any form.

60. *"Catvāri vāk parimitā padāni*
Tāni vidur brāhmaṇā ye manīṣiṇaḥ/
Guhā trīṇi nihitā neṅgayanti
Turīyaṁ vāco manuṣyā vadanti// (Ṛ. 1.106.45).

61. *AB.,* Vol. II, p. 764.

62. *Ib., l. c.*

63. Coomaraswamy, *op. cit.,* Vol. I, p. 24.

64. *Aṅguttara,* II., 245. Cf. my paper, 'Early Buddhist Notion of Beauty'; *Raj. Uni. Stud.,* 1964.

65. e. g., *Majjhima,* 1.119. (Nalanda ed.).

66. This may be seen in the *Nāṭyaśāstra* and the *Śilpaśāstras.*

67. In the *Nāṭyaśāstra* what is imitated is the 'world' or *loka.* The poets are expected to represent things according to their nature, real and conventional.

68. This may be seen in the theory of *sphoṭa* as well as in that of the four levels of speech. The analysis of the several types of meanings may also be recalled.

69. Iconography is the most striking example of this.

70. *Kāvyaprakāśa,* 1.2.

71. *Ib.,* 1.3.

72. Coomaraswamy, *Selected Papers,* Vol. I, p. 85.

73. *ŚB.,* Vol. I, p. 169.

74. e. g., *ŚB.,* Vol. I, p. 213.

75. Cf. *Ch.* 6.

76. Cf. my 'Reflections on Aesthetics from a Buddhist Point of View', *Journal of Buddhist Studies,* Delhi University, 1978.

77. *Vijñaptimātratāsiddhi, Viṁśikā,* thus begins by showing the similarity of the waking and dream worlds.

78. Cf. *Laṅkāvatāra.*

79. *Abhinavabhāratī* (Delhi), p. 485, *"rasāsvādaḥ smṛty-anumāna-laukika-sva-saṁvedana-vilakṣaṇa eva".*

80. *Ib.,* p. 487 *"alaukika evāyaṁ carvaṇopayogī vibhāvādivyavahāraḥ".*

81. Cf. Coomaraswamy, *op. cit.,* pp. 80, 88.

82. That is one reason why a merely geometrical or naturalistic perspective or naturalistic modelling have no necessary universality in art.

83. *sākṣātkārālambanam* ; cf. my paper on 'The Nature of Creative Imagination' presented at the Seminar in 'Creative Imagination & Social Transformation' at Nehru Memorial Museum, New Delhi, Feb. 7—Feb. 11, 1983.

84. *vibhāvādīnām alaukikatvam.*

85. *Kāvyaprakāśa,* 1.1.

86. Mammaṭa defines poetry as *śabdārthau,* Jagannātha Paṇḍitarāja as *śabdaḥ.*

87. *Vācyārtha,* which presupposes *yogyatā,* and *vyaṅgyārtha* which may not be a *prameya.*

88. Cf. *Kāvyaprakāśa,* 2.7.ff.

89. Its classical source is *Dhvanyāloka*.

90. See my *Mūlyamīmāṁsā*.

91. *Kāvyaprakāśa*, 1.5.

92. Cf. Bhaṭṭa Tauta's conception of *anuvyavasāya*.

93. Cf. Bhaṭṭa Nāyaka's conception of *Sādhāraṇīkaraṇa*.

94. *Tai*: *raso vai saḥ*, see my *Bhāratīya Paramparā Ke Mūla Svara*.

95. See my 'The Notion of Beauty in Early Buddhist Literature', *Rajasthan University Studies*, 1964.

96. Idealized form is free from the deviations attaching to actual instances. But it is a vivid presence in art.

97. *rasānuguṇavibhāvādirūpatā*.

SELECTED BIBLIOGRAPHY

(This list is highly selective and intended only to indicate *some* of the important sources utilized in the present work)

Chapter I

Bhagavadgītā with the commentary of Madhusūdana Sarasvatī, tr. & ann. Harihara Kripalu, Chowkhamba, Varanasi.

Bhagavadgītā, The Yoga of, expounded by Sri Krishna Prem, London, 1948.

Kaṭhopaniṣad, The Yoga of, by Sri Krishna Prem, Anand Publishing House, Allahabad.

Aurobindo, *Life Divine,* 2 Vols., (3 pts.), Arya Publishing House, Calcutta, 1939-40.

Aurobindo, *Synthesis of Yoga,* Vol. I.

Complete Works of Svāmī Vivekānanda, 11th ed., 8 Vols., Advaita Ashram, Calcutta, 1962.

G. C. Pande, *Bhāratīya Paramparā Ke Mūlasvara,* National Publishing House, New Delhi, 1981.

G. N. Kaviraj, *Bhāratīya Saṁskṛti Aur Sādhanā,* 2 Vols., Rāṣṭrabhāṣā Pariṣad, Patna, 1963.

Moti Lal Shastri, *Sattā-nirapekṣa Saṁskṛti-śabda evaṁ Sattā-sāpekṣa Sabhyatā-śabda Kā Cirantana Itivṛtta,* Mānavāśrama, Durgapura, Jaipur, *V.S.* 2015.

Chapters II & III

Aitareyabrāhmaṇa, 2 Vols., Ānandāśrama, Pune, 1930.

Aṣṭāviṁśatyupaniṣadaḥ, Nirṇayasāgara, Bombay.

Atharvavedasaṁhitā, Svādhyāya Maṇḍala, Aundh, *V.S.* 1995.

Avesta, 2 Vols., Vaidika Saṁśodhana Maṇḍala, Pune, 1962.

Bṛhaddevatā, 2 Vols., ed. Macdonell, reprinted, Motilal Banarsidass, Delhi, 1965.

Īśādidaśopaniṣadaḥ with Śaṅkara's commentary, Vāṇī-vilāsa Series, Kashi.

Nirukta, 2 Vols., Nirṇayasāgara, Bombay, 1921.

Ṛgveda-bhāṣyam by Dayānanda Sarasvatī, 9 Vols., Ajmer, *V.S.* 2020.

Ṛgveda-bhāṣyam by Dayānanda Sarasvatī, ed. Yudhiṣṭhira Mīmāṁsaka, 2 Vols., Bahalgarh (Hariyana), 1973.

Ṛgvedasaṁhitā with Sāyaṇa's commentary, 4 Vols., Vaidika Saṁśodhana Maṇḍala, Pune, 1933.

Ṛgveda with Commentaries, ed. Vishwabandhu, 8 Vols., Hoshiarpur, 1965-66.

Śatapathabrāhmaṇa, 2 Vols., Acyutagranthamālā, Kashi, *V.S.* 1994.

Siddhāñjana-bhāṣyam by Kapālī Śāstrī.

Taittirīyabrāhmaṇa, 3 Vols., Ānandāśrama, Pune, 1934.

Taittirīyasaṁhitā with Sāyaṇa's commentary, 8 Vols., 1901.

Tāṇḍyamahābrāhmaṇa, 2 Vols., Chowkhamba, Varanasi, 1936.

Vājasaneyisaṁhitā with the commentary of Uvaṭa and Mahīdhara, Nirṇayasāgara, Bombay, 1929.

Yajurveda-bhāṣyam, Dayānanda, 4 Vols., Ajmer, *V.S.* 2029.

Zend Avesta, 3 Vols., S.B.E.

Anirvana, *Vedamīmāṁsā,* Sanskrit College, Calcutta.

Aurobindo, *Hymns to Mystic Fire,* Pondicherry, 1972.

A. K. Coomaraswamy, *A New Approach to the Vedas,* London, 1933.

Griffith (tr.), *Hymns of the Ṛgveda,* 2 Vols., Reprint.

H. Grassmann, *Wörterbuch zum Ṛgveda,* Leipzig, 1873.

K. F. Geldner (tr.), *Der Ṛgveda,* 4 Vols., Harvard University Press, 1951-57.

Macdonell & Keith, *Vedic Index,* 2 Vols.

Suryakant, *Vaidika Kośa,* B.H.U., 1963.

Vedic Word-Concordance, 16 Vols., Hoshiarpur.

V. S. Agrawal, *Vision in Long Darkness,* Varanasi, 1963.

Winternitz, *History of Indian Literature,* (Eng. tr.), Vol. I, Calcutta, 1927.

Chapter IV

L'Abhidharmakośa de Vasubandhu, tr. and ann. La Vallee Poussin, Louvain, 1923-29.

Abhidharmakośabhāṣya with *Sphuṭārthā,* ed. Dvārikādāsa Śāstrī, 4 Vols., Varanasi, 1970.

Aṅgasuttāni, 3 Vols., ed. Muni Nathmal, Ladnu, *V.S.* 2031.

Ācārāṅgasūtra & Sūtrakṛtāṅga with Śīlāṅka's commentary, pub. Motilal Banarsidass, Indological Trust, Delhi, 1978.

Āpatamīmāṁsā of Samantabhadra, Varanasi, 1914.

Aṣṭasāhasrikāprajñāpāramitā, ed. P. L. Vaidya, Mithilā Institute, Darbhanga, 1960.

Bhagavatī Viyāhapannatti with Abhayadeva's commentary, Āgamodaya Samiti, Bombay, 1918-21.

Lalitavistara, ed. Lefman, 1902.

Laṅkāvatārasūtra, ed. B. Nanjio, Kyoto, 1956.

Madhyamaka-śāstra of Nāgārjuna, ed. P. L. Vaidya, Mithilā Institute, Darbhanga, 1960.

Mahābhārata, 4 Vols., Critical ed., Pune, 1971-75.

Mahāvastu Avadāna, 3 Vols., ed. R. G. Basak, Calcutta, 1963-68.

Mahāyānasūtrasaṅgraha, 2 Vols., ed. P. L. Vaidya, Mithilā Institute, Darbhanga, 1961-64.

Nyāyabindu with *Dharmottarapradīpa,* pub. K. P. Jayaswal Institute, Patna, 1955.

Pāli Tripiṭaka, 40 Vols., Nava Nāḷandā Mahāvihāra.

Pravacanasāra of Kundakunda, ed. A. N. Upadhye, Rājacandra Jain Sūtramālā.

Saddharmapuṇḍarīka, ed. N. Dutt, Calcutta, 1953.

Samayasāra of Kundakunda, Varanasi, 1974.

Sāṅgayogadarśana, Chowkhamba, Benares, 1935.

Sāṅkhyakārikā with *Māṭharavṛtti* and *Jayamaṅgalā,* Chowkhamba, Benares, 1970.

Sāṅkhyakārikā with *Yuktidīpikā,* Varanasi, 1970.

Sāṅkhyakārikā with the commentary of Gauḍapāda, Chowkhamba, Benares, 1940.

Sāṅkhyatattva Kaumudī, Chowkhamba, Benares, 1937.

Sāṅkhyapravacanabhāṣya, Bhāratīya Vidyā Prakāśana, Varanasi, *V.S.* 2022.

Sanmatiprakaraṇa of Siddhasena, Ahmedabad, 1963.

Tattvārthavārtika of Akalaṅka, Jñānapīṭha, Varanasi.

Tattvārthasūtra of Umāsvāti, commentary by Sukh Lal Sanghvi, Varanasi.

Vijñaptimātratāsiddhi of Hsuan Chwang, 2 Vols., tr. and ann. La Vallee Poussin, Paris, 1928-29.

Visuddhimaggo, ed. Kosambi, Bombay, 1940.

Yogaśāstra of Hemacandra, Delhi, 1963.

G. C. Pande, *Bauddha Dharma Ke Vikāsa Kā Itihāsa,* 2nd ed., Hindi Samiti, Lucknow.

—*R. K. Jaina Memorial Lectures on Jainism,* Delhi, 1978.

—*Śramaṇism and Its Contribution to Indian Culture,* Ahmedabad, 1977.

—*Studies in the Origins of Buddhism,* 3rd ed., Delhi, 1983.

Hariharananda Āraṇya, *Pātañjala Yogadarśana,* pub. by Calcutta University.

Chapter V

Brahmasiddhi, Madras, 1937.

Brahmasūtraśāṅkarabhāṣyam with 3 sub-commentaries, Bombay, 1934.

Brahmasūtraśāṅkarabhāṣyam with 9 sub-commentaries, Calcutta, 1933.

Saṅkṣepaśārīrakam, Benares, 1958.

Siddhāntaleśasaṅgraha, Acyuta Granthamālā, Benares, *V.S.* 2011.

Chapter VI

Āgamaprāmāṇya of Yāmunācārya, G.S.O., Baroda, 1976.

Ahirbudhnyasaṁhitā, 3 Vols., Adyar Library, Madras.

Ajitāgama, 2 Vols., Pondicherry, 1964, 1967.

Bhaktirasāyanam, Madhusūdana Sarasvatī, Varanasi, 1950.

Divyaprabandha, Vol. I, tr. Srinivas Raghavan, Vishvabharati, 1980.

Īśvarapratyabhijñāvimarṣiṇī of Abhinavagupta, 2 Vols., Kashmir Series of Texts and Studies.

Jayākhyasaṁhitā, G.O.S., Baroda, 1967.

Mālinīvijyottaratantram, Kashmir Series of Texts and Studies.

Mṛgendrāgama, Pondicherry, 1962.

Pāśupatasūtram, Trivandrum, 1940.

Rauravāgama, Vol. I, Pondicherry, 1961.

Śivajñānabodham, Benares, 1908.

Śivasūtras, Text with Vimarṣiṇī & tr. by Jaideva Singh, Delhi, 1979.

Spandakārikā, ed. and tr. Jaideva Singh, Delhi, 1980.

Śrībhāṣyam, 2 Vols., Madras, 1963.

Śrītantrāloka of Abhinavagupta, 12 Vols., Kashmir Series of Texts and Studies.

Tiruvācakam, tr. G. V. Pope, Oxford, 1900.

Tiruvācakam, Bharatiya Vidya Bhavan, Bombay.

Vedārthasaṅgraha of Rāmānuja, Deccan College, Pune.

Daniel Smith, *Descriptive Bibliography of the Printed Works of Pāñcarātra Āgamas,* Vol. I, G.O.S., Baroda.

H. C. Raychaudhuri, *Early History of the Vaiṣṇava Sect.*

J. C. Chatterji, *Kashmir Śaivism,* Srinagar, 1914.

J. S. M. Hooper, *Hymns of the Alvars,* O.U.P., 1929.

R. G. Bhandarkar, *Vaiṣṇavism, Śaivism and Minor Religious Systems.*

S. N. Dasgupta, *A History of Indian Philosophy,* Vol. V, Cambridge, 1955.

Susmita Pande, *Birth of Bhakti in Indian Religion and Art,* Books and Books, New Delhi, 1982.

Chapter VII

Dohākośa, ed. & tr. Rahula Sankrtyayana, Patna.

Guhyasamājatantram, G.S.O., Baroda.

Manusmṛti with the commentary of Kullūka, Chowkhamba, Varanasi.

Mārkaṇḍeyapurāṇam, Venkateshvar Press, Bombay.

Matsyapurāṇam, Venkateshvar Press, Bombay.

Prapañcasāra of Śaṅkarācārya, 2 Vols.

Śāradātilakam of Lakṣamaṇadeśika.

Śrīmadbhāgavatam, 2 Vols., Gita Press, Gorakhpur.

Śrīmadbhāgavatam with numerous commentaries, Devakinandan Press, Vrindavan.

Tripurārahasyam (Jñānakhaṇḍam), Varanasi, 1965.

Vāyumahāpurāṇam, Venkateshvar Press, Bombay.

Viṣṇupurāṇa, Gita Press, Gorakhpur.

F. E. Pargiter, *Ancient Indian Historical Tradition,* Delhi, 1972.

G. N. Kaviraj, *Tāntrika Sāhitya,* Hindi Samiti, Lucknow.

G. N. Kaviraj, *Tāntrika Vāṅmaya men Śākta Dṛṣṭi,* Bihar Rāṣṭrabhāṣā Pariṣad, Patna.

H. P. Shastri, *Bauddhagān O Dohā.*

R. C. Hazra, *Studies in the Puranic Records on Hindu Rites and Customs,* Dacca, 1940.

S. B. Dasgupta, *Introduction to Esoteric Buddhism.*

V. S. Agrawal, *Matsyapurāṇa—A Study,* Varanasi, 1963.

Chapter VIII

Ātmatattvaviveka of Udayana, Chowkhamba, Varanasi, 1940.

Nyāyamañjarī of Jayanta, Chowkhamba, Varanasi, 1934.

Pañcadaśī, Nirṇayasāgara Press, Bombay, 1935.

Pramāṇavārtika of Dharmakīrti, with Manorathanandin's commentary, Varanasi, 1968.

Prameyakamalamārtaṇḍa, Nirṇayasāgara Press, Bombay, 1941.

Ṣaḍdarśanasamuccaya of Haribhadrasūri, Jñānapīṭha, Varanasi.

Sarvadarśanasaṅgraha, Pune, 1928.

Ślokavārtika of Kumārila, Madras University.

Tattvasaṅgraha of Śāntarakṣita, 2 Vols., G.S.O., Baroda.

Upadeśasāhasrī of Śaṅkara, Nirṇayasāgara Press, Bombay, 1930.

Vedāntaparibhāṣā, Chowkhamba, Varanasi.

A. C. Mukherji, *The Nature of Self,* Allahabad, 1938.

K. C. Bhattacharya, *The Subject as Freedom,* Bombay, 1930.

Chapter IX

Gītā, Commentary of Śaṅkara, Gita Press, Gorakhpur.

Gītā, Commentary of Rāmānuja, Gita Press, Gorakhpur.

Gītā, Commentary of Madhusūdana Sarasvatī, Chowkhamba, Varanasi.

Gītā, Commentary of Tilaka, (Gītā-Rahasya), Hindi tr., Pune, 1933.

Aurobindo, *Essays on the Gītā*, 2 Series, Calcutta, 1949.

Sukthankar, *Meaning of the Mahābhārata*, Asiatic Society, 1957.

Chapter X

Apohasiddhi of Ratnakīrti, tr. with commentary by G. C. Pande, Jaipur, 1971.

Bṛhaddevatā, ed. Macdonell, Motilal Banarsidass, Delhi.

Laghumañjūṣā of Nāgeśa.

Nirukta with Durga's commentary, Nirṇayasāgara Press, Bombay.

Nyāyabindu of Dharmakīrti, tr. with commentary by G. C. Pande, Jaipur, 1972.

Vākyapadīya, ed. Raghunātha Śarmā, Varanasi.

Vyutpattivāda of Gadādhara, Chowkhamba, Varanasi.

Macdonell, *Vedic Mythology*, Varanasi, 1963.

V. S. Agrawal, *Mārkaṇḍeya Purāṇa—Eka Sāṁskṛ.ika Adhyayana*, Allahabad, 1961.

Chapter XI

Arthaśāstra, ed. Kangle, Bombay University.

Āryabhaṭīyam, tr. P. C. Sengupta, J.D.L. Calcutta University, 1927.

Bṛhatsaṁhitā, Sanskrit University, Varanasi.

Carakasaṁhitā, Chowkhamba, Varanasi.

Gaṇitasārasaṅgraha, Sholapur, 1963.

Mahābhāṣya, pub. Rohatak.

Nyāyabhāṣyam, Chowkhamba, Varanasi.

Pañcasiddhāntikā, Chowkhamba, Varanasi.

Praśastapādabhāṣyam with *Nyāyakandalī*, Sanskrit University, Varanasi.

Siddhāntaśiromaṇi, Chowkhamba, Varanasi.

Sūryasiddhānta, Chowkhamba, Varanasi.

Suśrutasaṁhitā, Calcutta, 1938.

Vedāṅgajyotiṣa, Mysore, 1936.

B. N. Seal, *Positive Sciences of the Ancient Hindus*, Delhi, 1958.

Bose, Sen & Subbarayappa, *Concise History of Science in India*, New Delhi, 1971.

P. C. Ray, *History of Hindu Chemistry*, 2 Vols., Calcutta, 1902, 1925.

S. C. Vidyabhushan, *History of Indian Logic*.

Stcherbatsky, *Bhuddhist Logic*, 2 Vols., Leningrad.

V. N. Misra, *The Descriptive Technique of Pāṇini*, Mouton.

Chapter XII

Abhinavabhāratī of Abhinavagupta, G.O.S. Baroda.

Amaruśatakam.

Bhagavadajjukīyam.

Bhāsanāṭakacakram, Pune.

Buddhacaritam of Aśvaghoṣa, Oxford, 1893.

Caturbhāṇi, ed. & tr. Motichandra, Bombay, 1959.

Daśakumāracaritam of Daṇḍin, Chowkhamba, Varanasi.

Dhvanyāloka Locana, Chowkhamba, Banaras.

Gāthāsaptaśatī, Nirṇayasāgara Press, Bombay.

Gītagovinda of Jayadeva.

Harṣacaritam, Nirṇayasāgara Press, Bombay.

Jātakaṭṭhavaṇṇanā, ed. Fausböll, London, 1877-97.

Kādambarī, Nirṇayasāgara Press, Bombay.

Kathāsaritsāgara, Nirṇayasāgara Press, Bombay.

Kāvyādarśa of Daṇḍin, Calcutta University.

Kāvyaprakāśa of Mammaṭa.

Kirātārjunīyam of Bhāravi, Nirṇayasāgara Press, Bombay.

Kumārasambhavam of Kālidāsa, Nirṇayasāgara Press, Bombay.

Mahābhāratam, 4 Vols., B.O.R.I., Pune, 1971-75.

Mattavilāsaprahaśanam.

Meghadūtam of Kālidāsa, Sāhitya Akademy.

Mṛcchakaṭikam, Nirṇayasāgara Press, Bombay.

Mudrārākṣasam, Chowkhamba, Varanasi.

Naiṣadhīyam of Śrīharṣa, Nirṇayasāgara Press, Bombay.

Nāṭyaśāstra of Bharata, Nirṇayasāgara Press, Bombay.

Pañcatantra of Viṣṇuśarmā, tr. Ryder.

Raghuvaṁśam of Kālidāsa, Nirṇayasāgara Press, Bombay.

Rāmāyaṇam, Bombay, 1930.

Rasagaṅgādhara, Nirṇayasāgara Press, Bombay.

Rūpakaṣaṭkam.

Śatakas of Bhartṛhari, Bhartiya Vidya Bhavan, Bombay.

Śākuntalam of Kālidāsa, Bombay.

Saundarananda of Aśvaghoṣa, Bhagalpur, 1948.

Śiśupālavadham of Māgha, Venkateshvar Press, Bombay.

Sūtrālaṅkāra of Vāmana, Atmaram & Sons, Delhi.

Theragāthā, Nalanda ed.

Therīgāthā, Nalanda ed.

Uttarajjhayaṇam, Jamnagar, 1938.

Uttararāmacaritam of Bhavabhūti, Nirṇayasāgara Press, Bombay.

Vakroktijīvita, Atmaram & Sons, Delhi.

Vāsavadattā of Subandhu.

Vyaktiviveka, Atmaram & Sons, Delhi.

Aurobindo, *Kālidāsa,* 2nd ed., Pondicherry, 1950.

H. K. Mukhopadhyaya, *Kavi Jayadeva O Śrī Gītagovinda,* Calcutta.

I. B. Horner, *Early Buddhist Poetry*, Colombo, 1963.

R. Panikkar, *Vedic Experience*, London, 1977.

Saunders, *Heart of Buddhism*, O.U.P., 1915.

Chapter XIII

Aparājitapṛcchā, G.O.S., Baroda.

Bharatakośa, Tirupati, 1951.

Bṛhaddeśī of Mataṅga, Trivandrum, 1928.

Mānasāra, ed. P. K. Acharya.

Mayamatam, T.S.S., No. 65.

Nāradīyaśikṣā, ed. in Satyavrata Sāmaśrami's "Uṣā" I, 4, Calcutta, 1890.

Nāṭyaśāstra of Bharata with *Abhinava-bhāratī*, 4 Vols., G.O.S., Baroda.

Samarāṅgaṇa-sūtradhāra, Baroda, 1925.

Saṅgītaratnākara, Madras, 1959.

Śilparatna, T.S.S., 1922.

Viṣṇudharmottarapurāṇa, Venkateshvara Press, Bombay.

A. K. Coomaraswamy, *Catalogue of the Indian Collections in the Museum of Fine Arts*, Boston, 1923-26.

—*Citralakṣana*, Ashutosh Mukerji Memorial Volume, Patna.

—*Figures of Speech or Figures of Thought*, London, 1946.

—*History of Indian and Indonesian Art*, Dover ed.

—*The Dance of Śiva*, London, 1925.

A. N. Tagore, *Ṣaḍaṅga*, Hindi tr., *Sammelan Patrikā*.

E. B. Havell, *The Ideals of Indian Art*, London, 1911.

Fergusson & Burgess, *Cave Temples of India*, London, 1880.

J. Griffiths, *Paintings in the Buddhist Cave Temples of Ajantā*, London, 1896-97.

Kapila Vatsyayan, *Classical Indian Dance in Literature and the Arts.*

M. A. Stein, *Ancient Khotan,* London, 1907.

—*Serindia,* London, 1921.

Marshall, Foucher & Majumdar, *Monuments of Sāñchī,* 3 Vols., Bhopal.

Mukund Laṭh, *A Study of Dattilam,* Delhi, 1978.

Percy Brown, *Indian Architecture (Buddhist and Hindu)*, Taraporewala, Bombay.

Ram Raz, *Essay on the Architecture of the Hindus,* London, 1834.

S. P. Gupta, *Roots of Indian Art.*

V. S. Agrawal, *Bhāratīya Kalā,* Vol. I, Varanasi, 1936.

T. A. G. Rao, *Elements of Hindu Iconography,* Motilal Banarsidass, Delhi.

INDEX